D1552683

THE
SPANISH
REVOLUTION
(1931-39)

THE SPANISH REVOLUTION (1931-39)

LEON TROTSKY

INTRODUCTION BY LES EVANS

PATHFINDER PRESS, NEW YORK

First Edition, 1973
Second Printing, 1973

Edited by Naomi Allen and George Breitman

Pathfinder Press, Inc.
410 West Street
New York, N.Y. 10014

Manufactured in the United States of America

CONTENTS

PART III: CIVIL WAR

APPENDIX

EDITORS' PREFACE

This is the first collection in English of Leon Trotsky's writings on the revolutionary developments in Spain during the decade of the 1930s. To the best of our knowledge, it contains everything by Trotsky on this subject in any language that was published by him during his lifetime or has been published since his death in 1940.

Nearly 40 percent of the articles in this book are translated into English for the first time or have appeared previously only in internal bulletins with restricted circulation. Most have been out of print for decades. Other articles are published here under Trotsky's name for the first time, since they were unsigned or were signed with pen names when first printed. The date preceding each article indicates when it was completed. Translations that were originally done in the thirties have been revised to correct obvious errors and to achieve uniformity in spelling of names, style, etc.

The source of each article and the name of its translator, if the latter is known, are presented in a note at the start of the article. Explanatory notes about the persons or events mentioned in the book follow the appendix. As further aids to the reader unfamiliar with the political developments in Spain during the thirties, prefatory notes precede each section of the book and a chronological outline of the decade follows the editors' preface.

We would like to express our debt to Louis Sinclair's *Leon Trotsky: A Bibliography* (Hoover Institution Press, Stanford, California, 1972), without which the present collection could not have achieved its comprehensiveness.

The Editors

SPAIN

CHRONOLOGY

1930 *January*   Dictator Primo de Rivera resigns; King Alfonso XIII appoints Berenguer to head interim government.

April   International Left Opposition (ILO) organized in Paris.

December   Liberal officers stage unsuccessful (Jaca) coup.

1931 *February*   Berenguer resigns.

April 12-14   Republicans carry all large towns in municipal elections; Alfonso goes into exile; republic declared; Alcalá Zamora is prime minister; Azaña is war minister; Maura is minister of interior; Caballero is minister of labor.

April 15   Government calls constituent Cortes (assembly).

May   Clashes between monarchists and workers in Madrid; several churches are burned.

June   Elections to Cortes give overwhelming majority to pro-republican parties; Socialists largest party in Cortes; Catholic Church is disestablished; Alcalá Zamora and Maura, both Catholics, resign; Alcalá Zamora becomes president of republic; Azaña is prime minister.

July-August   Strike wave; general strike in Seville crushed by republican government artillery.

1932 *January*   Uprisings in Catalonia organized by the FAI.

      August   Unsuccessful coup by monarchist general Sanjurjo.

1933 *January* 30   Hindenburg appoints Hitler chancellor.

      April   Municipal elections show big gains for rightists.

      July-   Trotsky leaves Turkey for France; ILO
      August   abandons perspective of reforming Comintern and decides on necessity of forming 4th International.

      September   Azaña resigns as prime minister; Lerroux forms government pending elections.

      October 29   Falange Española founded in Madrid.

      November   Elections to Cortes give rightists and monarchists control when CNT abstains; Lerroux confirmed as prime minister; begins to repeal reforms.

1934 *June*   Rural strike movement called by Anarchists; Macía dies; Companys takes over Catalan Generalitat (local government).

      October   Lerroux forms new government, with members of right-wing CEDA of Gil Robles; General strike of Socialists and Anarchists crushed; Lerroux calls in Franco to crush uprising of Asturian miners.

      October-   Fall of Oviedo, end of Asturian commune;
      November   5,000 killed in savage reprisals; 30,000 arrested as political prisoners.

1935 *June*   Norway grants Trotsky a visa.

      August   Seventh Congress of Comintern proclaims
                      Popular Front policy.

      September 25 Founding of the POUM.

1936 *January*   Lerroux resigns amid financial scandal;
                      Cortes dissolved.

      February 16   New elections bring Popular Front to
                      power; Azaña is prime minister again;
                      Anarchists and POUM support Popular
                      Front in the elections.

      March   Peasants in Estremadura seize land.

      April   General Mola issues circular calling for
                      insurrection; Socialist and Communist
                      youth groups merge; Hitler takes Rhine-
                      land.

      May 10   Azaña replaces Alcalá Zamora as pres-
                      ident; Casares Quiroga is prime minister.

      May-June   Mass strikes in France; French Popular
                      Front elected; Léon Blum is prime min-
                      ister; Daladier is minister of war.

      July 13   Spanish CP declares full support to gov-
                      ernment.

      July 17-21   Fascist rising begins in Morocco and
                      spreads to Spain; Quiroga refuses arms
                      to workers, and is replaced by Martínez
                      Barrio; General Miaja is minister of war;
                      Companys in Catalonia refuses to distrib-
                      ute arms; Giral replaces Martínez Barrio;
                      arms are distributed to workers.

      August 15   France and England sign noninterven-
                      tion pact.

August 21   Zinoviev and Kamenev executed in USSR
                   in first of big Moscow show trials.

September 4   Giral resigns; Largo Caballero becomes
                   prime minister on condition that CP join
                   government; Uribe (CP) is minister of
                   agriculture; six Socialists in cabinet in-
                   clude Prieto (minister of navy and air)
                   and Negrín (minister of finance).

September 26   CNT and POUM join Generalitat in Ca-
                   talonia; Nin becomes minister of justice.

October 10   Central government ends independence of
                   militias.

October 29   Siege of Madrid begins.

November   Central government reorganized to include
                   Anarchists (García Oliver, minister of jus-
                   tice); Caballero moves government to Va-
                   lencia. International Brigades arrive in
                   Madrid.

December 16   POUM expelled from government.

December 21   Letter from Stalin to Caballero insists
                   on protection of private property.

December 25   German-Japanese Anti-Comintern Pact
                   signed.

1937 *January* 9   Trotsky arrives in Mexico.

     April 25   Bombing of Guernica.

     May   Government attempt to seize Barcelona
                   telephone exchange from Anarchists leads
                   to new upsurge; Negrín replaces Caba-
                   llero as prime minister.

June 15-16   POUM outlawed by central government; leaders arrested.

October 31   Central government moved to Barcelona.

November 6   Italy signs Anti-Comintern Pact.

1938   *January* 11   Heavy bombardment of Barcelona begins.

April-June   Franco reaches coast and cuts republican Spain in half.

September   International Brigade fights final battles in Ebro campaign; Chamberlain and Daladier sign Munich Pact with Hitler.

November   International Brigades withdraw from Spain.

1939   *January* 26   Barcelona surrenders.

February 27   France and Britain recognize Franco while loyalists still hold a third of Spain.

March 4   Republican general Miaja broadcasts manifesto proposing surrender.

March 5-6   Hitler occupies Czechoslovakia.

March 28   Madrid and Valencia surrender; Spain signs Anti-Comintern Pact.

March 29   Active hostilities cease.

April 1   United States recognizes Franco.

August 24   Stalin-Hitler Pact signed.

INTRODUCTION

The publication of a comprehensive selection of Leon Trotsky's writings on the Spanish revolution of 1931-39 is a timely and much-needed addition to the literature of revolutionary Marxism. Many of these letters, resolutions, and pamphlets have long been out of print or appear here in English for the first time. Their interest is far from purely historical. In many respects Spain was a touchstone for the strategy and tactics of both revolution and counterrevolution for our century, and the experiences of that bitter struggle have lost little of their value in the intervening decades.

It is noteworthy that in the last few years we have seen a revival of the central tactic employed by the Communist and Socialist parties in the Spanish events: the Popular Front coalition between working class parties and the liberal bourgeoisie. Those who are disposed to view the Popular Unity government of Salvador Allende Gossens in Chile or the United Front regime of Sirimavo Bandaranaike in Ceylon, both of which were elected to office in 1970, as instruments for the construction of a socialist society would do well to review the record of the Popular Front in Spain.

The importance of the Spanish revolution stems not so much from its uniqueness as from its universality. Because Spain stood midway between underdevelopment and advanced capitalism it combined many features of the class struggle in both types of societies. There is much in the history of the Spanish peasantry that is reminiscent of Latin America. At the same time, the core of the revolutionary movement in Spain was proletarian, and the revolution and civil war encompassed many of the strategic problems of the workers' movement in Western Europe and the United States. For example, the multiplicity of major cities in Spain gave the civil war the character of a protracted struggle for control of the urban industrial centers. This struggle was fought out in positional rather than mobile or guerrilla warfare; the outcome was not to be decided by the capture of one or two major cities as might be the case in a smaller, less developed country.

The general tendency of Western historians has been to examine the Spanish conflict from a purely military and technical standpoint, weighing the quantities of arms, "volunteers," and air support provided to Franco by his German and Italian backers and comparing them to the more meager material resources mustered by the republic. This is an inadequate explanation for the ultimate triumph of the Falangist forces. As the Vietnam conflict has shown, even massive technical superiority can be stalemated or defeated by a revolutionary mobilization of the masses.

Social revolution — including civil war — is not merely a clash between ideologies or political personalities but a confrontation between social classes over the question of which class shall rule. In the epoch of modern capitalism there are only two serious contenders for power: those who already rule — the financial, manufacturing, and landholding bourgeoisie — and their principal antagonist, the industrial working class. The other sectors of society, the middle class of the cities — and the peasantry in the underdeveloped countries — in the last analysis adopt the leadership and the program of one or the other of the major combatants.

While technical factors undoubtedly play an important role in such a class battle, they are not decisive. If they were, socialist revolution would be impossible, because the old ruling class always enters the arena against the working class with the army, police, and the other organized repressive forces of society at its command. Yet in the twentieth century, a whole series of countries have nevertheless succeeded in breaking the power of capitalism and establishing workers' states, beginning with the Russian Revolution of October 1917 and extending up to the Cuban Revolution of the late 1950s.

The ultimate determinant of victory or defeat for the working class is the program, organizational methods, and caliber of the leadership of the insurgent revolutionary movement. This finds its highest and most conscious expression in the construction of a revolutionary political party on the Leninist model.

Trotsky, as a central leader of the successful October Revolution in Russia, understood this question very well. His writings on Spain are permeated with his appreciation of the urgent need to construct a mass revolutionary party of the Spanish working class and his contemptuous rejection of all the ersatz substitutes that claimed to be such a party. Indeed, the urgent need for a revolutionary party is the question above all others that occupied the attention of the exiled Russian revolutionist in his writings in the present book. In the first half of the book, before the civil war, this theme is expressed in his attempts to influence the development of the newly founded Spanish section of the International Left Opposition; in his later writings, after the civil war had begun, it leads him to try to educate the whole Fourth Internationalist movement to reject both the sectarians in its ranks who were opposed to supporting the loyalist military struggle against Franco in the civil war, and the centrists, who wavered on the question of Popular Frontism.

In assessing the causes of the failure of the Spanish revolution, it is important to weigh not only the objective obstacles, but also the organizational and theoretical shortcomings of the revolutionists on the scene, the subjective factor. This Trotsky does unsparingly, though with great fairness and perception. Even a cursory reading of his correspondence with the leaders of the Spanish Left Opposition is adequate to dispel the myth fostered by the apologists for Stalinism that Trotsky "failed to understand" the Leninist conception of party building or to apply it to concrete situations.

Spain was a testing ground for revolutionary programs and tendencies that have had their counterpart in countries throughout the world in this century. This is another measure in which the Spanish experience has a general application that transcends the particular time and place in which it unfolded. All the major tendencies of working class radicalism were well represented on the Spanish scene. These ranged from anarchism to reformist Social Democracy, the pro-Moscow Communist Party adhering to the doctrine of Stalinism, centrism (groups that wavered between revolutionary action and reformism), and revolutionary socialism.

Each of these tendencies in its own way was able to influence the outcome. In the process each had a chance to show what its program and proposals were worth in a real revolutionary situation.

The essential ingredient for victory, not only for socialism but also for the successful prosecution of the war against fascist rebellion, was missing. No mass revolutionary party was built in time.

The documents collected in this volume do not constitute a history of the Spanish revolution. They are the correspondence and polemics of an active revolutionist seeking to affect the events rather than to record them. In large part they take the form of concrete criticisms and tactical proposals directed to Trotsky's own followers in Spain and to those forces that at least verbally declared themselves in favor of a socialist revolution. To a lesser extent they include biting critiques of the programs of the nonrevolutionary organizations of the left.

For the benefit of readers unfamiliar with the Spanish left of the 1930s it will be useful to briefly trace the origins of the revolutionary crisis that erupted in 1931 and the relationship of forces among the workers' organizations at that time.

Social roots of the Spanish revolution

Spain entered the twentieth century as one of the most backward countries of Europe, saddled by a decaying ruling class and an absolute monarchy that rested on the twin pillars of the Catholic Church and the aristocratic officers' corps of the army. Despite the semifeudal appearance of the state superstructure, the core of the ruling class was capitalist. It was composed of an uneasy coalition between the owners of the vast landed estates of Castillian Spain (who produced for export to the capitalist world market) and the industrialists of Catalonia and the Basque provinces.

Spain had historically been torn between the centralizers of Castile who demanded a strong unitary government and the centrifugal demands of the Basques and Catalans for regional autonomy or independence, in keeping with their separate languages and cultures.

Spain was and remains predominantly an agricultural country. In 1936, 70 percent of its population of twenty-four million lived on the land. This rural populace, while brutally oppressed,

was not a peasant class in the main. Gerald Brenan estimates[1] *
that three-quarters of the population was made up of landless
agricultural laborers, that is, a rural semiproletariat. Brenan
provides some picture of the conditions of life for these people:

> . . . In 1930 they were earning on an average from
> 3 to 3.5 pesetas [1 peseta equaled US 12.5¢] for an eight-
> hour day during four or five months of the year. In
> summer — under the terrible heat of the Andalusian sun —
> they earned from 4 to 6 pesetas for a twelve-hour day.
> . . . During the rest of the year . . . during [up to] six
> months . . . they were unemployed. . . . Except at harvest
> time, when they were given beans, the only dish was *gaz-
> pacho*, a soup of oil, vinegar and water with bread floating
> on top. They took it hot for breakfast, cold for lunch, hot
> again at night. . . . Great numbers of these families did not
> own any furniture except a cooking pot and ate their meals
> like animals on the ground.

Spain's rulers prospered during World War I on the basis
of their exports of agricultural products to the belligerent nations of Europe. The foreign exchange accumulated in this
trade served to finance a rapid development of industry, particularly in Barcelona, the capital of Catalonia, and in Santander
and Bilbao on the northern Basque coast. This led in turn to the
growth of the Spanish proletariat in the separatist regions and
the expansion of a mass radical labor movement.

The foreign markets collapsed at the end of the war, deepening the radicalization. The ruling class then turned to its
traditional guardian, the military. In 1923 General Miguel
Primo de Rivera established a military dictatorship that was
to cover the last period of relative stability for the Spanish
ruling class until the crushing of the republic in 1939. Primo
de Rivera was able to hold onto power for eight years; but
the Great Depression that broke out in 1929 put an end for
the time being to the effort by Spanish absolutism to crush
all social protest under the heel of the armed forces. In 1930
the dictator was forced to resign and shortly afterward King
Alfonso XIII announced municipal elections that were held

---

*Notes for the Introduction begin on p. 49.

in April 1931. The vote went heavily against the monarchist and clerical parties. Unprepared for this outcome, the king went into exile; long silent and servile Spanish liberalism at last found its voice.

The republic of 1931 rested on a coalition of liberal bourgeois parties and the Spanish Socialist Party of Francisco Largo Caballero and Indalecio Prieto (both of whom were in the first cabinet). This bloc of parties from two antagonistic social classes was the forerunner of the Popular Front government that was to lead the republic from the elections of February 1936 through the civil war.

The bourgeois parties, whose most prominent leader was Manuel Azaña, were of course opposed to socialism. Their partnership with the Socialist Party, and later with the Communist Party, was based on the defense of democratic civil liberties and limited social reform. They had neither the will nor the means to break the power of the landed aristocracy or the industrial barons. Their reformist demagogy, however, raised hopes among the masses of city workers and agricultural laborers that they could not fulfill.

The loosening of the chains of absolutism under the republic had as its chief result a revolutionary upsurge of the Spanish masses. From 1931 the question of social revolution was posed, much to the horror of the republican liberals. Trotsky was among the first to see that this regime was a feeble creature, committed to the preservation of capitalist property relations but forced to balance precariously between the restless workers and the more resolute defenders of bourgeois reaction. Even before the republic was proclaimed, Trotsky declared of the republican bourgeoisie in his article "The Revolution in Spain" that "their fear of the masses is greater than their hostility to the monarchy." He was to dub Azaña "the Spanish Kerensky," an incidental figure to be swept aside by the real leaders of Spanish capitalism when they were prepared to deal a death blow to the insurgent mass movement that threatened their rule. The irony and tragedy of the Spanish revolution was that Azaña was kept in office not by the bourgeoisie, whose interests he valiantly attempted to serve to the end, but by the working class parties that sacrificed the possibility of socialist revolution in order to preserve the empty respectability conferred on the republic by Azaña's liberalism.

The organizations of the Spanish left

Anarchism. For a number of specific historical reasons the largest tendency among the Spanish workers was anarchism, or more correctly, anarcho-syndicalism — anarchism expressed not through a political organization but through the trade unions. It was the followers of Bakunin and not of Marx who first arrived in Spain, in 1868, as the representatives of the International Workingmen's Association, the First International. Anarchism established itself among the landless agricultural laborers of Andalusia, who were spread over a large geographical area and not concentrated and disciplined in large factories like the industrial workers of the more advanced countries.

The second major center of anarchism was among the pro-separatist and anti-authoritarian workers of Catalonia, in the factories of Barcelona. Here the general mood transmitted by the radical petty bourgeoisie as part of their struggle against the centralizers of Madrid was one of opposition to all authority. The doctrine of anarchism coincided with these libertarian sentiments not only in its revolutionary opposition to the injustice of bourgeois rule, but also, in a negative way, in its opposition to the self-disciplined organization of the workers to fight for their emancipation. The Anarchists stressed spontaneous struggle by the workers, eschewed all political action and organization as a bourgeois trap, and encouraged acts of individual terrorism against the representatives of the government.

A central tenet of anarchist belief, which was to immobilize and finally destroy Spanish anarchism as a social movement, was opposition to any and all forms of state government. Insofar as this opposition was directed at the bourgeois state it produced militant mass action. But in the course of the revolutionary crisis, the working class, if it is to be victorious, must pass beyond local organization to the creation of its own national state structure. If it fails to take this step the representatives of some other class will inevitably do so.

The principal Anarchist organization was the Confederación Nacional del Trabajo (CNT — National Confederation of Labor). Founded in 1911, the CNT claimed 1.5 million members in 1931. It was in turn dominated by the illegal Anarchist center, the Federación Anarquista Ibérica (FAI—Iberian Anarchist Federation), which was believed to have about 30,000 members in 1936.[2]

The leadership of the CNT-FAI was divided into a right and left wing, led respectively by José García Oliver and Buenaventura Durruti. As the revolutionary crisis deepened in the 1930s, culminating in the period of open military operations, this division was to play an important role in the destruction of Spanish anarchism and with it the most militant sector of the Spanish working class.

Beneath the cover of the traditional Anarchist abstention from elections and politics, García Oliver and the majority of the Anarchist leadership had long been moving in the direction of pure-and-simple reformist trade unionism. This leadership, unwilling to call the workers into battle to form a revolutionary government, ultimately abandoned its own cardinal principle of opposition to all governments by joining the bourgeois liberals in the Popular Front government. The key test of anarchism as a revolutionary theory was that in a real revolution its own leaders deserted it as a guide to action because it didn't work. Trotsky compared this doctrine to a raincoat full of holes: it was useless precisely when it rained.

The Spanish Socialist Party. The Spanish SP was an unusually left variety of Social Democracy. It formally decided not to join the Communist International only in 1921, and then only by a narrow majority. It too was divided into a right wing, led by Prieto, and a left wing, led by Largo Caballero. Though smaller than the Anarchists, the SP controlled an important union, the Unión General de Trabajadores (UGT—General Workers' Union), which claimed several hundred thousand members at the beginning of the 1930s. Its main centers were among the industrial workers of Madrid and Bilbao and among the miners of Asturias.

The Prieto forces were openly reformist and resembled the conservative Social Democratic parties of France and Germany. The Caballero wing was more contradictory. In words, especially after 1934, it called for arming the masses and for the dictatorship of the proletariat. In practice it conciliated with liberalism and participated in the class-collaborationist coalition governments of 1931 and 1936. On the other hand, until the beginning of 1936, when it was merged with the Stalinist youth, the Socialist Party youth movement was evolving rapidly in the direction of revolutionary Marxism. One of Trotsky's bitterest complaints against those who were identified as his followers in Spain was that they failed to recognize this revolutionary current among the Socialist youth and find a way to reach them in common action.

The Communist Party.[3] Initially the smallest of the major working class parties, the Spanish CP was to rise in the course of the civil war to virtual dominance of the republican government. Dolores Ibarruri ("La Pasionaria"), the party's most prominent leader, in a speech in Moscow in May 1934 estimated that with the inauguration of the republic in 1931 the CP could claim only 800 members.[4] Hugh Thomas put its membership at the beginning of 1936 at 10,000.[5]

This party, lacking roots in the Spanish working class and with few leaders of independent stature, served primarily as an instrument of Comintern policy and reflected the twists and turns of line initiated by Stalin in the turbulent decade of the 1930s. Stalin did not leave the application of Comintern decisions in Spain solely to the discretion of his local supporters in any case, but from 1933 onwards supplied a growing coterie of special "instructors." The most notorious of these were the Italians Vittorio Codovilla and Vittorio Vidali (Carlos Contreras) and the Hungarian Ernö Gerö.[6]

The Communist Party did not support the republican government of 1931. The Comintern was still in its ultraleft "third period," which lasted from 1928 to 1934. All of its affiliated parties during this time opposed collaboration with, or participation in, bourgeois governments, in keeping with the traditional position of the Marxist movement. Under Stalin's tutelage, however, they also rejected common action with other working class parties. This policy had its most disastrous result in Germany, where the Communist Party denounced the Social Democrats as "social fascists," refusing to seek a common front against the rise of Hitler. The Nazis' rise to power and the subsequent annihilation of the German CP prompted a belated shift by the Kremlin after 1933. But instead of returning to the Leninist tactic of a working class united front, the Stalinists moved to support of "democratic" capitalist governments under the slogan of the "Anti-Fascist People's Front."

The Comintern's right turn was formalized at its Seventh World Congress in 1935. In the Spanish elections of February

1936 the Communist Party would endorse the republican-SP coalition and instruct its deputies in the Cortes (parliament) to vote with the government.

Trotsky's attitude toward the Spanish Communist Party was conditioned by this evolution of the Comintern. Before Hitler's seizure of power, his perspective was to work to reform the parties under Stalin's influence. Trotsky and his followers in the International Left Opposition regarded themselves as an expelled faction of the Comintern and not as a fully separate party. While the ILO — and its Spanish adherents — maintained their own organization and press, they directed their appeals and criticisms to the rank and file of the Communist parties. This is expressed clearly in Trotsky's writings in this collection up to and including the selection entitled "Problems of the Spanish Left Opposition," which is dated December 1932. To describe the Comintern's political position during this time, Trotsky used the term "bureaucratic centrism," which signified inconsistency and left open the possibility of a return to a genuinely revolutionary policy by the Communist parties.

After the defeat in Germany, Trotsky and his followers abandoned any hope of reconstructing the Communist International. The German CP had proven incapable of mounting any serious resistance to fascism, which Trotsky saw as a symptom of its incurable degeneration. At this time he discarded the characterization of the Comintern as bureaucratic centrist. He no longer attributed its policies to criminal mistakes, but rather to the deliberate counterrevolutionary intention of the Stalinist bureaucracy. In its search for "peaceful coexistence" with the imperialist countries, it used the workers' movements as pawns to be sacrificed to its own diplomatic needs. Trotsky no longer considered it realistic to expect that the Stalinist bureaucracy could be reformed, and boldly proposed the formation of a new international and new parties. Thenceforth, this was the main task that dominated Trotsky's thoughts in regard to Spain.

The Spanish Left Opposition and the POUM

A number of prominent working class leaders rallied to the banner of the Left Opposition in Spain. These included Andrés Nin, who had been the secretary of the CNT and later of the Comintern's Red International of Labor Unions; and Juan

Andrade, who as an SP youth leader at the end of World War
I had been instrumental in winning a major section of the
Socialist youth to communism. They were talented revolutionists who won to the Spanish Bolshevik-Leninists, as the Opposition was then called, some of the best forces in the old Communist Party. Unfortunately, despite their great superiority
to those who prostrated themselves before Stalin, none of the
Spanish Oppositionists of this period were able to rise to the
needs of the impending revolution.

Organizationally the Spanish Left Opposition began to make
headway after 1931. By the end of 1932 it had become
one of the larger sections of the International Left
Opposition; and it continued to grow thereafter. These advances,
however, were one-sided, made at the expense of political clarity. A great part of this book is comprised of Trotsky's proposals and letters to Nin and others on the tactics and strategy
of the Spanish Left Opposition. While differences arose over
many subsidiary points, the essence of Trotsky's criticism of
Nin's leadership was that it was conciliatory — Nin tended to
adapt to the political *programs* of nonrevolutionary organizations in order to secure secondary tactical advantages. This
was particularly true of Nin's relations with the Catalan Federation of Joaquín Maurín, and to a lesser extent with the
Anarchists. Secondly, but stemming from the same desire for
accommodation and avoidance of conflict on the left, was a
marked tendency on Nin's part to abstain from steps that
would throw the Spanish Trotskyists into common mass organizations with the Socialist and Anarchist workers and youth,
where they would have an opportunity to win them for revolutionary politics.

Trotsky also had strong misgivings about the Spanish leadership's party-building methods. For him, the key to training
cadres was internationalism — not only in the programmatic but
also in the organizational sense. The International Left Opposition was a young organization, still in the process of learning
how to function under difficult conditions, how to shake off
accidental and alien elements, how to create an authoritative
collective leadership. Trotsky expected the Spanish leaders to
participate actively in the internal life, debates, and struggles
of the International Left Opposition; he insisted that this was
their duty not only to the ILO but to the Spanish Opposition-

ists as well. But Nin — perhaps because of his unhappy experiences with the Stalinized Comintern, perhaps because of his
inability to rise above the negative aspects of the Spanish
radical tradition — displayed a provincial disinterest in the daily
life of the ILO, except when its discussions or decisions concerned Spain. He was too preoccupied with Spanish problems
to have much time for the ILO, and he did not care to submit
the policies of the Spanish leadership to the scrutiny and criticism of some remote committee, which he felt could obviously
not understand the events and know what had to be done in
Spain as well as Nin, Andrade, and others who were on the
spot. So he remained aloof from the internal problems of the
ILO, or participated in them capriciously or subjectively.

Worst of all, from Trotsky's point of view, was the Spanish
leadership's failure to involve the ranks of their organization
in the discussions of the ILO. How else could they benefit
from the lessons of those discussions, and become a self-reliant
and well-informed Marxist membership? How else would they
learn to resist the pressures of their political environment?

Trotsky recognized that the ascendance of the republican
regime in April 1931 presaged a revolutionary crisis that
would enter its decisive phase in a few years' time. The key
task for the Spanish Oppositionists, he said, was to find a
road to the mass of radicalized workers in the CNT and draw
them away from their Anarchist misleaders. The organizational form he proposed to accomplish this was the united
front between left parties, which must be based on the freedom
of the revolutionists to criticize the programs of the other participants; and above all the formation of independent organs
of workers' political power, *juntas* (councils). Trotsky saw
these two steps as inseparable. He recognized that a united
front agreement between party leaderships without the correc-
tive of mass nonparty workers' councils would be heavily
weighted toward the bureaucratic apparatuses of the reformist
parties.

Before 1934, Trotsky visualized the road to the Anarchist
workers as passing through the official Communist Party. He
urged Nin and the Spanish Trotskyists to use their influence
to orient the members of the CP in this direction. After 1934,
the deepening radicalization of the 1930s internationally began
to bypass the Communist parties and seek a new channel

in the resurrection of viable left wings in the old Social Democracy. This prompted Trotsky to propose the temporary entry of the sections of the International Left Opposition into the Socialist parties in order to forge links with this new levy of young revolutionary workers and students. This policy was known as the "French turn," because it was first applied by the French Trotskyists who entered the Socialist Party of France in 1934.

Nin and Andrade resisted the orientation toward the Communist Party in the early 1930s and rejected the "French turn," and for symmetrical reasons. They were impressed with the self-sufficiency of their own organization, overestimated the importance of its numerical gains, and were nervous at the prospect of mixing too intimately in the hostile milieu of other parties. They therefore failed to see the implications of the designation the International Left Opposition adopted for itself as a faction of the Communist International. They preferred to ignore the numerically smaller and weaker Spanish CP and proceed directly to the construction of a new party. Trotsky warned them not to be deceived by appearances: the immense power of the Soviet Union stood behind the ineffectual Spanish Communist Party and to ignore this party could lead to disaster at a later stage.

Nin took a similar position toward the left-moving Socialist youth in 1934. A fusion with the SP youth would have jeopardized the organizational independence, or more accurately the comfortable routine, of the Opposition. To appreciate the opportunity that was thus missed, it is necessary to recall that in 1934 Largo Caballero publicly attacked the Communist International as "reformist" and declared himself sympathetic to the idea of building a fourth international. The Madrid Socialist youth newspaper *Renovación* appealed to the Trotskyists by name to join the SP and help to make it a Bolshevik party. Nin and Andrade did not accept the invitation. This paved the, way for the Stalinist merger with the SP youth at the beginning of 1936, providing the CP with its first mass base in Spain.

Even more significant were Nin's relations with the Maurín group in Catalonia. Maurín, like Nin and Andrade, had been a prominent leader of the Communist Party and was expelled at the end of the 1920s for his opposition to Stalinism. He took with him virtually the entire membership of the Catalan section of the party, the Catalan-Balearic Communist Federation, renamed in 1931 the Workers and Peasants Bloc (Bloque Obrero y Campesino). This group had broken with Stalin more over the ultraleftism of the third period line than over fundamental political disagreements. Maurín was aligned internationally with the right wing rather than the left wing in the Soviet party and the Comintern. His closest sympathies were with the Bukharin tendency in the Soviet Union.

On June 12, 1931, Trotsky wrote a public letter of scathing criticism of the Workers and Peasants Bloc. The very name, he said, suggested a nonproletarian party. Communism was not mentioned in the program, which contained a call for democratic revolution but not socialist revolution. The Bloc reprimanded the bourgeois republican government for its "mistakes," leaving unclear how it characterized the class basis of the government. It refrained from criticizing the domestic policy of Stalinism inside the Soviet Union. Moreover, Maurín was content to prosper in his own bailiwick and had no perspective of extending his Catalan organization to the level of a national party.

Nin was drawn to Maurín by long-standing ties of personal friendship. It is dismaying even after so many years to read the Trotsky-Nin correspondence [included here as an appendix] and see to what extent Nin's political course was dictated by such subjective considerations, a quality fatal in a revolutionary politician. In opposition to Trotsky's insistent advice, Nin engineered a fusion between the Spanish Trotskyists and the Maurín group, essentially on the basis of Maurín's and not Trotsky's program. This was consummated in September 1935 with the formation of the POUM.

The POUM has long been identified by the Stalinists and by many bourgeois historians as a "Trotskyist" party. It did not regard itself as such and Trotsky and the Fourth International certainly did not accept this characterization. Trotsky's final judgment of the POUM was that in verbally proposing revolutionary solutions to the Spanish crisis while hesitating to take the decisive action to put them into practice, it acted as the principal roadblock to the formation of a mass revolutionary socialist party in Spain.

From the republic of 1931 to the Popular Front

Events built steadily toward the inevitable civil war from the inauguration of the republican government in April 1931. The masses of workers and agricultural laborers expected rapid changes under the new regime. When these were not forthcoming, the masses began to challenge the ruling class directly, ignoring the edicts of the liberals. The "popular" government reacted with the methods of any capitalist regime: police clubs and bullets. In July and August a strike wave swept Spain. In Seville a general strike was crushed only when the army used artillery against the working class districts, leaving thirty persons dead and 200 wounded.

In January 1933 an Anarchist rising in the village of Casas Viejas in Cádiz was put down by the hated Civil Guard and the newly created "republican" Asaltos, the special police selected for their loyalty to the "democratic" government. At least a dozen prisoners were shot without trial.

In sullen retribution, the masses withheld their votes from the republican parties and the government fell, to be replaced by the ill-fated ministry of the ex-radical Alejandro Lerroux. This former priest-baiter-turned-reactionary leaned more and more heavily on the ancient pillars of Spanish conservatism: the church, the army, and the monarchist parties.

The smell of gunpowder was in the air. Even the most dull-witted reformists sensed that the tinder of the Spanish villages was awaiting the spark of social revolt. It became fashionable even in bourgeois circles to proclaim that the future of Spain would be decided not in the Cortes but in the clash of arms between the proletariat and the forces of reaction. In Madrid, José Antonio Primo de Rivera, the son of the former dictator, founded the Falange Española, the political party of Spanish fascism. Armed thugs began the systematic assassination of union leaders and left-wing politicians.

The whole tenor of liberal and radical politics in Spain shifted leftward — in words. In January 1934, at the insistence of the forces around Largo Caballero, the Socialist Party set up a committee to purchase and distribute arms to its members. Caballero's newspaper *El Socialista* wrote on the third anniversary of the republic:

Another 14 April? Much better something else: a Spanish October. The difference is this: April, frustrated hope,
lost illusion; October, firm eagerness, sure solution. . . .
April, citizens with ballot-papers; October, workers with
rifles. 7

Against Lerroux, Caballero could speak like a Leninist.
The test of these words would come in September 1936 when
Caballero would join the new "April" regime as Azaña's premier
and help to strangle the Spanish October. But for the moment
even the bourgeois politicians of the republican left could give
themselves over to such flights of verbal revolutionism. Azaña
himself, now in opposition, declared that while he preferred the
electoral road, "the day may come when we will have no other
remedy but to take up the carbine."8

In October 1934, Lerroux for the first time invited into his
cabinet representatives of the far right-wing Catholic party,
the CEDA (Confederación Española de Derechas Autónomas)
of Gil Robles. The working class parties immediately compared
this with Hindenburg's appointment of Hitler as chancellor in
Germany the previous year and saw in Lerroux's move an
attempt to impose a fascist government on Spain. The reaction
was swift. The Socialists and Anarchists opened a general
strike. In Asturias the miners seized Oviedo and declared a
socialist commune. The government called in General Franco
and the mercenary Army of Africa, the legionnaires of Spanish Morocco, to level the city. Oviedo fell on October 12. The
conquering troops exacted a fearful revenge on the workers
who had been so audacious as to challenge the established
order. The death toll in the fighting and the reprisals that
followed topped 5,000. The jails were filled with more than
30,000 political prisoners. The policy of massive executions
would be central to the strategy of fascist terror in the cities
that would fall to Franco in the civil war.

The victory of reaction in Asturias proved to be a pyrrhic
one, however. The workers had been beaten but they were not
intimidated. Hatred for the regime deepened and the ruling
parties entered a crisis that shattered the conservative coalition on which the government rested. New elections, held in
February 1936, returned Azaña to office at the head of a
Popular Front coalition of the bourgeois republican left, and

the Socialist and Communist parties. The Anarchists, in their first fateful step toward alliance with the liberal bourgeoisie, abandoned their principle of abstention in elections and encouraged their supporters to vote for the Popular Front.

Even the POUM, which had denounced the antirevolutionary concept of the Popular Front countless times in its press, gave "critical" support to the Popular Front slate and signed its procapitalist election manifesto. Nin and Andrade justified this with leftist excuses, arguing that they placed no confidence whatever in Azaña and his cohorts, but sought only to defeat the rightists and to secure the release of the political prisoners.

Trotsky retorted that such a step, whatever the rationalizations, could only have the effect of placing the Spanish working class under the leadership and discipline of their historic enemy, the bourgeoisie. "Andrade's conduct," he wrote, "is nothing else than *betrayal of the proletariat for the sake of an alliance with the bourgeoisie.*" (Emphasis in the original.) In particular Trotsky rejected Nin and Andrade's notion that the "anti-imperialist" struggle of backward Spain for national self-determination constituted a "special" condition. They claimed that such a special condition permitted them to form a *political* bloc on a common program with the parties of the "left" bourgeoisie. In his article "The Treachery of the POUM," written in January 1936, Trotsky mercilessly attacked the idea that any section of the Spanish bourgeoisie, liberal or otherwise, had any intention of solving the problems of backward Spain:

> The bloc of leaders of the Spanish working class with the left bourgeoisie does not include in it anything "national," for it does not differ in the least from the "Popular Front" in France, Czechoslovakia, Brazil, or China.

This judgment was confirmed all too unhappily for the Spanish working class in the course of the civil war.

As president of the republic, Azaña sought to temporize with reaction, to demonstrate to the army and the Falange that his government could assure stability and stave off a workers' insurrection. Like Allende in Chile three and a half decades later, he flattered the military hierarchy and used the governmental power to prevent the arming of the masses for their defense against the right. Azaña refused to purge the officers'

corps of the army, which stood as a tightly knit faction preparing to strike against the republic and through it at the
working class.

Trotsky's assessment of Azaña as the Spanish Kerensky became the common opinion of the generals and the rightist
parties. The class polarization had gone too deep to be settled
in the rarified atmosphere of the Cortes. It would be resolved
now in the working class districts of Barcelona and on the
plains of Aragon. Who was to rule Spain would be arbitrated
not in the rhetoric of parliament but in the language of machine
guns. Unfortunately, the right understood this far better than
the left.

Civil war

The fascist rising began on July 17, 1936, in Spanish Morocco. In the next three days almost all of the fifty garrisons
in Spain declared for fascism. The vast majority of the old
ruling class, including the industrial capitalists, joined the rebellion.

Azaña's instinctive reaction was to compromise. The only
possible defense against the fascist onslaught was the arming
of the workers' organizations. Instead, Azaña's prime minister,
Casares Quiroga, announced that anyone who gave arms
to the workers would be shot. This guaranteed a fascist victory in scores of cities and resulted in the deaths of tens of
thousands of workers. The liberal historian Hugh Thomas
writes:

> Nearly everywhere on July 18 the Civil Governors in
> the large towns followed the example of the Government
> in Madrid, and refused to co-operate fully with the work-
> ing-class organisations who were clamouring for arms.
> In most cases, this brought the success of the [fascist] ris-
> ings and signed the death warrants of the Civil Governors
> themselves, along with the local working-class leaders. . . .
> But had the liberal Government of Casares Quiroga dis-
> tributed arms, and ordered the Civil Governors to do so
> too, thus using the working class to defend the Republic
> at the earliest opportunity, it is possible that the rising
> would have been crushed.[9]

On July 18, Casares Quiroga resigned. Azaña, still hoping to come to an agreement with the fascists, appointed the conservative Martínez Barrio to form a "moderate" government to demonstrate the respectability of the republican regime to Franco. A hundred thousand workers took to the streets of Madrid crying "Treason!" and demanding arms. On July 19, a new cabinet was formed and arms were reluctantly distributed to the masses. This marked a new and decisive stage of the Spanish revolution.

Throughout republican Spain the real power began to pass to the armed workers organizations. In Catalonia the CNT and the POUM took arms by force when the regional government of President Luis Companys refused to arm the people. Some of the fiercest fighting of this period took place in Barcelona. The British socialist George Orwell, who arrived in Catalonia in December and served in the POUM militia, gave this account of the July fighting in the Catalan capital:

> It was the kind of effort that could probably only be made by people who were fighting with a revolutionary intention — i.e. believed that they were fighting for something better than the *status quo*. In the various centres of revolt it is thought that three thousand people died in the streets in a single day. Men and women armed only with sticks of dynamite rushed across the open squares and stormed stone buildings held by trained soldiers with machine-guns. Machine-gun nests that the Fascists had placed at strategic spots were smashed by rushing taxis at them at sixty miles an hour. [10]

In Catalonia the working class parties and trade unions formed militias that defeated the fascists on a broad front in Aragon. The most important of these was an Anarchist column commanded by Durruti.

The immediate task facing loyalist Spain was the creation of a military force and the organization of production for defense. Despite the Stalinist theory that Franco represented "feudalism" — a theory put forward to justify the alliance with the republican bourgeoisie — the fact was that in most places the factory owners had defected to fascist territory. Workers spontaneously seized the factories and put them into operation under their own control; workers' patrols were organized to replace the police; peasants took over the land. A social revolution on a gigantic scale was taking place. Orwell describes the Barcelona he saw on his arrival in December 1936:

> It was the first time that I had ever been in a town where the working class was in the saddle. Practically every building of any size had been seized by the workers and was draped with red flags or with the red and black flag of the Anarchists; every wall was scrawled with the hammer and sickle and with the initials of the revolutionary parties. . . . Every shop and café had an inscription saying that it had been collectivized. . . . There were no private motor cars, they had all been commandeered, and all the trams and taxis and much of the other transport were painted red and black. The revolutionary posters were everywhere, flaming from the walls in clean reds and blues that made the few remaining advertisements look like daubs of mud. 11

On July 21, the working class parties and trade unions organized the Central Committee of Anti-Fascist Militias of Catalonia, which immediately became the only real power in the area.

Two governments existed in republican Spain, both vying for power on behalf of opposed classes — a phenomenon that in the Russian Revolution had been named "dual power." On one side stood the spontaneously created factory committees, the militia units, and the peasant councils, supported by the Anarchists and the POUM. On the other was ranged the official republican government of Azaña, composed of a handful of liberal capitalist politicians cut off from their own social base and lacking any mass following in the republic. Trotsky was to call them the "shadow bourgeoisie"— the class on which their power had rested had gone over to Franco. The figureheads alone remained, dependent for their very political existence on the support of the Communist and Socialist parties, now the main prop of the regime.

This did not mean that Azaña and his ministers were prepared to adopt a program of socialist revolution to stay in power. On the contrary, they opposed all of the revolutionary social measures taken spontaneously by the mobilized workers and agricultural laborers. They argued that it was neces-

sary to sharply limit social reforms in order to avoid alien-
ating the liberal businessmen and the democratic governments
of France, Britain, and the United States, from whom they
hoped to secure aid.

In reality the liberal businessmen were already fighting at
Franco's side. The forlorn hope that the imperialist bourgeoisies
of the Western democracies could be persuaded to overlook
their real class interests and abandon Franco proved equally
illusory. Under the guise of neutrality Washington, Paris, and
London refused even to sell arms to the legal Spanish government while ignoring the substantial military aid provided
to Franco by Hitler and Mussolini. Ironically, the doctrine
of "nonintervention" was formulated by France's Social Democratic premier Léon Blum, who himself headed a Popular
Front government brought to power by Communist Party
votes.

The relationship of forces in republican Spain overwhelmingly
favored the organizations of proletarian power. Azaña was able
to maintain his rule for two reasons. The first was the wavering
and indecision of the leadership of the Anarchists and the
POUM. Instead of moving to unite the local workers' councils
on a national level and establish a workers' government they
waited until the liberals had regained the initiative — and then
joined the Popular Front government themselves in September
1936, grudgingly giving their assent to the forcible destruction
of all the achievements of the revolution.

The second factor was the policy of the Comintern. Militarily,
in conventional terms, the fascists had every advantage over
the republic. They commanded a trained army, a superior
air force, and an unlimited supply of arms, equipment, and
men from their German and Italian allies. The only defense
against such an apparatus, as every successful working class
revolution has shown, lay in the mass mobilization of the
workers and peasants. This was precisely what the Communist
Party, in its insistence on the maintenance of bourgeois property
relations and a regular army, rejected. Stalin was above all
concerned with securing a military alliance with the imperialist
democracies against Nazi Germany. In Spain he aimed to
prove to his prospective allies that he was uninterested in promoting the spread of revolution and was willing to use his
influence to contain the workers' movement within the limits
of bourgeois democracy. (This also proved illusory. Despite

Stalin's willingness to act as the hangman of the Spanish revolution, the "democratic" imperialists remained unimpressed and refused the cooperation he sought. In the end Stalin turned to Hitler, and the Kremlin's maneuverings to secure the Stalin-Hitler Pact were to play no small part in Moscow's final abandonment of the republic.)

It would be entirely wrong, of course, to accord the same weight to the two elements that coincided in the crushing of the workers movement by the loyalist regime and prepared the triumph of fascism. Indecision and capitulation on the part of people who view themselves as revolutionists is to be condemned, but it is not in the same category as the conscious policy of counterrevolution pursued by the Communist Party.

Stalin and his local representatives made no secret of their social program. Thus, Jesús Hernández, one of the leading figures of the Spanish Communist Party and editor of its newspaper *El Mundo obrero,* wrote:

> It is absolutely false that the present workers' movement has for its object the establishment of a proletarian dictatorship after the war has terminated. It cannot be said we have a social motive for our participation in the war. We communists are the first to repudiate this supposition. We are motivated exclusively by a desire to defend the democratic republic. 12

Seven months later another Spanish Stalinist was prepared to explicitly repudiate the workers' committees and take an open stand against the factory occupations. José Díaz, in his March 5, 1937, speech at a plenary session of the CP Central Committee, declared:

> If in the beginning the various premature attempts at "socialization" and "collectivization," which were the result of an unclear understanding of the character of the present struggle, might have been justified by the fact that the big landlords and manufacturers had deserted their estates and factories and that it was necessary at all costs to continue production, now on the contrary they cannot be justified at all. At the present time, when there is a government of the Popular Front, in which all the forces engaged in

the fight against fascism are represented, such things are not only not desirable, but absolutely impermissible. [13]

Stalin himself gave the same advice to the republican government. In a letter to Largo Caballero dated December 21, 1936, Stalin told the new prime minister to "attract the middle and lower bourgeoisie . . . [by] protecting them against confiscations," to promise the republican parties the retention of Azaña as president, and to respect the property "rights" and "legitimate" interests of foreigners "who are citizens of nations not supporting the rebels [i. e., France and Britain]." [14]

As the Anarchists and the POUM wavered, the government in Madrid began to reestablish its authority. In the first weeks censorship of the workers' press was reimposed. A drive was begun to dissolve the militias into the newly created "Popular Army" on the grounds of centralizing the conduct of the war. This was largely a spurious issue. The Anarchists and the POUM were equally in favor of centralizing military operations. The question was *to whom the military forces were going to be responsible.* The intention of Caballero's move was to cut off the working class parties from political influence in the armed forces.

A crucial turning point in the evolution of dual power was the entry of the Anarchists and the POUM into the regional government of Catalonia, the Generalitat, in September 1936. It was this step that caused Trotsky to finally sever all remaining connections with the POUM and to write off the possibility that under the pressure of events it could play a revolutionary role. On October 9 the Generalitat dissolved the Central Committee of the Anti-Fascist Militias, and subsequently expelled the POUM from the government.

As the power of the workers' committees waned, the government of the republic moved further and further to the right. This was epitomized by its attitude toward the Spanish colonies. Franco's main base of operations was Morocco, a colony subjugated by Spain only after many years of brutal desert warfare. Even from the standpoint of bourgeois democracy the republic could have proclaimed the independence of this oppressed colonial people. Strategically in the fight against Franco there was every reason to do so in order to win the

Moroccan people as allies in the fight against fascism. But Stalin and Azaña were afraid of alarming the British and French governments, which held vast colonial empires in Africa. And so the republic defended Spain's imperialist claims to rule Morocco.

Abd-el-Krim, the most outstanding military leader of the Moroccans in their war with Spain, appealed to Largo Caballero to use his influence to allow Krim to return from exile to Morocco, where he pledged to lead an insurrection against Franco. Caballero, dubbed the "Spanish Lenin" by the Stalinists, refused.

The May events in Barcelona and the suppression of the POUM

The greatest problem for the CP was Catalonia, where its influence had always been minimal. But with the arrival of Russian arms and foreign volunteers the Comintern now commanded a force with which it hoped to crush its rivals in the working class movement.

The Stalinists began their offensive against the Anarchist and POUM militias with a softening-up tactic. The CP used its control over the flow of Russian arms to deny weapons to those sections of the front defended by parties with which it was in political disagreement, thus handing over much territory to the fascists and promoting the slaughter of thousands of working class revolutionists, particularly on the Aragon front. This cynical policy has been documented by innumerable observers. Gerald Brenan, whose *Spanish Labyrinth* is one of the standard left-wing works on Spain during this period, testifies:

> To [the CP], winning the war meant winning it for the Communist party and they were always ready to sacrifice military advantage to prevent a rival party on their own side from strengthening its position. [15]

George Orwell, who fought on the Aragon front and was badly wounded there, gave this description of the pitiful lack of weapons:

> [The infantry] were far worse armed than an English public school Officers' Training Corps with worn out Mauser rifles which usually jammed after five shots; approximately

one machine-gun to fifty men; and one pistol or revolver to about thirty men. These weapons, so necessary in trench warfare, were not issued by the government and could be bought only illegally and with the greatest difficulty. . . .

A government which sends boys of fifteen to the front with rifles forty years old and keeps its biggest men and newest weapons in the rear, is manifestly more afraid of the revolution than of the fascists.[16]

In May of 1937, the Communist Party and its Russian advisors felt themselves strong enough to move against the left flank of the republican forces. The Anarchist leadership had joined the central government in November 1936, and in doing so had renounced the struggle for a workers' government. The POUM leaders, though out of the government, limited themselves to advising the Popular Front and the Anarchists to call a national congress of workers' organizations, which of course the government had no intention of doing. In the meantime the masses who followed the POUM and the Anarchists were growing restive as they watched the gains of the July revolution being taken away by their "allies" in the Popular Front.

The CP decided to stage a provocation. Using its agents in the Barcelona police it ordered the seizure of the telephone exchange. This building had been operated by the CNT since they captured it from the fascists at the cost of many lives in July 1936.

The Anarchist telephone operators refused to surrender the exchange and sharp fighting broke out between the workers and the Asaltos. Barricades went up throughout the city just as they had in the "Revolution of July 19." Thousands of workers poured into the streets to defend their organizations from this unprovoked assault by the police. Once again the question of power was directly posed.

Barcelona in May 1937 was the last possible moment that the workers could have created their own government in Spain and recouped what they had lost to the capitalist-Stalinist bloc. Instead, the leaders of the POUM and the Anarchists accepted a truce with the Popular Front, and on the basis of a pledge that there would be no reprisals, appealed to the workers to go home.

After the fighting had ended, troops were sent from Valencia, where the central government had moved in November 1936, to occupy the city. Anarchists, POUMists, and militia members were arrested on sight, as were members of the Spanish Bolshevik-Leninists, the organization of those who had remained loyal to Trotsky's program and tried against overwhelming odds to put it into practice.

The Communist Party had introduced a bill in the central government in Valencia demanding the outlawing of the POUM. This measure was finally passed on June 15-16, 1937. The Stalinists motivated this suppression of the left with a vile slander campaign, charging that the leaders of the POUM were paid agents of Franco. This was picked up and trumpeted by the Stalinist press around the world. The *Daily Worker,* the organ of the American CP, ran a blazing headline in its June 21, 1937, issue declaring: "Spanish Trotskyites Plot with Franco."

Even Largo Caballero had to protest against the CP's factional warfare. On May 11, the newspaper of his supporters, *Adelante,* declared editorially:

> If the Caballero government were to apply the measures of repression which the Spanish section of the Comintern is trying to incite, it would . . . destroy working-class unity and expose us to the danger of losing the war and wrecking the revolution.17

But by this time the Stalinists' grip on the Valencia government was too strong to be shaken from within. Caballero was finally deposed on May 15 and replaced by the more pliable Juan Negrín.

In June the CP began the final assault on the POUM. Hugh Thomas gives a graphic picture of the repression:

> In Barcelona . . . on the orders of Antonov-Ovsëenko, the Russian Consul General, the POUM headquarters at the Hotel Falcón was closed. It was immediately, and conveniently, turned into a prison. The POUM itself was declared illegal, and 40 members of its central committee arrested. Andrés Nin was taken off separately, but his friends all found themselves in an underground dungeon in Madrid. All members or associates of the POUM went

in fear of arrest, since the Stalinist habit of visiting the alleged crimes of the leaders upon all possible followers was well known. The Communist newspapers daily screamed accusations against those whom their party had arrested but did not bring to trial. . . . And a rumour spread that Andrés Nin had been murdered in prison. . . . In fact, he was in Orlov's prison in the dilapidated ex-cathedral city of Alcalá de Henares. . . . He was there undergoing the customary Soviet interrogation of suspected deviationists. [18]

When the Soviet interrogators became convinced that they could not use Nin in a show trial against the POUM, they decided to dispose of him. Hugh Thomas describes the shameful use made of the International Brigades in this execution:

> Eventually Vittorio Vidali (Carlos Contreras) suggested that a "Nazi" attack to liberate Nin should be simulated. So, one dark night, ten German members of the International Brigade assaulted the house in Alcalá where Nin was held. Ostentatiously, they spoke German during the pretended attack, and left behind some German train tickets. Nin was taken away in a closed van and murdered. [19]

The end of the republic

From this point on the fortunes of the republic began a steady decline. The war of attrition was to drag on for twenty-one months, but the revolution was already dead, and with it had passed any hope of halting Franco.

The end of the war is a bitter chronicle of demoralization, defeat, and betrayal by "loyal" officers out to save their own skins. The fascists drove to the coast at Vinaróz in April of 1938, cutting republican Spain in two. Stalin, now looking toward the alliance with Hitler that was to be consummated the next year in the Soviet-German Nonaggression Pact, was anxious to extricate himself from Spain and avoid the embarrassment of confronting German troops in the Spanish conflict.

The chronology of what followed was plain enough for anyone willing to read it: On September 22 the International Brigades fought their last battle in the Ebro campaign. On September 29 Chamberlain and Daladier signed the Munich Pact with Hitler, foreclosing the possibility of an anti-German alliance with the Soviet Union, to which Stalin had sacrificed the Spanish revolution. By November 15 the International Brigades were departing from Spain, leaving Stalin free to negotiate with Berlin.

The tragedy of the Spanish proletariat was not only that it was beaten in an open fight with its avowed enemy, fascism, but that it was betrayed by those who claimed to be its leaders. When the fascists took Barcelona on January 26, 1939, it fell without firing a shot. Hundreds of thousands of refugees fled across the frontier into France and into exile.

In March 1939, Madrid and Valencia surrendered to the fascists. The liberal politicians and the Communist Party functionaries had long prepared their escape hatches and fled abroad, but the Spanish working class could not flee.

Every condition for socialist victory had existed in Spain — save one. And that one, the existence of a mass revolutionary party that aimed at the establishment of a workers' government, proved to be indispensable.

Stalin acted in Spain on the assumption that with the aid of the Communist Party, bourgeois democracy could be preserved when the bourgeoisie had abandoned it. Moscow feared the socialist revolution as much as did the bourgeoisie, and in the name of "democracy" acted as the most ruthless agent of capitalism in the struggle with the workers' movement. Trotsky wrote in his pamphlet "The Lessons of Spain — The Last Warning" — the finest exposition of his views on the Spanish revolution — that Stalin "placed the technique of Bolshevism at the service of bourgeois property. In his bureaucratic narrow-mindedness, he imagined that 'commissars' by themselves could guarantee victory. But the commissars of private property proved capable only of guaranteeing defeat."

It is to be hoped that this collection of Trotsky's writings on Spain will help to arm the present generation of revolutionary youth so that the harsh experience of Spain need never be repeated.

                                        LES EVANS
                                        May 11, 1972

Notes for Introduction

1. Gerald Brenan, *The Spanish Labyrinth* (New York: Cambridge University Press, 1943), pp. 120-21.

2. Hugh Thomas, *The Spanish Civil War* (New York: Harper & Brothers, 1961), p. 40.

3. Strictly speaking I should deal with the Spanish Trotskyists and the party known as the POUM (Partido Obrero de Unificación Marxista — Workers Party of Marxist Unification) before coming to the CP, inasmuch as these forces were substantially larger than Spanish Stalinism from 1933 until well into the civil war years (the POUM in 1936 claimed 40,000 members). Because of the special place of the Spanish Left Opposition and the POUM in Trotsky's efforts to promote a revolutionary party in Spain, I will treat them in a separate section.

4. Stanley G. Payne, *The Spanish Revolution* (New York: W. W. Norton & Company, 1970), p. 144.

5. Thomas, op. cit., p. 99.

6. Vidali was later implicated in the machine-gun attempt on Trotsky's life in May 1940 in Mexico. Gerö acted as an agent of Khrushchev in the suppression of the Hungarian revolution in 1956.

7. *El Socialista*, April 29, 1934. Cited by Richard A. H. Robinson, in *The Origins of Franco's Spain* (Pittsburgh: University of Pittsburgh Press, 1970), p. 182.

8. From an interview with Lawrence Fernsworth in the summer of 1934. Fernsworth, *Spain's Struggle for Freedom* (Boston: Beacon Press, 1957), pp. 156-61.

9. Thomas, op. cit., p. 135.

10. George Orwell, *Homage to Catalonia* (Boston: Beacon Press, 1952), pp. 49-50.

11. Ibid., pp. 4-5.

12. *El Mundo obrero*, August 6, 1936. Cited by Felix Morrow in

Revolution and Counterrevolution in Spain (New York: Pioneer Publishers, 1938), p. 34.

13. *Communist International,* May 1937.

14. *New York Times*, June 4, 1939, p. 43. The *Times* published the full text of the letter, translated from the French, along with photostats of the first and last pages of the four-page original. An accompanying interview with Luis Araquistain, a confidant of Largo Caballero and his ambassador to France, testifies to the authenticity of the letter.

15. Brenan, op. cit., p. 326.

16. *Controversy*, August 1937.

17. Cited by Morrow, op. cit., p. 115.

18. Thomas, op. cit., pp. 453-54.

19. Ibid., pp. 454-55.

THE
SPANISH
REVOLUTION
(1931-39)

PART I:

From Monarchy to Republic

Under the impact of the financial crash of 1929, General Primo de Rivera polled the garrisons of Spain for a vote of confidence in January 1930. His fellow officers voted against him. The dictator's fall inaugurated a weak, semimilitary regime that was to give way almost directly to the republic.

King Alfonso XIII appointed General Dámaso Berenguer Fusté to head an interim government that the king hoped would prepare the way for a constitutional monarchy. The success of this venture depended on the organizational strength and mass base of the monarchist and clerical political parties. But since all parties had been illegal under Primo de Rivera, the party apparatuses of the bourgeois right and center were in disarray. Only the working class parties, which had carried on illegal work under the dictatorship, were prepared to take advantage of the new possibilities for political activity.

The Anarchists, as was their tradition, prepared to boycott any elections that might ensue. The Socialists, however, in the autumn of 1930 signed a pact at San Sebastian with representatives of the bourgeois republican parties pledging joint electoral action.

In December, republican officers led a military revolt against the monarchy, centered in the garrison at Jaca. This was suppressed and its organizers executed, but the popular outrage that followed prompted the king to form a new government and announce elections. Berenguer resigned, to be replaced in February 1931 by a civilian administration.

Convinced that the rightist parties could not win a majority in elections to the Cortes, the king called municipal elections instead for April 12. All the large towns voted solidly for the republican and Socialist parties. The monarchists maintained a majority of the total votes cast only through their fraudulent control of the rural vote through the system of *caciques* (local political bosses). When great crowds began gathering in the streets of Madrid proclaiming their hostility to the monarchy, Alfonso decided to abdicate. "Sunday's elections," he declared, "have shown me that I no longer enjoy the love of my people."

On April 14 a republic was declared and a new government

took office. The bourgeois parties dominated the cabinet. The first prime minister was Don Niceto Alcalá Zamora, an Andalusian lawyer who had been one of Alfonso's ministers before Primo de Rivera's coup. The ministry of the interior went to Miguel Maura, a prominent defender of the Catholic Church. The conservative Radical Party was given two posts, for its representatives Alejandro Lerroux and Diego Martínez Barrio. Thus far, the cabinet could hardly be distinguished from the far right-wing parties. The liberal republican "left" was represented by Manuel Azaña, who was minister of war; Casares Quiroga; Alvaro de Albornoz; Nicoláu d'Olwer; and Fernando de los Ríos, the last technically a member of the Socialist Party but in fact not bound by that party's discipline. The Socialist Party's actual representatives, Largo Caballero and Indalecio Prieto, were a minority of two in the overwhelmingly bourgeois government.

The new provisional government issued a "Juridical Statute" on April 15, which contained its program. It proposed calling a constituent Cortes to adopt a new constitution and formally elect a regular government. The statute pledged freedom of religion, guaranteed private property rights, and promised agrarian reform.

A Note on Trotsky's Exile: It would be useful for the reader to keep in mind where Trotsky was when he wrote the various documents collected in this book. Trotsky and his family were forcibly exiled from the Soviet Union by Stalin's order in February 1929, and lived in Turkey until July 1933. Under Trotsky's guidance, the International Left Opposition (Bolshevik-Leninists) had been organized in Paris in April 1930. The problems of its growth and development occupied a major part of his attention in 1930-31, when he was also busy writing *The History of the Russian Revolution.*

All the articles in Part I were written in Turkey, either on the island of Prinkipo or in Kadikoy, a suburb of Istanbul. With the exception of the pamphlet "The Revolution in Spain," they were written in the form of letters to the leaders of the newly formed Spanish section of the Left Opposition; from these letters Trotsky himself extracted portions for publication. It should be remembered that at the time of these articles Trotsky and the Left Opposition were guided by the strategy of reforming the Communist International and its affiliates.

1 TASKS OF THE SPANISH COMMUNISTS

May 25, 1930

Dear Comrades:

I warmly salute the appearance of the first issue of your newspaper. The Spanish Communist Opposition enters the arena at a particularly favorable and decisive moment.

The Spanish crisis is unfolding at this time with remarkable regularity, which affords the proletarian vanguard a certain amount of time to prepare itself. However, it is doubtful whether this period will last very long.

The Primo de Rivera dictatorship has fallen without a revolution, from internal exhaustion. In the beginning, in other words, the question was decided by the sickness of the old society and not by the revolutionary forces of a new society. This is not simply an accident. On the one hand, the dictatorial regime, in the eyes of the bourgeois classes, was no longer justified by the urgent need to smash the revolutionary masses; at the same time, this regime came into conflict with the economic, financial, political, and cultural needs of the bourgeoisie. But up to the last moment, the bourgeoisie avoided a showdown struggle with all its might. It allowed the dictatorship to rot and fall like wormy fruit.

Afterwards, the different classes, represented by their various political groups, were obliged to take clear-cut positions before the masses. And here we observe a paradox. The same bourgeois parties that because of their conservatism had refused to conduct a serious struggle, no matter how small, against the military dictatorship, now have put all the blame for that dictatorship on the monarchy and declared themselves republicans. As though the dictatorship had been hanging by a thread from the balcony of the royal palace the whole time,

A letter to the editors of *Contra la corriente*, the first Spanish Bolshevik-Leninist paper, which was published in exile in Belgium by Spanish emigres. From Leon Trotsky, *Ecrits*, Vol. III (1928-1940), Paris, 1959. Previously published in *La Vérité,* the organ of the Communist League of France, on June 13, 1930. Translated for this volume from the French by Constance Weissman.

and as though it had not been kept up at all by the support, sometimes passive, sometimes active, of the most substantial layers of the bourgeoisie who, with all their strength, paralyzed the activity of the petty bourgeoisie and trampled underfoot the workers of city and countryside.

And what is the result? While not only the workers, the peasants, the urban petty bourgeoisie, and the young intellectuals, but also almost all of the big bourgeoisie either are or call themselves republicans, the monarchy continues to exist and to function. If Primo did hang only by a thread from the monarchy, then by what thread did the monarchy hang, in such a "republican" country? At first glance, it appears to be an insoluble riddle. But the answer is not so complicated. The same bourgeoisie that was "tolerating" Primo de Rivera was actually supporting him, as today it supports the monarchy by the only means available, that is, by calling itself republican and thus adapting itself to the psychology of the petty bourgeoisie, the better to deceive and paralyze it.

For a bystander, this scene, despite its high drama, is not without its comical side. The monarchy is sitting on the back of the republican bourgeoisie, which is in no hurry to throw it off. The bourgeoisie, slipping stealthily among the restless masses with its precious load, answers the protests, complaints, and curses in the voice of a slapstick comedian: "Look at this creature on my back! It is my sworn enemy. I will list its crimes for you: pay attention!" etc., etc. And when the crowd, amused by this spectacle, begins to laugh, the bourgeoisie takes advantage of this favorable occasion to carry its load a little further on. If this is what is meant by struggling against the monarchy, then what is meant by a struggle in support of it?

The spirited demonstrations of the students are only an attempt by the younger generation of the bourgeoisie, and especially of the petty bourgeoisie, to find a solution to the instability into which the country fell after its supposed liberation from Primo de Rivera's dictatorship, of which the basic elements are still totally preserved. When the bourgeoisie consciously and obstinately refuses to resolve the problems that flow from the crisis of bourgeois society, and when the proletariat is not yet ready to assume this task, then it is often the students who come forward. During the development of

the first Russian revolution [1905], we observed this phenomenon more than once, and we have always appreciated its
symptomatic significance. Such revolutionary or semirevolutionary student activity means that bourgeois society is going
through a profound crisis. The petty-bourgeois youth, sensing
that an explosive force is building up among the masses, try
in their own way to find a way out of the impasse and to
push the political developments forward.

The bourgeoisie regards the student movement half-approv-
ingly, half-warningly; if the youth deal a few blows to the
monarchical bureaucracy, that's not so bad, as long as the
"kids" don't go too far and don't arouse the toiling masses.

By backing up the student movement, the Spanish workers
have shown an entirely correct revolutionary instinct. Of course,
they must act under their own banner and under the leadership of their own proletarian organization. It is Spanish communism that must guarantee this process and for that a correct policy is indispensable. That is why the appearance of
your newspaper, as I said before, coincides with an extraordinarily important and critical moment in the development
of the whole crisis; to be more precise, it coincides with a moment when the revolutionary crisis is being transformed into
a revolution.

The workers' strike movement, their struggle against industrial reorganization and unemployment, takes on a totally
different, incomparably more profound importance in the context of the extreme discontent of the petty-bourgeois masses
and of the sharp crisis in the system as a whole. The workers'
struggle must be closely linked to all the questions that flow
from the national crisis. The fact that the workers demonstrated
with the students is the first step, though still an insufficient
and hesitant one, on the proletarian vanguard's road of
struggle toward revolutionary hegemony.

Taking this road presupposes that the communists will
struggle resolutely, audaciously, and energetically for *democratic slogans*. Not to understand this would be to commit
the greatest sectarian mistake. At the present stage of the revolution, the proletariat distinguishes itself in the field of *political* slogans from all the "leftist" petty-bourgeois groupings
not by rejecting democracy (as the Anarchists and syndicalists
do) but by struggling resolutely and openly for it, at the same

time mercilessly denouncing the hesitations of the petty bourgeoisie.

By advancing democratic slogans, the proletariat is not in any way suggesting that Spain is heading toward a bourgeois revolution. Only barren pedants full of pat, ready-made formulas could pose the question this way.. Spain has left the stage of bourgeois revolution far behind.

If the revolutionary crisis is transformed into a revolution, it will inevitably pass beyond bourgeois limits, and in the event of victory the power will have to come into the hands of the proletariat. But in this epoch, the proletariat can lead the revolution — that is, group the broadest masses of the workers and the oppressed around itself and become their leader — only on the condition that it now unreservedly puts forth all the democratic demands, in conjunction with its own class demands.

First of all, these slogans will be of decisive importance for the peasantry. The peasantry cannot give the proletariat its confidence a priori by accepting the slogan of the dictatorship of the proletariat as a verbal pledge. The peasantry, being a large oppressed class, at a certain stage inevitably sees in the democratic slogan the possibility for the oppressed to overthrow the oppressors. The peasantry will inevitably link the slogan of political democracy with the slogan of the radical redistribution of the land. The proletariat will openly support both demands. At the proper time, the communists will explain to the proletarian vanguard the road by which these demands can be achieved, thus sowing the seeds for the future soviet system.

Even on national questions, the proletariat defends the democratic slogans to the hilt, declaring that it is ready to support by revolutionary means the right of different national groups to self-determination, even to the point of separation.

But does the proletarian vanguard itself raise the slogan of the secession of Catalonia? If it is the will of the majority, yes; but how can this will be expressed? Obviously, by means of a free plebiscite, or an assembly of Catalan representatives, or by the parties that are clearly supported by the Catalan masses, or even by a Catalan national revolt. Again we see, let us note in passing, what reactionary pedantry it would be for the proletariat to renounce democratic slogans. Meanwhile, as long as the national minority has not expressed its will, the proletariat itself will not adopt the slogan of separation, but it pledges openly, in advance, its complete and sincere support to this slogan in the event that it should express the will of Catalonia.

It is useless to say that the Catalan workers do not have the final word to say on this question. If they came to the conclusion that it would be unwise to divide their forces in the present crisis, which opens such sweeping opportunities to the Spanish proletariat, the Catalan workers would have to aim their propaganda toward maintaining Catalonia as a part of Spain, on one or another basis. As for me, I believe that political judgement suggests such a solution. Such a solution would be acceptable for the time being even to the most fervent separatists, since it is completely obvious that in the event of the victory of the revolution, it would be ever so much easier than it is today for Catalonia, as well as for other regions, to achieve the right of self-determination.

By supporting all really democratic and revolutionary movements of the popular masses, the communist vanguard will be leading an uncompromising struggle against the so-called republican bourgeoisie, unmasking its double-dealing, its treachery, and its reactionary character, and resisting its attempts to subject the toiling masses to its influence.

The communists never relinquish their freedom of political action under any conditions. It must not be forgotten that during a revolution temptations of this sort are very great: the tragic history of the Chinese revolution is irrefutable testimony to this.[1] * But while safeguarding the full independence of their organization and their propaganda, the communists nonetheless practice, in the broadest fashion, the policy of the united front,[2] for which the revolution offers a vast field.

The Left Opposition begins the application of the united-front policy with the official Communist Party. The bureaucrats must not be allowed to create the impression that the Left Opposition is hostile to the workers who follow the banner of the official Communist Party. On the contrary, the Opposition is ready to take part in all the revolutionary activity of the proletariat and to struggle side by side with those work-

---

*Notes for Part I begin on p. 401.

ers. If the bureaucrats refuse to act together with the Opposition, then they must bear the full responsibility for this refusal in the eyes of the working class.

The continuation of the Spanish crisis means the revolutionary awakening of millions among the toiling masses. Nothing
indicates that they will *suddenly* enlist under the banner of
communism. Instead, they will probably first reinforce the
party of the radical petty bourgeoisie, that is to say, primarily
the Socialist Party, especially its left wing, as was the case,
for example, with the German Independents during the 1918-
1919 revolution.[3] That is how the broad and real radicalization of the masses will be expressed, and not in a growth
of "social fascism."[4] Fascism could triumph anew — and this
time in a more "social" than "military" form, i. e., like the "social fascism" of Mussolini — only as a consequence of the defeat of the revolution and the disillusionment of the betrayed
masses who had believed in it. But in the face of the steady
development of recent events, a defeat can take place only
as a consequence of extraordinary errors on the part of the
communist leadership.

Verbal radicalism and sectarianism in combination with an
opportunist assessment of class forces, a policy of zig-zags,
bureaucratic leadership — in a word, everything that goes to
make up the essence of Stalinism — are the very things that can
reinforce the position of the Social Democracy,[5] the most dangerous enemy of the proletariat, as the experience of the German and Italian revolutionists showed with particular clarity.

Social Democracy must be politically discredited in the eyes
of the masses. But this cannot be achieved by means of insults. The masses trust only their own collective experience.
They must be given the opportunity during the preparatory
period of the revolution to compare in action the communist
policies with those of the Social Democrats.

The struggle to win over the masses will unquestionably
create the conditions for this, if the communists insist in full
view of the masses on a united front with the Social Democrats. Liebknecht had many areas of agreement with the
Independents, especially with their left wing.[6] There was an
outright bloc between the Bolsheviks and the Left Social Revolutionaries.[7] And right up to the insurrection we reached
a series of specific agreements with the Menshevik-Internation-

alists[8] and made dozens of proposals for a united front. We lost nothing from this policy. But, of course, what was involved was not a united front like the Anglo-Russian Committee,[9] which meant that at the time of a revolutionary general strike the Stalinists blocked with the strikebreakers. And of course it did not involve a united front in the spirit of the Kuomintang,[10] when, under the false slogan of a union of workers and peasants, a bourgeois dictatorship over the workers and peasants was ensured.

Such are the tasks and perspectives as they seem from the sidelines. I am sharply aware to what degree the above comments are lacking in concreteness. It is quite probable and even likely that I have left out a number of extremely important circumstances. You will see for yourselves. Armed with Marxist theory and Leninist revolutionary method, you will find your road by yourselves. You will know how to grasp the thoughts and sentiments of the working class and give them clear political expression. The purpose of my letter is only to recapitulate in a general way the principles of revolutionary strategy that have been confirmed by the experience of three Russian revolutions.

Warm regards and my best wishes for success.

Yours,
L. Trotsky

2   *SPANISH FASCISM*

November 21, 1930

In my article ["Tasks of the Spanish Communists"] I very carefully expressed the thought that after several years of dictatorship, after a bourgeois opposition movement, after all the superficial noise of the republicans, and after the student demonstrations, we must *inevitably* expect the workers to act; what is more, these interventions may catch the revolutionary

From the pamphlet "The Spanish Revolution in Danger," published by the Communist League of America in 1931, in a translation from the Russian by Morris Lewitt.

party unawares. Unless I am mistaken, several Spanish comrades thought that I exaggerated the symptomatic importance of the student demonstrations and, together with that, the perspectives for the revolutionary movement of the workers. Since then, however, the strike struggle has assumed gigantic proportions in Spain. It is altogether impossible to get a clear picture of who is leading these strikes.

Don't you think that Spain may go through the same cycle as Italy did, beginning with 1918-1919: ferment, strikes, a general strike, the seizure of the factories, the lack of leadership, the decline of the movement, the growth of fascism, and of a counterrevolutionary dictatorship? The regime of Primo de Rivera was not a fascist dictatorship because it did not base itself upon the reaction of the petty-bourgeois masses. Don't you think that the conditions for genuine Spanish fascism may be created as a result of the present unquestionable revolutionary upsurge in Spain, if the party of the proletarian vanguard remains passive and inconsistent, as in the past? The most dangerous thing in such a situation is the loss of time.

3   *THE CREATION OF SOVIETS*

December 12, 1930
What are the perspectives then? . . . As far as I can tell from your last letter, all the organizations and groups are drifting with the current, that is, they are participating in the movement to the extent that it drags them along. Not a single one of the organizations has a revolutionary program of action or a well-thought-out perspective. . . .

It seems to me that the slogan of soviets is suggested by the whole situation, if by soviets we mean the workers' councils that sprang up in Russia: at first, they were powerful strike committees. Not one of the early participants imagined that the soviets were the future organs of power. . . . Of course, soviets cannot be created artificially. But during each local

From "The Spanish Revolution in Danger."

strike that includes a majority of the trades and takes on a political character, it is necessary to encourage the creation of soviets. This is the only form of organization, under the circumstances, that is capable of taking the leadership of the movement and of imposing on it the discipline of revolutionary action.

I tell you frankly, I am very much afraid that the historians of the future may have to accuse the Spanish revolutionists of not having known how to take advantage of an exceptional revolutionary situation.

4   *FOR SPANISH SOVIETS*

January 8, 1931

(10) In Spain, conditions are apparently different from those in all the other countries. Spain is at present going through a period of clear and definite revolutionary upsurge. The heated political atmosphere must make it considerably easier for the Bolshevik-Leninists as the boldest and most consistent revolutionary wing to carry on their work. The Communist International has dispersed the ranks of Spanish communism, it has weakened and rendered impotent the official Communist Party. As in many other important cases, the Comintern leadership has passed up a revolutionary situation. The Spanish workers have been abandoned to their own fate at a most serious moment. Left almost without leadership, they are developing a struggle of revolutionary strikes with remarkable amplitude.

Under these conditions, the Spanish Bolshevik-Leninists are issuing the slogan of *soviets*. According to the theory of the Stalinists and the practice of the Canton insurrection,[11] it appears that soviets must be created only on the eve of the insurrection. Disastrous theory and disastrous practice! The soviets must be created when the real and living movement of

An excerpt from a letter to the Chinese Left Opposition that appeared in the *International Bulletin,* Communist Left Opposition, no. 5, August 1931. The full text of the letter is in *Writings of Leon Trotsky* (1930-31), Pathfinder Press, New York.

the masses manifests the need for such an organization. The soviets at first are formed as broad strike committees. This is precisely the case in Spain. There is no doubt that the initiative of the Bolshevik-Leninists (Opposition) will under these conditions find an echo among the proletarian vanguard. A broad perspective can open up in the near future for the Spanish Opposition. Let us wish our Spanish friends success.

5   *SOVIETS AND THE CONSTITUENT CORTES*

January 12, 1931
Will the elections actually take place on March 1?[12] . . .

In the immediate situation, it certainly appears that we could invalidate Berenguer's elections by an energetically applied boycott tactic; in 1905 that was how we invalidated the election of a legislative Duma that was merely consultative. What is the policy of the communists on this point? Do they distribute leaflets, appeals, proclamations on this subject?

But if the Cortes is to be boycotted, then in the name of what? In the name of the soviets? In my opinion, it would be wrong to pose the question that way. The masses of the city and countryside can be united at the present time only under democratic slogans. These include the election of a constituent Cortes on the basis of universal, equal, direct, and secret suffrage. I do not think that in the present situation you can avoid this slogan. Soviets are as yet nonexistent. The Spanish workers — not to speak of the peasants — do not know what soviets are; at any rate, not from their own experiences. Nevertheless, the struggle around the Cortes in the coming period will constitute the whole political life of the country. To counterpose the slogan of soviets, under these circumstances, to the slogan of the Cortes, would be incorrect. On the other hand, it will obviously be possible to build soviets in the near future only by mobilizing the masses on the basis of democratic slogans. This means: to prevent the monarchy from convening a false, deceptive, conservative Cortes; to as-

From "The Spanish Revolution in Danger."

sure the convocation of a democratic constituent Cortes; and
so that this Cortes can give the land to the peasants, and do
many other things, workers', soldiers', and peasants' soviets
must be created to fortify the positions of the toiling masses.

6   *THE REVOLUTION IN SPAIN*

January 24, 1931

1. *Old Spain*
The capitalist chain is again threatening to break at its weakest link; Spain is next in order. The revolutionary movement
is developing in that country with such vigor that world reaction is deprived in advance of the hope for a speedy restoration of order on the Iberian Peninsula.

Spain is unmistakably among the most backward countries
of Europe. But its backwardness has a singular character,
invested by the great historic past of the country. While the
Russia of the czars always lagged far behind its western neighbors and advanced slowly under their pressure, Spain knew
periods of great bloom, of superiority over the rest of Europe
and of domination over South America. The mighty development of domestic and world commerce increasingly overcame
the effect of the feudal dismemberment of the provinces and the
particularism of the national regions of the country. The growth
of the power and importance of the Spanish monarchy in those
centuries was inextricably bound up with the centralizing role
of mercantile capital and with the gradual formation of the
"Spanish nation."

The discovery of America, which at first enriched and
strengthened Spain, subsequently worked against it. The great
routes of commerce were diverted from the Iberian Peninsula.
Holland, which had grown rich, broke away from Spain.
Following Holland, England rose to great heights over Europe for a long time. By the beginning of the second half

Published in pamphlet form by the Communist League of America
in March 1931, in a translation from the Russian by Morris Lewitt.

of the sixteenth century, Spain had already begun to decline. This decline assumed an official character, so to speak, with the destruction of the Great Armada (1588). The condition that Marx called "inglorious and slow decay" settled down upon feudal-bourgeois Spain.

The old and new ruling classes — the landed nobility and the Catholic clergy with their monarchy, the bourgeois classes with their intelligentsia — stubbornly attempted to preserve the old pretensions but, alas, without the old resources. In 1820, the South American colonies finally broke away. With the loss of Cuba in 1898, Spain was almost completely deprived of colonial possessions. The adventures in Morocco only ruined the country, adding fuel to the already deep dissatisfaction of the people. [13]

Spain's retarded economic development inevitably weakened the centralist tendencies inherent in capitalism. The decline of the commercial and industrial life in the cities and of the economic ties between them inevitably led to the lessening of the dependence of individual provinces upon each other. This is the chief reason why bourgeois Spain has not succeeded to this day in eliminating the centrifugal tendencies of its historic provinces. The meagerness of the national resources and the feeling of restlessness all over the country could not help but foster separatist tendencies. Particularism appears in Spain with unusual force, especially compared with neighboring France, where the Great Revolution finally established the bourgeois nation, united and indivisible, over the old feudal provinces.

While not permitting the formation of a new bourgeois society, the economic stagnation also corroded the old ruling classes. The proud noblemen often cloaked their haughtiness in rags. The church plundered the peasantry, but from time to time it was plundered by the monarchy, who, as Marx said, had more in common with Asiatic despotism than with European absolutism.

How could this be? The comparison between czarism and Asiatic despotism, which has been made more than once, seems much more natural geographically and historically. But with regard to Spain, this comparison retains all its force as well. The difference is only that czarism was formed on the basis of the *extremely slow development* of the nobility and of the primitive urban centers, whereas the Spanish monarchy took shape under the conditions of the *decline* of the country and the *decay* of the ruling classes. If European absolutism generally could rise only thanks to a struggle by the strengthened cities against the old privileged estates, then the Spanish monarchy, like Russian czarism, drew its relative strength from the impotence of the old estates and the cities. This accounts for its obvious resemblance to Asiatic despotism.

The predominance of the centrifugal tendencies over the centripetal ones in the economy as well as in politics undermined the foundation of Spanish parliamentarism. The government's pressure on the electorate was decisive: throughout the last century, elections unfailingly gave the government a majority. Because the Cortes found itself dependent upon the successive ministries, the ministries themselves naturally sank into dependence upon the monarchy. Madrid held the elections but the king held the power.

The monarchy was doubly necessary to the disunited and decentralized ruling classes, which were incapable of governing the country in their own name. And this monarchy, reflecting the weakness of the whole state, was — between two upheavals — strong enough to impose its will on the country. In short, the state system in Spain can be called "degenerated absolutism, limited by periodic military coups." The figure of Alfonso XIII expresses the system very well, from the points of view of its degeneracy and absolutist tendencies and of its fear of coups. The king's maneuvering, his betrayals, his treason, and his victory over the temporary combinations hostile to him are not at all rooted in the character of Alfonso XIII himself but in the character of the whole governmental system; under new circumstances, Alfonso XIII only repeats the inglorious history of his great-grandfather, Ferdinand VII.

Alongside the monarchy, and in alliance with it, the clergy represents another centralized force. Catholicism, to this day, remains a state religion; the clergy plays a big role in the life of the country, being the firmest axis of reaction. The state spends many tens of millions of pesetas annually to support the church. [14]

The religious orders are extremely numerous; they possess great wealth and still greater influence. The number of monks and nuns is close to 70,000, equaling the number of high school students and more than twice the number of college students. It is no wonder that under these conditions 45 percent of the population can neither read nor write. Most of the illiterates, of course, are concentrated in the countryside.

If the peasantry in the epoch of Charles V (Carlos I) gained little from the might of the Spanish empire, it subsequently suffered the heaviest burden of the empire's decline.[15] For centuries it led a miserable, and in many provinces a famished, existence. Even today more than 70 percent of the population, the peasantry bears on its back the main burden of the state structure. Limited access to land and water, high rents and taxes, antiquated implements, primitive soil-tilling techniques, the requisitions of the church, high prices of industrial products, a surplus rural population, a great number of tramps, paupers, friars — that is the picture of the Spanish village. The condition of the peasantry has for a long time made this group a participant in the numerous uprisings. But these bloody outbursts were not national but local phenomena, dyed in the most varied and often the most reactionary colors. Just as the Spanish revolutions as a whole were small revolutions, so the peasant uprisings assumed the form of small wars. Spain is the classic country of guerrilla warfare.

2. *The Spanish army in politics*

Following the war with Napoleon,[16] a new political force was born in Spain — army officers, the younger generation of the ruling classes, inheritors of the ruins of the once-great empire, and in large measure declassed.

In this country of particularism and separatism, the army necessarily assumed great significance as a centralizing force. It became not only a prop of the monarchy, but also a vehicle for the discontent of all sections of the ruling classes. Like the bureaucracy, the officers are recruited from those elements, extremely numerous in Spain, that demand of the state, first of all, their means of livelihood. And as the appetites of the different groups of "cultured" society greatly exceed the state, parliamentary, and other positions available, the dissatisfaction of those left over nurtures the republican camp, which is just as unstable as all the other groupings in Spain. But insofar as a genuine and sharp social indignation is often concealed under this instability, the republican movement from time to time produces resolute and courageous revolutionary groups to whom the republic appears as a magic slogan of salvation.

The total size of the Spanish army is nearly 170,000 men, of whom over 13,000 are officers. Fifteen thousand marines should be added to this. The weapon of the ruling classes of the country, the commanding staff also drags the ranks of the army into its plots. This creates the conditions for an independent movement of the soldiers. In the past, noncommissioned officers have burst into politics without their officers and against them. In an uprising in 1836, the noncommissioned officers of the Madrid garrison compelled the queen to grant a constitution. In 1866, the artillery sergeants, dissatisfied with the aristocratic orders in the army, rose in insurrection. Nevertheless, the leadership in the past has remained with the officers. The soldiers, who were politically helpless, followed their dissatisfied commanders even though their own dissatisfaction was fostered by other, deeper social forces.

The contradictions in the army usually correspond to the branch of service. The more advanced the type of arms, that is, the more intelligence required on the part of the soldiers and officers, the more susceptible they are, generally speaking, to revolutionary ideas. While the cavalry is usually inclined to the monarchy, the artillery furnishes a big percentage of the republicans. No wonder the air force, the newest branch, appeared on the side of the revolution and brought with it elements of the individualist adventurism of their profession. The final say remains with the infantry.

The history of Spain is the history of continual revolutionary convulsions. Military coups and palace revolutions follow on each other's heels. During the nineteenth century and the first third of the twentieth, political regimes kept changing, and within each one of them ministries changed kaleidoscopically. Not finding sufficiently stable support in any of the propertied classes — even though they all needed it — the Spanish monarchy more than once fell into dependence upon its own army. But the atomization of the provinces put its stamp on the character of the military plots. The petty rivalry of the juntas was only the outward expression of the Spanish revolutions' lack of a leading class. Precisely because of this, the monarchy triumphed over each new revolution. A short time after the triumph of order, however, the chronic crisis once more broke through. Not one of the many regimes that supplanted each other sank deep enough roots into the soil. All of them quickly wore themselves out struggling with the difficulties growing out of the meagerness of the national income, which was inadequate to sustain the appetites and pretensions of the ruling classes. We saw in particular how shamefully the last military dictatorship ended its days. The stern Primo de Rivera fell even without a new military coup; he was simply deflated, like a tire that runs over a nail.

All the Spanish revolutions were the movements of a minority against another minority: the ruling and semiruling classes impatiently snatching the state pie out of each other's hands.

If by the term "permanent revolution" we are to understand a succession of social revolutions, transferring power into the hands of the most resolute class, which afterwards applies this power for the abolition of all classes, and subsequently the very possibility of new revolutions, we would then have to state that, in spite of the "uninterruptedness" of the Spanish revolutions, there is nothing in them that resembles the *permanent* revolution. They are rather the chronic convulsions expressing the intractable disease of a nation thrown backward.

It is true that the left wing of the bourgeoisie, particularly personified by the young intellectuals, long ago set itself the task of converting Spain into a republic. The Spanish students who, for the same general reasons as the officers, were recruited primarily from the dissatisfied youth, became accustomed to wielding an influence altogether out of proportion to their numbers. The domination of the Catholic reaction fed the flames of the opposition in the universities, investing it with an anticlerical character. Students, however, do not create a regime. In their highest echelons, the Spanish republicans are distinguished by an extremely conservative social program. They see their ideal in present-day reactionary France, calculating that along with the republic they will also acquire wealth. They are not at all disposed, or even able, to take the road of the French Jacobins; [17] their fear of the masses is greater than their hostility to the monarchy.

If the cracks and gaps of bourgeois society are filled in Spain with declassed elements of the ruling classes, the numerous seekers of positions and income, then at the bottom, in the cracks of the foundation, are the numerous slum proletarians, declassed elements of the toiling classes. Idlers in finery as well as idlers in rags form the quicksands of society. They are all the more dangerous for the revolution the less it finds its genuine base of support and its political leadership.

Six years of Primo de Rivera's dictatorship leveled and compressed all the dissatisfaction and rebelliousness. But the dictatorship bore within it the incurable vice of the Spanish monarchy: strong towards each of the separate classes, it remained impotent in relation to the historic needs of the country. This impotence brought about the wreck of the dictatorship on the submarine reefs of financial and other difficulties before the first revolutionary wave had a chance to reach it. The fall of Primo de Rivera aroused every kind of dissatisfaction and hope. Thus General Berenguer has become the doorman for the revolution.

3. *The Spanish proletariat and the new revolution*

In this new revolution, we meet, at first glance, the same elements we found in a series of previous revolutions: the perfidious monarchy; the splinter factions of the conservatives and liberals who despise the king and crawl on their bellies before him; the right-wing republicans, always ready to betray, and the left-wing republicans, always ready for adventure; the conspiratorial officers, of whom some want a republic and others a promotion; the restless students, whose fathers view them with alarm; finally, the striking workers, scattered among the different organizations; and the peasants, reaching out for pitchforks and even for guns.

It would, however, be a grave error to assume that the present crisis is unfolding according to and in the image of all those that preceded it. The last decades, particularly the years of the world war, produced important changes in the economy and social structure of the country. Of course, Spain still remains at the tail end of Europe. But the country has experienced its own industrial development, in both extractive and light industry. During the war, coal mining, textiles, the construction of hydroelectric stations, etc., were greatly advanced. Industrial centers and regions sprang up all over the country. This created a new relationship of forces and opened up new perspectives.

The successes of industrialization did not at all mitigate the internal contradictions. On the contrary, the circumstance under which the industry of Spain, a neutral country, flourished under the golden rain of the war was transformed into a source of new difficulties at the end of the war when the increased foreign demand disappeared. Not only did the foreign markets disappear — Spain's share in world commerce is now ever smaller than it was prior to the war (1.1 percent as against 1.2 percent) — but the dictatorship was compelled, with the aid of the highest tariff walls in Europe, to defend its domestic market from the influx of foreign commodities. The high tariff led to high prices, which diminished the already low purchasing power of the people. That is why industry after the war did not rise out of its lethargy, which is expressed by chronic unemployment on the one hand, and the sharp outbursts of the class struggle on the other.

Now even less than in the nineteenth century can the Spanish bourgeoisie lay claim to that historic role which the British and French bourgeoisies once played. Appearing too late, dependent on foreign capital, the big industrial bourgeoisie of Spain, which has dug like a leech into the body of the people, is incapable of coming forward as the leader of the "nation" against the old estates, even for a brief period. The magnates of Spanish industry face the people hostilely, forming a most reactionary bloc of bankers, industrialists, large landowners, the monarchy, and its generals and officials, all devouring each other in internal antagonisms. It is sufficient to state that the most important supporters of the dictatorship of Primo de Rivera were the Catalan manufacturers.

But industrial development raised the proletariat to its feet and strengthened it. Out of a population of twenty-three million — which would be considerably greater if not for emigration — there are nearly one and a half million industrial, commercial, and transportation workers. To them should be added about an equal number of agricultural workers. Social life in Spain was condemned to revolve in a vicious circle so long as there was no class capable of taking the solution of the revolutionary problem into its own hands. The appearance of the Spanish proletariat on the historic arena radically changes the situation and opens up new prospects. In order to grasp this properly, it must first be understood that the establishment of the economic dominance of the big bourgeoisie and the growth of the proletariat's political significance definitely prevent the petty bourgeoisie from occupying a leading position in the political life of the country. The question of whether the present revolutionary convulsions can produce a genuine revolution, capable of reconstructing the very basis of national life, is consequently reduced to whether the Spanish proletariat is capable of taking the leadership of the national life into its hands. There is no other claimant to this role in the Spanish nation. Moreover, the historic experience of Russia succeeded in showing with sufficient clarity the specific gravity of the proletariat, united by big industry in a country with a backward agriculture and enmeshed in a net of semifeudal relations.

The Spanish workers, it is true, already took a militant part in the revolutions of the nineteenth century, but always on the leash of the bourgeoisie, always in the second line, as a subsidiary force. The independent revolutionary role of the workers was reinforced in the first quarter of the twentieth century. The 1909 uprising in Barcelona showed what power was pent up in the young proletariat of Catalonia.[18] Numerous strikes that developed into direct uprisings broke out in other parts of the country too. In 1912, a strike of the railroad workers took place. The industrial regions became fields of valiant proletarian struggles. The Spanish workers revealed a complete freedom from routine, an ability to respond quickly to events and to mobilize their ranks boldly on the offensive.

The first postwar years, or more correctly, the first years after the Russian Revolution (1917-1920), were years of great battles for the Spanish proletariat. The year 1917 witnessed a revolutionary general strike. Its defeat, and the defeat of a number of subsequent movements, prepared the way for the Primo de Rivera dictatorship. When the collapse of the latter once more posed in all its magnitude the question of the further destiny of the Spanish people, when the cowardly search for old cliques and the impotent lamentations of the petty-bourgeois radicals showed clearly that salvation cannot be expected from this source, the workers, by a series of courageous strikes, cried out to the people: *We are here!*

The "left" European bourgeois journalists and, trailing after them, the Social Democrats, with their scientific pretensions, love to philosophize on the theme that Spain is simply going to reproduce the Great French Revolution, after a delay of almost one hundred and fifty years. To expound revolution to these people is equivalent to arguing with a blind man about colors. With all its backwardness, Spain has passed far beyond France of the eighteenth century. Big industrial enterprises, 10,000 miles of railway, 30,000 miles of telegraph, represent a more important factor for the revolution than historical reminiscences.

Endeavoring to take a step forward, the well-known English weekly *The Economist* says with regard to the Spanish events: "We have the influence of Paris of 1848 and 1871 rather than the influence of Moscow of 1917." But Paris of 1871 is a step from 1848 toward 1917. The counterposition is an empty one.

The conclusion L. Tarquin reached last year in *La Lutte de classes* was infinitely more serious and profound:[19] "The proletariat (of Spain), supported by the peasant masses, is the only force capable of seizing power." This perspective is laid out as follows: "The revolution must bring about the dictatorship of the proletariat which would carry out the bourgeois revolution and would courageously open the road to socialist reconstruction." This is the way — the only way — the question can now be posed.

4. *The program of the revolution*

The republic is now the official slogan of the struggle. The development of the revolution, however, will drive not only the conservatives and liberals but also the republican sections of the ruling classes to the banner of the monarchy.

During the revolutionary events of 1854, Cánovas del Castillo wrote: "We are striving for the preservation of the throne, but without a camarilla which will disgrace it." Now this great idea is developed by Señor Romanones and others.[20] As though a monarchy is even possible without camarillas, especially in Spain! . . .

A combination of circumstances is possible, to be sure, in which the possessing classes are compelled to sacrifice the monarchy in order to save themselves (for example: Germany!). It is quite likely, however, that the Madrid monarchy, even with two black eyes, will survive until the dictatorship of the proletariat.

The slogan of the republic, of course, is also the workers' slogan. But for them establishing a republic is not merely a matter of replacing the king with a president, but also of thoroughly purging the feudal refuse from the whole of society. Here the first consideration is the agrarian question.

The relationships in the Spanish countryside present a picture of semifeudal exploitation. The poverty of the peasants, particularly in Andalusia and Castille, the oppression by the landowners, authorities, and village chiefs have already more than once driven the agricultural workers and the peasant poor to the road of open mutiny. Does this mean, however, that even during a revolution bourgeois relations can be purged of feudalism? No. It only means that under the current conditions in Spain, capitalism must use feudal means to exploit the peasantry. To aim the weapon of the revolution against the remnants of the Spanish Middle Ages means to aim it against the very roots of bourgeois rule.

In order to break the peasantry away from localism and reactionary influences, the proletariat needs a clear revolutionary democratic program. The yearning for land and water, the bondage caused by the high rents, acutely pose the question of *confiscation of privately owned land* for the benefit of the poor peasants. The burden of state finances, the unbearable government debt, bureaucratic pillage, and the African adventures pose the need for a *cheap government,* which can be achieved not by the owners of large estates, not by bankers and industrialists, not by the liberal nobility, but only by the toilers themselves.

The domination of the clergy and the wealth of the church put forward the democratic problem: *to separate church and state and to disarm the church, transferring its wealth to the people.* Even the most superstitious sections of the peasantry will support these decisive measures when they are convinced that the budgetary sums that have up to now gone to the church, as well as the wealth of the church itself, will, as a result of secularization, go not to the pockets of the freethinking liberals but to the cultivation of the exhausted peasant holdings.

The separatist tendencies present the revolution with the democratic task of *national self-determination.* These tendencies were accentuated, to all appearances, during the period of the dictatorship. But while the "separatism" of the Catalan bourgeoisie is only a pawn in its play with the Madrid government against the Catalan and Spanish people, the separatism of the workers and peasants is only the shell of their social rebellion. One must distinguish very rigidly between these two forms of separatism. Precisely, however, in order to draw the line between the nationally oppressed workers and peasants and their bourgeoisie, the proletarian vanguard must take the boldest and most sincere position on the question of national self-determination. The workers will fully and completely defend the *right* of the Catalans and Basques to organize their state life independently in the event that the majority of these nationalities express themselves for complete separation. But this does not, of course, mean that the advanced workers will push the Catalans and Basques on the road of secession. On the contrary, the economic unity of the country with *extensive autonomy of national districts*, would represent great advantages for the workers and peasants from the viewpoint of economy and culture.

The monarchy's attempt to ward off the further development of the revolution with the aid of a new military dictatorship is not at all out of the question. But what is out of the question is the serious and long-term success of such an attempt. The lesson of Primo de Rivera is still too fresh. The chains of the new dictatorship would have to be wound over the sores that have not yet healed from the chains of the old one. According to the newspaper dispatches, the king would like to try; he looks about anxiously for a suitable candidate but finds no volunteers. One thing is clear: the breakdown of a new military dictatorship would be very costly to the monarchy and its distinguished representative, and the revolution would acquire a mighty impulsion. "Place your bets, gentlemen!" the workers can say to the ruling classes.

Can the Spanish revolution be expected to skip the parliamentary stage? Theoretically, this is not excluded. It is conceivable that the revolutionary movement will, in a comparatively short time, attain such strength that it will leave the ruling classes neither the time nor the place for parliamentarism. Nevertheless, such a perspective is rather improbable. The Spanish proletariat, in spite of its combativeness, still recognizes no revolutionary party as its own, and has no experience with soviet organization. And besides this, there is no unity among the sparse communist ranks. There is no clear program of action that everyone accepts. Nevertheless, the question of the Cortes is already on the order of the day. Under these conditions, it must be assumed that the revolution will have to pass through a parliamentary stage.

This does not at all exclude the tactic of a boycott of Berenguer's fictitious Cortes, just as the Russian workers successfully boycotted Bulygin's Duma in 1905 and brought about its collapse.[21] The specific tactical question of the boycott has to be decided on the basis of the relation of forces at a given stage of the revolution.

But even while boycotting Berenguer's Cortes, the advanced workers would have to counterpose to it the slogan of a *revolutionary constituent Cortes*. We must relentlessly disclose the fraudulence of the slogan of the *constituent* Cortes in the mouth of the "left" bourgeoisie, which, in reality, wants a *conciliationist* Cortes by the good graces of the king and Berenguer, for the purpose of haggling with the old ruling and privileged cliques. A genuine constituent assembly can be convoked only by a revolutionary government, as a result of a victorious insurrection of the workers, soldiers, and peasants.

We can and must counterpose the revolutionary Cortes to the conciliationist Cortes; but, to our mind, it would be incorrect *at the present stage* to give up the slogan of the revolutionary Cortes. To counterpose the slogan of the dictatorship of the proletariat to the problems and slogans of revolutionary democracy (for a republic, for an agrarian revolution, for the separation of church and state, the confiscation of church properties, national self-determination, a revolutionary constituent assembly) would be the most sterile and miserable doctrinairism. Before the masses can seize power, they must unite around the leading proletarian party. The struggle for democratic representation in the Cortes, at one or another stage of the revolution, can immeasurably facilitate the solution of this problem.

The slogan of *arming the workers and peasants* (the creation of a workers' and peasants' militia) must inevitably acquire an ever greater importance in the struggle. But at the *present stage*, this slogan too must be closely tied to the questions of defending the workers' and peasants' organizations, the agrarian revolution, the assuring of free elections, and the protection of the people from reactionary military coups.

A radical program of *social legislation*, particularly unemployment insurance; shifting the burden of taxation to the wealthy classes; free popular education — all these and similar measures, which in themselves do not exceed the framework of bourgeois society, must be inscribed on the banner of the proletarian party.

Alongside these, however, demands of a transitional character must be advanced even now: nationalization of the railroads, which are all privately owned in Spain; nationalization of mineral resources; nationalization of the banks; workers' control of industry; and, finally, state regulation of the economy. All these demands are bound up with the transition from a bourgeois to a proletarian regime; they prepare this transition so that, after the nationalization of the banks and industry, they can become part of a system of measures for a planned economy, preparing the way for the socialist society.

Only pedants can see contradictions in the combination of democratic slogans with transitional and purely socialist slogans. Such a combined program, reflecting the contradictory construction of historic society, flows inevitably from the diversity of problems inherited from the past. To reduce all the contradictions and all the tasks to one lowest common denominator — *the dictatorship of the proletariat* — is a necessary, but altogether insufficient, operation. Even if one should run ahead and assume that the proletarian vanguard has grasped the idea that only the dictatorship of the proletariat can save Spain from further decay, the preparatory problem would nevertheless remain in full force: to weld around the vanguard the heterogeneous sections of the working class and the still more heterogeneous masses of village toilers. To contrast the bare slogan of the dictatorship of the proletariat to the historically determined tasks that are now impelling the masses towards the road of insurrection would be to replace the Marxist conception of social revolution with Bakunin's.[22] This would be the surest way to ruin the revolution.

Needless to say, democratic slogans under no circumstances have as their object drawing the proletariat closer to the republican bourgeoisie. On the contrary, they create the basis for a victorious struggle against the leftist bourgeoisie, making it possible to disclose its antidemocratic character at every step. The more courageously, resolutely, and implacably the proletarian vanguard fights for democratic slogans, the sooner it will win over the masses and undermine the support for the bourgeois republicans and Socialist reformists. The more quickly their best elements join us, the sooner the democratic republic will be identified in the mind of the masses with the workers' republic.

For the correctly understood theoretical formula to be transformed into a living historic fact, it must penetrate the consciousness of the masses on the basis of their experience and their needs. To do this, it is important to avoid getting bogged down in details, so as not to distract the attention of the masses; the program of the revolution must be expressed in several clear and simple slogans, which will vary in accordance with the dynamics of the struggle. This is precisely what revolutionary politics consists of.

5. *Communism, anarcho-syndicalism, Social Democracy*

As usual, the leadership of the Comintern started out by overlooking the Spanish events.[23] Manuilsky, the "leader" of the Latin countries, only recently declared that the Spanish events do not deserve attention. There you are! In 1928, these people declared France to be on the eve of the revolution. After having so long accompanied funerals with wedding music, they could not but greet a wedding with a funeral march. For them to act otherwise would mean to betray themselves. When it appeared, nevertheless, that the events in Spain, not foreseen in the calendar of the "third period,"[24] continued to develop, the leaders of the Comintern were simply silent. This, at any rate, shows far greater prudence. But the December events made further silence impossible.[25] Once more in rigid conformity with tradition, the leader of the Latin countries made a 180-degree turn: we have in mind his December 17 article in *Pravda*.

This article calls the dictatorship of Berenguer, like the dictatorship of Primo de Rivera, a "fascist regime." Mussolini, Matteoti, Primo de Rivera, MacDonald, Chiang Kai-shek, Berenguer, Dan — all these are variations of fascism.[26] Once there is a ready epithet, why bother to think? To be thorough, only the "fascist" regime of the Abyssinian Negus remains to be included in this catalog. *Pravda* informs us that the Spanish proletariat not only is more and more "adopting the program and slogans of the Spanish Communist Party," but also has already "become conscious of its role of hegemony in the revolution." Simultaneously, the official dispatches from Paris speak of peasant soviets in Spain. It is known that under Stalinist leadership the soviet system is adopted and realized first of all by the peasants (China!). If the proletariat has already "become conscious of its role of hegemony," and the peasants have started to build soviets, all this under the leadership of the official Communist Party, then the victory of the Spanish revolution must be considered guaranteed — at any rate, till the time when the Madrid agents are accused by Stalin and Manuilsky of incorrectly applying the general line which, on the pages of *Pravda*, once more appears before us as general ignorance and light-mindedness. Corrupted to the very marrow by their own policy, these "leaders" are no longer capable of learning anything!

In reality, in spite of the mighty sweep of the struggle, the subjective factors of the revolution — the party, the mass organizations, the slogans — are extraordinarily behind the tasks of the movement, and it is this backwardness that constitutes the main danger today.

The semispontaneous spread of strikes, which have brought victims and defeats or have ended with no gains, is an absolutely unavoidable stage of the revolution, the stage of the awakening of the masses, their mobilization, and their entry into struggle. For it is not the cream of the workers who take part in the movement, but the masses as a whole. Not only do factory workers strike, but also artisans, chauffeurs, and bakers, construction, irrigation, and, finally, agricultural workers. The veterans stretch their limbs, the new recruits learn. Through the medium of these strikes, the class begins to feel itself a class.

However, the spontaneity — which at the present stage constitutes the strength of the movement — may in the future become the source of its weakness. To assume that the movement can continue to be left to itself without a clear program, without its own leadership, would mean to assume a perspective of hopelessness. For the question involved is nothing less than the seizure of power. Even the stormiest strikes do not solve this problem — not to speak of the ones that are broken. If the proletariat were not to feel in the process of the struggle during the coming months that its tasks and methods are becoming clearer to itself, that its ranks are becoming consolidated and strengthened, then a decomposition would set in within its own ranks. The broad layers aroused by the present movement for the first time would once more fall into passivity. In the vanguard, to the extent to which the ground slipped from under its feet, moods favoring partisan acts and adventurism in general would begin to revive. In such an eventuality, neither the peasantry nor the city poor would find authoritative leadership. The awakened hopes would very quickly be converted into disappointment and exasperation. A condition would be created in Spain reproducing, in a certain measure, the situation in Italy after the autumn of 1920.[27] The dictatorship of Primo de Rivera was not fascist but a typical Spanish dictatorship of a military clique supporting itself on certain parts of the wealthy classes; but with the conditions pointed out above — the passivity and the hesitancy of the revolutionary party, and the spontaneity of the mass movement — genuine fascism would find a base in Spain. The big bourgeoisie would conquer the unbalanced, disappointed, and despairing petty-bourgeois masses and would direct their restlessness against the proletariat. Of course, we are far from that point yet. But no time should be lost.

Even if we should assume for a moment that the revolutionary movement led by the left wing of the bourgeoisie — officers, students, republicans — leads to victory, then the fruitlessness of this victory would in the final analysis prove it equal to defeat. The base of support of the Spanish republicans, as we have already said, is completely on the present property relations. We can expect them neither to expropriate the big landowners, nor to liquidate the privileges of the Catholic church, nor to cleanse the Augean stables of the civil and military bureaucracy. The monarchist camarilla would simply be replaced by a republican camarilla, and we would have a new edition of the short-lived and fruitless republic of 1873-1874.[28]

The fact that the Socialist leaders trail behind the republican leaders is quite in the nature of things. Yesterday, the Social Democracy clung with its right arm to the dictatorship of Primo de Rivera. Today it clings with its left arm to the republicans. The principal aim of the Socialists, who do not and cannot have an independent policy, is participation in a solid bourgeois government. To this end, they would not refuse to make peace even with the monarchists, if it came to that.

But the right wing of the anarcho-syndicalists is in no way insured against the same fate; in this connection, the December events are a great lesson and a stern warning.

The National Confederation of Labor (CNT — Confederación Nacional del Trabajo) indisputably embraces the most militant elements of the proletariat. Here the selection has gone on for a number of years. To strengthen this confederation, to transform it into a genuine organization of the masses, is the obligation of every advanced worker and, above all, of the communists. This can also be assisted by work inside the reformist trade unions, tirelessly exposing the betrayals of their leaders and calling upon the workers to unite in a single trade union confederation. The conditions of revolution will be of extraordinary assistance to this work.

But at the same time we have no illusions about the fate of anarcho-syndicalism as a doctrine and a revolutionary method. Anarcho-syndicalism disarms the proletariat by its lack of a revolutionary program and its failure to understand the role of the party. The anarchists "deny" politics until it seizes them by the throat; then they prepare the ground for the politics of the enemy class. This is what happened in December!

If the Socialist Party were to acquire a leading position over the proletariat during the revolution, it would be capable of only one thing: spilling the power conquered by the revolution into the republican sieve, from which the power would then automatically pass to its present possessors. The great conception would result in a miscarriage.

As far as the anarcho-syndicalists are concerned, they could head the revolution only by abandoning their anarchist prejudices. It is our duty to help them do this. In reality, it may be assumed that a part of the syndicalist leaders will go over to the Socialists or will be cast aside by the revolution; the real revolutionists will be with us. The masses will join the communists, and so will the majority of the Socialist workers.

The advantage of a revolutionary situation lies in the fact that the masses learn fast. The evolution of the masses will inevitably produce differentiations and splits not only among the Socialists but also among the syndicalists. Practical agreements with *revolutionary* syndicalists are inevitable in the course of the revolution. These agreements we will loyally fulfill. But it would be truly fatal to introduce into these agreements elements of duplicity, concealment, and deceit. Even in those days and hours when the communist workers have to fight side by side with the syndicalist workers, there must be no destruction of the principled disagreements, no concealment of differences, nor any weakening of the criticism of the wrong principled position of the ally. Only under this condition will the progressive development of the revolution be secured.

6. *The revolutionary junta and the party*

The events of December 15, when the workers rose up simultaneously not only in the big cities, but also in the remote villages, demonstrate how much the workers themselves are striving for unity of action. They utilized the signal of the republicans because they didn't have a loud enough signalman of their own. The defeat of the movement apparently did not call forth a shadow of dismay. The masses viewed their own actions as experience, as a school, as preparation. This is an extremely characteristic feature of "revolutionary ascent."

In order to enter the broad road, the proletariat needs even now an organization rising over all the present political, national, provincial, and trade union divisions in their ranks and corresponding to the sweep of the present revolutionary struggle. Such an organization, democratically elected by the workers of the factories, mills, mines, commercial enterprises, railway and marine transport, by the proletarians of the city and village, can only be the soviet. The epigones[29] have done immeasurable damage to the revolutionary movement of the whole world, fixing in many minds the prejudice that soviets can only be created by the needs of an armed insurrection and only on the brink of this insurrection. In reality, the soviets are created when the revolutionary movement of the working masses, even though still far from an armed insurrection, creates the need for a broad, authoritative organization, capable of leading the economic and political struggles embracing simultaneously the different enterprises and the different trades. Only if the soviets are rooted in the working class during the preparatory period of the revolution will they be able to play a leading role at the time of a direct struggle for power. It is true that the word "soviet" after thirteen years of existence of the Soviet regime has now acquired a somewhat different meaning than it had in 1905 or in the beginning of 1917, when the soviets appeared not as organs of power but only as the militant organizations of the working class. The word "junta," directly tied to all of Spain's revolutionary history, expresses this thought better than anything else. On the order of the day in Spain stands the creation of workers' juntas.

With the present state of the proletariat, the building of juntas presupposes the participation in them of the communists, anarcho-syndicalists, Social Democrats, and the nonparty leaders of the strike struggles. To what extent can we count on the participation of the anarcho-syndicalists and the Social Democrats in the soviets? This cannot be foretold from a distance. The sweep of the movement will undoubtedly compel many syndicalists, and perhaps some of the Socialists, to go further than they wish, provided that the communists are able to present the idea of the workers' juntas with the necessary energy. Under the pressure of the masses, the practical questions of the building of soviets, the ratio of representation, the time and method of elections and so forth, can and should become the object of *agreement* not only of all the communist factions among themselves but also with those syndicalists and Socialists who consent to the creation of juntas. The communists, of course, appear at all stages of the struggle with their banner unfurled.

In spite of the newest Stalinist theory, it is hardly likely that the peasant juntas, as elected organs, will appear in any considerable number, prior to the seizure of power by the proletariat. In the preparatory period in the village, different forms of organization will develop sooner, based not upon elections but upon individual selection: peasant unions, committees of the village poor, communist nuclei, a labor union of agricultural workers, and so forth. The propagation of the slogan of *peasant juntas*, based on a revolutionary agrarian program, can even now, however, be put on the agenda.

The correct posing of the question of "soldiers' juntas" is very important. Because of the very character of military organization, soldiers' soviets can appear only in the final period of the revolutionary crisis, when the state power loses control over the army. In the preparatory period, it will be a matter of organizations of an intimate character, groups of revolutionary soldiers, party nuclei, and, in many cases, personal connections of workers with individual soldiers.

The republican uprising in December 1930 will undoubtedly go down into history as the transition between two epochs of revolutionary struggle. It is true that the left wing of the republicans established connections with the leaders of workers' organizations in order to bring about unity of action. The unarmed workers had to play the role of cheerleaders for the republicans, who were the chief performers. This act was performed fully enough to reveal once and for all the incompatibility of an officers' plot with a revolutionary strike. Against the military plot, which opposed one branch of the service to another, the government found sufficient forces within the army itself. And the strike, deprived of an independent aim and of its own leadership, was necessarily reduced to nothing as soon as the military uprising was crushed.

The revolutionary role of the army, not as an instrument of officers' experiments but as an armed part of the people, will be determined, in the last analysis, by the role of the worker and peasant masses in the course of the struggle. For the revolutionary strike to be victorious, it will have to bring about the confrontation of the workers with the army. No matter how important the purely military features of such a clash may be, politics outweighs them. The masses of soldiers can be won over only by clearly explaining the social tasks of the revolution. But it is precisely the social tasks that frighten the officers. It is natural that the proletarian revolutionists should direct their attention even now to the soldiers, creating nuclei of conscious and daring revolutionists in the regiments. The communist work in the army, politically subordinated to the work among the proletariat and the peasantry, can be developed only on the basis of a clear program. But when the decisive moment arrives, the workers, by the sheer weight of numbers and the force of their assault, must sweep a large part of the army to the side of the people or, at any rate, neutralize it. This broad revolutionary posing of the question does not exclude a military "plot" of the advanced soldiers and officers sympathizing with the proletarian revolution, in the period directly preceding the general strike and insurrection. But such a "plot" has nothing in common with military coups: its task is of an auxiliary character and consists of insuring the victory of the proletarian uprising.

For a successful solution of all these tasks, three conditions are required: a party; once more a party; again a party!

How will the relations between the various existing communist organizations and groups be arranged, and what will be their fate in the future? It is difficult to judge from a distance. Experience will show. Great events unmistakably put to the test ideas, organizations, and people. Should the leadership of the Comintern appear incapable of offering anything to the Spanish workers except a wrong policy, apparatus commands, and splits, then the genuine Communist Party of Spain will be constituted and tempered outside the official framework of the Communist International. One way or another — a party has to be created. It must be united and centralized.

The working class can under no circumstances build its political organization on the basis of federations. A Communist Party is needed — not in the image of the future state order of Spain but as a steel lever for the demolition of the existing order. It can be organized only on the principle of democratic centralism.

The proletarian junta will become the broad arena in which every party and every group will be put to the test and scrutinized before the eyes of the broad masses. The communists will counterpose the slogan of the united front of the workers to the practice of coalitions of Socialists and a part of the syndicalists with the bourgeoisie. Only the united revolutionary front will enable the proletariat to inspire the necessary confidence among the oppressed masses of the village and city. The realization of the united front is conceivable only under the banner of communism. The junta requires a leading party. Without a firm leadership, it would remain an empty organizational form and would inevitably fall into dependence upon the bourgeoisie.

The Spanish communists have ahead of them glorious historic tasks. The advanced workers of the world will follow with rapt attention the course of the great revolutionary drama, which will sooner or later require not only their sympathy but also their cooperation. We will be ready!

7 *FOR COMMUNIST UNITY*

January 31, 1931
The Spanish communists must reconstruct their unity. This slogan will undoubtedly be tremendously attractive in the next period, and will increase in popularity along with the growth of communist influence. This is why it seems to me that the slogan of the united front in relation to the syndicalist and the Socialist workers should be supplemented by the slogan for unification of the communists (on a definite program).

From "The Spanish Revolution in Danger."

8 *THE BOYCOTT TACTIC*

February 5, 1931
. . . I think that you will hardly be able to cast aside the slogan of the revolutionary constituent Cortes. Peasants account for more than 70 percent of Spain's population. How will they understand the slogan "workers' republic"? The Socialists and the republicans, on the one hand, and the priests, on the other, will tell the peasants that the workers want to wrap the peasants around their little fingers and to command them. What will you reply to this? I know of only one reply under the circumstances: we want the workers and peasants to drive out the officials appointed from above and, in general, all the oppressors and their accomplices, and to express their own free will on the basis of universal suffrage. The peasants may be *led* to the workers' republic, that is, to the dictatorship of the proletariat, in the process of the struggle that will take place for the land, etc. But it is impossible to propose to the peasants a dictatorship of the proletariat as an a priori formula.

. . . The communists obviously committed an error by failing to take the initiative in the boycott. They alone, at the head of the revolutionary workers, could have given the boy-

From "The Spanish Revolution in Danger."

cott campaign a bold and militant character. The sentiment for
boycott, nevertheless, is clearly very widespread in the opposition parties and is a reflection and symptom of the profound
restlessness among the popular masses. The latest dispatches
seem to confirm the news that the republicans and Socialists
have come out in favor of the boycott. If the communists had
vigorously confronted them at the proper time, the republicans
and Socialists would have infinitely more difficulty in renouncing this plan for a boycott. In the meantime, Berenguer and
his government have bound themselves up very tightly with
the March 1 elections. Had the boycott compelled Berenguer
to make a retreat of some sort, it would have had formidable
consequences in the sense of raising the revolutionary consciousness of the masses, particularly if the leaders of this boycott
tactic had been the communists.

9   WORKERS' REPUBLIC AND
CONSTITUENT CORTES

February 13, 1931
In regards to the "workers' republic," one is by no means
compelled to give up this slogan. But at present, the slogan
has more a propagandistic than an agitational character. We
must explain to the advanced workers that we are marching
towards the workers' republic but that to begin with the peasants have to be brought around to this concept. But it will
hardly be possible to bring the peasants to support a workers' republic, which means in fact the dictatorship of the proletariat, except through intermediary experiences, including
those of a parliamentary character. The peasantry will accept
the dictatorship of the proletariat only after exhausting all
other possibilities. It is true that in Spain all the possibilities
have already been tried. But there nevertheless still remains
the chance for "complete," "consistent" democracy achieved by
revolutionary means. That is what the constituent Cortes is.
Of course, we make no fetish of this slogan. Should developments move faster, we will know at the right time to substitute
another slogan.

From "The Spanish Revolution in Danger."

10 BERENGUER'S RESIGNATION

February 15, 1931
I recollect that I wrote to you by way of "speculation" how good it would have been had the boycott forced the monarchy to its knees, or at least to one knee. Now this is an accomplished fact. The immediate political significance of Berenguer's resignation is not great, in and of itself, but its symptomatic significance is tremendous. The impotence of the monarchy; the degeneration of the ruling cliques; their lack of self-confidence; fear, fear, fear of the people, of the revolution, of the morrow; their attempts by means of extreme concessions to forestall the most terrific consequences: these stand out in the resignation of Berenguer and the semicapitulation of the king. Marvelous! Truly marvelous! One could not imagine anything better! The superstitious respect for power in the consciousness of the people will be relentlessly undermined by all this. A wave of satisfaction, of confidence, of daring will go through millions of hearts, warming them, inspiring them, spurring them on.

The general revolutionary situation in which the proletarian party must act is now eminently favorable. The whole question now lies with the party itself. Unfortunately, the communists were not the stars in the boycotters' performance. That is why they did not achieve any important victories in the campaign of the last two or three months. In periods of stormy revolutionary flux, the authority of the party grows rapidly, feverishly — if, in decisive turns, at new stages, the party immediately advances the necessary slogan, whose correctness is soon confirmed by the events. . . . In the course of the last few weeks and months, opportunities have been allowed to escape. But it does no good to look back now. We must look ahead. The revolution is only beginning. We can win back a hundredfold what we have allowed ourselves to lose.

The constitutional-parliamentary problem is becoming the center of official political life. We cannot adopt a nonchalant attitude toward this. The slogan of the revolutionary constituent Cortes must now be advanced, to my mind, with double force.

From "The Spanish Revolution in Danger." Alfonso XIII had appointed General Dámaso Berenguer Fusté to head an interim government in January 1930, when Primo de Rivera resigned.

We must not recoil from using distinctly democratic formulations. For example: universal suffrage without discrimination
because of sex, from the age of eighteen, with no restrictions.
Eighteen years for Spain, a southern country, is perhaps even
too old. We should stake everything on the youth. . . .

. . . The question of the united front of all communist factions, the official party included, will inevitably come up on
the agenda. The masses will feel in the coming weeks and
months the strong need for a united and serious revolutionary
leadership. Squabbling among the communists will irritate
the masses. They will force unity — not forever, because events
may once more fling the various factions in different directions.
But for the coming period, the rapprochement of the communist factions seems to me absolutely inevitable. Here too,
as in the question of the boycott, as well as in every other live
political question, that faction will win that takes the initiative
in uniting the communist ranks. The communist left must
itself become united and organized to be able to take the initiative. It is necessary to create immediately a well-organized faction of the Left Opposition, no matter how small it may be
to begin with, which will publish its own bulletin and its own
theoretical organ. Of course, this does not exclude the participation of the Left Communists in broader organizations;
on the contrary, it assumes it, but at the same time organizing
the Left Opposition is the indispensable condition for this participation.

11   SOLDIERS' AND WORKERS' JUNTAS

March 13, 1931

A few words on the soldiers' juntas. Would you like to see
them arise as *independent* organizations? This is a very serious
question for which a definite line of conduct must be marked
out at the very outset, leaving open, of course, the right to
introduce corrections if experience indicates the need.

In Russia in 1905, matters did not reach the point of soldiers' soviets. The appearance of soldier deputies in the work-

From "The Spanish Revolution in Danger."

ers' soviets had an episodic character. In 1917 the soldiers' soviets played a gigantic role. In Petrograd the soldiers' soviet was combined with the workers' soviet from the very beginning. Moreover, the soldiers were the overwhelming majority. In Moscow, the workers' and peasants' soviets existed independently. But this was essentially for organizational reasons: the immense army consisted then of some ten to twelve million peasants.

In Spain we have a peacetime army inconsequential when compared with the population, or even when compared with the proletariat. Is the rise of independent soldiers' soviets inevitable under these conditions? From the standpoint of proletarian policy, we are interested in drawing the soldiers' delegates into the workers' juntas to the extent that the latter are created. Juntas composed only of soldiers could arise only at the culmination of the revolution, or after its victory. Workers' juntas might (and should!) arise earlier, on the basis of strikes, the boycott of the Cortes, or later, on the basis of participation in elections. We can therefore draw the soldier delegates into the workers' juntas long before soldiers' juntas can be created. But I go further: if we take the initiative in time and create workers' juntas and assure their influence on the army, then perhaps in consequence we will be able to prevent the rise of *independent* soldiers' juntas in danger of falling under the influence of careerist officers rather than of revolutionary workers. The small size and importance of the Spanish army speaks in favor of such a perspective. But, on the other hand, this small army has its independent revolutionary political traditions — more than in any other country. To a certain degree, this may interfere with the soldiers' representation through the workers' juntas.

You see that on this question I have not decided to express myself categorically; and I doubt if the comrades who are close to the situation can render a categorical decision here. I would rather put the question up for consideration; the sooner the broad circles of advanced workers begin to discuss the key questions, the easier it will be to solve them. At any rate, the course taken should be towards incorporating the soldiers' delegates into the workers' councils. If it should be only partially successful, even that much would be good. But precisely with this aim in mind, the moods in the army and in the various branches of service, the different types of arms, all should be studied in time and in great detail.

In conclusion, it would be a good idea to attempt collectively to make up a political chart of Spain with the aim of determining more precisely the relationship of forces in each region, and the relationship among the regions. Such a chart should also have the workers' districts, the revolutionary centers, the trade union and party organizations, the garrisons, the relationship of forces between the Reds and the Whites, the districts of peasant movements, etc. No matter how few in numbers the Oppositionists may be, nevertheless they can take the initiative in various places for such a study, collaborating with the best representatives of other workers' groups. Thus, the elements of the general staff of the revolution would be created. The central nucleus would give this work the necessary unity and cohesion. This preparatory, at first seemingly "academic," work will acquire a tremendous, perhaps even a decisive, significance in the future. In an epoch such as the one Spain is now passing through, the greatest of sins is to waste time.

12   *TO SAY WHAT IS*

April 12, 1931

Dear Comrades:

I have finally received the long-awaited news that the Communist Left Opposition has begun publication of its theoretical organ, *Comunismo*. I don't doubt for a moment that this publication will be well received. Spain is going through a revolutionary period. In such a period, the awakened intellect of the proletarian vanguard seeks avidly to understand questions, not in a detached fashion but in all their internal complexities. Revolutionary epochs have always been periods of the development of theoretical curiosity among historically progressive classes.

Letter to the editorial board of *Comunismo*, the theoretical journal of the Spanish Left Opposition. From Leon Trotsky, *Ecrits*, Vol. III (1928-1940). Translated for this volume from the French by Constance Weissman.

No theory but Marxism can give answers to the gigantic problems now facing the Spanish communists. We must also point out in an absolutely categorical manner that no group except the Left Opposition is capable at present of giving the Spanish workers an authentic Marxist interpretation of the conditions of the revolution, its motivating forces, its perspectives, and its goals. Whereas the official centrist faction of the Communist International subordinates the problems of the proletarian revolution to the interests and needs of bureaucratic prestige,[30] which has been seriously compromised and does not permit critical discussion of any question, the Left Opposition proposes as its goal to say what is. Clarity, theoretical precision, and consequently political honesty is what renders a revolutionary tendency invincible. May *Comunismo* grow and thrive under this banner!

I promise my energetic support and above all a most diligent collaboration. And I invite our cothinkers from all countries to do the same. I am sending you the rough draft of a manifesto on the USSR which I just finished in the last few days. I hope that the advanced communists in Spain will give the internal questions of the first workers' state the same attention that the communists of the USSR and all countries should give to the problems of the Spanish revolution.

Long live *Comunismo*! Long live the Spanish Bolshevik-Leninists! Long live the revolutionary Spanish proletariat!

PART II:

From
Republic
to
Civil War

The Alcalá Zamora government announced elections to the Cortes for June 1931. In May, sharp clashes broke out in Madrid between monarchists and crowds of workers, while Anarchists burned a number of churches in reprisals against the corrupt pro-monarchist clergy.

The June elections were swept by the pro-government parties. The various rightist parties captured a total of only 60 seats in the Cortes to 116 for the Socialist Party alone. The rest of the seats were divided as follows: Radical Socialists, 60; Azaña's Republican Action Party, 30; Lerroux's Radicals, 90; Catalan Esquerra, 43; Alcalá Zamora's Progressive Party, 22; and 16 seats to the Gallegan Nationalists of Casares Quiroga. All of these last-named parties supported the republic.

Within the new Cortes the most hotly contested issue was the privileged position of the church. Outside, among the radicalized workers and agricultural laborers, the issues were land reform, workers' control, and wages. The divisions among the bourgeois parties over clericalism were not reflected in their attitude toward the workers' movement; there the republican government employed the same methods of forcible suppression as its monarchist predecessors.

In July and August the CNT organized a series of local general strikes. The most sharply fought of these was in Seville, where Azaña ordered the military to use artillery against the workers' districts.

The republican coalition, united in opposition to the working class, began to splinter over the question of the church. In October, Alcalá Zamora and Maura resigned in a gesture of support for the church hierarchy. Azaña became prime minister, while Lerroux and his Radical Party broke with the republican bloc to move first to the bourgeois center and finally to the far right. Alcalá Zamora chose not to desert the government altogether and accepted the titular post of president of the republic.

The constitution passed by the June Cortes provided for the

formation of a Spanish federation that could give certain aspects of local autonomy to the Catalan and Basque provinces. This was followed by the Statute of Catalan Autonomy, passed at the beginning of 1932, which provided for the reorganization of the Barcelona municipal government as a "Generalitat," a regional governing body for Catalonia with limited powers. The Basques then demanded a similar statute for their region.

To win the confidence of the monarchist generals, Azaña supported them in their persecution of republican junior officers. The generals meanwhile had bolder plans. In August 1932 the commander of the customs guards, General José Sanjurjo, led a rising against the government. Backed by sections of the monarchists and the nascent fascist movement, and promised support by Mussolini, the coup nevertheless failed and its principal organizers were jailed.

After Sanjurjo's defeat, the initiative for a time passed to the workers' organizations. The Anarchists seized the town of Casas Viejas in January 1933. The brutal suppression of this rebellion by the government quickly alienated many Socialist and Anarchist workers from the regime. Municipal elections in April showed a marked decline of the government's support. By mid-summer, Azaña felt compelled to resign, and new elections were called for November. This time the vote went heavily against the republicans and Socialists.

The Socialist Party dropped from 116 to 58 seats in the Cortes elections of November 1933. The government parties secured a total of only 99, compared to 104 for Lerroux's Radicals and 207 for the openly rightist parties. The largest party in the Cortes was now the newly formed ultrareactionary CEDA of Gil Robles. The Communist Party and the Falange of José Antonio Primo de Rivera each won a single seat.

Lerroux became prime minister. He immediately faced a series of violent strikes called mainly by the Anarchists. Apart from crushing these strikes, the government's main preoccupation was repealing the limited reforms enacted under Azaña.

The Asturian rising of the Anarchists and left Socialists began October 4, 1934, in protest of Lerroux's inclusion of representatives of the CEDA in the government. This was accompanied by a revolt in Catalonia led by the bourgeois Catalan nationalists of Luis Companys. Both uprisings were put down by the military. Companys and Largo Caballero were among those imprisoned in the wave of reprisals by the government after the defeat of the workers of Asturias.

The suppression of the Asturian commune was followed by a series of governmental crises, capped by a major financial scandal that directly implicated the leaders of the Radical Party. Finally, Alcalá Zamora dissolved the Cortes on January 4, 1936, and called new elections for February 16. The left, with the exception of the Anarchists and the small Spanish section of the International Left Opposition, were grouped in the Popular Front electoral bloc with a common slate. The rightist parties formed a counter bloc under the name "National Front." The bourgeois center of Lerroux was split several ways but all of its components suffered a marked loss of support. The following are the results of the second and final round of the elections:

	Seats
Popular Front	
Socialists	99
Republican Left (Azaña)	87
Republican Union (Martínez Barrio)	39
Esquerra (Catalan Separatists)	36
Communists	17
	278
National Front	
CEDA (Gil Robles)	88
Agrarians (landowners)	11
Monarchists (led by Calvo Sotelo)	13
Independents	10
Traditionalists (Carlists*)	9
Others	3
	134
Center	
Center Party (led by Portela Valladares)	16
Lliga (Catalan industrialists)	12
Radicals (Lerroux)	4
Progressives (Alcalá Zamora)	6
Basques (led by José Antonio Aquirre**)	10
Others	7
	55

* The wing of the monarchists who defended the claim to the throne of the descendants of Don Carlos rather than those of King Ferdinand.

** The Basque Nationalists were soon to go over to the Popular Front.

Azaña became prime minister. Ignoring the support he had received from the Communist and Socialist parties, his government was composed entirely of members of the bourgeois partners in the Popular Front, drawn mainly from his own party.

A Note on Trotsky's Exile: When the Spanish republic was installed in 1931, Trotsky applied to the new government for a visa to allow him and his family to move to Spain, but the government of the self-styled "republic of labor" was not quite that liberal. He finally left Turkey in July 1933, when the French government gave him a visa.

This change in residence coincided with a fundamental change in his political orientation, for it was at that time, shortly after Hitler had come to power, thanks in great part to the criminally erroneous policies of the Stalinized Comintern, that he abandoned the perspective of reforming the Comintern and began to advocate the building of the Fourth International and new revolutionary parties throughout the world. His preoccupation with these problems may account for the fact that he did not publish much about Spain in the next two or three years.

Nine months after his arrival in France, the government ordered him to leave, but he had to remain until June 1935, when the Norwegian government granted him a visa. Thus he was in Norway in July 1936, when the Spanish civil war began, a few days after he had completed his book *The Revolution Betrayed.* All of Part II up to "Letter to All Members of the Spanish Left Opposition" was written in Turkey, either at Kadikoy or Prinkipo; the next four articles were written in France; and the last six were written in Norway.

TEN COMMANDMENTS
OF THE SPANISH COMMUNIST

April 15, 1931

1. The monarchy has lost power, but it hopes to win it back. The possessing classes are still firmly in the saddle. The bloc of republicans and Socialists has based itself upon the republican upheaval in order to hold back the masses from the road of the socialist revolution. No faith in words. Give us deeds! In the first place, arrest the most prominent leaders and supporters of the old regime, confiscate the property of the monarchy and its most discredited henchmen! Arm the workers!

2. The government, supporting itself on the republicans and Socialists, will make every effort to extend its base towards the right, in the direction of the big bourgeoisie, and will seek to capitulate in order to neutralize the church. The government is an exploiters' government created to protect them from the exploited. The proletariat is in irreconcilable opposition to the government of the "Socialist" republican agents of the bourgeoisie.

3. The participation in power of the Socialists means that violent clashes between the workers and the Socialist leaders will increase. This opens up great possibilities for the revolutionary policy of the united front. Every strike, every demonstration, every approach of the workers to the soldiers, every step of the masses towards the real democratization of the country will henceforth collide with the resistance of the Socialist leaders acting as the men of "order." It is therefore all the more important for the communist workers to participate in a united front with the Socialist, syndicalist, and nonpartisan workers, and to draw them under their leadership.

4. The communist workers today constitute a small minority in the country. They cannot aspire to power immediately. At the present moment, they cannot set themselves as a practical task the violent overthrow of the republican-Socialist government. Any attempt of this sort would be a catastrophic adventure. The masses of workers, soldiers, and peasants must

From "The Spanish Revolution in Danger."

pass through the stage of Socialist-republican illusions in order to rid themselves of these illusions all the more radically and conclusively, so that they are not trapped by phrases, can look the facts straight in the face, and stubbornly prepare the second revolution, the proletarian revolution.

5. The task of the communists in the present period is to win the majority of the workers, the majority of the soldiers, the majority of the peasants. How can this be done? By carrying on agitation, by training cadres, by "explaining patiently" (to use Lenin's expression), by organizing — all this on the basis of the experience of the masses and with the active participation of the communists in the experience: a broad and audacious united-front policy.

6. The communists do not take any step, with the republican-Socialist bloc or with any part of it, that either directly or indirectly might restrict or weaken the communist freedom of criticism and agitation. Everywhere the communists will tirelessly explain to the masses of the people that in the struggle against every form of monarchist counterrevolution they will be in the front ranks, but that for such a struggle no alliance is needed with the republicans and the Socialists, whose policy will inevitably be based on concessions to the reaction and will tend to cover up its intrigues.

7. The communists issue the most radical democratic slogans: complete freedom for the proletarian organizations; freedom of local self-administration; election of all officials by the people; admission to suffrage of men and women from the age of eighteen, etc.; formation of a workers' militia and later on of a peasants' militia, confiscation of all properties of the monarchy and the church for the benefit of the people, above all, for the unemployed and the poor peasants and for improving the conditions of the soldiers; complete separation of church and state.

All civil rights and political privileges for the soldiers; election of officers in the army. The soldier is not an executioner of the people, nor an armed mercenary of the rich, nor a praetorian guard, but a revolutionary citizen, blood brother to the worker and the peasant.

8. The central slogan of the proletariat is that of the *workers' soviet*. This slogan must be proclaimed tirelessly and popularized constantly, and at the first opportunity we must proceed to put it into practice. The workers' soviet does not mean the im-

mediate struggle for power. This is undoubtedly the perspective, but one that the masses can attain only through their
own experience and with the help of the enlightening work
of the communists. The workers' soviet today means assembling
the scattered forces of the proletariat, struggling for the unity
of the working class, for its independence. The workers' soviet
takes up the questions of strike benefits; of feeding the unemployed; of contacts with the soldiers in order to prevent
bloody encounters with them; of contacts between the city and
country in order to assure the alliance of the workers with the
poor peasants. The workers' soviet includes representatives of
the army corps. It is in this way and only in this way that
the soviet will become the organ of the proletarian insurrection and later on the organ of power.

9. The communists must immediately work out a revolutionary agrarian program. Its basis must be the confiscation
of the lands of the privileged and rich classes, of the exploiters,
beginning with the monarchy and the church, for the benefit
of the poor peasants and the soldiers. This program must
be concretely adapted to the different parts of the country. In
each province, according to its own economic and historic
peculiarities, a commission must be created for the concrete
elaboration of the agrarian program, in close cooperation
with the revolutionary peasants of the locality. We must know
how to understand the will of the peasants in order to express
it in a clear and accurate manner.

10. The so-called left Socialists[1]* (among whom there are
many honest workers) will invite the communists to make
a bloc and even to unite the various organizations. To this
the communists answer: "We are ready, in the interests of the
working class and for the solution of definite concrete tasks,
to work hand in hand with any group and with any proletarian organization. Precisely towards this end do we propose
to create soviets. Workers' representatives, belonging to different parties, will discuss within these soviets all the timely
questions and all the immediate tasks. The workers' soviet
is the healthiest, most natural, most open, and most honest
form of this alliance for common work. In the workers' soviet
we communists will propose our slogans and our solutions,
and we will endeavor to convince the workers of the correct-

*Notes for Part II begin on p. 406.

ness of our course. Each group must enjoy full freedom of criticism in the workers' soviet. In the struggle for the practical tasks proposed by the soviet, we communists will always be in the front ranks." This is the form of collaboration that the communists propose to the Socialist, the syndicalist, and the nonpartisan workers.

By insuring unity in their own ranks, the communists will win the confidence of the *proletariat* and the great majority of the poor peasants. *They will take power* arms in hand, and they will open up the era of the socialist revolution.

14 REPRESSIVE MEASURES OF THE REPUBLICAN GOVERNMENT

April 20, 1931

Many features of similarity between the February regime in Russia and the present republican regime in Spain strike the eye.[2] But there are also deep differences: (a) Spain is not at war and you have no slogan of struggle for peace; (b) you don't have workers' soviets yet, not to speak of soldiers' soviets. From the press I do not even see that this slogan is being raised among the masses; (c) the republican government from the very outset applies repressive measures against the left proletarian wing, which we did not have in February because the bayonets were at the disposal of the workers' and soldiers' soviets and not in the hands of the liberal government.

The last circumstance has a tremendous significance for our agitation. The February regime, in the political sphere, immediately realized full and almost absolute democracy. The bourgeoisie maintained itself by the good will of the masses of workers and soldiers. Your bourgeoisie maintains itself not only on good will but also on the organized violence that it took over from the old regime. You do not have complete and unconditional freedom of assembly, speech, press, etc.

From "The Spanish Revolution in Danger."

The electoral basis of your new municipalities is very far from democratic. Meanwhile, in a revolutionary epoch, the masses are particularly sensitive to every inequality in rights, to every form of police rule. This should be utilized. In other words, it is necessary for the communists at present to come forward as the party of the most consistent, decisive, and intransigent defenders of democracy.

On the other hand, it is necessary to proceed immediately with the formation of workers' soviets. The struggle for democracy is an excellent point of departure for this. *They* have their own municipal government; *we* workers ñeed our own city juntas to protect our rights and our interests.

15   *THE CATALAN FEDERATION*

April 23, 1931

The Catalan Federation should strive to enter the general Spanish communist organization. Catalonia is the vanguard. But if this vanguard will not march in step with the proletariat and later on with the peasantry of all of Spain, the Catalan movement will at best be concluded as a magnificent episode in the style of the Paris Commune.[3] The peculiar position of Catalonia is driving in this direction. The national conflict may heat up the steam to such an extent that the Catalan explosion will occur long before the situation in Spain as a whole has matured for a second revolution.

It would be the greatest historical misfortune if the Catalan proletariat, under the influence of the national ferment, permitted itself to be drawn into a decisive struggle before it has had the chance to consolidate itself with the proletariat of all of Spain. The strength of the Left Opposition in Barcelona, as well as in Madrid, can and should lie in raising all these questions to a historical level. . . .

From "The Spanish Revolution in Danger." The Catalan Federation had originated in the Communist Party and had broken with the CP over tactical questions. Its leader, Joaquín Maurín, was a close personal friend of Andrés Nin.

16   *UNIFY THE COMMUNIST RANKS!*

April 24, 1931

The fate of the Spanish revolution depends completely upon whether an authoritative and combative Communist Party will be constituted in Spain in the coming months. With the system of artificial splits imposed upon the movement from without, this is not realizable.

In 1917, the Bolshevik Party consolidated around itself all the currents akin and close to it. Carefully guarding the unity of its ranks and its discipline in action, the party at the same time opened up the possibility of a broad and many-sided consideration of the basic problems of the revolution (the March council, the April conference, the pre-October period).⁴ Are there other ways that the proletarian vanguard of Spain can elaborate its views and become imbued with that indomitable conviction in their correctness which alone will permit it to lead the masses of the people towards the decisive battle?

The mere fact — I offer it as an example — that the official Communist Party is compelled in the present situation to characterize Andrés Nin as a counterrevolutionist⁵ cannot but lead to a monstrous confusion, primarily in the communist ranks themselves. Amidst ideological confusion, the party cannot grow. The defeat of the Spanish revolution, which is inevitable if the dismemberment and weakness of the communist ranks continue, will lead almost automatically to the establishment of *genuine* fascism in Spain in the style of Mussolini. It is not necessary to speak of the consequences this would have for the whole of Europe and for the USSR. On the other hand, a favorable development of the Spanish revolution, under the conditions of the far-from-terminated world crisis, would open up tremendous possibilities.

The profound differences on a series of questions pertaining to the USSR and the world labor movement should not stand in the way of making an honest attempt at a united front in the arena of the Spanish revolution. It is not yet too late! The policy of artificial splits must be stopped immediately in Spain, advis-

A letter to the Political Bureau of the Communist Party of the Soviet Union. Never answered, this letter was made public on June 12, 1931, and was published in "The Spanish Revolution in Danger."

ing—not ordering, but just that, advising—the Spanish communist organizations to convene as soon as possible a unity conference that would assure all tendencies, under the necessary discipline of action, at least that degree of freedom of criticism that in 1917 was enjoyed by the various currents of Russian Bolshevism, who were incomparably more experienced and hardened.

There can be no doubt that if the official Spanish party understands the disproportion between its weakness and its tremendous tasks, and makes a serious attempt to unify the communist ranks, it will meet the fullest support on the part of those revolutionary communists who at present have their own separate organizations for reasons you already know, nine-tenths of which lie outside of the conditions of the Spanish revolution.

In order not to create even external difficulties, I made this proposal of mine not in the press but in the present letter. The course of events in Spain—there can be no doubt about this—will every day confirm the necessity of uniting the communist ranks. The responsibility for a split in the given instance will be a tremendous historical responsibility.

17 THE PROGRESSIVE CHARACTER OF CATALAN NATIONALISM

May 17, 1931

As to the so-called nationalism of the Catalan Federation, this is a very important and serious question. Mistakes on this point may have fatal consequences.

The revolution in Spain raised all the problems with a new force, including the national question. The chief carrier of the national tendencies and illusions is the petty-bourgeois intelligentsia, striving to find support among the peasantry against the centralizing role of big capital and the state bureaucracy. At the present stage, the leading role of the petty bourgeoisie

From "The Spanish Revolution in Danger."

in the national liberation movement, as in every revolutionary democratic movement in general, inevitably brings into the movement numerous prejudices of various kinds. From this source national illusions also seep in among the workers. In general and as a whole, this is probably the situation at present in Catalonia; perhaps also in the Catalan Federation. But what has been said does not at all diminish the *progressive, revolutionary democratic* character of the Catalan national struggle — against the Spanish great-power chauvinism, bourgeois imperialism, and bureaucratic centralism.

It must not be forgotten for a minute that Spain as a whole and Catalonia in particular are at present governed not by Catalan national democrats but by Spanish bourgeois imperialists in alliance with the landowners, old bureaucrats, and generals, and with the support of the Spanish national socialists. This whole fraternity stands on the one hand for the continued subjugation of the Spanish colonies, and on the other for the maximum bureaucratic centralization of Spain itself, that is, for the suppression by the Spanish bourgeoisie of the Catalans, the Basques, and the other nationalities. At the present stage of developments, with the given combination of class forces, Catalan nationalism is a progressive revolutionary factor; Spanish nationalism is a reactionary imperialist factor. The Spanish communist who does not understand this difference, ignores it, does not advance it to the front rank, but on the contrary covers up its significance, risks becoming an unconscious agent of the Spanish bourgeoisie and being lost to the cause of the proletarian revolution.

What is the danger of petty-bourgeois national illusions? That they are capable of dismembering the proletariat of Spain along national lines, which is a very serious danger. But the Spanish communists can successfully fight against this danger in only one way: by pitilessly denouncing the violence of the bourgeoisie of the ruling nation and in that way winning the confidence of the proletariat of the oppressed nationality. Any other policy would be tantamount to supporting the reactionary nationalism of the imperialist bourgeoisie of the ruling nation against the revolutionary democratic nationalism of the petty bourgeoisie of an oppressed nation.

18 *THE NEED FOR A SYSTEMATIC PICTURE*

May 20, 1931
You write that the lies of *l'Humanité* cause resentment in Catalonia.[6] This can be easily imagined. But resentment alone
is insufficient. The Opposition press must give a systematic
picture of what is happening in Spain.

This matter has a tremendous importance. The reeducation
of the cadres of international communism will be based upon
the living experience of the Spanish revolution. There must
be systematic correspondence from Barcelona and Madrid — or,
rather, not simply correspondence but political documents of
first-rate significance. Without this, the Stalinists are capable
of creating around the Catalan Federation such an atmosphere
of isolation and hostility that this may by itself push the advanced Catalan workers on the road of adventure and catastrophe.

From "The Spanish Revolution in Danger."

19 *THE SPANISH REVOLUTION AND THE DANGERS THREATENING IT*

May 28, 1931
*The leadership of the Comintern in the face of the Spanish
events*
The Spanish revolution is growing. In the process of struggle, its internal forces are growing. But together with them
the dangers are growing. We do not speak of the dangers that
proceed from the ruling classes and their political servants,
the republicans and Socialists. Here it is a matter of open
enemies and the tasks in relation to them are entirely clear.
But there are also internal dangers.

The Spanish workers look confidently upon the Soviet Union,
the product of the October Revolution. This mood represents
a valuable capital for communism. The defense of the Soviet

From "The Spanish Revolution in Danger."

Union is the duty of every revolutionary worker. But we must not permit the workers' faith in the October Revolution to be abused for the purpose of foisting upon them a policy that runs counter to all the lessons taught by October.

It must be said clearly. It must be said so that the vanguard of the Spanish and the international proletariat will hear: *The present leadership of the Comintern threatens the proletarian revolution in Spain with an immediate danger.* Any revolution can be ruined, even the most promising one; this was proved by the experience of the German revolution of 1923[7] and still more clearly by the experience of the Chinese revolution of 1925-27. In both instances, the immediate reason for the defeat was the wrong leadership. Spain is next in line. The leaders of the Comintern have learned nothing from their own mistakes. Worse yet, in order to cover up their past mistakes, they are compelled to defend them and to elaborate them. To the extent that it depends upon them, they are preparing the same fate for the Spanish revolution as for the Chinese.

For two years, the advanced workers were misled by the luckless theory of the "third period," which weakened and demoralized the Comintern. The leadership finally sounded the retreat. But when? Precisely at a moment when the world crisis created a radical break in the situation and revealed the first possibilities for a revolutionary offensive. The internal developments in Spain, in the meantime, were occurring unnoticed by the Comintern. Manuilsky kept declaring — and Manuilsky at the present time acts in the capacity of a Comintern leader! — that events in Spain are in general not deserving of attention.

In our sketch of the Spanish revolution, written prior to the April overturn ["The Revolution in Spain"], we expressed ourselves to the effect that the bourgeoisie, playing with different shadings of republicanism, will with all its strength and up to the very last moment retain its alliance with the monarchy. "A combination of circumstances is possible, to be sure," we wrote, "in which the possessing classes are compelled to sacrifice the monarchy in order to save themselves (for example: Germany!)." These lines gave the Stalinists an excuse — after the event, of course — to speak about an incorrect prognosis.* People who themselves have foreseen nothing demand of others not

---

* The American Stalinists excel all the others. It is difficult to imagine the Herculean pillars of vulgarity and stupidity that officials, who

a Marxist prognosis but theosophic forecasts about the day and the form in which the events will take place; this is the manner in which the ignorant and the superstitious sick demand miracles of medicine. The task of a Marxist prognosis is to help orient our ideas in the general direction of developments and to help forearm us against "surprises."

The fact that the Spanish bourgeoisie decided to part with the monarchy is to be explained by two equally important reasons. The stormy deluge of mass resentment forced the bourgeoisie to attempt to convert the generally despised Alfonso into a scapegoat. But such a serious maneuver, which has a serious risk connected with it, was available to the Spanish bourgeoisie only because the masses had confidence in the republicans and the Socialists and because during the change of regimes the communist danger could be ignored. The historic variant that has taken place in Spain is consequently a result of the force of mass pressure on the one hand, and the weakness of the Comintern on the other. One must begin by establishing these facts. It is a basic rule of tactics: if you want to get stronger, do not begin with an exaggeration of your forces. But this rule is not for the epigone bureaucracy.

On the eve of events, Manuilsky foretold that in general nothing serious would happen; then a day after the change of regimes the irreplaceable Péri,[8] the purveyor of false information from the Latin countries, began sending telegram after telegram to Moscow about how the Spanish proletariat was almost unanimously supporting the Communist Party and how the Spanish peasants were building soviets. *Pravda* printed this nonsense, supplementing it with the nonsense about the "Trotskyists" being at the tail of the Zamora government. Meanwhile, Zamora was jailing Left Oppositionists and continues to jail them.[9] Finally, on May 14, *Pravda* printed a programmatic editorial, "Spain in Flames," which constitutes a distillation of the ramblings and mistakes of the epigones, translated into the language of the Spanish revolution.

What about the Cortes?

Pravda attempts to use as its point of departure the irre-

get paid for it and whom nobody controls, are capable of talking themselves into. — L. T.

futable truth that bare propaganda is insufficient: "The Communist Party must tell the masses what they should do today." What does *Pravda* itself propose in this connection? To organize the workers "for the disarming of reaction, for the arming of the proletariat, for the election of factory committees, for the realization of the seven-hour working day, etc." "Etc."—that is just how it is put. The slogans enumerated are incontestable, even though they are presented without any internal cohesion and without the sequence that should flow from the logic of the development of the masses. But what is shocking is that the leading article in *Pravda* does not so much as mention the *election to the Cortes*, as though this political event did not even exist in the life of the Spanish nation, or as if the workers had nothing to do with it. How is this silence to be understood?

From external appearances, the republican insurrection took place, as is known, through the medium of the municipal elections. Of course, the insurrection had deeper underlying reasons and we spoke about them long before the collapse of the Berenguer ministry. But the liquidation of the monarchy by "parliamentary" methods was entirely for the benefit of the bourgeois republicans and the petty-bourgeois democrats. A great many workers in Spain imagine now that the basic questions of social life can be decided with the aid of the ballot. This illusion can be shattered only by experience. But one must know how to assist this experience. How? By turning one's back on the Cortes, or on the contrary by participating in the elections? This question demands an answer.

Besides the editorial mentioned above, the same paper carried a "theoretical" article (in the issues dated May 7 to May 10), which pretends to be a Marxist analysis of the internal forces of the Spanish revolution and a Bolshevik determination of its strategy. This article too does not say a single word about the Cortes. Boycott the elections or participate in them? In general, *Pravda* is completely silent about the slogans and the tasks of political democracy, even though it calls the revolution democratic. What does this silence signify? The elections can be *participated in*; they can be *boycotted*. But can they be *ignored?*

With regard to the Berenguer Cortes, the tactic of boycott was perfectly correct. It was clear beforehand that either Alfonso would succeed for a certain period in again resorting to the road of military dictatorship or else the movement would roll over the head of Berenguer with his Cortes. Under these conditions, the communists had to take the initiative in the struggle to boycott the Cortes. *This is precisely what we insisted on with the aid of those meager resources that we had at our disposal.* * Had the Spanish communists come out resolutely and in time for a boycott, even if only by distributing short statements on the subject, their authority would have been considerably greater at the moment when the Berenguer ministry was overthrown. The advanced workers would have said to themselves: "These people are capable of foreseeing things." Unfortunately the Spanish communists, thrown off the track by the leadership of the Comintern, did not understand the situation and made preparations to participate in the elections, but again without any confidence. The events rolled over their heads, and the first victory of the revolution brought the communists almost no increase in influence.

Now the Zamora government has undertaken to convene a constituent Cortes. Is there any basis for thinking that the convocation of this Cortes will be interrupted by a second revolution? There is no basis whatever. Powerful movements of the masses are quite possible, but without a program, without a party, without a leadership, these movements cannot bring about a second revolution. To call for boycott would now be to call for self-isolation. It is necessary to participate most actively in the election.

The parliamentary cretinism of the reformists and
the antiparliamentary cretinism of the Anarchists

Parliamentary cretinism is a revolting sickness, but antiparliamentary cretinism is not much better. We see this most clearly in the fate of the Spanish anarcho-syndicalists. The revolution poses political questions directly and *at the present stage* gives them a parliamentary form. The attention of the working class cannot but be concentrated on the Cortes, and the anarcho-syndicalists will vote on the sly for the Social-

---

* The Left Opposition has no daily press. We are compelled to develop thoughts in private letters that should form the contents of daily articles. In the supplement to this work, we give extracts from such letter-articles in chronological order. — L. T.

ists or perhaps the republicans. To fight against parliamentary illusions without fighting simultaneously against the antiparliamentary metaphysics of the anarchists is less possible in Spain than anywhere else.

In a series of articles and letters, we demonstrated the tremendous importance of democratic demands for the further development of the Spanish revolution. Unemployment relief, the seven-hour working day, the agrarian revolution, regional autonomy — all these vital, basic questions are in one way or another connected in the consciousness of the great majority of the Spanish workers — the anarcho-syndicalists included — with the future Cortes. In the period of Berenguer, the Cortes granted by Alfonso had to be boycotted — in the name of a *revolutionary constituent Cortes.* From the very beginning, the question of suffrage had to be advanced to the foreground of agitational work. Yes, the prosaic question of suffrage! Soviet democracy, needless to say, is incomparably higher than bourgeois democracy. But soviets do not fall from the sky. To achieve them takes work.

There exist Marxists who have a lofty contempt for such a slogan, for example, as universal, equal, direct, and secret suffrage for all men and women from the age of eighteen. Nevertheless, had the Spanish communists advanced this slogan in time and defended it in speeches, articles, pamphlets, and leaflets, they would have acquired tremendous popularity. Precisely because the Spanish people are inclined to exaggerate the creative power of the Cortes, every awakened worker, every revolutionary peasant woman wants to participate in the elections. We do not solidarize ourselves for a moment with the illusions of the masses; but we must utilize whatever is *progressive* about these illusions to the utmost, otherwise we are not revolutionists but contemptible pedants. The mere lowering of the voting age directly affects many hundreds of thousands of workers and peasants, both men and women. And which ones? The young and active ones, those who are called upon to create the second revolution. To set this young generation against the Socialists, who seek the support of the older workers, is quite an elementary and incontestable task of the communist vanguard.

Furthermore, the Zamora government wants to put a constitution through the Cortes providing for a bicameral legislature. The revolutionary masses who have just overthrown the monarchy and who are imbued with an impassioned, even if very vague, striving towards equality and justice will respond warmly to the agitation of the communists against the plan of the bourgeoisie to foist a "house of lords" upon the backs of the people. This *small* question can play a tremendous role in the agitation, create severe difficulties for the Socialists, and drive a wedge between the Socialists and the republicans, that is, divide even for a time the enemies of the proletariat and — what is a thousand times more important — drive a wedge between the working masses and the Socialists.

The demand for a seven-hour working day, advanced by *Pravda*, is quite correct, extremely important, and timely. But can this bare demand be advanced, ignoring the political surroundings and the revolutionary democratic tasks? By speaking *only* of the seven-hour day, of factory committees and arming the workers, by ignoring "politics," and by not having a single word to say in all its articles about the elections to the Cortes, *Pravda* goes all the way to meet anarcho-syndicalism, fosters it, covers up for it. In the meantime the young worker, whom the republicans and the Socialists deprive of suffrage — although bourgeois legislation considers him sufficiently mature for capitalist exploitation — and on whom they want to impose a second house, will tomorrow, in the struggle against this abomination, want to turn his back on anarchism and stretch out his hand for a rifle. To counterpose the slogan of *arming the workers* to the reality of the political processes that grip the masses at their vitals means to isolate oneself from the masses — and the masses from arms.

The slogan of *national self-determination* has acquired exceptional significance in Spain today. But this slogan too exists on a democratic plane. We are not concerned, of course, with calling upon the Catalans and the Basques to separate from Spain; but it is our duty to insist on their right to do this should they themselves want it. But how is it to be determined whether or not they want it? Very simply: through universal, equal, direct, and secret vote of the districts concerned. There is no other method at present. In the future, national questions, as well as all others, will be decided by soviets as the organs of the dictatorship of the proletariat. But we can only lead the workers towards soviets. We cannot force soviets on the workers at any desired moment; still less can we force upon the people the soviets that the proletariat will create only in the future. In the meantime, it is necessary to answer today's question. In May, the municipalities of Catalonia found themselves called upon to elect their deputies to elaborate a temporary constitution for the province, that is, to determine its relation to Spain as a whole. Can the Catalan workers have an indifferent attitude to the attempts of the petty-bourgeois democracy, subordinated as always to big capital, to decide the fate of the Catalan people with the aid of anti-democratic elections? Without the slogans of political democracy to supplement and concretize it, the slogan of national self-determination is a senseless formula, or still worse, it is dust thrown in the eyes.

For a certain time, all the questions of the Spanish revolution will in one way or another be refracted through the prism of parliamentarism. The peasants will wait with the greatest anxiety for what the Cortes will say about the *agrarian question.* Is it hard to see the significance of a communist agrarian program unfolded from the forum of the Cortes under present conditions? But to do this, it is necessary to have an agrarian program and to gain access to the parliamentary forum. The Cortes will not solve the land question, this we know; that will require the fighting initiative of the peasant masses themselves. But to take such an initiative the masses need a program and a leadership. The communists need the forum of the Cortes as a bond with the masses; and from this bond will develop actions that will submerge the Cortes. This is the essence of the revolutionary dialectic with regard to parliament.

Nevertheless, how is it to be explained that the leadership of the Comintern is silent on this question? Only by the fact that it is a captive of its own past. Too loudly have the Stalinists rejected the slogan of a constituent assembly for China. The Sixth Congress officially condemned the slogans of political democracy for colonial countries as "opportunism."[10] The example of Spain, a country incomparably more advanced than China and India, reveals all the inconsistency of the decisions of the Sixth Congress. But the Stalinists are bound hand and foot. Not daring to call for a boycott of parliamentarism, they simply pass over it in silence. Let the revolution perish, but long live the leaders' reputation for infallibility!*

What kind of revolution is ahead in Spain?
The theoretical article quoted above, which seems to have been especially written to muddle the brain, after attempting to determine the class character of the Spanish revolution, continues literally: "Taking all this into consideration [!] it would, however [!], be incorrect to characterize the Spanish revolution *at the present stage* as a socialist revolution" (*Pravda,* May 10, 1931). This sentence alone sums up the analysis. Are there people in the world, the reader must ask himself, capable of thinking that the Spanish revolution "at the present stage" can be characterized as socialist, without taking the risk of landing in an insane asylum? Where then did *Pravda* get the idea that this sort of "outline" was necessary, and moreover in such a mild and reserved form: "Taking all this into consideration, it would, however, be incorrect . . ."?

This is explained by the fact that the epigones, to their misfortune, read in Lenin's writings the phrase about the "growing over" of the bourgeois-democratic revolution into a socialist revolution. Not understanding Lenin, forgetting or distorting the experiences of the Russian Revolution, they make the concept of "growing over" a basis for the grossest opportunist meanderings. It is not — let us say it outright — a matter of academic subtleties, but a life-and-death question for the proletarian revolution.

Only very recently, the epigones expected that the dictatorship of the Kuomintang would "grow over" into the workers' and peasants' dictatorship, and the latter into a socialist dic-

---

* The Italian group "Prometeo" (the Bordigists) rejects revolutionary democratic slogans in general for all countries and all peoples. This sectarian doctrinairism, which coincides in practice with the position of the Stalinists, has nothing in common with the position of the Bolshevik-Leninists. The International Left must reject any shadow of responsibility for such ultraleft infantilism. It is precisely the fresh experiences in Spain that bear witness that in the process of crushing the regime of the fascist dictatorship in Italy the slogans of political democracy will undoubtedly play an extremely important role. To enter the Spanish or Italian revolution with the program of Prometeo is tantamount to plunging into water with hands tied behind the back. Such a swimmer always runs the risk of drowning. — L. T.

tatorship of the proletariat. In this connection they imagined —
Stalin developed this theme with particular profundity — that
on one flank of the revolution, the "rightist elements" would
gradually split away, while on the other flank the "leftist elements" would grow stronger; this is what the organic process
of "growing over" was supposed to consist of. Unfortunately,
the magnificent theory of Stalin-Martinov is entirely contrary
to the class theory of Marx. 11

The character of the social regime, and consequently also
the character of every revolution, is determined by the character of the class that holds the power in its hands. The power
can pass from the hands of one class into the hands of another only through a revolutionary overthrow, and not by
any means through an organic "growing over." This basic
truth the epigones have trampled underfoot — first for China
and now for Spain. And we see the learned wizards of *Pravda,*
who cover their heads with skull caps, put a thermometer
under Zamora's tongue, and debate: Can we or can we not
acknowledge that the process of "growing over" has brought
the Spanish revolution over into the socialist stage? And these
sages — let us give their wisdom its due — come to the conclusion: No, so far we cannot.

Having presented such a valuable sociological survey, *Pravda* enters into the sphere of prognosis and directives. "In Spain,"
it says, "the socialist revolution cannot be an *immediate task
of the day*. The most immediate task [!] is the workers' and
peasants' revolution against the landowners and the bourgeoisie" (*Pravda,* May 10, 1931). That the socialist revolution is not an "immediate task of the day" in Spain is indisputable. Yet it would have been much better and more accurate
to say that the *armed uprising with the aim of the seizure of
power by the proletariat is not an "immediate task of the day"
in Spain.* Why? Because the dispersed vanguard of the proletariat does not as yet lead the class behind it, and the class
does not lead behind it the oppressed masses of the village.
Under such conditions, a struggle for power would be adventurism.

But under these circumstances, what is the meaning of the
additional phrase, "the most immediate task is the workers'
and peasants' revolution against the landowners and the bourgeoisie"? Does it mean that in between the present bourgeois

republican regime and the dictatorship of the proletariat there looms before us a *distinct* "workers' and peasants' revolution"? And furthermore, does it mean that this distinct intermediary "workers' and peasants' revolution," as distinguished from the socialist revolution, is an "immediate task" in Spain? Does it mean that on today's agenda stands a new overthrow? By means of an armed uprising or by some other means? In precisely what way will the workers' and peasants' revolution "against the landowners and the bourgeoisie" be distinguished from the proletarian revolution? What combination of class forces will lie at its foundation? What party will lead the first revolution in contrast to the second? Wherein lie the differences in the programs and methods of these two revolutions?

We would seek in vain for an answer to these questions. The blurring and confusion of thought is covered up by the word "growing over"; in spite of all the contradictory reservations, these people dream of a process of evolutionary transition from a bourgeois into a socialist revolution, through a series of organic stages, disguised under different pseudonyms: Kuomintang, "democratic dictatorship," "workers' and peasants' revolution," "people's revolution"— and what is more, the decisive moment in this process when one class wrests the power from another is unnoticeably dissolved.

The problem of the permanent revolution[12]

To be sure, the proletarian revolution is at the same time a peasant revolution; but under contemporary conditions, a peasant revolution *without* a proletarian revolution is impossible. We can say to the peasant quite correctly that our aim is to create a workers' and peasants' republic just as, after the October Revolution, we called the government of the proletarian dictatorship in Russia a "workers' and peasants' government." But we do not counterpose the workers' and peasants' revolution to the proletarian revolution; on the contrary, we consider them identical. This is the only correct way of putting the question.

Here we once more touch the very heart of the problem of the so-called permanent revolution. In the struggle against this theory, the epigones have come to a complete break with the class point of view. After the experience of the "bloc of the four classes" in China, it is true, they became more careful. But because of this their confusion has only grown, and they now strain all their energy to confuse others.

Fortunately, however, events have now lifted the question out of the sphere of the "Red professors" whose specialty is philosophizing over old texts. It is no longer a matter of historical reminiscences, nor of picking out quotations, but of a new, magnificent historical experience unfolding before our eyes. Here two viewpoints have been brought face to face on the field of revolutionary struggle. Events will speak the last word. To slip out from under their control is impossible. The Spanish communist who does not give timely consideration to the essence of the questions connected with the struggle against "Trotskyism" will stand theoretically disarmed before the fundamental questions of the Spanish revolution.

What is the "growing over" of the revolution?

Yes, Lenin in 1905 advanced the hypothetical formula of a "bourgeois-democratic dictatorship of the proletariat and the peasantry." If there ever existed a country where an independent democratic agrarian revolution *preceding* the seizure of power by the proletariat might have been expected, this country was Russia, where the agrarian problem dominated the whole of national life, where revolutionary peasant movements existed for decades, where an independent revolutionary agrarian party existed with a great tradition and widespread influence among the masses.

However, even in Russia there proved to be no place for the intermediary revolution between the bourgeois and the proletarian. In April 1917, Lenin repeated and repeated for the benefit of Stalin, Kamenev, and others who were clinging to the old Bolshevik formula of 1905: There is not and there cannot be a "democratic dictatorship" other than the dictatorship of Miliukov-Tseretelli-Chernov.[13] The *democratic dictatorship,* by its very nature, is a *dictatorship of the bourgeoisie over the proletariat.* Only the dictatorship of the proletariat can take the place of such a "democratic dictatorship." Whoever invents intermediary, middle-of-the-road formulas is either a wretched visionary or a charlatan. This is the conclusion Lenin drew from the living experience of the February and October revolutions. We stand entirely on the ground of these experiences and these conclusions.

Nevertheless, what does Lenin's "growing over" of the democratic into a socialist revolution signify under such conditions? Nothing of the kind imagined by the epigones and the windbags like the Red professors.

The fact is that the dictatorship of the proletariat does not at all coincide mechanically with the inception of the socialist revolution. The seizure of power by the working class occurs in definite national surroundings, in a definite period, for the solution of definite tasks. In backward nations, such *immediate* tasks have a democratic character: the national liberation from imperialist subjugation and the agrarian revolution, as in China; the agrarian revolution and the liberation of the oppressed nationalities, as in Russia. We see the same thing at present in Spain, even though in a different combination. Lenin even said that the proletariat in Russia came to power in October 1917 primarily as an *agent of the bourgeois-democratic revolution.* The victorious proletariat began with the solution of the democratic tasks, and only gradually, by the logic of its rule, did it take up the socialist tasks; it took up seriously the collectivization of agriculture only in the twelfth year of its power. This is precisely what Lenin called the growing over of the democratic revolution into the socialist.

It is not the bourgeois power that grows over into a workers' and peasants' and then into a proletarian power; no, the power of one class does not "grow over" from the power of another class, but is torn from it with rifle in hand. But after the working class has seized power, the democratic tasks of the proletarian regime inevitably grow over into socialist tasks. An evolutionary, organic transition from democracy to socialism is conceivable only under the *dictatorship of the proletariat.* This is Lenin's central idea. The epigones have disfigured all this, have confused and distorted it, and now they poison the consciousness of the international proletariat with their falsifications.

Two variants: opportunist and adventurist

What is at issue — let us repeat — is not academic subtleties but vital problems of the revolutionary strategy of the proletariat. It is not true that the "workers' and peasants' revolution" is on the agenda in Spain. It is not true that a new revolution, that is, an immediate struggle for power, is *at present* on the agenda in Spain in general. No; the question on the agenda is the struggle for the masses, for their liberation from republican illusions and from confidence in the Socialists, for their revolutionary consolidation. This second revolution will come, but it will be the revolution of the proletariat leading behind it the poor peasants. Between a bourgeois regime and the dictatorship of the proletariat, there will be no room for any sort of distinct "workers' and peasants' revolution." To count on such a revolution and to adapt one's policy to it, is to foist a Kuomintang on the proletariat, and to ruin the revolution.

The confusionist formulations of *Pravda* open two roads that have also been followed to the end in China: the opportunist and the adventurist. If *Pravda* today does not yet dare to "characterize" the Spanish revolution as a workers' and peasants' revolution, then who knows if we will not be confronted with it tomorrow when Zamora-Chiang Kai-shek will be replaced by a true Wang Ching-wei, that is to say, a left Lerroux.14 Will not then the wise diagnosticians — Martinov, Kuusinen, and their associates — decide that this is the workers' and peasants' republic that should be "supported conditionally" (the formula of Stalin in March 1917), or "supported completely" (the formula of the same Stalin towards the Kuomintang in 1925-27)?

But there is also an adventurist possibility which is perhaps more suited to the centrist moods today. The *Pravda* editorial speaks about the fact that the Spanish masses "are also beginning to direct their blows against the government." But can the Spanish Communist Party advance the slogan of the overthrow of this government as a *task of the day?* In its learned investigations, *Pravda* says, as we are already aware, that the immediate task is the workers' and peasants' revolution. If we are to understand this "stage" not in the sense of "growing over" but in the sense of the overthrow of the power, then the adventurist variant becomes completely clear. The weak Communist Party may say to itself in Madrid, as it said to itself (or as it was commanded to say) in December 1927 in Canton: "We are not yet ready, of course, for the proletarian dictatorship; but as it is a question of an intermediary stage, a workers' and peasants' dictatorship, then let us attempt even with our weak forces to stage an uprising — perhaps something will come of it." It is really not difficult to foresee that after the criminal neglect of the first year of the Spanish revolution has been revealed, the ones responsible for the loss of time will start to whip up their agents with a cat-o'-nine-tails and may lead them into a tragic adventure in the style of Canton.

The perspectives of the "July days"

How real is the danger? It is quite real. It is rooted in the inner conditions of the revolution itself, which add an ominous character to the omissions and confusion of the leaders. The possibility of a new mass explosion is contained in the present Spanish situation, which corresponds more or less to the battles of 1917 in Petrograd that have passed into history as the "July days," which did not result in the crushing of the revolution thanks only to the correctness of the Bolshevik policy.[15] It is necessary to pause on this question, which is a burning one for Spain.

We come across a prototype of the "July days" in all the old revolutions too, beginning with the Great French Revolution, with varying, but as a general rule unfavorable, and often catastrophic outcomes. Such a stage is built into the mechanism of the bourgeois revolution insofar as the class that sacrifices most for its success and places the most hope in it receives from it least of all.

The regularity of the process is quite clear. The possessing class, having come to power through the revolution, is inclined to think that the revolution has by that exhausted its mission, and is concerned more than anything else with proving its reliability to the forces of reaction. The "revolutionary" bourgeoisie provokes the indignation of the masses by the very measures with which it strives to gain the good graces of the overthrown classes. The disillusionment of the masses proceeds very quickly, even before its vanguard has had a chance to cool off from the heat of the revolutionary battles. It appears to those at the head of the movement that by a new blow it can finish or correct what it previously did not carry out resolutely enough. From this comes the impulse for the new revolution, unprepared, without a program, without looking back at the reserves, without a thought for the consequences. On the other hand, the bourgeoisie, which has come to power, acts as though it were waiting for a stormy uprising from below in order to attempt to settle matters with the people. Such is the social and psychological basis for that supplementary semirevolution, which more than once in history became the provocation for a victorious counterrevolution.

In 1848, the "July days" in France fell in June and assumed an immeasurably more awesome and tragic character than in Petrograd in 1917. The so-called June days of the Parisian proletariat grew out of the February revolution. The Parisian workers, with the February rifles in their hands, could not but react to the contradiction between the magnificent program and the sorry reality, the unbearable contrast, which struck at their stomachs and hearts every day. Without a plan, without a program, without a leadership, the June days of 1848 were like a powerful and ungovernable reflex of the proletariat. The insurgent workers were mercilessly crushed. Thus the democrats paved the way for Bonapartism.[16]

The gigantic conflagration of the Paris Commune stood in the same relation to the September revolution of 1870 as the June days did to the February revolution of 1848.[17] The March 1871 uprising of the Parisian proletariat was least of all a matter of strategic calculation. It arose from a tragic combination of circumstances, supplemented by one of those provocations for which the French bourgeoisie is so inventive when fear spurs on its malice. In the Paris Commune, the reflex protest of the proletariat against the deceit of the bourgeois revolution rose to the level of a proletarian revolution for the first time, but it rose only to fall again.

At present, the bloodless, peaceful, glorious revolution in Spain (this list of adjectives is always the same) is preparing its own "June days" before our very eyes, if we use the French calendar, or "July days," according to the Russian calendar. The Madrid government, soaked with phrases that often seem to be translations from the Russian language, promises strong measures against unemployment and land-hunger, but it does not dare to touch a single one of the social ulcers. The coalition Socialists help the republicans sabotage the tasks of the revolution. The head of Catalonia, which is the most industrialized and revolutionary region of Spain, preaches a millennial kingdom without oppressed nations and oppressed classes, but at the same time he does not dare to lift a finger in order really to help the people cast off even some of the most hated of the old chains. Macia hides behind the Madrid government,[18] which in turn hides behind the constituent assembly, as if life were waiting upon this assembly! As if it were not clear in advance that the coming Cortes will only be an enlarged replica of the republican-Socialist bloc, which is primarily concerned with maintaining the status quo.

Is it hard to foresee the feverish mounting of the workers' and peasants' rebelliousness? The discordance between the progress of the mass revolution and the policy of the new ruling classes — that is the source of the irreconcilable conflict that, in its future development, will either bury the first revolution — the April one — or produce a second one.

If the Bolshevik Party had been obstinate in evaluating the July movement in Petrograd as "untimely" and had turned its back upon the masses, the uprising, such as it was, would inevitably have fallen under the dispersed and discordant leadership of anarchists, adventurists, the incidental figures of the revolt of the masses, and would have exhausted itself in hopeless, bloody convulsions. But on the other hand, if the party, standing at the head of the movement, had given up its overall evaluation of the situation and had allowed itself to be swept into decisive battles, the uprising would undoubtedly have assumed an audacious scope; the workers and soldiers under the leadership of the Bolsheviks would have conquered power temporarily in Petrograd in July, only in order to set the stage for the crushing of the revolution afterwards. Only the correct leadership of the Bolshevik party avoided both variants of fatal danger: the spirit of the June days of 1848 and the spirit of the Paris Commune of 1871. The blow dealt to the masses and the party in July 1917 was very heavy. But it was not a decisive blow. The victims were counted by the tens, but not by the tens of thousands. The working class emerged from this trial neither beheaded nor debilitated. It preserved its fighting cadres intact. These cadres learned a great deal and led the proletariat to victory in October.

Precisely from the viewpoint of the "July days," the fiction of the "intermediary," middle-of-the-road revolution, which is supposed to be next in order in Spain, constitutes a terrific danger.

The struggle for the masses and the workers' juntas

It is the duty of the Left Opposition to uncover and expose mercilessly, and once and for all to discredit in the minds of the proletarian vanguard the formula of a separate "workers' and peasants' revolution" distinct from the bourgeois and the proletarian revolutions. Do not believe in it, communists of

Spain! It is an illusion and a deception. It is a diabolical
snare which will be transformed tomorrow into a noose around
your neck. Do not believe in it, advanced workers of Spain!
Study the lessons of the Russian Revolution and the lessons
of the defeats of the epigones.

A perspective of struggle for the *dictatorship of the proletariat* is opening up before you. To accomplish this task, you
must consolidate around you the working class and arouse
the millions of village poor to the aid of the workers. This is
a gigantic task. Upon you, the Spanish communists, lies a vast
revolutionary responsibility. Do not close your eyes to your
weakness; do not be seduced by illusions. The revolution does
not believe in words. It tests everything, and what is more
it tests it in blood. Only the dictatorship of the proletariat
can overthrow the rule of the bourgeoisie. There is not, there
will not be, and there cannot be any "intermediary" revolution
more "simple," more "economical," more adapted to your forces.
History will not invent for you any transitional dictatorship,
a dictatorship of a second order, a dictatorship at a discount.
Whoever speaks to you about it is deceiving you. Make your
preparations for the dictatorship of the proletariat, prepare
seriously, stubbornly, tirelessly!

However, the immediate task of the Spanish communists is
not the struggle for power, but the struggle for the masses,
and furthermore this struggle will develop in the next period
on the basis of the bourgeois republic and to a great degree
under the slogans of democracy. The creation of workers' juntas is undoubtedly the principal task of the day. But it is absurd to counterpose the juntas to democratic slogans. The
struggle against the privileges of the church, the abuses of
the monastic orders and monasteries — a purely democratic
struggle — produced a mass explosion in May that created
favorable conditions for the election of workers' deputies; unfortunately, those conditions were allowed to slip away.

At the present stage, juntas are the organizational forms
for the united proletarian front — for strikes, for the expulsion
of the Jesuits, for participation in the elections to the Cortes,
to establish contact with the soldiers, as well as to provide
support to the peasant movement. Only through juntas embracing the basic core of the proletariat can the communists
assure their hegemony in the proletariat, and thus also in the

revolution. Only to the extent that the influence of the communists grows among the working class will the juntas be transformed into organs of struggle for power. At one of the later stages — we do not yet know when — the juntas, as organs of the power of the proletariat, will find themselves opposed to the democratic institutions of the bourgeoisie. Only then will the last hour of bourgeois democracy have struck.

Every time the masses are drawn into struggle, they invariably feel — and cannot help but feel — an acute need for an authoritative organization rising above the parties, factions, sects, and capable of uniting all the workers for joint action. This is the form that the juntas elected by the workers must take. It is necessary to know how to put forward this slogan to the masses on appropriate occasions — and such occasions arise now at every step. But to counterpose the slogan of soviets as organs of the dictatorship of the proletariat to the realities of the present struggle means to convert the slogan of soviets into a suprahistorical divinity, into a superrevolutionary icon, which individual saints may worship but which the masses will never follow.

The problems of tempo of the Spanish revolution

But is there still time to apply correct tactics? Isn't it too late? Haven't all the opportunities been missed?

It is extremely important to determine the exact tempo with which the revolution is developing — if not to determine the basic strategic line, then at least to determine the tactics. For without correct tactics, the best strategy may lead to ruin. Of course, to guess the tempo far in advance is impossible. The tempo has to be examined in the course of the struggle, making use of the most varied indicators. Moreover, in the course of events the tempo may change very abruptly. But we must nevertheless keep before our eyes a definite perspective in order to introduce the necessary correctives into it in the course of experience.

The Great French Revolution took over three years to reach its highest point, the dictatorship of the Jacobins. The Russian Revolution produced the dictatorship of the Bolsheviks within eight months. Here we see a tremendous difference in tempo. If in France events had developed faster, the Jacobins would not have had the time to take shape, because they did not exist as a party on the eve of the revolution. On the other hand, had the Jacobins represented a power on the eve of the revolution, events would probably have proceeded faster. That is one of the factors determining the tempo. But there are also others, perhaps more decisive ones.

The Russian Revolution of 1917 was preceded by the revolution in 1905, which Lenin called a dress rehearsal. All the elements of the second and third revolutions were prepared beforehand, so that the forces participating in the struggle moved as if according to plan. This hastened extraordinarily the period of the revolution's rise to its culmination.

Nevertheless, it must be kept in mind that the decisive factor in relation to the tempo in 1917 was the *war*. The agrarian question might have been postponed for months, perhaps for a year or two, but the question of death in the trenches could bear no postponement. The soldiers were saying: "What good is the land to me if I am not alive?" The pressure of twelve million soldiers was a factor in the extraordinary acceleration of the revolution. Without the war, in spite of the "dress rehearsal" of 1905 and the presence of the Bolshevik Party, the pre-Bolshevik period of the revolution might have lasted not eight months, but perhaps a year or two or more.

These general considerations have an unmistakable significance for determining the possible tempo of development of the events in Spain. The present generation of Spaniards has known no revolution, has gone through no "dress rehearsal" in the past. The Communist Party went into the events in an extremely weak condition. Spain is not carrying on any foreign war; the Spanish peasants are not concentrated by the millions in the barracks and trenches, and are not in immediate danger of extermination. All these circumstances compel us to expect a slower development of events and consequently permit us to hope for a lengthier period in which to prepare the party for the seizure of power.

But there are factors that pull in the opposite direction and may provoke premature attempts at decisive battle that are equivalent to a defeat of the revolution: the weakness of the party accentuates the strength of the spontaneous elements in the movement; the anarcho-syndicalist traditions have the same effect; finally, the false orientation of the Comintern opens the gates to explosions of adventurism.

The conclusion from these historical analogies is clear: the situation in Spain (where there is no recent revolutionary tradition, no strong party, no foreign war) leads to a condition in which the *normal birth* of the dictatorship of the proletariat will, from all indications, prove to be delayed for a considerably longer period than in Russia and therefore there are circumstances that strengthen to an extraordinary degree the danger of a *miscarriage of the revolution.*

The weakness of Spanish communism, which is the result of a wrong official policy, makes it extremely susceptible to the most dangerous conclusions from the wrong directives. A weakling does not like to look his weakness in the eye, he is afraid of being late, he is nervous and runs ahead. The Spanish communists may be particularly afraid of the Cortes.

In Russia, the Constituent Assembly, which was repeatedly postponed by the bourgeoisie, was convened only after the decisive encounter and was liquidated without any difficulties. The Spanish constituent Cortes is being convened at an earlier stage in the development of the revolution. The communists in the Cortes will be a negligible minority, assuming that they get into it at all. From here it is not far to the thought: try to overthrow the Cortes as quickly as possible, utilizing some kind of a spontaneous attack by the masses. Such an adventure will not only fail to solve the problem of power, it will also throw the revolution back for a long time, and in all probability will break its back. The proletariat will be able to wrench the power out of the hands of the bourgeoisie only if the majority of the workers strive passionately toward power and if the majority of the oppressed people have confidence in the proletariat.

Precisely on the question of the parliamentary institutions of the revolution, the Spanish comrades should refer not so much to the Russian experience as to the experience of the Great French Revolution. The dictatorship of the Jacobins was preceded by three parliaments. Upon these three steps, the masses mounted to the dictatorship of the Jacobins. It is ridiculous to think — as the Madrid republicans and Socialists do — that the Cortes will really put a stop to the revolution. No, it can only give a new impetus to the development of the revolution, assuring it at the same time a more regulated evolution. Such a perspective is extremely important for an orientation in the course of events, for a remedy for nervousness and adventurism.

Of course this does not mean that the communists act as a brake on the revolution. It means still less that the communists separate themselves from the movement and from the upsurges of the masses of town and village. Such a policy would ruin the party, which is still confronted with the challenge of gaining the confidence of the revolutionary masses. Only because the Bolsheviks led all the battles of the workers and soldiers were they in a position to hold the masses back from a catastrophe in July.

If the objective conditions and the treachery of the bourgeoisie were to force the proletariat into a decisive battle under unfavorable conditions, the communists, of course, would take their place in the front ranks of the fighters. A revolutionary party will always prefer to subject itself to a defeat together with the masses, rather than stand aside moralizing, and leave the workers without leadership under the bayonets of the bourgeoisie. A party beaten in battle will root itself deeply in the hearts of the masses and will sooner or later take revenge. But a party that has deserted the class at the moment of danger will never come to life again. However, the Spanish communists are by no means confronted with such a tragic dilemma. On the contrary, there is every reason to calculate that the disgraceful policies of the Socialists in power and the sorry bewilderment of the anarcho-syndicalists will push the workers further and further towards communism, and that the party — provided it has a correct policy — will have sufficient time to prepare itself and to lead the proletariat to victory.

For the unity of the communist ranks!

One of the most malicious crimes of the Stalinist bureaucracy is the systematic splitting of the weak communist ranks in Spain, a split that did not result from the events in the Spanish revolution but was injected in advance in the form of directives, issuing from the struggle for existence of the Stalinist bureaucracy. The revolution always creates in the proletariat a powerful attraction to the left wing. In 1917, all the currents and groups that were near in spirit to Bolshevism fused with it, even those that had fought against it in the past. Not only did the party grow rapidly; it also had an extremely stormy internal life. From April to October, and later, in the years of the civil war, the struggle of tendencies and groupings in the Bolshevik Party attained an extraordinary acuteness at certain moments. But we do not see any splits. We do not even see individual expulsions.

The mighty pressure of the masses welds the party together. The internal struggle trains the party and makes its own road clear to it. In this struggle, all the members of the party gain a deep confidence in the correctness of the policy of the party and in the revolutionary reliability of the leadership. Only such a conviction in the rank-and-file Bolshevik, won through experience and ideological struggle, gives the leadership the chance to lead the whole party into battle at the necessary moment. And only a deep confidence of the party itself in the correctness of its policy inspires the working masses with confidence in the party. Artificial splits forced from outside; the absence of a free and honest ideological struggle; the branding of friends as enemies; the creation of myths serving to split the communist ranks — this is what now paralyzes the Spanish Communist Party. It must wrench itself out of the bureaucratic grip that condemns it to impotence. The communist ranks must be assembled on the basis of open, honest discussion. A unity conference of the Spanish Communist Party must be prepared.

The situation is complicated by the fact that not only the official Stalinist bureaucracy in Spain, small in numbers and weak, but also the Opposition organizations formally outside of the Comintern — the Catalan Federation, the Madrid autonomous group[19] — have no clear program of action, and what is worse yet, are to a considerable extent contaminated with the prejudices that the epigones of Bolshevism have sowed so generously for the last eight years. On the question of the "workers' and peasants'" revolution and the "democratic dictatorship" and even the "workers' and peasants' party," the Catalan Oppositionists do not possess the necessary clarity. This doubles the danger. The struggle for the restoration of the unity of the communist ranks must be combined with the struggle against the ideological decay and falsifications of Stalinism.

This is the task of the Left Opposition. But here too the truth must be stated: the Left Opposition has barely approached the solution of these tasks. The fact that the Spanish comrades adhering to the Left Opposition have not as yet established their own press is an inexcusable waste of time and the revolution will not leave it unpunished. We know under what difficult conditions our cothinkers find themselves: unremitting police persecution under Primo de Rivera, under Berenguer and under Zamora. Comrade Lacroix, for instance, emerges from prison only to return there again.[20] The apparatus of the Comintern, impotent when it comes to revolutionary leadership, shows great ingenuity in the domain of persecution and slander. All this makes our work extremely difficult. Nevertheless, it has to be done. We must assemble the forces of the Left Opposition throughout the country, establish a journal and a bulletin, group together the working class youth, organize groups, and fight for unity of the communist ranks on the basis of a correct Marxist policy.

20   *ANARCHO-SYNDICALISM AND THE CATALAN FEDERATION*

May 31, 1931

As far as I can judge, the anarcho-syndicalists are following a policy of conciliation toward the despicable regime of Colonel Macía, the Barcelonese agent of the Madrid imperialists. The anarcho-syndicalist leaders have become the sub-lieutenants, and in fact the agents, of national civil peace in Catalonia.

The Catalan Federation, as far as I can tell, has adopted a conciliatory position toward the anarcho-syndicalists; that is to say, it has replaced the revolutionary policy of the united front with the opportunist policy of defending and flattering the anarcho-syndicalists and thereby the Macía regime. It is precisely in this that I see one of the sources of explosion that can be so dangerous at a certain stage.

It is not the task of the trade unions to hold back the workers, but on the contrary to mobilize and organize them for the offensive. Above all, the unions must arouse the workers of

From Leon Trotsky, *Ecrits*, Vol. III (1928-1940). Translated for this volume from the French by Constance Weissman.

the backward regions of Catalonia and the rest of Spain. The task of the Catalan Federation does not consist of building up the prestige of the anarcho-syndicalist confederation but rather of carrying out a constant step-by-step criticism, and of denouncing to the workers its tacit bloc with the petty-bourgeois counterrevolution of Macía.

So that the restraining of actions that are premature and unreasonable cannot be transformed into a Menshevik suffocation of the revolution, we must have a clear strategic line, and the advanced workers must understand it well so that they can tirelessly explain it to the broad masses. The Catalan Federation obviously has no strategic line. Its leaders are afraid to ponder on the fundamental problems of the revolution; otherwise they would not have that infantile and stupid fear of "Trotskyism," which expresses the entire extent of their political thought. . . .

21   *THE CATALAN FEDERATION'S PLATFORM*

June 12, 1931
Dear Comrades:

I have just read for the first time in *La Lutte de classes* the platform of the so-called Workers and Peasants Bloc, the name under which the Catalan Federation acts. I admit that the document is thoroughly and correctly translated in *La Lutte de classes.* The document as a whole, from beginning to end, produces a painful impression. Everything I have written in my latest work, "The Spanish Revolution in Danger," against the official policy of the Comintern on the Spanish question applies to the Catalan Federation. Moreover, the latter commits errors which the leadership of the Comintern has already renounced, at least verbally.

1. The document is issued by the "Workers and Peasants Bloc." What is this? A pseudonym for the Catalan Federation? The bloc, that is, the union of the workers and peasants, is a gigantic political task that the proletarian vanguard must accomplish. This task must be written into its platform. Instead

From *The Militant*, August 1, 1931. *The Militant* was then the newspaper of the Communist League of America.

of this, the "Workers and Peasants Bloc" becomes the name of the revolutionary organization. This is nothing more than a new edition of the workers' and peasants' party. Yet even the Sixth Congress of the Comintern renounced this reactionary idea — as part of its criticism of the Left Opposition.

2. In all their documents the word "communism" does not appear a single time. Anyone who hides his communism from the masses ceases to be a communist.

3. They speak of the democratic revolution, of the democratic republic, of the popular revolution, without the slightest attempt at a class analysis. The government is accused of indecision, of vacillation, etc. . . . But nowhere is it called a government of the bourgeoisie, an enemy of the people. Their criticism of the Zamora government is an exact replica of the criticism addressed by the Mensheviks and the Social Revolutionaries to the government of Kerensky-Prince Lvov.[21] They are silent on the subject of the Macía government.

4. The document speaks of a "rational construction of society" without explaining what this means. It is the language of the "true" socialists before 1848. Then it says: "The republic must signal a new social organization." What kind — a bourgeois regime or a socialist regime? The platform plays hide-and-seek with capitalism and with socialism.

5. The fact that Alfonso was given a chance to flee abroad is presented as the "first profound *mistake* of the provisional government." Mistake? Is this to mean that Zamora is not sufficiently "sensible" in his revolutionary policy? This is how the Russian Mensheviks put the question. To call a deliberate counterrevolutionary calculation on the part of the bourgeoisie a "mistake" means to whitewash the bourgeoisie and to cover up for it to the masses.

6. "The republic must be a victory not only for the bourgeoisie but also for the workers." What is the meaning of this mealy-mouthed, vulgarly democratic, and profoundly false phrase? Where and when has a republic existed that satisfied at the same time the interests of the bourgeoisie and those of the workers? From the republican bourgeoisie, we can and should demand democratic rights and social reforms, ceaselessly exposing the bourgeois, even the arch-democratic, republic as a machine that the bourgeoisie uses to squeeze the sweat and blood out of the workers and the peasants.

7. The reference to the republic of 1873 is accompanied by this incredible moral: "Thus a complete division was created

between the power and the people." The abstraction of the people is separated from the abstraction of the power. Perhaps the bourgeoisie separated itself from the *working* people? It is necessary to refer to the example of 1873, not in order to insist that the bourgeoisie become softer, better, more generous, more tender, but in order to teach the masses not to believe for a single instant in the "softer," "more generous," "more tender" bourgeoisie. That is how the Marxists put the question.

8. The platform calls upon the "working masses to organize themselves in all the provinces on the basis of revolutionary juntas." To what end? No program is indicated. Not only is there no mention that juntas of this kind will have to guarantee the revolutionary passage of power into the hands of the workers and the poor peasants, but there is also no program of transitional demands: the seven-hour working day, workers' control of production, organization through revolutionary juntas of workers and soldiers for the agrarian uprising. They do not so much as mention that the junta is an organization of the proletariat and the exploited masses *against* the class that is in power, that is, *against the bourgeoisie*. The junta is taken as a "revolutionary organization" in the spirit of the Spanish petty-bourgeois tradition.

9. In speaking of the importance of the agrarian uprising, the platform refers to the French and Russian revolutions. Not a word about the experience of the Chinese revolution, which has just been strangled under our very eyes by the leadership of the Comintern. Did the Comintern "solve" the agrarian question in China correctly? Not a word about that. The communist who has not profited by the lessons of the Chinese revolution has no right to address himself to the masses in order to teach them and to issue appeals to them, especially in a country in the midst of a revolution.

10. The platform says: "We support a state for each nation." What does this mean for Spain? What nations are involved? The pan-Spanish state organization is defined as follows: "The Union of Iberian Republics." What does this mean? If it means a federation, it would be better to say so.

11. "The defense of the revolution must be the supreme law." Defense against whom? The bourgeoisie in power defends *its* revolution against the proletariat. Whoever conceals this fact behind hollow phrases about defense *in general* of the revolution *in general* against enemies *in general* helps the bourgeoisie

to stifle the proletariat under the banner of the revolution.

12. The "Workers and Peasants Bloc," that is, the workers' and peasants' party, promises at the end of its platform to "fight with all its strength for the complete realization of the democratic revolution." Does this mean the bourgeois republic on the basis of democratic parliamentarism? Then that must be said; but in this case, it is necessary at least to put forward demands for democratic electoral rights because, before the "rational" republic and the "rational organization of society" can be realized on the Iberian Peninsula, it is necessary for the bourgeois republic of Zamora at least to give the working man and woman and the peasant man and woman the right to vote.

13. The name of the Socialist Party is not mentioned in the platform. Not a word is said about the anarcho-syndicalists. The official Communist Party is not mentioned. One might say that the "Workers and Peasants Bloc" is prepared to act in a void.

These are the immediate objections that I believe it is necessary to make on the basis of the text published in *La Lutte de classes*. It is possible that the Catalan Federation has already introduced into its platform some change, correction, or amendment. I am ready, of course, to welcome every step of the Federation in the direction of Marxism. But the document as it stands represents a pure "Kuomintangism" transported to Spanish soil. The ideas and methods against which the Opposition fought implacably when it was a question of the Comintern's Chinese policy find their most disastrous expression in this document.

As far as I know, the leaders of the Catalan Federation systematically dissociate themselves from the Left Opposition. This is not enough; the Left Opposition must dissociate itself in a clear and precise manner from the ideas and methods that are expressed by the leaders of the Catalan Federation in the document that we have just analyzed briefly. A false point of departure during a revolution is inevitably translated in the course of events into the language of defeat. The Spanish Left Opposition, weak as it is, can render enormous services to the proletariat and to the Spanish revolution. But in order to fulfill this mission, it must establish in its own ranks a regime of *clarity, honesty, and intransigence.* That is my call to our Spanish friends.

22   *THE CHARACTER OF THE REVOLUTION*

June 18, 1931

The course of events today puts on the agenda an imposing question about which the Left Opposition can and must have its say. I speak of the *Spanish revolution*. It is not a question now of criticism in retrospect; for the International Left Opposition, it is a question of making an active intervention in the events in order to prevent a catastrophe.

We have few forces. But the advantage of a revolutionary situation consists precisely in the fact that even a small group can become a great force in a brief space of time, provided that it gives a correct prognosis and raises the correct slogans in time. I refer not only to our Spanish section, directly involved by the events, but also to all our sections, because the further the revolution advances, the more it will draw the attention of the workers throughout the world. The verification of the political lines will take place before the eyes of the world proletarian vanguard. If we are really the left wing, if we are really strong through our correct revolutionary conception, we must show this strength especially sharply during a revolutionary situation. If we are really internationalists, we must do this work on an international scale.

We must squarely pose two fundamental questions: (1) the question of the general character of the Spanish revolution and the *strategic* line that flows from it; and (2) the question of the correct tactical utilization of democratic slogans and of parliamentary and revolutionary possibilities. I tried to say everything essential on these questions in my last work on Spain ["The Spanish Revolution in Danger."] Here I want only to express myself briefly on the general questions on which we must *take the offensive against the whole line of the Communist International.*

Should we look forward in Spain to an intermediate revolution between the accomplished republican revolution and the future proletarian revolution, a so-called "workers' and peasants'" revolution, with a "democratic dictatorship"? Yes or no? The whole strategic line is determined by the reply to this question. The official Spanish party is up to its neck in ideological confusion on this fundamental question, a confusion

From *The Militant,* July 18, 1931.

that was sown and is still being sown by the epigones and that finds its expression in the program of the Communist International. From day to day, in the light of living facts, we have the chance to expose all the emptiness, all the absurdity, and at the same time the terrific danger represented by the fiction of a middle-of-the-road, intermediate revolution.

The leading comrades of all the sections must remember that we, the left wing, are precisely the ones who must place ourselves upon *a solid scientific* basis. Thoughtless dabbling with ideas, journalistic charlatanism in the style of Landau and his associates,[22] are contrary to the very essence of a proletarian revolutionary organization. The fundamental questions of the revolution must be studied in the same way that engineers study the resistance of matter or doctors study anatomy and pathology. The problem of the permanent revolution, thanks to the events in Spain, has now become the central problem of the International Left Opposition.

The questions of democratic slogans, of the utilization of the elections, and later on of the Cortes, are questions of revolutionary tactics subordinated to the general question of strategy. But the most correct strategic formulas are worth nothing without a tactical solution to these formulas at a given moment.

But matters look very bad in Spain from this point of view. According to the French newspaper dispatches, the leader of the Catalan Federation, Maurin,[23] is reported to have said in his Madrid speech that his organization will not participate in the elections because it does not believe in their "sincerity." Could this possibly be true? That would mean that Maurín is not approaching the problems of revolutionary tactics from the point of view of the mobilization of the forces of the proletariat, but from the point of view of morality and petty-bourgeois sentimentalism. Two weeks ago I would have thought that the bourgeois press was talking nonsense; but after acquainting myself with the platform of the Catalan Federation, I am obliged to acknowledge that this news, monstrous as it may seem, is nevertheless not impossible and must not be excluded in advance.

On this line, we must inaugurate a merciless struggle in our own ranks. It is entirely absurd and unworthy to quarrel with various groups on the subject of the functions, the rights, and the prerogatives of the Secretariat at a time when we have no common ground in principle with these groups. I have in mind above all the "Prometeo" group, which is in disagreement with the Bolshevik-Leninists on all the fundamental questions of strategy and tactics.[24] Nobody must be allowed to stifle these profound differences by noisy quarrels on organizational questions and by unprincipled "blocs" that degenerate inevitably into intrigues behind the scenes.

After the Russian experience, the question of democratic slogans in the revolution was posed anew in the course of the struggle in China. However, not all of the European sections had the chance to follow all stages of this struggle. For this reason, the discussion on these questions had a more or less academic character for certain comrades and for certain groups. But today, these questions are the very incarnation of the struggle, and of life. Can we permit ourselves to be bound hand and foot at such an important historical turning point? Just as during the Sino-Russian conflict, which threatened to let loose a war, we could not lose ourselves in discussions over whether it was necessary to support the Soviet Union or Chiang Kai-shek, so today, face to face with the Spanish events, we cannot admit even indirect responsibility for the sectarian, semi-Bakuninist superstitions of certain groups.

My practical proposals are summed up as follows:

1. All the sections must place the problems of the Spanish revolution on the agenda.

2. The leaders of our sections must form special commissions, which should have as their tasks to gather material to go deeply into the questions, and above all to follow attentively the activity of the official parties and the manner in which they pose the problems of the Spanish revolution.

3. All the important documents of Spanish communism (of all its tendencies) must be communicated regularly, at least in the form of extracts, for the information of all our national sections.

4. After the necessary preparation, each national section of the Opposition must open the attack against the policy of the Comintern in the Spanish revolution. This offensive can have different forms: articles in the paper, critical resolutions, open letters, interventions at meetings, individual work and work by groups, etc. But all these forms must be rigorously coordinated.

5. Following a certain preparatory work in the national

sections, as well as in the International Secretariat, it will be indispensable to work out a *Manifesto of the International Left Opposition* on the Spanish revolution, which should be done in the most concrete manner possible and in intimate collaboration with the Spanish section. This manifesto will have to be given the widest possible circulation.

These are the concrete proposals. I beg you to discuss them and at the same time to send a copy to all the national sections so that the discussion will follow simultaneously in all of them.

23   "DOWN WITH ZAMORA-MAURA!"

June 24, 1931

In a letter to Comrade Lacroix, I presented some supplementary considerations on the subject of the situation in Spain. Unfortunately I don't have enough information to know how the various groups of Spanish communists pose the political questions of the day. To analyze the revolutionary situation in such a case is more difficult than playing chess blindfolded. On all questions there remain some points on which I require additional elaboration. I now want to raise these questions with you, and through you with the Spanish communists and all the sections of the International Opposition.

The main part of my article on the dangers threatening the Spanish revolution is devoted to proving that between the bourgeois republican revolution of April of this year and the proletarian revolution to come, there is no room for a special "workers' and peasants' revolution." In passing, I noted that this does not mean that the party of the proletariat has to devote itself to the peaceful assembling of forces until "the final and decisive conflict." Such a conception would be a philistine antirevolutionary one. While there cannot be either an intermediary *revolution* or an intermediary *regime*, there can and will be intermediary mass actions, strikes, demonstrations, clashes with the police and the troops, tumultuous revolutionary convulsions in which the communists will naturally be in the front ranks of the fight. What may be the historical meaning

---

From *The Militant,* July 25, 1931. Miguel Maura was minister of the interior under Alcalá Zamora.

of those intermediary fights? On the one hand, they may introduce democratic changes in the bourgeois republican regime.
On the other hand, they will prepare the masses to conquer
power in order to create a proletarian regime.

The participation of the communists in these fights, and above
all their participation in the leadership of these struggles, requires of them not only a clear understanding of the development of the revolution as a whole, but also the capacity to
put forward at the right moment sharp, specific, fighting slogans that by themselves don't derive from the "program" but
are dictated by the circumstances of the day and lead the masses forward.

The enormous role of the Bolshevik slogan "Down with the
ten capitalist ministers" is well known. This slogan was adopted
in 1917 at the time of the coalition between the conciliators and
the bourgeois liberals. The masses still trusted the Socialist
conciliators but even the most trusting masses always have
an instinctive distrust of the bourgeoisie, of the exploiters, and
of the capitalists. It is upon this distrust that the tactic of the
Bolsheviks was based during that specific period. We didn't
say "Down with the Socialist ministers," we didn't even advance
the slogan "Down with the Provisional Government" as a fighting slogan of the moment, but instead we hammered inces-
santly on the same theme: "Down with the ten capitalist ministers." This slogan played an enormous role, because it gave
the masses the opportunity to learn from their own experience
that the Socialist conciliators thought much more of the capitalist ministers than of the working masses.

Slogans of that type are best fitted for the present stage of
the Spanish revolution. The proletarian vanguard is fully interested in pushing the Spanish Socialists to take power into
their hands. For that to happen, it is necessary to split the
coalition. The present task is the fight to drive the bourgeois
ministers from the coalition. The achievement of this task even
in part is conceivable only in connection with important political events, under pressure of new mass movements, and so
on. Thus, in Russia, under the constant pressure of the masses,
first Guchkov[25] and Miliukov, then Prince Lvov, were ousted
from the coalition government; Kerensky was put at the head
of the government; the number of "Socialists" in the government rose, and so on. After Lenin's arrival, the Bolshevik
Party did not solidarize itself for one moment with Kerensky

and the conciliators, but it helped the masses to push the bourgeoisie out of power and to test the government of the conciliators in practice. That was an indispensable stage in the
Bolshevik rise to power.

Insofar as it is possible for me to judge from a distance,
the elections to the Cortes will show an extreme weakness of
the rightist republicans of the Zamora and Maura type, and
will bring about an overwhelming majority of petty-bourgeois
conciliators of various stripes: Radicals, Radical Socialists,
and "Socialists."[26] In spite of this, we can almost certainly
expect the Socialists and the Radical Socialists to cling with
all their forces to their allies on the right. The slogan "Down
with Zamora-Maura" is quite timely. It is only necessary to
make one thing clear: the communists are not agitating in
favor of the Lerroux ministry, nor are they assuming any
responsibility for the Socialist ministry; but at every given
moment they deliver their strongest blows against the most
determined and consistent class enemy, thereby weakening the
conciliators and clearing the way for the proletariat. The communists say to the Socialist workers: "Unlike us, you believe
your Socialist leaders; then force them at least to take power.
In *this* we shall honestly help you. And when they are in power,
we will see by what happens which of us is right."

We have already approached this question in connection with
the composition of the Cortes. But other events, for instance,
repressions against the masses, may give an extreme acuteness to the slogan "Down with Zamora-Maura." At this new
stage, a victory in that field, i.e., the resignation of Zamora,
would assume almost the same importance for the subsequent
development of the revolution as the resignation of Alfonso in
April. In order to issue such slogans, we must not let ourselves
be guided by doctrinaire abstractions, but by the state of consciousness of the masses and the way they react to the various
partial successes. Simply counterposing the slogan of the "dictatorship of the proletariat" or "workers' and peasants' republic" to the present regime is entirely inadequate because these
slogans do not move the masses.

In this connection, the question of *social fascism* again arises.
This silly invention of the ultraleft bureaucracy is currently
becoming in Spain the greatest obstacle on the road to revolution. Let us turn again to the Russian experience. The Men-

sheviks and Social Revolutionaries, then holding the power, conducted an imperialist war, defended the capitalists, persecuted the soldiers, the peasants, and the workers, made arrests, introduced the death penalty, condoned the killing of Bolsheviks, forced Lenin into illegal existence, kept the other Bolshevik leaders in prison, spread the most ignominious calumnies against them, etc., etc. All that is more than enough to call them in retrospect "social fascists." But in 1917 that word did not exist at all, which as everyone knows did not prevent the Bolsheviks from coming to power. After the terrible persecution of the Bolsheviks in July and August, the Bolsheviks sat together with the "social fascists" in the bodies set up to fight against Kornilov.[27] From his secret hiding place in the beginning of September, Lenin proposed a compromise to the Russian "social fascists": "Break with the bourgeoisie, take power, and we Bolsheviks will peacefully fight for power within the soviets."

If there had been no difference between the conciliators and the Kornilovists, who were the real "fascists" of that time, the struggle of the Bolsheviks jointly with the conciliators against the Kornilovists would not have been possible. Yet that struggle played the greatest role in the development of the revolution by throwing back the attack of the generals' counterrevolution and by helping the Bolsheviks to tear the masses once and for all away from the conciliators.

It is precisely the nature of petty-bourgeois democracy to vacillate between communism and fascism. During the revolution, these vacillations become particularly sharp. To regard the Spanish Socialists as a variety of fascists means to renounce beforehand all possibility of profiting from their inevitable vacillations to the left, to cut ourselves off from the Socialist and trade union workers.

To conclude, I must emphasize that merciless criticism of Spanish anarcho-syndicalism is an extremely urgent task that cannot be postponed for a single day. The top leaders of anarcho-syndicalism represent the most deceptive, treacherous, and dangerous form of conciliationism with, and servility toward, the bourgeoisie. Among the rank-and-file anarcho-syndicalists, there are potentially very great forces for the revolution. Our basic task here is the same as in regard to the Socialists: set the rank and file against their leaders. This

task, however, must be carefully adapted to the specific spirit
of trade union organization and to the specific character of
the Anarchist deception. I shall deal with this in one of my
next letters.

I insist once more: the articles, resolutions, platforms, etc.,
of the revolutionary organizations and groups in Spain must
be assembled and translated into French and sent to all the
sections for translation into other languages.

24

MAURIN AND THE
ANARCHO-SYNDICALISTS

June 29, 1931

We must submit Maurín to pitiless and incessant criticism;
events will completely confirm our criticism. In a short time
Maurín will be only a comical figure with his provincial re-
flections, his corroded doctrines, and his primitive slogans. Everything lies in knowing who will succeed him. The Left Opposition cannot become a leading force in Spain without being
one in Catalonia.

The second urgent question regards the anarcho-syndicalists.
It is essential to publish a pamphlet against anarcho-syndicalism and to distribute it widely not only in Spain but also
in other countries. Have you read Monatte's articles, in which
he expresses his hope to see the Spanish anarcho-syndicalists
counterpose a genuinely "Anarchist" state to the Bolshevik
state?[28] The whole fate of world Anarchism, or rather of the
fragments left over from the Russian Revolution, is intimately
bound up today with the fate of Spanish anarcho-syndicalism.
And since anarcho-syndicalism in Spain is moving inevitably
to the most pitiful and ridiculous bankruptcy, there is no doubt
that the Spanish revolution will be the tombstone of Anarchism.
But it is necessary to be sure that the tombstone of anarcho-
syndicalism does not at the same time become the tombstone
of the revolution.

If Maurín is the temporary screen for the Stalinists, anarcho-
syndicalism is a temporary screen for the Socialists and the

From *The Militant*, September 5, 1931.

republicans, that is, for the bourgeoisie. Just as Maurín can hand the advanced Catalan workers over to the centrist bureaucracy, so the anarcho-syndicalists can hand over the whole revolution to the bourgeoisie.

The theoretical and practical struggle against anarcho-syndicalism is now on the agenda. It is obvious that this struggle must be conducted on the basis of the united-front policy, trade union unity, etc. But we must unmask the leaders of anarcho-syndicalism, and above all expose that pitiful lay priest Pestaña,[29] who will undoubtedly play the most infamous and cowardly role in the subsequent development of the revolution. . . .

The samples of Maurín's speeches produce a painful impression. Unlike us, you see, he considers the Five-Year Plan an acquisition of the revolution![30] Can it be that he has read nothing?

By the way, the Reuters Press Agency and other agencies along with it are spreading false telegrams concerning alleged articles and interviews with me on the Five-Year Plan (complete failure, falsehood, etc. . .). It is extremely important to expose and to deny these infamies. In the present case, the bourgeoisie uses against the Stalinists the latters' own technique of falsehood and calumny.

25 THE ELECTION RESULTS AND THE TACTICS THEY INDICATE

July 1, 1931

1. I have before me a local Turkish newspaper of July 1 in French with the first information on the results of the Spanish elections. Indeed everything up to now rigorously follows a "planned" succession of events. The movement toward the left took place as if according to plan. Let us hope that our Spanish comrades will analyze the results of the elections very carefully, after gathering all the material. We must find out how the workers, and particularly the anarcho-syndicalists, voted. In certain districts, the answer should be quite clear from the electoral statistics. It is most important, of course, to learn

From *The Militant,* July 25, 1931.

how the peasants in the various provinces voted. At the same time, it is necessary to gather all the "agrarian programs" that were presented by the various parties in the various parts of the country. All this is very urgent and very important work.

2. As expected, the Socialists appear to have won a great victory. This is the crux of the parliamentary situation: the Socialist leaders consider themselves lucky because they do not have a majority in the Cortes, and because their coalition with the bourgeoisie is thus justified by parliamentary statistics. The Socialists do not want to take power, for they justly fear that a Socialist government will only be a stage on the road to the dictatorship of the proletariat. From Prieto's speech[31] it is clear that the Socialists intend to support the coalition as long as it is possible to hold back the proletariat by doing so and then, when the pressure of the workers becomes too strong, to pass into opposition, under some radical pretext, leaving it to the bourgeoisie to discipline and crush the workers. In other words, we have before us a variant of Ebert and Tseretelli.[32] Let ·us remember that Ebert's line was successful, while Tseretelli's failed, and that the decisive factor in both cases was the strength of the Communist Party and its policy.

3. We must immediately expose the plan of the Socialists (their game of playing to lose), unmasking them on each particular question. Of course, this concerns the Spanish Left Opposition above all. But exposing them alone is not enough. There must be a clear political slogan, corresponding to the character of the present stage of the Spanish revolution. The results of the elections make that slogan absolutely clear: the workers must break the coalition with the bourgeoisie and force the Socialists to take power. The peasants must help the workers, if they want to get the land.

4. The Socialists will say they cannot give up the coalition because they do not have a majority in the Cortes. Our answer to that is to call for democratic elections to the Cortes on the basis of a truly universal and equal suffrage for men and women from eighteen years of age. In other words, to the nondemocratic, falsified Cortes, we counterpose at this stage a truly popular, truly democratic, honestly elected Cortes.

5. If the communists, at this stage, turn their backs on the Cortes, opposing to it the slogan of the soviets and the dictatorship of the proletariat, they would only demonstrate that

they cannot be taken seriously. There is not a single communist in the Cortes (according to the Turkish press). Of course, the revolutionary wing is always stronger in action, in the struggle, than in parliamentary representation. Nevertheless, there is a certain relationship between the strength of a revolutionary party and its parliamentary representation. The weakness of Spanish communism is fully disclosed. Under these conditions, to speak of the overthrow of bourgeois parliamentarism by the dictatorship of the proletariat would simply mean to play the part of imbeciles and babblers. The task is to gather strength for the party on the basis of the parliamentary stage of the revolution and to rally the masses to us. That is the only way that parliamentarism can be overcome. But precisely for that purpose it is indispensable to develop a fierce agitation under the most decisive and extreme democratic slogans.

6. What should be the criteria for advancing the slogans? On the one hand, we must consider the general direction of the revolutionary development, which determines our strategic line. On the other hand, we must take into account the level of consciousness of the masses; the communist who does not take that into consideration will break his neck.

Let us consider for a moment the way in which the Spanish workers en masse should view the present situation. Their leaders, the Socialists, have power. This increases the demands and tenacity of the workers. Every striker will not only have no fear of the government but will also expect help from it. The communists must direct the thoughts of the workers precisely along those lines: "Demand everything of the government, since your leaders are in it." In reply to the workers' delegations, the Socialists will say that they do not have a majority yet. The answer is clear: with truly democratic suffrage and an end to the coalition with the bourgeoisie, a majority is guaranteed. But this is what the Socialists do not want. Their situation places them in conflict with bold, democratic slogans. If we simply counterpose the dictatorship of the proletariat or the soviets to the Cortes, we will succeed only in driving the workers to the Socialists, for both will say: The communists want to rule us. But under the slogan of democracy and of an end to the coalition between the Socialists and the bourgeoisie, we drive a wedge between the workers and the Socialists and prepare the next stage of the revolution.

7. All the considerations mentioned above would remain a dead letter if we were to limit ourselves only to democratic slogans in the parliamentary sense. There can be no question of this. Communists participate in all strikes, in all protests and demonstrations, arousing more and more numerous strata of the population. Communists are with the masses and at the head of the masses in every battle. On the basis of these battles, the communists put forward the slogan of the soviets, and at the first opportunity build soviets as the *organizations of the proletarian united front*. At the present stage, the soviets can be nothing else. But if they emerge as the combat organizations of the proletarian united front, then under the leadership of the communists they will inevitably become, at a certain stage, organs of insurrection and then organs of power.

8. In boldly developing our agrarian program, we must by no means forget about the independent role of the agricultural workers. They are the main instruments of the proletarian revolution in the rural districts. With the peasants, the workers have an alliance, but the agricultural workers are a part of the proletariat itself. This important distinction must always be kept in mind.

9. I learn from *La Vérité*[33] that the Stalinists accuse the whole Left Opposition as well as me personally of being against the immediate confiscation of landed property. Indeed, it can never be foreseen in what direction the bureaucratic demagogues will turn next. What does the "immediate" confiscation of the land mean? By whom? By what organizations? The inimitable Péri, it is true, asserted back in April that the Spanish peasants were creating soviets, and that every worker was following the communists. Naturally, we agree that the soviets (or juntas or committees) should *immediately* take the land of the large landlords into their own hands. But it is still necessary to arouse the peasants. And for that it is necessary to tear the workers away from the influence of the Socialists. One cannot be done without the other. Or maybe the Stalinists want to say that we are protecting the landlords' property? But even in calumny there has to be some logic. How can defending the landlords' property be derived from the position of permanent revolution? Let them try to explain that to us.

We, for our part, will recall that when the Stalinists in China pursued the policy of the bloc of four classes, the Politburo, under Stalin's leadership, sent a telegram to the Central Committee of the Chinese Communist Party demanding the curbing of the peasant movement in order not to repel the "revolutionary generals." In the agrarian program, Stalin and Molotov[34] included a small limitation: the confiscation of landlords' estates, except those of the officers. And since all the landlords, their sons, and their nephews entered Chiang Kai-shek's army, "revolutionary" officership became the insurance on landlords' property.

This shameful chapter in the history of Stalinist leadership cannot be crossed out. At the time, the Opposition found a copy of that telegram in the minutes of the Politburo, and exposed and denounced this ignominious treason to the agrarian revolution. Now these gentlemen attempt to attribute to us in Spain the crime that they themselves committed in China. But no: now the Opposition has sections in almost every country, and we will not permit them to spread lies and filth about us with impunity. In the living experience of the Spanish revolution, the Left Opposition will clear up all the basic problems and will make a gigantic step forward. It is not in vain that revolution is the locomotive of history.

26 SPANISH COMMUNISM AND THE CATALAN FEDERATION

July 8, 1931

The most harmful, dangerous, and even the most ominous development would be to reinforce the idea in the minds of the workers of Catalonia, Spain, and the whole world that we are in solidarity with the Catalan Federation's politics or bear responsibility for them, or even that we are closer to the Federation than to the centrist grouping. The Stalinists present it this way with all their might. Up to now, we haven't fought against this vigorously enough. It is all the more important and urgent to dispel this misunderstanding, which would compromise us terribly and block the development of the Catalan and Spanish workers.

Of course, the denunciation of the Catalan Federation is a task that devolves primarily on our supporters in Catalonia

From *The Militant,* August 1, 1931.

itself. They should declare their position in a clear, open, precise criticism, a criticism that leaves nothing unsaid about Maurín's politics, that mixture of petty-bourgeois prejudices, ignorance, provincial "science," and political crookedness.

In the elections to the Cortes, the Federation received almost 10,000 votes. This is not much. Of course, in a revolutionary epoch, a truly revolutionary organization is capable of growing fast. There is, however, a circumstance that diminishes greatly the significance of these 10,000 votes: in the Cortes elections, the Catalan Federation obtained fewer votes from Barcelona — the most important revolutionary center — than it did in the Barcelona municipal elections. This fact, trifling at first glance, has an enormous symptomatic significance. It demonstrates that while in the most remote corners of the country there is a movement of workers toward the Federation — although still pretty weak — in Barcelona Maurín's confusion does not attract but repels the workers. Of course, the inevitable bankruptcy of Macía can help even Maurín as the lesser of two evils. But the impotence of the present leadership of the Federation is completely demonstrated by the elections to the Cortes. It really takes special "talents" to tax one's ingenuity so as not to increase one's influence in Barcelona during the three months of the revolution.

What does the Federation represent in the language of revolutionary politics? Is it a communist organization? And if so, exactly what kind — right, left, or center? There is no doubt that those who vote for the Federation are revolutionary workers, potential communists. But they are not yet at all clear in their minds. And where can clarity come from if these workers are led by confusionists? Under these conditions, the most determined, bold, and resolute workers are going to throw themselves inevitably on the side of the official party. The latter obtained only 170 votes in Barcelona and about 1,000 in all of Catalonia. But don't think these are the worse elements. On the contrary, most of these elements could be with us and they will be when we unfurl our banner.

At the start of the 1917 revolution, the majority of the Russian Social Democratic organizations had a mixed character and included in their ranks Bolsheviks, Mensheviks, conciliators, etc. The tendency towards unification was so great that at the conference of the Bolshevik Party at the end of March, a few days before Lenin's arrival, Stalin declared himself for

unification with the Mensheviks. Certain provincial organizations remained mixed right up to the October Revolution. I see
the Catalan Federation as a similar sort of mixed organization,
indeterminate, which includes future Bolsheviks and future Mensheviks. That justifies a policy of attempting to bring about
political differentiation within the ranks of the Federation. The
first step on this road is to denounce the political vulgarity
of Maurínism. Here we must be merciless.

The analogy between the Catalan Federation and the united
organizations in Russia is limited, however, in important respects. The unified organizations did not exclude any existing
Social Democratic grouping. Each had the right to struggle
for its opinions inside the united organization. It is completely
different within the Catalan Federation. There "Trotskyism" is
banned. Each confusionist has the right to defend his confusion there, but the Bolshevik-Leninist cannot openly lift his
voice. And so this mixed, eclectic, united organization excludes
the left wing from the outset; but by that very fact, it becomes
a chaotic bloc of centrist and right-wing tendencies. Centrism
can develop either to the left or to the right. The centrism of the
Catalan Federation, which rejects the left wing during the revolution, is destined for a shameful destruction. The task of the
Left Opposition is to hasten this destruction by its merciless
criticism.

But there is another fact that must be considered exceptionally important. The Catalan Federation is officially for the
unification of all the communist organizations and groupings.
It is certain that the rank-and-file members sincerely and loyally desire this unity although they have all sorts of illusions
about this slogan. We do not share these illusions in any way.
We struggle for unity because we hope to successfully carry
out among the cadres of a united party the progressive work
of ideological differentiation on the basis of questions and
tasks that are not dragged in extraneously but that flow from
the development of the Spanish revolution itself.

However, in every way, we support the fight for communist unification. For us, the fundamental condition of this unification is the right to struggle for our slogans and our points
of view among the cadres of the unified organization. We can
and we should promise complete loyalty in this fight, but this
basic condition of membership has been ruled out from the
beginning by the Federation itself. While fighting under the

flag of unity, it bans the Bolshevik-Leninists from its own ranks. Under these conditions, to rely on the Catalan Federation to play the leading role in the fight for the unity of the Communist Party would be the greatest absurdity on our part. Maurín is getting ready to play first fiddle at the unification congress. Can we tolerate in silence this disgusting hypocrisy? In fighting the Left Opposition, Maurín is imitating the Stalinist bureaucracy in order to win its favor. In reality, he is saying to the Stalinists: give me your blessing and above all your subsidies, and I promise to fight the Bolshevik-Leninists not through compulsion but with all sincerity.

Maurín's unification activity is only a form of blackmailing the Stalinists. If we kept quiet on that, we would not be revolutionaries but passive accomplices to political blackmail. We must mercilessly denounce Maurín's role, that is, his "unification" charlatanism, without lessening for a single instant our struggle for real unification of the communist ranks, and without weakening our struggle to win the communist ranks to our banner.

Nine-tenths of the work of the International Left Opposition today should be concentrated on Spain. All other expenses must be cut down in favor of the possibility of putting out a Spanish weekly with regular publications in Catalan, and simultaneously issuing pamphlets in considerable quantities. We must consider limiting all other expenses without exception in order to send the greatest possible help to the Spanish Opposition.

The International Secretariat, in my opinion, should devote nine-tenths of its forces to the questions of the Spanish revolution. The fact that all kinds of Landaus exist in the world must simply be forgotten. We must turn our back on all the quarrels, all the intrigues and intriguers without wasting a single minute on them.

The Spanish revolution is on the agenda. The most important documents must be translated without delay and submitted to the necessary criticism. The next issue of the *International Bulletin* should be entirely devoted to the Spanish revolution. It is equally necessary to take a series of organizational measures. For that, human and material resources are necessary. Both must be found.

There is and there can be no greater crime than to waste time.

27 THE NATIONAL QUESTION IN CATALONIA

July 13, 1931

Once more on the subject of the timely questions of the Spanish revolution.

1. Maurín, the "leader" of the Workers and Peasants Bloc, shares the point of view of separatism. After certain hesitations, he has reconciled himself with the left wing of petty-bourgeois nationalism. I have already written that Catalan petty-bourgeois nationalism at the present stage is progressive — but only on one condition: that it develops its activity outside the ranks of communism and that it is always under the blows of communist criticism. To permit petty-bourgeois nationalism to disguise itself under the banner of communism means, at the same time, to deliver a treacherous blow to the proletarian vanguard and to destroy the progressive significance of petty-bourgeois nationalism.

2. What does the program of separatism mean?— the economic and political dismemberment of Spain, or in other words, the transformation of the Iberian Peninsula into a sort of Balkan Peninsula, with independent states divided by customs barriers, and with independent armies conducting independent Hispanic wars. Of course, the sage Maurín will say that he does not want this. But programs have their own logic, something Maurín doesn't have.

3. Are the workers and peasants of the various parties of Spain interested in the economic dismemberment of Spain? Not at all. That is why to identify the decisive struggle for the right to self-determination with propaganda for separatism means to accomplish a fatal task. Our program is for Hispanic federation with the indispensable maintenance of economic unity. We have no intention of *imposing* this program upon the oppressed nationalities of Spain *with the aid of the arms of the bourgeoisie.* In this sense, we are sincerely for the right to self-determination. If Catalonia separates, the communist minority of Catalonia, as well as of Spain, will have to conduct a struggle for federation.

4. In the Balkans, the old prewar Social Democracy already put forward the slogan of the democratic Balkan federation

From *The Militant,* September 19, 1931.

as the way out of the madhouse created by the separated states. Today, the communist slogan in the Balkans is the Balkan Soviet Federation (by the way, the Comintern adopted the slogan of the Balkan Soviet Federation, but at the same time it rejected this slogan for Europe!). How can we, under these conditions, adopt the slogan of the Balkanization of the Spanish peninsula? Isn't it monstrous?

5. The syndicalists, or at least certain of their leaders, declare that they will fight against separatism even with arms in hand. In this case, the communists and the syndicalists would find themselves on opposite sides of the barricades, because without sharing the separatist illusions, while criticizing them, on the contrary, the communists must stand up unflinchingly against the hangmen of imperialism and their syndicalist lackeys.

6. Should the petty bourgeoisie succeed — against the advice and criticism of the communists — in dismembering Spain, the negative results of such a regime will not take long to manifest themselves. The workers and peasants of the various sections of Spain will speedily arrive at this conclusion: yes, the communists were right. But this means precisely that we must not assume a particle of responsibility for Maurín's program.

7. Monatte hopes that the Spanish syndicalists will create a new "syndicalist state." Instead of this, the Spanish friends of Monatte are integrating themselves successfully into the bourgeois state. It is the story of the luckless hen who sits on duck's eggs. Today, it is very important to follow all that the Spanish syndicalists say and do. This will open up possibilities for the Left Opposition in France to deal a harsh blow to French anarcho-syndicalism. One cannot doubt for a single instant that under revolutionary conditions the anarcho-syndicalists will discredit themselves at every step.

The brilliant idea of the syndicalists consists of controlling the Cortes without participating in it! To employ revolutionary violence, to fight for power, to seize power — all this is not permitted. In its place, they recommend the "control" of the bourgeoisie which is in power. A magnificent picture: the bourgeoisie breakfasts, lunches, and dines, and the proletariat led by the syndicalists "controls" these operations — on an empty stomach.

28   *A TURN BY THE STALINISTS?*

July 30, 1931

According to the information of Comrade N., the Central Committee of the Spanish Communist Party has made a decisive turn in its policy. . . .

From the words of Comrade N., it appears that the Spanish CP's Central Committee, while formally retaining the slogan of the "democratic dictatorship," has changed its policy decisively on two points: first, it takes the road of struggle for democratic slogans; second, it is ready to apply the policy of the united front.

We have here a clear and unquestionable victory of the Left Opposition. How deep and serious the turn of the Spanish Stalinists may be is another question. Moreover, any answer to it depends to a considerable degree on our policy. But in any case, the very fact of the turn is a direct result of the criticism of the Left Opposition. . . . Only the faction of the Left Opposition is a progressive force within communism. . . . Upon its successes depend the successes of communism, and particularly the successes of the Spanish revolution.

But how shall we react to the turn of the Spanish Stalinists? On this score we already have substantial experience, though, it is true, primarily an experience in mistakes. When the French Stalinists, to a considerable degree under the influence of our criticism, decided to retreat from the fantastic policy of the "third period," the old leadership of the League declared in advance that adventurism was giving way to opportunism, and that the Left Opposition should go its way as if nothing had happened. [35] At the time, we criticized this formalistic and lifeless policy, which had as its consequence the fact that the French League missed the extremely favorable opportunity to approach the proletarian core of the party. Let us hope that this mistake will not be repeated in Spain.

In a brief letter, Comrade N. underlines two facts having an exceptionally important significance for the policy of the Spanish Left Opposition for the present period: the official party has taken, or at any rate has proclaimed, a series of steps directed towards the policy of the Bolshevik-Leninists; on the other hand, the leadership of the Catalan Federation

From *The Militant,* September 26, 1931.

sinks ever deeper into the confusion of opportunism and petty-bourgeois nationalism. The official party, heretofore, has done everything to identify the Left Opposition with the blunders of Maurín. At the present time, we are offered an exceptionally favorable opportunity to dispel all misunderstanding. . . .

The Left Opposition should subject the turn of the Spanish CP's Central Committee to a serious analysis — without naive credulity, but also without sectarian prejudices. Whatever we have gained should be clearly stated and taken into consideration. Where differences remain, they should be characterized without any softness and embellishment.

The faster and the more decisively the Left Opposition reacts to the turn by approaching the party, the more advantageous it will be to the Left Opposition, to the party, to the Spanish revolution.

29   THE ROLE OF STRIKES IN A REVOLUTION

August 2, 1931
The purpose of this letter is to exchange our views on the occasion of the tumultuous strike wave in Spain.36 In my second pamphlet on the Spanish revolution ["The Spanish Revolution in Danger"], I indicated one of the *possible* perspectives: the revolutionary movement develops violently without the correct leadership and concludes in an explosion that the counterrevolutionary forces may exploit in order to smash the proletariat. As I pointed out in the pamphlet, this perspective does not, of course, mean that the role of the communists should be to hold back the revolutionary movement. I do not doubt that in this respect we will have no differences, but I would like to analyze this question more thoroughly, because it may come to be of great practical importance.

First of all, it is necessary to make clear that this violent elemental outburst of strikes is the inevitable outcome of the character of the revolution itself, being in a certain sense its

From *Fourth International,* October 1943. *Fourth International* was the theoretical journal of the Socialist Workers Party.

basis. The overwhelming majority of the Spanish proletariat does not know what organization means. During the time the dictatorship lasted, a new generation of workers grew up, lacking in independent political experience. The revolution awakens — and in this lies its force — the most backward, down-trodden, the most oppressed toiling masses. The strike is the form of their awakening. By means of the strike, various strata and groups of the proletariat announce themselves, signal to one another, verify their own strength and the strength of their foe. One layer awakens and infects another. All this together makes the present strike wave absolutely inevitable. Least of all do the communists have to be afraid of it, for this is the very expression of the creative force of the revolution. Only through these strikes, with all their mistakes, with all their "excesses" and "exaggerations," does the proletariat rise to its feet, assemble itself as a unit, begin to feel and to conceive of itself as a class, as a living historical force. Never have revolutions developed under a conductor's stick. Excesses, mistakes, sacrifices are the very nature of any revolution.

Had the Communist Party told the workers: "I am still too weak to guide you; therefore, wait a little, don't press too much, don't start the fight by striking, give me a chance to become stronger," the party would have made itself hopelessly ridiculous, the awakening masses would have stepped over it, and instead of becoming stronger, the party would have only weakened.

Even if you have correctly foreseen a historical danger, this does not mean that you may eliminate it by mere reasoning. The danger can be removed only if you possess the necessary strength. But in order to be such a force, the Communist Party must enter wholeheartedly into the arena of the developing "elemental" or semi-elemental strike movement, not in order to hold it back, but in order to learn to direct it, and in the very process of the struggle, acquire authority and strength.

It would be a mistake to think that the present movement was provoked by the anarcho-syndicalists. The latter are themselves under indomitable pressure from below. The leading group of the syndicalist nucleus would like to slow up the movement. Individuals like Pestaña are certainly negotiating behind the scene with the employers and administration about the best means of liquidating the strikes. Tomorrow, many of these gentlemen will prove to be the executioners of the workers, and like the Russian Mensheviks will preach against "strike fever" as they shoot them.

One cannot doubt that along this line will grow the differentiation among the anarcho-syndicalists. The most revolutionary wing, the further it goes, will find itself ever more in conflict with the syndico-reformists. From this, left-wing putschists, heroic adventurists, individual terrorists, and others will inevitably surge up.

Needless to say, we cannot encourage any kind of adventurism. But we must make sure in advance that not the right wing, which combats the strikes, but the left revolutionary syndicalist wing will come closer to us. It will be all the easier to overcome all kinds of adventurist elements, the sooner the revolutionary syndicalists are convinced that the communists are fighters — not rationalizers.

The official party is being accused of an adventuristic policy in the field of strikes. I personally cannot judge in the matter due to my lack of information. The general attitude of the party in the previous period, however, leads one to think that this charge is probably justified. But precisely for that reason there is a danger that having burnt its fingers the party may abruptly turn to the right. The greatest misfortune would be if the working masses came to the conclusion that the communists, just like the syndicalists like Pestaña, would like to instruct them dogmatically, from the top downward, and not to rise with them from the bottom upward.

In summary, the danger of the June days remains without any doubt the gravest in perspective; but the most immediate danger for the communists may become abstract arguing, "trying to appear intelligent," abstract coaxing, which revolutionary workers will regard as pessimistic croaking.

The Left Opposition must not forget for a single moment that the dangers arising from the development of the revolution should be overcome not by watchful caution but by audacity, audacity, and more audacity.

30
MORE ON SOVIETS AND THE "BALKANIZATION" ARGUMENT

September 1, 1931

I have received your letter of August 25. You ask yourself the question: shall we summon the workers to join the party or the Federation? The local conditions speak in favor of the Federation. The general Spanish conditions speak in favor of the party.

From the practical point of view, that is, from the point of view of the relationship of forces at the given moment, it is difficult to solve this problem, but it seems to me that our principled position is really of decisive importance: we declare that we are a faction of the party, a faction of thé Comintern. The main struggle against us is carried on along the line that we are "enemies" of the USSR and of the Comintern. Even Maurín lives on the crumbs that fall from this table.

If we call upon the workers to join the Federation, we compromise ourselves throughout the rest of Spain and internationally. Do we gain at all on the Catalan scale? If we consider the present results of our collaboration with the Federation, we find that it is bringing us more harm than benefit. The entire press of the Comintern, and *Pravda* in particular, has held us responsible for Maurín's opportunist confusionism. Comrade Mill's articles in *La Vérité* also contributed greatly to this.[37] Despite this collaboration, we have been forced to break with the Federation and we have left almost empty-handed. In other words, the experience of collaboration with the Federation has weakened us in Spain as a whole as well as internationally, without helping us any in Catalonia.

It is time to strike a balance. In my opinion, we ought to execute an abrupt political turn to avoid being confused with Maurín any longer — a confusion that has been to his advantage and our own disadvantage.

The most correct procedure would be to call upon the workers to join the Left Communist faction, to build it, and to demand admission into the party. But such a policy requires an official center, no matter how small, of the Left Opposition in Cata-

From *The Militant,* December 19, 1931.

lonia. If you remember, I have insisted on this from the first day of your arrival in Barcelona, but alas without success. Even now I see no other road. . . .

Maurín has issued the slogan: "All power to the proletariat." I think you are quite right in pointing out that he has chosen slogans of this sort in order to provide himself with a bridge to the syndicalists and to lend himself the appearance of greater strength than he actually possesses. Unfortunately, the chase after appearances is very strong in politics, and very disastrous in revolutionary politics.

I ask myself — at times — why are there no soviets in Spain? What is the cause of this?

On the slogan of soviets

In a previous letter, I expressed several ideas in this connection. I have developed these much more amply in an article I sent you on workers' control in Germany.[38] It appears that the slogan of "juntas" is associated in the minds of the Spanish workers with the slogan of soviets; and for this reason it seems too sharp, too decisive, too "Russian" to them. That is to say, they look at it in a different light than did the Russian workers at a corresponding stage. Are we not confronted here with a historical paradox in that the existence of soviets in the USSR acts to paralyze the creation of soviets in other revolutionary countries?

This question must be given the utmost attention in private conversations with workers in different parts of the country. At any event, if the slogan of soviets (juntas) fails as yet to meet with a response, then we must concentrate on the slogan of factory committees. I dealt with this topic in the above-mentioned article on workers' control. On the basis of factory committees, we can develop the soviet organization without referring to them by name.

Workers' control

On the question of workers' control, you are, in my opinion, absolutely correct; to renounce workers' control merely because the reformists are for it — in words — would be an enormous stupidity. On the contrary, it is precisely for this reason that we should seize upon this slogan all the more eagerly and compel the reformist workers to put it into practice by means of a united front with us, and on the basis of this experience to push them into opposition to Caballero and other fakers.[39]

We succeeded in creating soviets in Russia only because the demand for them was raised, not by us alone, but by the Mensheviks and the Social Revolutionaries as well, although, to be sure, they had different aims in mind. We cannot create any soviets in Spain precisely because neither the Sosialists nor the syndicalists want soviets. This means that the united front and organizational unity with the majority of the working class cannot be created under this slogan.

But here is Caballero himself, under the pressure of the masses, forced to seize upon the slogan of workers' control and thereby opening wide the doors for the united-front policy and forging an organization that embraces the majority of the working class. We must grab this with both hands. Certainly, Caballero will try to transform workers' control into the control of the capitalists over the workers. But that question already pertains to another subject, that of the relationship of forces within the working class. If we succeed in creating factory committees all over the country, then in this revolutionary epoch that we are witnessing, Messrs. Caballero and his associates will have lost the decisive battle.

The separatist movement and the Iberian Soviet Federation

You describe how one might unintentionally aid Madrilenian liberalism by proclaiming that the Balkanization of the Iberian Peninsula is inconsistent with the aims of the proletariat, and by proclaiming it without further elaboration. You are quite right. If I have not underscored it sufficiently in my preceding letter ["Maurin and the National Question"] I am prepared to do so ten times over right now.

The analogy between the two peninsulas really needs to be completed. There was a time when the Balkan Peninsula was unified under the domination of the Turkish gentry, the militarists, and the proconsuls. The oppressed people longed to overthrow their oppressors. If our opposition to partitioning the peninsula had been counterposed to these aspirations of the people, we would have been acting as lackeys to the Turkish pashas and beys. On the other hand, however, we know that the Balkan peoples, liberated from the Turkish yoke, have been at one another's throats for decades. In this matter, too, the proletarian vanguard can apply the point of view of the permanent revolution: liberation from the imperialist yoke, which is the most important element of the democratic revolution, leads immediately to the Federation of Soviet Republics as the state form for the proletarian revolution. Not opposing the democratic revolution, but on the contrary supporting it completely even in the form of separation (that is, supporting the struggle but not the illusions), we at the same time bring our own independent position into the democratic revolution, recommending, counseling, encouraging the idea of the Soviet Federation of the Iberian Peninsula as a constituent part of the United States of Europe. Only under this form is my conception complete. Needless to say, the Madrid comrades and the Spanish comrades in general should use particularly great discretion with regard to the Balkanization argument.

31   *A NARROW OR BROAD FACTION?*

September 27, 1931
Dear Friend:

First of all, I should like to clear up for myself the disputed question in the Left Opposition: a narrow or broad faction? I have received your opinion and that of Comrade Lacroix on this subject. Comrade M[olinier] has not yet submitted the report that he promised.[40]

I must admit that the basis for this dispute is not clear to me. Yesterday, with regard to Catalonia, as I can see from your letter, the question was posed in the following manner: should we call upon the workers to enter the official Communist Party or the Catalan Federation? From your last letter it appears that the Catalan Federation expels the Left Opposition from its ranks, that is to say, it proceeds in the same manner as the party. This fact by itself is quite logical. The right wing and the centrists manifest the same hostility toward

---

From *The Militant,* November 14, 1931.

the Bolshevik-Leninists in all countries, beginning with the USSR. It would be odd for Spain to be an exception to this. On the contrary, in view of the revolutionary situation in Spain, all the political processes (including all the mistakes) arrive at their logical conclusion very swiftly.

But is it still possible to speak seriously of the Left Opposition calling on the workers to enter the Catalan Federation? I cannot understand it! We can, to be sure, try to create our nuclei in the Catalan Federation with the aim of recruiting a maximum of followers in the event of the inevitable collapse of the Maurín organization. We can send individual comrades into the Federation with this aim. But can we openly call upon nonparty workers to enter the Federation? Never. It would be the most monstrous mistake, and would not only weaken but even disgrace the Left Opposition.

Formally, the question of the official party is posed differently, since we have not renounced the idea of winning over the Comintern, and consequently each of its sections. It has always appeared to me that many comrades have underestimated the possibilities for the development of the official Communist Party in Spain. I have written to you about this more than once. To ignore the official party as a fictitious quantity, to turn our backs on it, seems to me to be a great mistake. On the contrary, with regard to the official party, we must stick to the path of uniting the ranks. Nevertheless, this task is not so simple. As long as we remain a weak faction, this task is in general unachievable. We can only produce a tendency toward unity inside the official party when we become a serious force.

The opponents of the "broad faction" reply to this: But if we group about us a broad section of workers, we automatically transform ouselves into a second party. I must admit that this argument astonishes me. If we are to reason in such a formal manner, then in order to avoid the danger of a second party, the Bolshevik-Leninist must altogether disappear from the face of the earth. That is just what the Stalinists want. Political Malthusianism is the most unnatural of all the varieties of Malthusianism. Any political tendency that has confidence in its forces cannot help looking forward to uniting the largest possible masses around it. It is possible to come to the party by different roads. If the Left Opposition becomes stronger than the present official party, that will furnish us the possibility of struggling with a hundredfold greater effectiveness for the unity of the communist ranks than at present when the Opposition is still weak. Isn't this clear?

But, the partisans of the "narrow faction" will answer, the Left Opposition can only take into its ranks conscious followers. Indeed! But does not the same thing hold true for the party? It all comes down to this: the Left Opposition must not attract to itself new workers; no, it is obliged to refer them to the ranks of the party, where they will be taught that the Trotskyists are "counterrevolutionists." Then, and only then, will the Opposition have the right to disillusion these workers, to reeducate them, to cure them of the contagious Stalinist slanders. Really, I cannot understand such a complicated mechanism.

Growth and scope of the Opposition

It seems to me that the Opposition has not only the right but also the duty to group about itself all those who come to it, who respond to its appeals and whom it is able to reach. Naturally, at first, they will be far from convinced and conscious Bolshevik-Leninists. But this only imposes the necessity of occupying ourselves seriously with the education of our followers. Within the scope of this education, will also enter the question why we are for one party and why the Stalinists are for two parties. If the flow towards us proves to be too tempestuous (which is hardly to be feared!), then we can form a circle of sympathizers. A local organization of the Opposition numbering twenty members can assemble around it two or three hundred sympathizers. In this circle of sympathizers, it will be necessary to clear up the difference between Leninism and centrism. After the circle has reached a certain level under our direction, it can invite the representatives of the official party to present their views before it. On this basis, a discussion will arise between our followers and the Stalinists. Only this will bring about a serious reconciliation between the Left Opposition and the party and create a far more secure path toward a united party than the Malthusian measures against reproduction.

The Left Opposition would become a sect if it were to come

to the conclusion that its task is only *criticism* of the actions of the official party and of the mass organizations of the proletariat. The Spanish revolution is a fact. There has already been a tremendous amount of time lost without all this, including time lost by the Spanish Left Opposition. Next year we will not be able, merely by snapping our fingers, to reproduce the revolutionary situation that we are passing up today. It is precisely in Spain that the Opposition can grow within a brief time into a large force. But the first condition for that is not to be afraid of becoming a force but to strive toward that.

That is all I can say in the meantime on the disputed question on the basis of incomplete information. I will be happy to receive additional information.

32   *GREETINGS TO "EL SOVIET"*

September 29, 1931
Dear Friends:

You are preparing to publish a weekly. This is a serious step forward. Let us hope that others will follow swiftly after this one.

In Spain, as elsewhere, communism is divided into three factions: right-wing, centrist, and left-wing. The right represents a combination of communism with Social Democracy, trade unionism, or syndicalism, according to national conditions. In Spain, as in other countries, the official representation of the Comintern is in the hands of the centrists, that is, people who vacillate between revolutionary Marxism and various phases of "communist" opportunism.

The strength of centrism in the Comintern lies in the fact that it supports itself on the state power in the USSR. Under the present conditions, centrism is not only an ideological current, not only a faction, but also a powerful bureaucratic

From *The Militant,* October 31, 1931. *El Soviet* was the short-lived newspaper of the Spanish Left Opposition.

state apparatus. In conducting a perfunctory, confused, and contradictory policy, with not only the authority but also the material resources of the Comintern at its disposal, centrism has created cruel ravages in the world vanguard of the proletariat, and has already led several revolutions to catastrophes.

In Spain, through the fault of the centrist bureaucracy, the Communist Party proved to be a miserably small force at the beginning of the revolution. At the same time that it imposes a false policy on the national sections, the Stalinist bureaucracy permits no criticism of itself and thereby obstructs the education of the proletarian vanguard, preventing the formation of a vigorous Communist Party, independent and self-confident. That is the chief danger threatening the Spanish revolution, which is developing so powerfully before our own eyes.

The principled position of the Bolshevik-Leninists (Left Opposition) has been confirmed by gigantic international developments, particularly by the entire advance of the Spanish revolution. The official Communist Party, thrown off guard at each step in the progress of the revolution, corrects its mistakes in little parcels, basing itself on *our criticism*, utilizing *our principled line*, because centrism in itself is empty and barren.

But for the Bolshevik-Leninist faction, a correct principled position is not enough; it is necessary to apply it precisely to daily events. Revolutionary strategy requires a corresponding tactic.

The importance of the weekly consists in that it brings the Spanish Left Opposition face to face with all the current happenings and forces it to give its immediate fighting reply to them. With the creation of the weekly, the Spanish Opposition rises to a higher stage.

The proletariat, especially in an epoch of tempestuous convulsions, can be assembled only on the basis of a consistent revolutionary position. This is your historic mission, Spanish Leninists. You must increase your efforts twofold, threefold, tenfold. The voice of the Bolshevik-Leninists must resound in all parts of the country, at all the mass meetings. Yours are proud tasks. The revolution does not wait. Woe to those who lag behind! With all my heart I hope that you may not prove to be lagging behind!

33   *THE LEADERSHIP CRISIS IN SPAIN*

November 26, 1931

1. The Spanish revolution has created the general political premises for an immediate struggle for power by the proletariat. The syndicalist traditions of the Spanish proletariat have now been revealed as one of the most important obstacles in the way of the development of the revolution.

The Comintern was caught unawares by the events. The Communist Party, totally impotent at the beginning of the revolution, occupied a false position on all the fundamental questions. The Spanish experiences have shown — let it be recalled once more — what a frightful instrument of the disorganization of the revolutionary consciousness of the advanced workers the present Comintern leadership represents! The extraordinary delay of the proletarian vanguard lagging behind the events, the politically dispersed character of the heroic struggles of the working masses, the actual assurances of reciprocity between anarcho-syndicalism and Social Democracy — these are the fundamental political conditions that made it possible for the republican bourgeoisie, in league with the Social Democracy, to establish an apparatus of repression, and by dealing the insurgent masses blow for blow, to concentrate a considerable amount of political power in the hands of the government.

By this example, we see that fascism is not at all the only method of the bourgeoisie in its struggle against the revolutionary masses. The regime existing in Spain today corresponds best to the conception of a Kerenskiad, that is, the last (or next-to-last) "left" government, which the bourgeoisie can only set up in its struggle against the revolution. But this kind of government does not necessarily signify weakness and prostration. In the absence of a strong revolutionary party of the proletariat, a combination of semi-reforms, left phrases, and gestures still more to the left, and reprisals, can prove to be of much more effective service to the bourgeoisie than fascism.

An excerpt from *Germany, The Key to the International Situation.* Published as a pamphlet by Pioneer Publishers early in 1932, in a translation from the Russian by Morris Lewitt. The full text is available in *The Struggle Against Fascism in Germany,* by Leon Trotsky, Pathfinder Press, New York.

Needless to say, the Spanish revolution has not yet ended
It has not solved its most elementary tasks (the agrarian
church, and national questions) and is still far from having
exhausted the revolutionary resources of the popular masses
More than it has already given, the bourgeois revolution wil
not be able to give. With regard to the proletarian revolution
the present internal situation in Spain may be characterized
as prerevolutionary, but scarcely more than that. It is quite
probable that the offensive development of the Spanish revolution will take on a more or less protracted character. In this
manner, the historical process opens up, as it were, a new
credit account for Spanish communism.

34 *BALANCE SHEET OF THE SPANISH SECTION*

December 22, 1931
7. The Spanish section has made certain advances, and established contacts that permit it to hope for new successes. But
it is clear that measured on the scale of the magnificent revolutionary movement of the Spanish masses, the successes of
the Spanish Opposition are pretty small. However, this is primarily because the Spanish Opposition did not exist before the
revolution. It formed itself in the fire of the events, and in the
process time was lost and wasted with experiments whose fruitlessness was clear in advance (for example, in Catalonia).

The extreme weakness of the Spanish Opposition at the
beginning of the revolution expressed itself in that, regardless
ot the exceptionally favorable situation in the country, our
Spanish comrades until recently did not create the opportunity
to issue a weekly paper. Help from abroad did not suffice or
did not arrive in time. *El Soviet* of Barcelona was suspended.
It cannot remain unsaid that the reasons the Spanish Opposition gives to explain the suspension of *El Soviet* are completely

An excerpt from a letter sent to all the sections of the Left Opposition
from an unnumbered and undated internal bulletin of the Communis
League of America, 1932. Other parts of this letter were publishec
in *The Militant*, February 13, 1932. The full text appears in *Writings
of Leon Trotsky* (1930-31), Pathfinder Press, New York.

unacceptable. Instead of saying clearly and openly: "We have no means, we are weak, send help!" the Spanish comrades declare that they do not want to submit to the censor. When revolutionists are not in a position to shake off the censor, then they must on the one hand adapt themselves to it legally, and on the other hand say every bit of what is necessary in the illegal press. But they must not disappear from the scene by pointing to the censorship and to their own revolutionary pride, for that means to carry out a decorative but not a Bolshevik policy.

The Spanish revolution has now entered a period of slackening that separates the bourgeois stage from the proletarian. How long this stage will last cannot be foretold. In any event, the Spanish Opposition now has the opportunity to do more systematic and planful preparatory work. Cadres must be developed; there is no time to lose. The theoretical monthly organ *Comunismo* is one of the most important weapons in this connection. A serious bulletin for internal discussion must be created. The education of cadres is unthinkable on the basis only of national questions. If the Spanish comrades have devoted very little time to international questions in the course of the past year, this was easily attributable to the youthfulness of the Opposition and the furious pace of revolutionary events. This undoubtedly explains why the intervention of the Spanish Opposition in international questions was extremely infrequent and had an episodic character that was not always propitious.

35 MESSAGE TO THE CONFERENCE OF THE SPANISH LEFT OPPOSITION

March 7, 1932
Dear Comrades:

The very fact that the conference of the Spanish Left Opposition is being convoked in itself represents an undeniable achievement for which I sincerely congratulate you.

I deeply regret that circumstances have kept you from pub-

Published in the English edition of the *International Bulletin* of the Communist Left Opposition, no. 17, April 1933.

lishing in convenient time the draft resolutions, and thus from giving foreign comrades an opportunity to take part in these deliberations before the conference. For this reason, with no opportunity to pronounce my views more concretely on the questions on your agenda, I here confine myself to a few short remarks. It is quite possible that their elementary character renders them superfluous. I should be the first to rejoice if this is so.

1. First of all, it seems to me that in the regional reports it is necessary to clarify just what part the Bolshevik-Leninists have taken in the genuine acts and struggles of Spain's working class. That is the central question. A political group that stayed outside of the actual movement and occupied itself with criticisms after the events, especially under revolutionary conditions, would be rejected by the working class. I do not doubt for a moment that the majority of the Bolshevik-Leninists in the regions have participated in all the mass movements, even when they regarded them as not conforming to their own purposes. A revolutionist criticizes not from the outside but from the very heart of the movement itself. On January 9, 1905, the Bolsheviks, together with the workers, marched to the czar to lead the republican propaganda, with far greater success.

I do not doubt that on this fundamental question we shall not have the slightest difference among us. If I nevertheless raise the question it is because the experience of other countries has shown that certain isolated elements are preparing to link themselves with the Left Opposition, elements that under the pretext of "Marxist criticism" actually dodge the revolutionary struggle. For these gentlemen, the revolutionary movement is never sufficiently "conscious," "mature," and "noble," for them to indulge themselves in coming out on the streets with the workers. At an opportune moment, we must purge the organization of people who, in the crucial moment of the struggle, are inclined to profoundly contemplate their navels.

That is why I advise, in connection with the critical work of the Opposition, that its direct participation in the struggle be clarified in the regional reports. A concrete report on this subject would be very useful for our entire international press.

2. Another question to which I would like to call your attention touches upon the international character of our work.

Opportunists like Maurín and his Madrid imitators built up their entire policy on their national peculiarities. Not to know these peculiarities would of course be the greatest idiocy. But underneath them we must know how to discover the motivating forces of international developments and grasp the dependence of national peculiarities upon the world combination of forces. The tremendous advantage of Marxism and consequently of the Left Opposition consists precisely in this international manner of solving national problems and national peculiarities.

For your young organization a particular task is carefully following the work of the other sections of the International Left Opposition in order always to do your work in conformity with the interests of the whole. Without international criteria, without regular international links, without control over the work of a national section, the formation of a true revolutionary proletarian organization is impossible in our epoch.

3. Germany stands at the center of the world picture right now.[41] I do not doubt that your conference will devote all necessary attention to the burning problems of the German revolution. This is a question of immeasurable as well as immediate importance for the Spanish Opposition. The more clearly the Spanish Bolshevik-Leninists pose and decide the problems of the German revolution before the eyes of the official party and the proletariat of Spain, the more smashing a blow they will deal to bureaucratic centrism, and the more quickly they will concentrate about them the sympathies and support of the advanced workers of Spain.

In confining myself to these short remarks, I warmly wish you success in the work of your conference. Forward! There are mighty tasks and decisive struggles; may your conference forge the necessary weapons for these struggles.

With communist greetings,
L. Trotsky

36

THE INTERNATIONAL RELATIONS
OF THE SPANISH SECTION

March 7, 1932

Dear Comrades:

Lately I have received from Spain several letters and documents that bring out the existence of certain misunderstandings between the Spanish comrades and the majority of the International Left Opposition. The best thing to do in such a case is to attempt to clarify these misunderstandings in time, in such a way that the temporary and minor misunderstandings are set apart from the important and principled ones.

1. Comrades Lacroix and Nin had a conflict with the French Comrade Molinier over a purely practical question. I was and still am of the opinion that Comrades Lacroix and Nin, who are entirely uninformed about the situation, raised an erroneous charge against Comrade Molinier in these practical questions. For my part, I hurried to clarify this misunderstanding. After that, I considered this incidental question as settled, since there were no political or principled questions involved.

The views of Comrades Lacroix and Nin concerning Comrade Molinier are their personal affair and there is no need to refer to this question.

2. Because of this, Comrade Lacroix is in error when he thinks that we have a difference with him in regard to Comrade Molinier. No, the difference (if it is not a misunderstanding) concerns the relation of the Spanish Opposition to all debated issues of the International Left Opposition; that is, it concerns the principled and fundamental questions of the Left Opposition. This is the only question that interests me.

3. Experience has proven that within the ranks of the Left Opposition in the different countries there are elements who are entirely at variance with us. The example of Gorkin alone shows that simply to recognize the fundamental principles of the Left Opposition is not sufficient.[42] Organizations and revolutionists are controlled in their work, that is, through applying their principles. Because of this, very small events may throw a clear

A letter to the Central Committee of the Spanish Left Opposition. From an unnumbered and undated internal bulletin of the Communist League of America, 1932.

light on this or that person or group in the sense that a small symptom often reveals a great infirmity.

In this respect, I want to give an example. In Germany, as you know, a left socialist party, Sozialistische Arbeiter Partei [SAP — Socialist Workers Party], has arisen.[43] Its leaders recognize the proletarian dictatorship and the Soviet system. Urbahns, who was once with us, mistook this recognition as proof of the communism of this new party.[44] Otto Bauer and Léon Blum, the notorious mercenaries of French imperialism, are called "comrades" in the papers of this party. An opponent may object that the word "comrade" is rather small in comparison to the proletarian dictatorship and the Soviet system. Well, it is my opinion that the recognition of the dictatorship of the proletariat and the Soviet system is in the way of mere phrases with these leaders of the SAP, and the small expression 'Comrade Léon Blum" completely betrays their real feelings. It is necessary in politics to understand how to orient oneself in regard to such small signs, and all the more so when they do not lead to greater events that could become the actual proof.

4. Rosmer, Naville, Gérard, and others in France, Landau in Germany, and Overstraeten in Belgium were in agreement with all the "principles" of the Left Opposition.[45] But in practice they were in agreement with nothing. Rosmer, Naville, and others have systematically opposed the ideas of the Left Opposition and each attempt to draw closer to the party, to the trade union, and to the international organization, and have thereby hindered the success of the Left Opposition. The struggle against them extended over more than a year and a half. They have supported the elements at variance with us in the different countries, simultaneously building their own faction and paralyzing our work. The break with this group, which was at variance with us, proved to be unavoidable, and I did not hesitate one moment to proceed to this break despite the fact that I was intimately connected with Rosmer through a personal friendship of more than fifteen years.

5. Are the Spanish Oppositionists acquainted with the course of this struggle with Overstraeten, Urbahns, Landau, Rosmer, Naville, and others? I have in mind here not only the leaders of the Spanish Opposition, but the organization as a whole. If the Spanish Oppositionists remain unacquainted with this struggle,

176 *The Spanish Revolution (1931-39)*

then that must be considered a great shortcoming. We cannot develop true revolutionists without giving the young communists the chance to follow the day-to-day elaboration of the Bolshevik policies not only in the Spanish section but in the other sections of the International Opposition as well. Only in this manner can we gain experience, build and strengthen the revolutionary consciousness. This is precisely the most important part of the democratic party regime that we strive to establish.

6. In elaborating my question as to whether the Spanish Oppositionists are informed of the course of the international ideological struggles, I am compelled to again refer to small evidences, which to my mind have a great symptomatic meaning. While Landau had already put himself outside our ranks, while Rosmer had already deserted our organization, nevertheless both were mentioned in your review (*Comunismo*) as contributors. That startled me very much. What would you say if the French or German Opposition papers carried Gorkin as one of their contributors? That would be an act inimical to our Spanish friends. I put the question to Comrade Lacroix and I received a reply that this whole matter was merely one of a technical misunderstanding. Please be assured that I did not intend for one moment to exaggerate the importance of the error. But I had to come to the conclusion that our Spanish friends are not yet sufficiently attentive to the life of the International Opposition. Undoubtedly you agree that just as socialism cannot be built in one country, a Marxist policy cannot be pursued in one country alone.

7. In regard to this, new evidence has presented itself that gives reason to fear that this matter is more serious than it originally appeared. That showed itself particularly clearly in the question of the constitution of the International Secretariat.[46] This question did not only appear yesterday. There is a long story to that. There are innumerable documents on this question, particularly those written by myself. I am once more compelled to ask if these documents are known to the Spanish comrades? Are they translated into Spanish?

It is true that I have myself met some comrades in the ranks of the Left Opposition who speak of the internal ideological struggles in a belittling sense, calling them "quibbles, intrigues." Such comrades have not learned in the school of Marx and Lenin. In order to prepare ourselves for the great struggles, we must learn to be steadfast and uncompromising in all the current principled questions, even when they are of a minor character. It is most frequently the case that those comrades who call the principled struggles "intrigues" are precisely the ones who display the ability for real intrigues when someone steps on their corns. A lack of concern about principled questions and an exaggerated sensitivity in personal questions characterize many of those who landed by accident in the ranks of the Left Opposition.

8. One of these accidental persons is undoubtedly Comrade Mill. Due to the absence of Russian-speaking comrades in other countries, the Russian Opposition was forced to resort to Comrade Mill, who was little known to it, as its unofficial representative in the International Secretariat. Comrade Mill accepted this representation. I was in constant correspondence with Comrade Mill. A big volume could be bound together from my letters to him. All the answers of Comrade Mill have shown me not only that he lacks even elementary revolutionary training and understanding of the meaning and importance of the organization, but also that he does not want to learn and cannot learn the ABC of communist policy. Mill repeats very glibly the general phrases about socialism in one country, but when a definite political line has to be defended he changes his course under the influence of some sort of intangible mood.

In the course of several months, Comrade Mill participated in the struggle against Landau and Naville, and their leader, Rosmer. One had to assume that Mill understood the meaning of this struggle, which led to a break with a whole series of groups and persons. But that did not at all prevent Mill from proposing a bloc by letter to Rosmer against the leadership of the French League and against the Russian Opposition. This manner of acting, if we are to take matters seriously, is *treachery*. A man who is capable of such political somersaults does not deserve to be recognized as a revolutionist. Are you in accord with this, comrades, or not?

9. I conducted a correspondence with the International Secretariat through Comrade Mill in Russian in order to save time. Comrade Mill systematically concealed those of my letters from the secretariat that contained proposals, remarks, and criticisms that did not appeal to him, and on the contrary drew on isolated parts of my letters that he could use against the Secretariat, thereby systematically misleading them.

10. The Russian Opposition broke with Mill. The French

condemned him strongly. The German Opposition considered
his manner of acting to be impermissible. The Belgian Opposition condemned Mill, and the Italian Opposition in the person
of Comrade Souvo, a member of the IS, condemned the bloc of
Comrade Mill with Rosmer. Are these facts known to the
members of the Spanish Opposition or aren't they? I hope that
they are. How then explain the fact that the Central Committee
of the Spanish Left Opposition has established the candidacy
of Mill as their representative in the International Secretariat?

A step of this sort takes on the character of a hostile political
demonstration against the Russian, French, Belgian, and other
national sections whose decisions most probably will not be
delayed. It is clear that if you have any serious differences with
us, you not only have the right but are duty-bound to express
them by means of words as well as deeds. In this case you
must express yourselves clearly and openly.

11. Your support of Comrade Mill appears inexplicable as
well for the following reasons: Comrade Mill wrote two letters
from Spain in which he threw the Left and the Right Opposition
into one pot and in this manner led the entire Left Opposition
astray. It is hard to conceive of a more scandalous confusion,
especially on the part of the permanent secretary. When I protested against his letters, Comrade Mill replied that he had
been misled by Comrade Nin. Isn't it clear that Mill thereby
only emphasized his complete inability to judge elementary
political questions by himself?

I have proposed to collectively draw up an international
manifesto on the Spanish revolution. Despite my repeated demands, Comrade Mill did not even lift a finger in this important matter because his entire attention was consumed by the
factional struggle and by the behind-the-scenes combinations
against the most important sections of the Opposition. These
are the facts.

How then, comrades, are we to explain the circumstance
that you have so demonstratively expressed your lack of confidence in the French, Russian, German, Belgian, and other
sections of the Left Opposition? You must probably have deep
grounds of principle for this. *Our* principled considerations
I have explained above, and not for the first time. Now I am
awaiting with the greatest interest and attention *your* principled
considerations.

12. I will mention just one more episode. You have voted

against the entrance of the representative of the Russian Opposition, Comrade Markin, into the International Secretariat on the basis that he belongs to the Molinier-Frank faction — that Comrade Markin belongs to the same faction to which I belong; but we work in complete solidarity with them.[47] What basis have you then to attempt to deprive the Russian Opposition of its representation in the International Secretariat? You must have very serious reasons for this. Please explain them. We will direct all our attention towards them.

In his last letter, Comrade Lacroix asked me not to return to the question of the French comrade Molinier with whom he has had the conflict mentioned in point 1. I am perfectly in accord and I believe that we can entirely leave aside the small and personal episodes that have no principled or political significance.

In his letter, Comrade Lacroix says that the International Conference must solve the disputed questions. That is also quite correct. But the International Conference must be prepared for by a discussion of the most important political and organizational differences in all the sections. Therefore, I turn to you, dear comrades, with this letter, of which I am sending copies to the leaderships of all the national sections. I do not doubt that with our united forces we will be able to lay aside the misunderstandings and find a common language with you.

With communist greetings,
L. Trotsky

37 *TO THE SPANISH YOUTH*

June 13, 1932
Dear Comrades:

I learned with joy that you are undertaking the publication of your own paper. A revolutionary tendency that does not educate the youth will die stillborn. In the present world, communism is the only task of great magnitude that demands a whole series of generations for its complete realization. The proletarian revolution requires continuity. To assure this continuity is the mission of the youth; that is to say, it is your

From the March 1933 *Young Spartacus*, the monthly paper of the Young Spartacus League, the youth group of the CLA.

mission. Marxism shows how this is to be done.

The strength of Marxism is in the unity of scientific theory with revolutionary struggle. On these two rails, the education of the communist youth should progress. The study of Marxism outside the revolutionary struggle can create bookworms but not revolutionaries. Participation in the revolutionary struggle without the study of Marxism is unavoidably full of danger, uncertainty, half-blindness. To study Marxism as a Marxist is possible only by participating in the life and struggle of the class; revolutionary theory is verified by practice, and practice is clarified by theory. Only the truths of Marxism that are conquered in struggle enter the mind and the blood.

A letter from the Soviet Union, which I received some days ago, states that despite the monstrous persecutions, arrests, and deportations, new organizations and new Left Opposition (Bolshevik-Leninist) groups have been formed in every industrial center, especially among the youth. No repression can break revolutionary continuity as long as it supports itself on revolutionary theory.

I hope with all my heart that your paper will successfully accomplish the task before it: to unite theory with practice. This will not be easy. You will make mistakes; but we too, the old ones, who possess some revolutionary experience, make mistakes very often, more often than necessary. You will learn by your mistakes. The second and the third step will be more certain than the first.

I warmly greet the young proletarian communists of Spain in the name of the thousands and thousands of our cothinkers, the Russian Bolshevik-Leninists, who are carrying on the struggle in the factories and the mines and who are dispersed in the prisons and the exile camps of the Stalinist bureaucracy.

Yours,

L. D. Trotsky

38

THE SPANISH KORNILOVS AND THE SPANISH STALINISTS

September 20, 1932

As in the past, *Pravda* keeps quiet about Germany. But to make up for that it carries in its September 9 issue an article on Spain. The article is very highly instructive. It is true that it casts only an indirect light on the Spanish revolution; but in return it brilliantly illuminates the political convulsions of the Stalinist bureaucracy.

The article says: "After the defeat of the general strike in January,[48] the Trotskyists [here follow some ritualistic insults — L. T.] asserted that the revolution was beaten and that the period of defeats had come." Is this true? If there are revolutionaries in Spain who in January of this year were ready to bury the revolution, they do not have and can not have anything in common with the Left Opposition. A revolutionary cannot recognize the revolution as finished until objective indications leave no room for any doubt. Only miserable impressionists and not Bolshevik-Leninists can make pessimistic predictions on the basis of a dampening of spirits.

In our article "The Spanish Revolution and the Dangers Threatening It," we examined the question of the line of general development of the Spanish revolution and its possible tempo. The Russian Revolution took eight months to reach its culmination. But this prolongation is not at all obligatory for the Spanish revolution. The Great French Revolution gave power to the Jacobins only after almost four years. One of the causes of the slow development of the French Revolution lay in the fact that the Jacobin party itself was only formed in the fire of events. These conditions exist in Spain: at the moment of the republican revolution, the Communist Party was still in its infancy. For this reason, as well as others, we would consider it probable that the Spanish revolution would develop slowly through a series of stages, including the parliamentary stage.

We recalled at that time that the tide of revolution permits ebbs and flows. Incidentally, the art of leadership consists

---

Published in French in Leon Trotsky, *Ecrits,* Vol. III (1928-1940), and translated for this volume from the French by Constance Weissman.

in not ordering an offensive at the moment of ebb, and in not retreating at the moment of floodtide. For that reason it is necessary, above all, not to confuse special "conjunctural" vacillations with its fundamental rhythm.

After the defeat of the January general strike, it was evident that what was involved was a partial ebbing of the revolution in Spain. Only babblers and adventurers can ignore the ebb. But only panic-mongers and deserters can speak of the liquidation of the revolution as a consequence of a partial retreat. Revolutionists are the last to leave the battlefield. Any revolutionist who buries the living revolution himself deserves the firing squad.

The partial retreat and lull of the Spanish revolution gave impetus to the counterrevolution. After defeat in a big battle, the masses fall back and quiet down. An insufficiently tempered leadership is often inclined to exaggerate the extent of the defeat. All this encourages the extremist wing of the counterrevolution. Such is the political mechanism of the monarchist attempt of General Sanjurjo.[49] But what especially awakens the masses like the crack of a whip is the emergence of the mortal enemy of the people into the arena. It is not rare in such cases for the revolutionary leadership to' be caught unawares.

"The swiftness and ease with which the generals' revolt was smashed," writes *Pravda,* "shows that the forces of the revolution are not broken. The revolutionary upsurge has received a new push from the events of August 10." This is perfectly true. One could also say that this is the only correct passage in the whole article.

Was the Spanish Communist Party taken unawares by the events? Judging only by testimony in *Pravda,* one would have to answer affirmatively. The article is entitled "The Workers Defeat the General." Evidently, without the revolutionary intervention of the workers against the monarchist coup d'etat, Zamora and not Sanjurjo would have been forced to go into exile. In other words, at the price of their heroism and their blood, the workers helped the republican bourgeoisie hold on to the power. Pretending not to see that, *Pravda* writes: "The Communist Party fought . . . against the right-wing coup d'etat in such a way as to give not even a shadow of support to the present counterrevolutionary government."

What the Communist Party intends is one thing; but what counts now is the result of its efforts. The monarchist wing of the propertied classes tried to remove the republican wing, although the republicans had taken pains not to provoke the monarchists. But the proletariat entered the picture. "The Workers Defeat the General." The monarchists go into exile and the republican bourgeoisie stays in power. How, in the face of such facts, can it be maintained that the Communist Party has not given "a shadow of support to the present counter-revolutionary government?"

From what has been said, does it follow that the Communist Party should wash its hands of the conflict between the monarchists and the republican bourgeoisie? Such a policy would have been suicidal, as was shown by the experience of the Bulgarian Communists in 1923.[50] Only if the Spanish workers were strong enough to take power themselves could their intervention in a decisive struggle against the monarchists not have given momentary aid to their enemy, the republican bourgeoisie. In August 1917, the Bolsheviks were much stronger than the Spanish Communists were in August 1932. But even the Bolsheviks could not possibly have won power by themselves in the struggle against Kornilov. Thanks to the victory of the workers over the Kornilovists, Kerensky's government lasted another two months. Let us recall once again that battalions of Bolshevik sailors guarded Kerensky's Winter Palace against Kornilov.

The Spanish proletariat has shown itself to be strong enough to overcome the revolt of the generals, but too weak to take power. Under such conditions, the heroic struggle of the workers could not help but strengthen — even if only temporarily — the republican government. Only harebrains who substitute rubber-stamp epithets for analysis are capable of denying this.

The misfortune of the Stalinist bureaucracy is that neither in Spain nor in Germany does it see the real contradictions that exist in the enemy camp, that is, the living classes and their struggle. The "fascist" Primo de Rivera is replaced by the "fascist" Zamora allied to "social fascists." It is not surprising that with such a theory, the intervention of the masses in the conflict between the monarchists and the republicans took the Stalinists by surprise. With the proper instinct, the masses threw themselves into the struggle, dragging the communists with them. After the victory of the workers over the generals, *Pravda* began to gather up the debris of its theory in order to glue the pieces together again as though nothing had happened. This is the principal meaning of the stupid blustering which would have it that the Communist Party had not given a "shadow of support" to the bourgeois government.

In reality, the Communist Party not only gave *objective* support to the government but also, as can be seen in the article itself, did not know how to differentiate itself *subjectively* from it. On this matter, we read: "We didn't succeed, in all cells or in all the provincial organizations, in showing sufficiently the true face of the Communist Party and in counterposing it to the maneuvers of the social fascists and republicans. That would have demonstrated that the party fights not only against the monarchists but also against the 'republican' government which is a cover for the monarchists." It is well known throughout Stalinist writings what the words "not in all cells," "not in all the organizations," etc. are meant to say. They are designed to conceal the cowardice of the thought. When, on February 15, 1928, Stalin recognized for the first time that the kulak was not an invention of the Left Opposition, he wrote in *Pravda,* "In some departments, in certain provinces . . ." the kulak has appeared. Because mistakes can only be admitted as coming from those who implement the directives, they obviously can arise only "in some areas." The party is thus only equal to the sum of its provincial parts.

In reality, the quotation that we just gave, if it is stripped of its bureaucratic evasions, means: In the struggle against the monarchists, the party did not know how to "show its face." It did not know how to counterpose itself to the "social fascists" and to the republicans. In other words, not only did the party give provisional military support to the bourgeois and Social Democratic government but it also did not know how to strengthen itself at the government's expense in the process of the struggle.

The weakness of the Communist Party — which is the result of the policy of the epigones of the Communist International — did not allow the proletariat to reach for power on August 10, 1932. At the same time, the party was forced to take part and did take part in the struggle as the left wing of the provisional general front; on its right was the republican bourgeoisie. The leadership of the coalition did not forget for a single instant to show *its* "face" in curbing the struggle and restraining the masses, and immediately after the victory over the generals it proceeded to fight against the communists. As far as the Spanish Stalinists were concerned, they could not, according to the testimony of the Russian Stalinists, demonstrate that "the party fights not only against the monarchists, but also against the 'republican' government."

That is the crux of the matter. On the eve of the events, the party smeared all its enemies with the same color. At the climax of the battle, it was itself streaked by the color of the enemy and was temporarily lost in the front of republicans and Social Democrats. Only those who have not understood the origin of bureaucratic centrism can be astonished by this. In theory (if this word can be used here), it protects itself against opportunist deviations by a general refusal to make any political and class distinctions: Hoover, von Papen, Vandervelde, Gandhi, Rakovsky, all are "counterrevolutionaries," "fascists," "agents of imperialism."[51] But every sudden change in events, every new danger, in practice forces the Stalinists to enter the struggle against an enemy and to kneel before the other "counterrevolutionaries" and "fascists."

In face of the war, the Stalinists voted for a diplomatic, prudent, and spineless resolution at Amsterdam, proposed by General von Schoenaich, the French freemasons, and the Indian bourgeois Patel,[52] whose highest ideal is Gandhi. In the German Reichstag, the Communists suddenly declared that they are ready to vote for the "social fascist" president in order to prevent the election of a national-socialist president, that is to say, they place themselves completely on the ground of the "lesser evil." In Spain, at the moment of danger, they show themselves incapable of opposing the republican bourgeoisie. Is it not clear that what we are dealing with here is not occasional mistakes, not "certain" cells, but the hereditary vice of bureaucratic centrism?

The intervention of the mass of workers into the conflict between the two camps of exploiters has given a serious forward impulse to the Spanish revolution. The Azaña government found itself obliged to order the confiscation of manorial estates, a measure which, a few weeks earlier, was as remote as the Milky Way.[53] If the Communist Party had noticed the differences between the real classes and their political organizations, if it had foreseen the real march of events, if it had criticized and exposed its enemies on the basis of their *real* sins and crimes, then the masses would have seen the Azaña government's new agrarian reform as the effect of Communist Party policy and would have said to themselves: We must go forward with more energy under its leadership.

If the German Communist Party had embarked confidently and decisively on the line of the united front, which the whole situation called for, and if it had criticized the Social Democrats not for their "fascism" but for their weakness, their waverings, their cowardice in the struggle against Bonapartism and fascism, then the masses would have learned something by the common struggle and by the criticisms, and they would have aligned themselves more decisively behind the Communist Party.

In view of the current policy of the Communist International, the masses are convinced at each new turn of events that not only do their class enemies not do what the communists had predicted but also that the Communist Party itself at the crucial moment abandons everything it had taught. This is why confidence in the Communist Party does not grow. And that is why the danger arises in part that Azaña's weak agrarian reform will only profit the bourgeoisie and not the proletariat.

Under exceptional and favorable conditions, the working class can triumph even with bad leadership. But exceptionally favorable conditions are rare. The proletariat must learn to win under less favorable conditions. Besides, the leadership of the Stalinist bureaucracy — as experience in every country shows, and as the events of each new month confirm — prevents the communists from utilizing favorable conditions to strengthen their ranks, to maneuver actively, to distinguish among groupings of enemies or semi-enemies and allied forces. In other words, 'the Stalinist bureaucracy has become the most important internal obstacle on the road to victory for the proletarian revolution.

39   THE STATE OF THE LEFT OPPOSITION

December 16, 1932

The most important result of the trip to Copenhagen was undoubtedly the coming together of Oppositionists from many
countries. The original intention was to call together a dozen
comrades from the areas nearest to Denmark in order to take
the necessary safety measures. In point of fact, however, twenty-
four comrades (of whom two were delayed) arrived, among
them the most responsible functionaries of several sections.
Including sympathizers, there was a total of thirty people.

If Stalin informed the capitalist police by radio of a "Trotskyist conference" meeting in Copenhagen, that was a lie. Since
it came about by accident, the trip to Copenhagen necessarily
caught the Left Opposition by surprise. The preparatory work
for the conference was still in the early stages. There could
be no question of accepting a platform of programmatic theses
in Copenhagen. Even the European sections were far from
completely represented, and not all the comrades who arrived
had plenary powers. Unfortunately a conference did not take
place and in the course of events could not have taken place.

Needless to say, however, the comrades who came took full
advantage of the opportunity to get to know each other and
to discuss in informal consultations the most urgent and burning problems. The unforeseen, hastily improvised meeting of
two dozen Bolshevik-Leninists from seven European countries
will undoubtedly be recorded as an important achievement in
the history of our international faction.

The Left Opposition has grown considerably. The cadres
of functionaries know the history of the Left Opposition in the

---

An excerpt from the *Internal Bulletin,* CLA, no. 9, 1933. Signed "G.
Gourov." Full text appears in *Writings of Leon Trotsky* (1932-33).

Trotsky went to Copenhagen in November 1932 to deliver a lecture
on the anniversary of the Russian Revolution. He went in the hope
that he would be allowed to stay in Denmark, but he was forced to
return to Turkey.

The presence of several Oppositionists in Copenhagen during his
stay gave Trotsky the opportunity to hold an informal meeting at
which they discussed the affairs of the European Left Opposition
groups, as Trotsky describes. This letter was written upon Trotsky's
return to Turkey and was sent to all the sections of the Left Opposition.

various countries, orient themselves freely in theoretical and political questions, and both together and separately embody a considerable political experience. The consultations, which lasted several days, solidly fused the comrades together, a fact that will have fruitful effects on our entire future work. Without falling victim to official optimism, we can say with assurance that all the participants in the consultation left it with a new supply of confidence.

The Spanish Opposition

One question threw a shadow over the consultation: the situation of the Spanish Opposition. If we could observe certain nuances within the International Left Opposition with regard to the sicknesses and mistakes of the Spanish Opposition, these nuances were thrust completely into the background in the course of the consultation, before the feeling of common concern. All the participants were completely in accord with the view that we must have an open and complete discussion with the Spanish comrades, and that this discussion must not be limited this time to the leaders of the Opposition; only if all the members of the sections are made familiar with the questions in dispute can the Spanish Opposition be brought onto the right road.

It would be criminal to close our eyes any further before the real situation or to palliate it; if we do not succeed in clarifying completely and in time through an open discussion all disputed questions — and too many of them have piled up — then the pressure of events may divide us into different camps.

Unfortunately the Spanish section was not represented at the consultation. At the last minute certain obviously accidental circumstances proved an obstacle, but I take the liberty of expressing my certainty that the leading Spanish comrades, if they had locked themselves less into their environment and had shown more interest in their international organization, would have found their way to the Copenhagen consultation without difficulty.

But that is precisely the chief misfortune of the Spanish Opposition, that its leaders have persistently kept their organization away from the internal life and the internal struggles of the other sections, and thereby have shut it off from access to an irreplaceable international experience. But insofar as the Spanish section through its official position was after all compelled to mix into international questions, its leaders, influenced neither by the experience of the other sections nor by the public opinion of their own organization, let themselves be guided by personal connections, sympathies, or antipathies. For a Marxist analysis of the situation and of the differences of opinion, they substituted all too often — we must say it openly — a petty-bourgeois psychologizing and sentimentalizing. So it was in the case of the Catalan Federation (Maurín), where several Barcelona comrades' confidence in "friendly personal relations" for a long time took the place of principled struggle against petty-bourgeois nationalism and thereby put a brake on the development of the Left Opposition in the most decisive period. So it was in the case of Landau, whom *Comunismo* surprisingly listed as a collaborator after Landau had shown his utter inadequacy, remained in the minority, and finally left the Left Opposition. So it was in the differences of opinion within the French section, where the Spanish comrades privately agreed that Rosmer's ideas and methods were worthless, but in public supported Rosmer, indirectly if not directly, on the ground that Rosmer "appealed to them" more than his opponents. So it was in the question of Mill, whom the leading Spanish comrades thought it possible to choose as their representative on the International Secretariat, after Mill's political worthlessness had been completely exposed. In all these cases, we have not heard from Madrid or Barcelona even a hint of principled grounds or political explanation.

The same features revealed themselves in no less sharp and painful a form in the inner life of the Spanish organization. The crisis that broke out in the leadership caught not only the International Opposition but also the Spanish section by surprise. The members of the Central Committee resigned, one after the other. The whole leadership was concentrated de facto in the hands of Lacroix alone. Then, just as surprisingly, it appeared that Comrade Lacroix was outside of the Central Committee, in fact for a time outside of the Opposition, while the leadership went over to Barcelona. Why? What do the differences of opinion consist of? What are the grounds of the crisis? Nobody knows, at least nobody outside of the narrow circle of the initiated. Such a regime is absolutely impermissible in a revolutionary organization, and can bring it only defeats. By refraining from participation in the struggle over principled questions, by substituting personal evaluations for political differences of opinion, the Spanish comrades themselves fall victim to inevitable personal conflicts and "palace revolutions."

Such subjective arbitrariness in politics would be completely impossible if the Central Committee of the Spanish section worked under the control of its own organization. But this is not the case. In their own defense, several leaders of the Spanish Opposition pointed more than once to the insufficiently high theoretical and political level of the Spanish Oppositionists. Obviously an objection that will not hold water! The level of a revolutionary organization rises all the faster, the more it is brought into the discussion of *all* questions, the less the leaders try to think, act, and behave as guardians for the organization.

The first condition for party democracy consists of providing all-sided *information*. The beginning must be the international documents on the Spanish Opposition; the Spanish Central Committee must obligate itself to communicate these documents to all members of the Opposition; every Spanish Bolshevik-Leninist must study, think through, and judge not only the experience with Mill but also the essence of the crisis of the Spanish Central Committee itself. Through this the Spanish Oppositionists will learn much more than through a dozen abstract articles on democratic centralism and the correct relation to "human beings. . . . "

40

PROBLEMS OF THE SPANISH LEFT OPPOSITION

December 1932

The Spanish revolution created exceptionally favorable objective conditions for the rapid development of communism. But the lack of cadres who were in any way trained made it very difficult for the Left Opposition as well as for the official party to take advantage of a truly historic situation. Although the Spanish section surpasses a number of other sections in numbers — this must be credited to the revolutionary upsurge — its ideological consolidation and the character of its leadership present a most unsatisfactory picture.

In order to understand the reasons for this, we must establish the most important mistakes of the leading cadres of the Spanish Opposition.

In Catalonia, where the proletariat offers a natural milieu for the rapid growth of Bolshevik-Leninist influence, the leading comrades lost time in an inexcusable manner; instead of coming out openly under their own banner even as a small nucleus, they played hide-and-seek with principles during the most critical months of the revolution, first engaging in diplomacy with the petty-bourgeois nationalist and provincial phrasemaker Maurín, and then hanging on to his tail.

Things were not much better in the rest of Spain, where the Left Opposition, while ignoring the official party and substituting revolutionary sentimentalism for the Marxist education of cadres, failed for a long time to draw the necessary distinction between itself and the groups of the Right Opposition.

No less harmful was the fact that the leading comrades sub-

Unsigned. An excerpt from "The International Left Opposition, Its Tasks and Methods," which Trotsky began in December 1932, and which was adopted in expanded form at an international preconference of the ILO in Paris, February 4-8, 1933.

This part of the resolution was intended for internal circulation only, and was published in the *Internal Bulletin* of the CLA, no. 11, March 31, 1933. All of the resolution that was written or edited by Trotsky can be found in *Writings of Leon Trotsky* (1932-33); other sections, added at the preconference, are in the same *Internal Bulletin* or in *The Militant,* which printed the text in its issues of March 6, 8, 10, 18, and 25, 1933.

mitted to the influence of the worst aspects of the Spanish revolutionary tradition, turned their backs on the international
experience, and while verbally declaring their solidarity with the
Left Opposition, in actual fact supported, directly or indirectly,
all the muddleheads and deserters (Landau, Rosmer, Mill, etc.).

On the question of *faction or independent party*, the Spanish
section at its last conference took an ambiguous position, to
say the least, by declaring itself in favor of setting up its own
list of candidates at parliamentary and other elections. This
decision, which is contrary to the policy of the Left Opposition
and was in no way prepared for in practice, remained a
platonic but nonetheless harmful demonstration.

On the road of alienation from the Bolshevik-Leninists, the
leaders of the Spanish Opposition went so far as to consider
it possible to change the name of their organization. By assuming the name of "Left Communists"—an obviously false
name from the standpoint of theory — the Spanish comrades
put themselves into contradiction with the International Left
Opposition and at the same time approached the name taken
by the Leninbund, the Rosmer group, etc.[54] No serious revolutionary will believe that such an important step was taken
by accident, without a political reason. At the same time, no
Marxist will approve a policy that does not openly declare its
aims on principled questions, but takes refuge in diplomacy
and maneuver.

By its demand that the international conference be opened
to all groups declaring themselves adherents of the Left Opposition, including those that split away and were expelled,
the Spanish Opposition shows how far removed it has been
and continues to be from the real development of the International Left and how little of its internal logic it has absorbed.

While accusing the other sections of wrong organizational
policies, without attempting to justify their accusations, the
Spanish comrades at the same time have in fact proven the
entire falsity of their own methods. The struggle that suddenly
broke out between the two groups in the Central Committee
has led the Spanish section to the verge of a split. The organization as a whole was taken utterly by surprise since
neither of the two contending groups has been able up to now
to formulate the principled foundations of this bitter struggle. [55]

On its present ideological foundation, the Spanish section

cannot develop any further. Taking clear account of the fact that the correction of the mistakes that were made and the creation in Spain of an organization firm in principle and organized in a revolutionary manner can only be the result of long and systematic work, the preconference proposes the following immediate measures:

a) All important international documents on the questions in dispute must be translated into Spanish and be brought to the knowledge of all the members of the section. Concealing of facts must be stopped. What is said here refers particularly to the Mill case, in which the leaders of the Spanish section not only supported an obviously unprincipled person against the International Opposition, but even now, in defense of the mistakes they have made, permit themselves completely inappropriate insinuations against the International Opposition.

b) Both contending groups within the Central Committee must give up the idea of an unprincipled split and of organizational measures, and make the necessary provisions so that the discussion on the disputed questions will run through normal channels and have the participation of all members of the organization without exception.

c) The internal discussion must be carried on in a bulletin whose editorial staff must guarantee the most complete impartiality toward each of the contending groups (through a joint editorial committee).

d) All the principled questions of the International Left must be placed on the agenda, and sympathies, antipathies, and personal insinuations must not be allowed to become substitutes for clear political positions.

e) A comprehensive discussion must prepare the way for a new national conference.

The preconference directs the Secretariat to follow the internal development of the Spanish section with special attention, to help it carry out the measures stated above and other suitable measures, in full coordination with the tasks and methods of the Left Opposition. [56]

41

LETTER TO COMRADE LACROIX

March 25, 1933

Dear Comrade Lacroix:

My correspondence with Comrade Nin had a political character, not a personal one. Since the same disagreements were repeated at each new stage, I considered it necessary to make available the most important extracts from my correspondence with Nin *to all the members of the Spanish section.* Without the formation of an educated collective opinion in the Marxist method, no progress will be possible in the Spanish section.

I did not publish this correspondence for the purpose of helping one group against another, much less when you used the same ideas and methods that I have criticized in Comrade Nin. The struggle of your two groups has taken on a sharp and venomous personal character. It is inexcusable, and cannot be discussed normally except by linking today's differences with yesterday's on the basis of Marxist methodology. On this basis, and only on this basis, I would be very pleased to collaborate with you, as well as with Comrade Nin. My best communist greetings.

From *Boletín Interior* de la Izquierda Comunista Española, no. 2, July 15, 1933. Translated for this volume from the Spanish by Naomi Allen.

In the dispute between Lacroix and Nin, Nin tried to prove that Trotsky supported Lacroix; Trotsky's real position in the factional struggle is clear from this letter.

42   *LETTER TO ALL MEMBERS*
              OF THE SPANISH LEFT OPPOSITION

April 24, 1933
Dear Comrades:
   The other day I received a copy of the written reply of the Barcelona Central Committee to the Organizational Commission for the convocation of a national antifascist conference. This letter, dated April 5, 1933, is a document that should be studied by every member of the Spanish Opposition who is devoted to the cause of communism.
   What is the point of either an international antifascist congress or a national antifascist conference? The Left Opposition (Bolshevik-Leninists) explained this question in detail in documents and articles on the Amsterdam congress against war and in a number of subsequent declarations. The Stalinist bureaucracy isolated the communist proletarian vanguard by means of a false policy, which has made a united front of the workers impossible, particularly one against fascism and war. In order to camouflage its bankruptcy, the Comintern from time to time organizes a masquerade in imitation of a united front. It brings scattered groups of communist workers together with powerless individuals, pacifists, left democrats, and others, picturing such purely theatrical congresses, conferences, and committees as "a united front of the masses." We ourselves, at one time, took part in the Amsterdam congress, but only in order to *expose* this sham and thus draw the attention of the communist workers to the correct course. Needless to say, our attitude toward the coming antifascist congress is the same.
   On this matter the Barcelona Central Committee has taken a position exactly opposite to that of the Bolshevik-Leninists. The letter of April 5 ceremoniously informs the Organizational Commission that the Left Opposition has joined the "united front" as if there were actually a united front involved rather than a mockery of the united front policy.
   Helping the Stalinists embellish reality, the letter of the Barcelona CC repeats the general phrases about how a united

Copy of original Russian provided by Pierre Broué. Signed "G. Gourov." Translated for this volume by Marilyn Vogt.

front against fascism is realizable despite the existence of differences. However, this elementary idea, true in relation to the mass *proletarian* organizations, loses its meaning in relation to bourgeois individuals, pacifists, democratic writers, and others. Moreover, the letter of the Barcelona CC declares: "A pacifist can be just as opposed to war as a revolutionary communist can, and even more so. It is perfectly logical for these people to be found in a united front against those who are their enemies."

It is hard to believe that these words could have been written by people who consider themselves Marxists, who have some sort of concept of Lenin's politics and of the decisions of the first four congresses of the Comintern, not to mention the decade of work by the International Left Opposition, and particularly its declaration on the Amsterdam congress.57

How can a pacifist be a greater enemy of war than a revolutionary communist? Marxist theory and political experience teach us that pacifism is an instrument of imperialism. Pacifists decry war during times of peace, but when war comes they quietly yield to militarism under the pressure of their own isolation and impotence, and more often than not they are transformed into its lackeys. The same thing applies to the struggle against fascism.

The purpose of the united front policy is to bring the Social Democratic and syndicalist workers into a rapprochement with the communist workers (and with communism) through the process of joint struggle against the class enemy. As far as isolated individuals from the bourgeois camp are concerned, that is a matter of tenth-rate significance. The best of them will support the workers more surely, to the extent that the policy of the united proletarian front is pursued correctly, and the masses are drawn together firmly. But abandonment of mass politics for the pursuit of individuals with big names is the worst kind of adventurism and political charlatanism.

Instead of exposing the very idea of an alliance between the Stalinist bureaucracy and bourgeois individuals, the Barcelona CC expresses confidence that the Organizational Commission views the tasks of the congress just as the CC itself does, and for that reason the CC "gladly" proffers its "loyal collaboration." What is this: diplomacy? If so, it is the kind that can deceive only our friends and co-thinkers. And why would Marxists become involved in diplomacy over this sort of issue, one that requires maximum clarity? No, one is forced to conclude that the Barcelona CC has a position totally contrary to Marxism on this major question in proletarian politics.

The struggle of leading Spanish comrades against the fundamental views and principles of the International Left Opposition (Bolshevik-Leninists) did not begin yesterday. It can be said without exaggeration that during the past three years there was hardly one serious Spanish or international question on which the leading Spanish comrades held a correct position. Mistakes, of course, are always possible, and in a young organization they are inevitable. But it is essential that an organization, and most of all its leaders, learn from their mistakes. Then it can go forward. The unfortunate thing here is that the comrades who are now on the CC of the Spanish Opposition do not allow the organization to discuss issues; instead, on every occasion, they substitute personal attacks and petty, insignificant accusations for principled discussion of differences. The struggle between Comrade Nin's group and that of Comrade Lacroix has, of course, a significance of its own. But the struggle that the group of Nin, Fersen, and others is conducting against the International Left Opposition as a whole,58 which violates the most fundamental principles of Marxism at every step, is a hundred times more important.

In any factional struggle personal conflicts and mutual accusations occur: that is inevitable. However, a revolutionary who determines his political position on the basis of purely personal episodes, accusations, sympathies, and antipathies is no good at all. Such a method is typical of petty-bourgeois radicals, incapable of rising to the level of Marxist principles. Petty-bourgeois squabbles have to date poisoned the leadership of the Spanish Opposition, preventing it from orienting itself correctly and paralyzing the development of the entire organization, despite the exceptionally favorable objective conditions. If rank-and-file members of the Spanish Opposition, real Bolshevik-Leninists, want to break out of this impasse, they will have to brush aside the debris of personal squabbles and examine political differences on the basis of their merit. It is necessary to study the entire history of these differences. But first and foremost, it is necessary to place the unprincipled

CC document of April 5, 1933, at the center of the discussion. It is essential that every member of the Spanish Opposition understand that the root cause of the unending conflicts between Barcelona, on the one hand, and Paris, Brussels, Berlin, Vienna, New York, etc., etc., on the other, is the fact that the Barcelona CC has an anti-Marxist position and steadfastly refuses to abandon it.

With this letter, I am appealing to all members of the Spanish section because my attempts over the past three years to achieve a mutual understanding with the leading Spanish comrades has thus far accomplished nothing. With communist greetings.

43

THE IMPERMISSIBLE CONDUCT OF COMRADE NIN

August 10, 1933
Dear Comrades:

The recent letters and documents coming from the Central Committee of the Spanish section, led by Comrade Nin, provoke a feeling that can only be termed indignation. Most astonishing is the tone of these letters. They are strewn with the most caustic charges and offensive expressions, employed without a shadow of reason. In many cases they are simply insults. This tone alone testifies to how remote Nin and his close friends are from the spirit of revolutionary comradeship and a feeling of elementary personal responsibility. Only people devoid of any inner discipline could write this way, especially with respect to the organization — which in their deepest convictions they judge to be foreign and hostile.

The "charges" advanced by the Nin group have been disproven many times over. A representative of this group was at the preconference where he had the chance to present all his claims and accusations. What was the result? *The politics of Nin and his friends were condemned by all the sections*

From *La Révolution Espagnole* (1936-1939), "Supplément à Etudes Marxistes," no. 7-8, Paris, and translated for this volume from the French by J. R. Fidler.

of the International Left Opposition without exception. One might have thought that this fact alone should have made Nin and his friends at least a little more prudent. Instead, they doubled and tripled the insults they directed from their center against the whole International Left Opposition.

For the moment, I want to touch on only one point: the Nin group dares to accuse the International Opposition of having — it seems, unjustly — expelled Rosmer, Landau, and the others from its ranks. However, the documents and the facts testify that it is precisely the contrary: Rosmer wanted to bring about the expulsion from the League of some comrades who were undesirable to him, and he remained in the League as a small minority; after that, he quit the League. Personally, I found myself with respect to that incident in constant correspondence with Nin. I shared with him all the measures I was taking to keep Rosmer from taking an obviously wrong step, resulting not from revolutionary considerations, but from personal whim. Nin, despite his friendship for Rosmer, wrote to me that *"common sense is not on Rosmer's side."* To my repeated questions, written to know if it was impossible for Nin still to carry out some supplementary steps to hold Rosmer back from an erroneous course, Nin proposed absolutely nothing, recognizing thereby that all possible measures had been exhausted.

So also with respect to Landau. No one, as is known, proposed to expel him. He was only asked to take part in the democratically called conference of the German section. . . . I submitted a resolution that was extremely conciliatory in its content and tone, *to which Nin adhered in writing "entirely and unreservedly."* We know that afterwards Landau *"expelled"* the majority of the Central Committee of the German section, and refused to participate in the conference, where he was to remain in a hopeless minority.

As a member of the International Bureau at that time, Nin participated in our entire policy and bears complete responsibility for it. Now, without providing facts or documents, he shifts the responsibility for Landau and Rosmer onto the International Left Opposition, forgetting or keeping silent about his own responsibility. How is such a method of action to be characterized?

Let us allow, for a moment, that Nin later came to conclude that our method of action with regard to Rosmer, Landau, and the others, was incorrect. He should then have said: *"WE have made such and such an error; we must correct it in such and such a way."* This would have been an absolutely legitimate course of action. All that is necessary is to say clearly *how* to correct the "errors." The Rosmer and Landau groups have publications and develop viewpoints that differ more and more from our positions on certain essential questions. If the issue of Rosmer and Landau was put forward not as an underhanded maneuver but with a practical aim — to bring the Rosmer-Landau group back into the International Left Opposition — the duty of Comrade Nin would then have consisted of evaluating their viewpoints and drawing the appropriate conclusion: are these positions compatible with the positions of the Bolshevik-Leninists? Are we being asked to make specific concessions, and exactly which ones? Or, on the contrary, must Rosmer and Landau renounce some specific positions and methods in order to rejoin the Left Opposition? To pose the question in such a serious, principled, and at the same time practical manner would have opened the opportunity to discuss and perhaps take this or that other practical step. Nin's present method of proceeding shows he is not concerned with any practical results whatsoever: all he wants is an artificial pretext for insinuations about the International Left Opposition.

What is even sadder is that Comrade Nin needs to act in this disloyal way in order to cover his own political vacillations and a whole series of errors, which have prevented the Spanish Left Opposition from winning the place opened up to it by the conditions of the Spanish revolution. Now, as a result of the radically incorrect policy of Comrade Nin, the Spanish section is growing not stronger but weaker. Unfortunately, discussing political questions with Comrade Nin leads to nothing: he beats about the bush, engages in diplomacy, equivocates, or what is even worse, replies to comrades' political arguments with personal insinuations.

I ask you to bring this letter to the attention of all the sections, beginning with the Spanish section. I would like this letter to come to the attention of all our friends in South America: they will join all the more closely with our international organization, and they will work in their national arena with

ll the more success, the more rapidly they are persuaded
of the falseness and danger of the politics of Comrade Nin.

Communist greetings,
L. Trotsky

P. S. This letter was already written when my friends showed
me the documents of Comrade Nin and others in reply to the
letter of Comrades Shachtman and Frank. 59 Since that letter
had been written at Prinkipo, Comrade Nin detects an intrigue,
a "comedy," etc. . . . He implies that I am hiding behind the
signers of the letter. For what reason? It is not out of fear of
Nin and his associates, for I have many times expressed myself, I hope unequivocally, on the "politics" of Nin. My correspondence with him is now accessible to the comrades. I
have not the least interest in hiding my opinion that Comrade
Nin's activity is pernicious. Why should I hide behind the
backs of Shachtman and Frank? Even if the initiative for
the letter had come from me, that would not have changed
its contents in the least. What counts are the facts and the
arguments of the letter, and they are crushing for Nin. Now,
the truth of the matter is that the responsibility for initiating
and writing the letter lies totally and exclusively with the comrades who signed it. I became acquainted with the text of the
letter only when I read it. And what right have Nin and his
associates to represent Shachtman and Frank as incapable
of having a judgment about these intrigues and of expressing
it on their own initiative? If Nin has some doubt about the
exact weight of this letter, let him inquire of the American
and French sections and their central and local bodies. I am
sure he will receive a clear if somewhat discomforting reply.

With his methods of shabby subterfuge, Nin defends his
personal insinuations by quoting my comment — hardly a personal one — that politics is expressed through people. He forgets
only that people can produce both good and bad politics,
and that each politics selects the people suited to it and trains
them accordingly.

44

ON ENTRY INTO THE SPANISH SOCIALIST PART'

November 1, 1934

I have not as yet received any documents on the recent even!
in Spain generally, and on the role played by our section
But the general line of development suffices to draw the con
clusion that our Spanish comrades should have joined th
Socialist Party there at the very outset of the internal differer
tiation that began to prepare that party for the armed strug
gle.[60]   Our position in the Spanish situation would today b
more favorable.

An excerpt from a letter to the International Secretariat, publishe
in an unnumbered and undated internal bulletin of the Communi
League of America, 1934. Signed "Crux." Full text is in *Writings*
Leon Trotsky (1934-35).

45

THE CONSEQUENCE OF PARLIAMENTARY REFORMISM

November 9, 1934

12. But the Defeats in Austria and Spain . . .

The impotence of parliamentarianism under the conditions c
crisis of the whole capitalist system is so obvious that th
vulgar democrats in the camp of the workers (Renaude
Frossard, and their imitators)[61] do not find a single argumer
to defend their petrified prejudices. All the more readily do the
seize upon every defeat and every failure suffered along th
revolutionary road. The development of their thought is this
if pure parliamentarianism offers no way out, armed struggl
does no better. The defeats of the proletarian insurrections i
Austria and in Spain are now, of course, their choice argumen
In fact, in their criticism of the revolutionary method the theore

An excerpt from *Whither France?*, translated by John G. Wright an
Harold Isaacs (Pioneer Publishers, 1936); reprinted in 1968 by Mer
Publishers. Full text is in *Leon Trotsky on France* (1934-39). The de
feat Trotsky refers to is the crushing of the Asturian miners.

ical and political bankruptcy of the vulgar democrats appears still more clearly than in their defense of the methods of decaying bourgeois democracy.

No one has said that the revolutionary method automatically assures victory. What is decisive is not the method in itself but its correct application, the Marxist orientation in events, powerful organization, the confidence of the masses won through long experience, a perspicacious and bold leadership. The issue of every struggle depends upon the moment and conditions of the conflict and the relation of forces. Marxism is quite far from the thought that armed conflict is the only revolutionary method, or a panacea good under all conditions. Marxism in general knows no fetishes, neither parliamentary nor insurrectional. There is a time and place for everything. There is one thing that one can say at the beginning:

On the parliamentary road the socialist proletariat has nowhere and never conquered power nor ever, as yet, even drawn close to it.

The governments of Scheidemann, Hermann Müller, MacDonald had nothing in common with socialism. [62] The bourgeoisie permitted the Social Democrats and Labourites to come to power only on condition that they defend capitalism against its enemies. They scrupulously fulfilled this condition. Purely parliamentary, antirevolutionary socialism nowhere and never resulted in a socialist ministry. It did succeed in producing loathsome renegades who exploited the workers' party to carve out cabinet careers — Millerand, Briand, Viviani, Laval, Paul-Boncour, Marquet. [63]

On the other hand, historical experience shows that the revolutionary method can lead to the conquest of power by the proletariat — in Russia in 1917, in Germany and Austria in 1918, in Spain in 1930. In Russia there was a powerful Bolshevik Party, which prepared for the revolution over a long period of years and knew solidly how to take over power.

The reformist parties of Germany, Austria, and Spain did not prepare the revolution, did not lead it, but suffered it.

Frightened by the power that had come into their hands against their own will, they benevolently handed it over to the bourgeoisie. In this way they undermined the confidence of the proletariat in itself, and further, the confidence of the petty bourgeoisie in the proletariat. They prepared the conditions for the growth of fascist reaction and fell victims to it.

Civil war, we have said, following Clausewitz, is a continuation of politics but by other means. This means that the result of the civil war depends for one-fourth, not to say one-tenth, upon the development of the civil war itself, its technical means, its purely military leadership, and for three-fourths, if not for nine-tenths, on the political preparation.

Of what does this political preparation consist? Of the revolutionary cohesion of the masses, of their liberation from servile hopes in the clemency, generosity, and loyalty of "democratic slave owners," of the education of revolutionary cadres who know how to defy official public opinion and who know how to display towards the bourgeoisie one-tenth the implacability that the bourgeoisie displays towards the toilers. Without this temper, civil war when conditions force it— *and they always end by forcing it*— will take place under conditions most unfavorable for the proletariat, will depend upon many hazards, and even then, in case of military victory, power can escape the hands of the proletariat. Whoever does not foresee that the class struggle leads inevitably to armed conflict is blind. But he is ño less blind who fails to see behind this armed conflict and its outcome the whole previous policy of the classes in struggle.

What was defeated in Austria was not the method of insurrection but Austro-Marxism and in Spain unprincipled parliamentary reformism. . . .

In Spain events took a different course but the causes of the defeat were basically the same. The Socialist Party, like the Russian Social Revolutionaries and Mensheviks, shared power with the republican bourgeoisie to prevent the workers and peasants from carrying the revolution to its conclusion. For two years the Socialists in power helped the bourgeoisie disembarrass itself of the masses by crumbs of national, social, and agrarian reforms. Against the most revolutionary strata of the people, the Socialists used repression.

The result was twofold. Anarcho-syndicalism, which would have melted like wax in the heat of revolution had the workers' party pursued a correct course, was strengthened and drew around it the militant layers of the proletariat. At the other pole, social catholic demagogy succeeded in skillfully exploiting the discontent of the masses with the bourgeois-socialist government.

When the Socialist Party was sufficiently compromised, the bourgeoisie drove it from power and took over the offensive on the whole front. The Socialist Party had to defend itself under the most unfavorable conditions, which had been prepared for it by its own previous policy. The bourgeoisie already had a mass support at the right. The anarcho-syndicalist leaders, who during the course of the revolution committed all the mistakes typical of these professional confusionists, refused to support the insurrection led by the traitor "politicians." The movement did not take on a general character but remained sporadic. The government directed its blows at the scattered sections of the workers. The civil war forced by the reaction ended in the defeat of the proletariat.

From the Spanish experience it is not difficult to draw conclusions against socialist participation in a bourgeois government. The conclusion itself is indisputable but utterly insufficient. The alleged "radicalism" of Austro-Marxism is in no sense any better than Spanish ministerialism. The difference between them is technical, not political. Both waited for the bourgeosie to give them "loyalty" for "loyalty." Both led the proletariat to catastrophe.

In Spain as in Austria it was not revolutionary methods that were defeated but opportunist methods in a revolutionary situation. It is not the same thing!

We shall not stop here on the policy of the Communist International in Austria and in Spain. We refer the reader to the files of *La Vérité* and a series of pamphlets of recent years. In an exceptionally favorable situation the Austrian and Spanish Communist Parties, fettered by the theory of the "third period" and "social fascism," etc., found themselves doomed to complete isolation. Compromising the methods of revolution by the authority of "Moscow" they barred, thereby, the road to a truly Marxist, truly Bolshevik policy. The fundamental faculty of revolution is to submit to a rapid and pitiless examination all doctrines and all methods. The punishment almost immediately follows the crime.

The responsibility of the Communist International for the defeats of the proletariat in Germany, Austria, and Spain is incommensurable. It is not sufficient to carry out a "revolutionary" policy (in words). A *correct* policy is needed. No one has yet found any other secret of victory.

46 *PASSIVITY IN THE FACE OF GREAT EVENTS*

December 16, 1934

. . . Much more disturbing is the passivity of our Spanish comrades (with a few honorable exceptions) during the great revolutionary events. We have always criticized the leaders of the Spanish section as being permeated with a purely propagandistic and timid spirit. Each comrade can and should reread the international discussions with the Spanish leadership. And here is what makes it significant: the Spanish comrades have declared themselves frankly hostile to the French turn. A new confirmation that their "intransigence" on this question is only the facade on a passivity that is purely propagandistic and journalistic. For our part, we will always repeat: of all the errors committed by all the sections, the greatest was committed by the Spanish section, which did not have the sense to join the Socialist Party in time at the beginning of the preparation for the armed struggle. . . .

An excerpt from a letter to the International Secretariat, published in *Bulletin intérieur* du Groupe bolchevik-léniniste de la SFIO (French Socialist Party), no. 4, January 1935. Translated for this volume from the French by Naomi Allen.

47   *LETTER TO A COMRADE*

October 18, 1935
Comrade:

The most recent issue of *La Batalla*[64] contains the manifesto of the Unification Congress of the Workers and Peasants Bloc with the Left Communists. I direct your attention to the one paragraph that speaks of international affiliation.

From the personal archives of Jean Rous; printed by permission. Unsigned. Translated for this volume from the French by Naomi Allen. In this letter, Trotsky takes as his point of departure an error in transiation. The phrase in the POUM's international resolution which was translated as "works objectively for the reconstruction of the unity of the revolutionary forces" should have been translated as "whose objective is to work for the reconstruction of the revolutionary forces."

The new party claims adherence to the [London Bureau or] Revolutionary Socialist Unity (IAG).[65] It is natural for Spain as it was natural for Holland; in these two cases, the majority had belonged to the IAG before the fusion. But the explanation of this adherence in the manifesto is most inadequate. The document affirms that this international organization (IAG) "works objectively for the reconstruction of the unity of revolutionary forces on a new foundation." What does this "objectively" mean? One could say that the proletariat is *objectively* forced to take the road of revolution: by that, one would be referring to the laws of capitalist development. But how can one speak of the same "objective" necessity for small propaganda organizations? The whole meaning of their existence is in their *subjective* effort: What is their program? What is their goal? These subjective criteria determine entirely the role that they *can* play in the workers' movement.

But precisely these decisive questions are unanswered. They speak only of "revolutionary unity on a new foundation." But we are interested in knowing what this "new foundation" is. That of the SAP or that of revolutionary Marxism and of the Fourth International? In the Dutch party, a bitter struggle is developing on this question. The longer the new Spanish party refuses to make its formulas precise in this discussion, the more heated and destructive the conflict that will inevitably engulf the contradictory tendencies.

We can only insist in a friendly way on the need for theoretical and political precision in the interests of the future of the new Spanish party.

48   *THE TREACHERY OF THE POUM*

January 23, 1936

The Spanish organization of "Left Communists," which was always a muddled organization, after countless vacillations to the right and to the left, merged with the Catalan Federation

---

From the *New Militant*, February 15, 1936. In 1934 the CLA merged with the American Workers Party of A. J. Muste and the new group was called the Workers Party. Its newspaper was the *New Militant*.

of Maurín into a party of "Marxist (?) Unification" on a centrist program. Some of our own periodicals, misled by this name, have written about this party as though it were drawing close to the Fourth International. There is nothing more dangerous than to exaggerate one's own forces with the aid of . . . a credulous imagination. Reality will not be restrained thereby from bringing cruel disillusion!

The newspapers report that in Spain all the "left" parties, both bourgeois and working class, have made an electoral bloc on the basis of a *common program,* which in the nature of things differs in no way from the program of the French Popular Front and all other fake programs of the same type. Here we find "reform of the tribunal of constitutional guarantees," as well as rigid support of the "principle of authority" (!), as well as the "freeing of justice from all influences of a political and economic order" (the freeing of capitalist justice from the influence of capital!). And more of the same. The program records the *rejection* of the nationalization of the land by the bourgeois republican members of the bloc, but "in return," along with the customary cheap promises in favor of the peasantry (credits, higher prices for agricultural products, etc.), the program declares for the "recovery (!) of industry" and protection for small industry and petty merchants. Then follows the inevitable "control over the banks," which — since the bourgeois republicans, according to the text of the program, reject workers' control — boils down to control over the banks . . . by the bankers themselves, through the medium of their parliamentary agents like Azaña and similar gentlemen. Finally, the foreign policy of Spain will be laid down in accordance with the "principles and methods of the League of Nations." Is anything left out?

Signatories to this infamous document are the representatives of two left bourgeois parties, the Socialist Party, the General Workers Union (UGT), the Communist Party (of course!), the Socialist Youth (too bad!), "Syndicalist Party" (Pestaña), and finally the "Workers Party of Marxist Unification" [POUM] (Juan Andrade).[66]

Most of these parties stood at the head of the Spanish revolution during the years of its upsurge and they did everything in their power to betray it and trample it underfoot. The new angle is the signature of the party of Maurín-Nin-Andrade. The former Spanish "Left Communists" have turned into a mere tail of the "left" bourgeoisie. It is hard to conceive of a more ignominious downfall!

A few months ago in Madrid, Juan Andrade's book was published, *The Reformist Bureaucracy and the Labor Movement*, which contains, along with quotations from Marx, Engels, Lenin, and other authors, an analysis of the causes underlying the degeneration of the labor bureaucracy. Juan Andrade forwarded his book to me twice, each time with glowing dedications, in which he calls me his "leader and teacher." This fact, which under different conditions would have only made me happy, compels me at present to announce all the more decisively in public that I never taught anybody *political betrayal*. And Andrade's conduct is nothing else than *betrayal of the proletariat for the sake of an alliance with the bourgeoisie*.

In this connection, it is in order to recall that the Spanish "Left Communists," as their very name indicates, posed on every appropriate occasion as incorruptible revolutionists. In particular, they thunderously condemned the French Bolshevik-Leninists for entering the Socialist Party. Never! Under no conditions! To enter temporarily into a mass political organization in order to carry on an uncompromising struggle in its ranks against the reformist leaders for the banner of the proletarian revolution — that is opportunism; but to conclude a political alliance with the leaders of a reformist party on the basis of a deliberately dishonest program serving to dupe the masses and cover up for the bourgeoisie — that is valor! Can there be any greater debasement and prostitution of Marxism?

The POUM is a member of the celebrated London Bureau of "Revolutionary Socialist Parties" (the former IAG). The leadership of this bureau is now in the hands of Fenner Brockway, secretary of the Independent Labour Party (ILP).[67] We have already written that, despite the antiquated and apparently incurable pacifist prejudices of Maxton[68] and others, the ILP has taken an honest revolutionary position on the question of the League of Nations and its sanctions. Each of us has read with pleasure a number of excellent articles in the *New Leader*. During the last parliamentary elections, the Independent Labour Party refused to give even electoral support to the Labourites, precisely because the latter supported the League of Nations. In itself this refusal was a tactical error. Wherever the ILP was unable to run its own candidates, it should have supported a Labour candidate against a Tory. But this is incidental. In any case, even talk of any "common programs" with the Labourites was excluded. Internationalists would have combined support in elections with an exposure of the crawling of the British social patriots before the League of Nations and its "sanctions."

We take the liberty of putting a question to Fenner Brockway: Just what is the purpose of this "International" of which he is the secretary? The British section of this "International" rejects giving even mere electoral support to Labour candidates if they support the League of Nations. The Spanish section concludes a bloc with *bourgeois* parties on a common program of support to the League of Nations. Is not this the extreme in the domain of contradictions, confusion, and bankruptcy? There is no war as yet, but the sections of the London "International" are already pulling in completely opposite directions. What will happen to them when the ominous events break?

But let us return to the Spanish party of "Marxist Unification." How ironic is the name "Marxist Unification" . . . with the bourgeoisie. The Spanish "Left Communists" (Andrés Nin, Juan Andrade, and others) have more than once tried to parry our criticism of their collaborationist policies by citing our lack of understanding of the "special conditions" in Spain. This is the customary argument put to use by all opportunists. But the first duty of a genuine proletarian revolutionist lies in translating the *special* conditions of his country into the international language of Marxism, which is understandable even beyond the confines of one's own country.*

But today there is no need for these theoretical arguments. The bloc of leaders of the Spanish working class with the left bourgeoisie does not include in it anything "national," for it does not differ in the least from the "Popular Front" in France, Czechoslovakia, Brazil, or China. The POUM is merely slavishly conducting the same policy that the Seventh Congress of the Comintern foisted on all its sections, absolutely inde-

---

* In search of a justification for their policy, Maurin and Nin point to the Spanish electoral system that makes it exceptionally difficult for a new party to field independent candidates (see the resolution of the Central Committee, *La Batalla*, number 234). But this argument is worthless. Electoral *technique* cannot justify the *politics* of betrayal, which a *joint program* with the bourgeoisie amounts to. — L. T.

pendently of their "national peculiarities."[69] The real difference in the Spanish policy this time lies only in the fact that a section of the London International has also adhered officially to the bloc with the bourgeoisie. So much the worse for it. As far as we are concerned, we prefer clarity. In Spain, genuine revolutionists will no doubt be found who will mercilessly expose the betrayal of Maurín, Nin, Andrade, and their associates, and lay the foundation for the Spanish section of the Fourth International!

49

TASKS OF THE FOURTH INTERNATIONAL IN SPAIN

April 12, 1936

The situation in Spain has again become revolutionary.

The development of the Spanish revolution is taking place at a slow tempo. For this reason, the revolutionary elements have acquired a fairly long period of time in which to take shape, to rally the vanguard around themselves, in order to measure up to their task at the decisive moment. We must now say openly that the Spanish "Left Communists" have allowed this exceptionally favorable interval to slip by, and have revealed themselves to be in no way better than the Socialist and "Communist" traitors. Not that there was any lack of warning. All the greater therefore is the guilt of Andrés Nin, Juan Andrade, and the others. With a correct policy, the "Left Communists" as a section of the Fourth International might have been at the head of the Spanish proletariat today. Instead, they are vegetating in the confused organization of Maurín — without a program, without perspectives, and without any political significance. Marxist action in Spain can begin only by means of an irreconcible condemnation of the whole policy of Andrés Nin and Andrade, which was and remains not only false but also criminal.

What does the removal of President Zamora mean? It means that political developments have once more entered into an acute stage. Zamora was, so to speak, the stable pole of the

A letter to a Spanish comrade. From the *New Militant*, May 2, 1936.

ruling echelons. Under different conditions, he played the same role that Hindenburg played in Germany for a certain period of time, that is, during the time when the reaction (even the Nazis) on one side, and the Social Democracy on the other placed their hopes in him.

Modern Bonapartism is the expression of the most extreme class antagonisms in the period when these antagonisms have not yet led to *open* struggle. Bonapartism may find its point of support in the quasi-parliamentary government, but also for that matter in the "supraparty" president; this depends exclusively on the circumstances. Zamora was the representative of the Bonapartist equilibrium. The sharpening of the antagonism led to a state of affairs in which both of the main camps sought first to use Zamora and then to get rid of him. The right wing did not succeed in doing this ᶜin its time, but the "Popular Front" did. This means, however, the beginning of an *acute revolutionary period.*

Both the profound ferment in the masses and the continual violent explosions demonstrate that the workers of town and country, as well as the poor peasants, deceived over and over again, are continually directing all their forces toward a revolutionary solution. And what role does the Popular Front play in the face of this powerful movement? The role of a gigantic *brake*, built and set into motion by traitors and servile scum. And only yesterday Juan Andrade signed the thoroughly despicable program of this Popular Front!

After Zamora's removal, Azaña, hand in hand with the new president of the republic, must take over the role of the stable Bonapartist pole; that is, he must try to elevate himself above the two camps in order to be better able to direct the arms of the state against those revolutionary masses who assisted him to power. The workers' organizations, however, remain completely enmeshed in the net of the Popular Front. The convulsions of the revolutionary masses (without a program, without a leadership worthy of confidence) thus threaten to throw the gates wide open to the counterrevolutionary dictatorship!

That the workers are driving ahead in a revolutionary direction is shown by the development of all their organizations, most particularly by that of the Socialist Party and the Socialist Youth. Two years ago we raised the question of the entry of the Spanish Bolshevik-Leninists into the Socialist Party.

This proposal was rejected by the Andrés Nins and Andrades with the disdain of conservative philistines: they wanted "independence" at all costs, because it left them in peace and put them under no obligations. And yet, affiliation to the Socialist Party in Spain would have yielded immeasurably better results under the given circumstances than was the case, for example, in France (on the condition, of course, that in Spain the terrible mistakes committed by the leading French comrades had been averted). Meanwhile, however, Andrade and Nin united with the confusionist Maurín, in order jointly to trot along behind the Popular Front.* The Socialist workers, however, in their striving for revolutionary clarity, fell victim to the Stalinist deceivers. The fusion of the two youth organizations [Socialist and Stalinist] signifies that the best revolutionary energies will be abused and dissipated by the Comintern's mercenaries. And the "great" revolutionists, Andrés Nin and Andrade, remain on the sidelines in order to carry on, together with Maurín, completely impotent propaganda for the "democratic socialist" revolution, that is, for a social democratic betrayal.**

---

* The "turn" of *La Batalla* toward the Popular Front does not inspire confidence. One cannot say on Monday that the League of Nations is a band of brigands; on Tuesday urge voters to vote for the program of the League of Nations; on Wednesday explain that yesterday it was only a question of electoral action, and that today one has to resume one's own program. The serious worker must ask: and what are these people going to say on Thursday and Friday? Maurín appears to be the very incarnation of a petty-bourgeois revolutionist: superficial, agile, and versatile. He studies nothing, he understands little, and he spreads confusion all around him. — L. T.

** Marx wrote in 1876 on the falseness of the term "Social Democrat": Socialism cannot be subordinated to democracy. Socialism (or communism) is enough for us. "Democracy" has nothing to do with it. Since then, the October Revolution has vigorously demonstrated that the socialist revolution cannot be carried out within the framework of democracy. The "democratic" revolution and the socialist revolution are on opposite sides of the barricades. The Third International theoretically confirmed this experience. The "democratic" revolution in Spain has already been carried out. The Popular Front is renewing it. The personification of the "democratic" revolution in Spain is Azaña, with or without Caballero. The socialist revolution is yet to be made in uncompromising struggle against the "democratic" revolution and its Popular Front. What does this "synthesis," "democratic socialist revolution" mean? Nothing at all. It is only an eclectic hodge-podge. — L. T.

Nobody can know what form the next period in Spain will take. In any case, the upsurge that has borne the clique of the Popular Front to power is too mighty to ebb in a short period of time and to leave the battlefield free to the reaction. The truly revolutionary elements still have a certain period of time, not too long, to be sure, in which to take stock of themselves, gather their forces, and prepare for the future. This refers above all to the Spanish supporters of the Fourth International. Their tasks are as clear as day:

1. To condemn and denounce mercilessly before the masses the policy of *all* the leaders participating in the Popular Front.

2. To grasp in full the wretchedness of the leadership of the "Workers Party of Marxist Unification" and especially of the former "Left Communists" — Andrés Nin, Andrade, etc. — and to portray them clearly before the eyes of all the advanced workers.

3. To rally around the banner of the Fourth International on the basis of the "Open Letter."[70]

4. To join the Socialist Party and the United Youth in order to work there as a faction in the spirit of Bolshevism.

5. To establish fractions and other nuclei in the trade unions and other mass organizations.

6. To direct their main attention to the spontaneous and semi-spontaneous mass movements, to study their general traits, that is, to study the temperature of the masses and not the temperature of the parliamentary cliques.

7. To be present in every struggle so as to give it clear expression.

8. To insist always on having the fighting masses form and constantly expand their committees of action (juntas, soviets), elected ad hoc.

9. To counterpose the program of the conquest of power, the dictatorship of the proletariat, and the social revolution to all hybrid programs (à la Caballero, or à la Maurín).

This is the real road of the proletarian revolution. There is no other.

50 *IS A RAPPROCHEMENT WITH NIN POSSIBLE? I*

June 3, 1936

. . . If I have understood your letter from Paris, you are dissatisfied with our behavior toward Andrés Nin, behavior that you find "sectarian." You do not and cannot know the political and personal history of our relations.

You can easily imagine how happy I was when Nin arrived abroad. For several years, I corresponded with him quite regularly. Some of my letters were veritable "treatises" on the subject of the living revolution, in which Nin could and should have played an active role. I think that my letters to Nin over a period of two or three years would make up a volume of several hundred pages: that should indicate how important I regarded Nin and friendly relations with him. In his answers, Nin affirmed over and over again his agreement in theory, but he always avoided discussing practical problems. He asked me abstract questions about soviets, about democracy, etc. . . . but he never said one word about the general strikes that were occurring in Catalonia.

Of course, no one is obligated to be a revolutionary. But Nin was the head of the Spanish Bolshevik-Leninists, and by that fact alone, he had a serious responsibility, which he failed to carry out in practice, all the while throwing dust in my

---

Excerpt from a letter to Victor Serge. French translation provided by Pierre Broué, with the authorization of Colette Chambelland and Jean Maitron, who are preparing a complete edition of Serge's correspondence, the originals of which are in the archives of the Musée social. Translated for this volume from the French by Naomi Allen.

Victor Serge (1890-1947) was born in Belgium of Russian parents and became an anarchist in his youth, for which he was sentenced to five years in prison. Attracted to Bolshevism after the 1917 revolution, he moved to the Soviet Union and worked for the Comintern. Arrested as an Oppositionist and then freed in 1928, he was rearrested in 1933. Thanks to a campaign by intellectuals in France, he was released and allowed to leave the country in 1936. He soon developed differences with the Fourth Internationalist movement, especially over the POUM, and left. He wrote several important historical works, as well as novels, including *From Lenin to Stalin, The Birth of Our Power, Memoirs of a Revolutionary*, and *Russia: Twenty Years After*.

eyes. Believe me, dear friend, I have a certain gift for these things: if I am guilty of anything with regard to Nin, it is of having nourished illusions for too long on his account, and thereby of having given him the opportunity of maintaining under the banner of Bolshevism-Leninism the passivity and confusionism of which there is already a surfeit in the Spanish workers' movement — and I mean in its highest echelons. If in Spain there had been, instead of Nin, a serious revolutionary worker like Lesoil or Vereecken,[71] it would have been possible, during those years of revolution, to accomplish significant work there.

Pushed by the ambiguity of his position, Nin systematically supported in all countries those who, for one reason or another, launched a struggle against us and generally ended up as pure and simple renegades. How did the rupture come about? Nin announced that he was absolutely opposed to the tactical entry of our comrades into the French Socialist Party. Then, after long hesitations, he declared that in France it was a correct tactic and that he should act in the same way in Spain. But instead of that, he joined with the provincial organization of Maurín, which had no perspective at all, but which allowed him to lead a peaceful existence. Our International Secretariat wrote him a critical letter. Nin responded by breaking off relations and publishing something on the subject in a special bulletin.

If I were not afraid of wasting your time, I would send you the file of my correspondence with Nin; I have kept copies of all my letters. I am sure that you, like other comrades who have become familiar with this correspondence, would accuse me of excessive patience, a "conciliatory spirit," and not of sectarianism. . . .

51   *IS A RAPPROCHEMENT WITH NIN POSSIBLE? II*

June 5, 1936

. . . In my last letter, there were some omissions. Let us start with Nin. If you think that there is some possibility of his returning to us, why wouldn't you try to get him back? I personally cherish no hope of seeing Nin become a revolutionary, but I could be wrong. Find out for yourself, if you think it necessary. I could only approve of that step.

Of course, we could not be satisfied with verbal assurances from Nin (at which he is quite prolific), but with actual deeds. At this moment, Nin is allied with the sworn enemies of the Fourth International, who hide their petty-bourgeois hatred of revolutionary Marxism behind hollow phrases on the subject of "organizational" differences, as if serious people could break with revolutionaries and ally themselves with opportunists because of secondary differences.

If Nin wants to return to us, then he must openly raise the banner of the Fourth International in Spain. The pretexts that he invokes for refusing to do so are in the same class as those that Blum invokes with regard to the class struggle, which, according to him, while being a good thing in general, is, however, not appropriate for our epoch. Blum's politics consist of class collaboration, although "in theory" he recognizes the class struggle. Nin recognizes the Fourth International in words, but in deeds he helps Maurín, Walcher, Maxton, and his other allies wage a bitter struggle against the Fourth International, exactly like the struggle that the pacifists like Longuet and Ledebour waged against the revolutionary internationalist partisans of the Third International during the last war.[72] . . .

Excerpt from a letter to Victor Serge. French translation provided by Pierre Broué, with the authorization of Colette Chambelland and Jean Maitron. Translated for this volume from the French by Naomi Allen.

52 *THE POUM AND THE POPULAR FRONT*

July 16, 1936

7) I now come to Spain. In one of the latest letters, Comrade Sneevliet in the name of the Central Committee of the party took up the defense of the Maurín-Nin party against my allegedly exaggerated or too sharp attacks.[73] This appears to me not only unjustified but also incomprehensible. The struggle with Maurín does not date from yesterday. His *entire* policy during the revolution was nationalistic-provincial and petty bourgeois; reactionary in its entire essence. I recorded this fact publicly more than once from the beginning of the revolution on. Nin, too, with the vacillations proper to him, acknowledged this. The program of the "democratic-socialist" revolution is a legitimate child of the Maurínist spirit; it corresponds essentially to the program of a Blum and not of a Lenin.

As for Nin, during the whole revolution he proved to be a completely passive dilettante who does not in the slightest degree think of actually participating in the mass struggle, of winning the masses, of leading them to the revolution, etc. He contented himself with hypercritical little articles on Stalinists, on Socialists, etc. This is now a very cheap commodity! During the series of general strikes in Barcelona he wrote me letters on all conceivable questions but did not so much as mention the general strikes and his own role in them. In the course of those years we exchanged hundreds of letters. I always tried to elicit from him not empty literary observations on everything and nothing, but practical suggestions for the revolutionary struggle. To my concrete questions, he always replied: "as to that, I shall write in my next letter." This "next letter," however, never arrived — for years.

The greatest misfortune for the Spanish section was the fact

Excerpt from a letter to the Central Committee of the RSAP (Revolutionary Socialist Workers Party), the Dutch section of the Fourth Internationalist movement. From the *Internal Bulletin,* Socialist Workers Party, no. 5, August 1938. The full letter is in *Writings of Leon Trotsky* (1935-36). The Socialist Workers Party was founded on New Years Day by the left-wing members who had been expelled from the American Socialist Party.

that a man with a name, with a certain past and the halo of a martyr of Stalinism, stood at its head and all the while led it wrongly and paralyzed it.

The splendid Socialist Youth came spontaneously to the idea of the Fourth International. To all our urgings that all attention be devoted to the Socialist Youth, we received only hollow evasions. Nin was concerned with the "independence" of the Spanish section, that is, with his own passivity, with his own petty political comfort; he didn't want his captious dilettantism to be disturbed by great events. The Socialist Youth then passed over almost completely into the Stalinist camp. The lads who called themselves Bolshevik-Leninists and who permitted this, or better yet, who caused this, have to be stigmatized forever as criminals against the revolution.

At the moment when Nin's bankruptcy became clear even to his own supporters, he united with the nationalist-Catalan philistine Maurín, breaking off all relations with us by the declaration that "the International Secretariat understands nothing of Spanish affairs." In reality Nin understands nothing of revolutionary policy or of Marxism.

The new party soon found itself in the tow of Azaña. But to say about this fact: "it is only a small, temporary technical electoral agreement," seems to me to be absolutely inadmissible. The party undersigned the most miserable of all Popular Front programs of Azaña and simultaneously also its death sentence for years to come. For at every attempt at criticism of the Popular Front (and Maurín-Nin are now making such desperate attempts) they will always receive the stereotyped reply from the radical bourgeois, from the Social Democrats and the communists: But didn't you yourselves take part in the creation of the Popular Front and sign its program? And if these gentlemen then try to make use of the rotten subterfuge: "it was only a technical maneuver of our party"— they will only make themselves ridiculous.

These people have completely paralyzed themselves, even if they were now unexpectedly to display a revolutionary will, which is not, however, the case. The small crimes and betrayals, which remain almost unobserved in normal times, find a mighty repercussion in the time of revolution. It should never be forgotten that the revolution creates special acoustic conditions. All in all, I cannot understand how it is that extenuating circumstances are sought for the Spanish betrayers, while at the same time our Belgian friends, who are fighting with preeminent courage against the enormous POB machine and the Stalinists, and who have quite substantial successes to show, are publicly disparaged in the *Nieuwe Fakkel*.[74]

8) In the latest number of *La Batalla* there is an appeal of the Maurín-Nin party to our South American sections, which represents an attempt to group the latter around the so-called Party of Marxist Unification on a purely national basis. Like every section of the London Bureau, the Spanish "Marxist" party of confusion tries to penetrate the ranks of the Fourth International, to split them, etc. There you have the little cur who snaps at our heels. Must we not say openly to our South American organizations, which still have in their ranks SAPist parliamentarians, etc., what the difference is between us and the London Bureau and why Nin breaks with us in Europe and wants to appear in South America as the pious unifier of all the revolutionary forces? This contemptible hypocrisy, which always characterizes centrism, must be mercilessly exposed. This alone would suffice to prove the *absolute necessity* of our theses on the London Bureau.

9) The question of questions at present is the Popular Front. The left centrists seek to present this question as a tactical or even as a technical maneuver, so as to be able to peddle their wares in the shadow of the Popular Front. In reality, the Popular Front is the *main question of proletarian class strategy* for this epoch. It also offers the best criterion for the difference between Bolshevism and Menshevism. For it is often forgotten that the greatest historical example of the Popular Front is the February 1917 revolution. From February to October, the Mensheviks and the Social Revolutionaries, who represent a very good parallel to the "Communists" and the Social Democrats, were in the closest alliance and in a permanent coalition with the bourgeois party of the Cadets,[75] together with whom they formed a series of coalition governments. Under the sign of this Popular Front stood the whole mass of the people, including the workers', peasants', and soldiers' councils. To be sure, the Bolsheviks participated in the councils. But they did not make the slightest concession to the Popular Front. Their demand was *to break* this Popular Front, to destroy the alliance with the Cadets, and to create a genuine workers' and peasants' government.

All the Popular Fronts in Europe are only a pale copy and often a caricature of the Russian Popular Front of 1917, which could, after all, lay claim to a much greater justification for its existence, for it was still a question of the struggle against czarism and the remnants of feudalism.

PART III:

Civil War

The new government was hardly installed before the generals began to plan its overthrow. Franco, who had masterminded the assault on Oviedo in October 1934, was transferred by Azaña to a relatively unimportant command in the Canary Islands. Before he took up his post, Franco established links with the military-monarchist conspirators in General Mola's headquarters.

In April, Mola issued a secret circular to his supporters calling for preparations for a coup to be ready in twenty days. Mola wrote:

> It will be borne in mind that the action, in order to crush as soon as possible a strong and well-organized enemy, will have to be very violent. Hence, all directors of political parties, societies or unions not pledged to the [fascist] Movement will be imprisoned; such people will be administered exemplary punishments so that movements of rebellion or strikes will be strangled.

Villagers in Estremadura, discontented with the slow pace of the land reform, began to seize large tracts of land. The government ordered the Civil Guard against the peasants.

Seeking to consolidate its power against the right as well as against the left, the Popular Front used its votes in the Cortes in April to depose Alcalá Zamora as president of the republic, replacing him in May with Azaña, while Casares Quiroga became prime minister.

Franco, meanwhile, arranged to be flown secretly to North Africa, where he would take command of the Moroccan legionnaires and begin the fascist revolt.

The uprising began on July 17. The garrisons on the mainland followed suit between the 18th and the 21st. The fascists captured roughly a third of Spain in the initial week, mainly in the northwest, with the exception of the Basque provinces.

Azaña, after dropping Casares Quiroga and his conservative

226 *The Spanish Revolution (1931-39)*

successor Martínez Barrio as prime ministers, settled on José Giral, an undistinguished professor of chemistry, to lead the republic in civil war. This third government in as many days still was composed entirely of representatives of the bourgeois parties. The principal leaders of the Socialist and Communist parties and the Anarchist FAI, however, pledged to support the Popular Front. This regime was to last until September, when Giral was replaced by Largo Caballero and the Socialist and Communist parties were brought directly into the cabinet. The Anarchists, represented by García Oliver, Federica Montseny, Juan Peiro, and Juan López Sánchez, entered the government in November during the siege of Madrid. At the same time, the republican government fled Madrid for Valencia.

The CP-inspired attempt to seize the Barcelona telephone exchange from the Anarchist workers took place on May 2, 1937, followed by the fall of Largo Caballero on the 15th and the appointment of Juan Negrín as prime minister on the 17th. In October 1937, after the crushing of the POUM, Negrín moved the central government again, this time to Barcelona.

After the suppression of the POUM, the Communist Party had accomplished the job that the republican liberals and Social Democrats had feared to attempt, and the CP was no longer so useful to the bourgeois government. Negrín and Prieto, who was now war minister, began to maneuver to restrict the power of the CP, although the Stalinists were still quite strong in the governmental apparatus. In October 1937 Prieto prohibited officers from attending meetings of political parties and abolished many of the military posts of commissar, held mainly by Stalinists.

Negrín also refused the CP's demand for new elections to the Cortes, in which the Communist Party was still represented by only sixteen members.

From December 1937 through February 1938 came the battle of Teruel, in which the republican forces took the city from the fascists and then lost it again at terrible cost. The fascists claimed to have found 10,000 republican dead when they finally re-entered the city. The CP began a campaign for the ouster of Prieto, whom they blamed for the defeat. Prieto was dismissed on April 8, but that did not stop the fascist advance in Catalonia and Valencia. At the same time, the fascist general Alonso Vega took the town of Vinaroz on the Mediterranean coast. This victory was consolidated with the fall of Castellón on June 14, and the republic was permanently cut in two.

The battle of the Ebro, the last major offensive of the republic, began on the night of July 24-25. The republican advance was contained by August 2. After that the fascists began to retake the ground they had lost. The withdrawal of the International Brigades from Spain followed in November.

By late 1938 industrial production began to collapse in the republic, in part because of the now nearly complete fascist naval blockade, but also in large part because of the demoralization of the ranks of the Anarchist workers under the persecution of the Stalinist-controlled police.

In October the surviving leaders of the POUM were brought to trial, more than a year after their arrest. Caballero and other prominent figures testified in defense of the POUM, and the Stalinists' case collapsed.

On December 23, the fascists began the final assault on Catalonia, taking Barcelona on January 26, 1939. The refugees who fled across the border into France numbered some 500,-000. Most of the republican government, including Azaña and Companys, fled with them.

France and Britain, who had refused to sell arms to the republic throughout the war, officially recognized Franco's government on February 27, while the loyalists still held a third of the country.

At this point the "republican" officer corps, led by Colonel Casado in Madrid, decided to make their own peace with Franco behind the backs of the republican government. Casado banned the Communist Party press in Madrid for urging continued resistance. The CP had by this time decimated the radicalized working class and had few forces with which to resist when the bourgeois army turned against it. General José Miaja Menant, an old career officer who had been singled out for special support by the Communist Party, joined Casado in the treacherous effort to establish a new government of capitulation in Madrid. At midnight on March 4 the plotters broadcast a manifesto on Madrid radio repudiating the Negrín government and proposing peace with Franco. Casado ordered the arrest of members of the government and of the Communist Party. Negrín, along with the top leaders of the CP and the remaining Russian advisors, chose this moment to make their escape from Spain, and on March 6 they flew to France.

Meanwhile in Madrid heavy fighting broke out between units loyal to Casado and those commanded by the Communist Party. The CP had the upper hand, but leaderless, its local commanders lost the initiative, and Casado drove them from Madrid and opened negotiations with Franco.

This last demoralizing betrayal finished the republic. The fascists began a final advance uncontested by the republican troops, who began to disband en masse. The end came on March 28, 1939.

A Note on Trotsky's Exile: The Spanish civil war was only a month old when the Soviet government startled the world by staging the first of three big Moscow trials in which the chief defendant (in absentia) was Trotsky, accused of trying to restore capitalism in the USSR with the support of the imperialists. Trotsky's efforts to defend himself were quickly stifled by the Norwegian government, which submitted to Soviet pressure and interned him until the end of 1936. The first six articles in Part III were written in Norway before he was forbidden to talk to reporters or write letters and public articles.

Trotsky's final place of exile was Mexico, where he arrived in January 1937. All the remaining articles in Part III were written in Coyoacán, a suburb of Mexico City, where he lived until he was assassinated by an agent of Stalin in August 1940. Many of them were written to influence internal disputes over Spain that were taking place in his movement, which had reorganized itself as the Fourth International in September 1938.

53 *THE POPULAR FRONT IN CIVIL WAR*

July 1936

> The collision of the two camps in France, Belgium, and Spain is absolutely inevitable. The more the leaders of the Popular Front "reconcile" the class antagonisms and dampen the revolutionary struggle, the more explosive and convulsive character will it assume in the immediate future, the more sacrifices it will cause, and the more defenseless the proletariat will find itself against fascism. ["The New Revolutionary Upsurge and the Tasks of the Fourth International," paragraph 16.]

The events have brought a confirmation of this prediction even before the present theses could be published.

The July days deepen and supplement the lessons of the June days in France with exceptional force. For the second time in five years, the coalition of the labor parties with the radical bourgeoisie has brought the revolution to the edge of the abyss. Incapable of solving a single one of the tasks posed by the revolution, since all these tasks boil down to one, namely, the crushing of the bourgeoisie, the Popular Front renders the existence of the bourgeois regime impossible and thereby provokes the fascist coup d'etat. By lulling the workers and peasants with parliamentary illusions, by paralyzing their will to struggle, the Popular Front creates the favorable conditions for the victory of fascism. The policy of coalition with the bourgeoisie must be paid for by the proletariat with years of new torments and sacrifice, if not by decades of fascist terror.

The Popular Front government reveals its total inadequacy precisely at the most critical moment; one ministerial crisis follows the other because the bourgeois Radicals fear the armed workers more than they do the fascists. The civil war takes

---

This is the postscript to "The New Revolutionary Upsurge and the Tasks of the Fourth International," a resolution written by Trotsky and adopted by an international conference in Geneva in July 1936. It was published for the International Secretariat by the Workers Party of Canada, and was reprinted in the *Internal Bulletin*, SWP, no. 4, 1938. The full text of the resolution is in *Writings of Leon Trotsky* (1935-36).

on a lingering character. Whatever the immediate outcome of the civil war in Spain may be, it strikes a death blow at the Popular Front in France and other countries. It must henceforth become clear to every French worker that the bloc with the Radicals signifies the legal preparation of a military coup d'etat by the French general staff under cover of the minister of war Daladier.

The administrative dissolution of the fascist leagues while the bourgeois state apparatus is maintained, as the Spanish example shows, is a lie and a deception. Only the armed workers can resist fascism. The conquest of power by the proletariat is possible only on the road of armed insurrection against the state apparatus of the bourgeoisie. The smashing of this apparatus and its replacement by workers', soldiers', and peasants' councils is the necessary condition for the fulfillment of the socialist program. Without carrying out these tasks, the proletariat and the petty bourgeoisie have no way out of misery and need, and no way of being saved from the new war.

54
LETTER TO THE
INTERNATIONAL SECRETARIAT

July 27, 1936
Dear Comrades:

The events in Spain, however they conclude (and I'm counting on a favorable outcome), will be of historic importance for the development of the Fourth International in France as everywhere.

The question of the Popular Front is now posed with absolute clarity before all the workers. Many French Socialists are asking themselves (see, for example, the article in *Le Populaire*

From Leon Trotsky, *Le Mouvement communiste en France,* 1919-1939, edited by Pierre Broué (Les Editions de Minuit, Paris, 1967). Previously published on August 15, 1936, in *La Lutte ouvrière*, the newspaper of the Revolutionary Socialist Party of Belgium, the Belgian section of the Fourth International. Translated for this volume from the French by Walter Blumenthal.

that miserable Maurice Paz):[1]* "Why is it that the leaders
the Spanish Popular Front, who have held power since
ebruary, did not take the necessary steps to deal with the
my? What a blunder! etc." What these people do not under-
and is that it is not a question of "a blunder" but entirely
ie of *class* interests. When the bourgeoisie is constrained
conclude an alliance between its left wing and the workers'
ganizations, it needs the officer corps more than ever as
counterweight—for the most important question, that is,
e question of the protection of property, is then posed.

This was no blunder at all! The Popular Front government
Spain was not a government, but simply a ministry. The
al government resided in the General Staff, in the banks,
c. The French Radicals[2] were authorized to form an al-
ance with the workers on condition that they did not touch
e officer corps. But as the workers continue to press their
emands, the entire state machine will ultimately come down
pon their heads. The SAPists consider the Popular Front
n enrichment of proletarian tactics. If they cannot see its
ass character, that is because they are good for nothing.
*he Radicals are seen only as the right wing of the Popular
'ront; in reality they are there to represent the ruling class,
nd it is through them that finance capital maintains its rule,
oth within the Popular Front and over the proletariat.*

In France, the question is posed more clearly and more
cutely than in Spain. Daladier keeps the army under his
rotection.[3] It is not a question of holding off the half-dozen
fficers who are fascist braggarts; the *entire* officer corps is
oroughly hostile to the working class. If you wish to hold
em off, then "you disorganize the army." But Hitler is at
ie gates! The bourgeoisie—and the Radical bourgeoisie in-
luded—cannot allow anyone to touch its officer corps. Neither
o the "Communists" want anyone touching it, for it is with
iis officers' corps that they must "defend" the Soviet Union.
nd tomorrow this same officer corps will attack the Pop-
lar Front—that is, above all, the working class—they will
stablish a military dictatorship and form an alliance with
litler against the USSR. In times like ours, rich in catas-
:ophes, at every turn of events the criminal consequences of

---

opportunist politics appear with ten times as much vigor!

Today we can also grasp more clearly the crime committed at the beginning of this year by the POUM leaders Maurín and Nin. Any thinking worker can and will ask these people: "Did you foresee nothing? How could you have signed the Popular Front program and have us put our confidence in Azaña and his associates, instead of instilling in us the greatest distrust in the Radical bourgeoisie? Now we must pay for your errors with our blood." The workers must feel particular anger towards Nin and his friends because they belonged to a tendency that a few years ago had provided a precise analysis of Popular Front politics, concretizing and clarifying it at each stage. And Nin cannot invoke ignorance as his excuse — a wretched excuse for any leader — because he ought to have at least read the documents he once signed.

The Spanish events will open new and great possibilities for the Fourth International in Spain and France as everywhere — precisely at the expense of the centrist tendencies. We have good reason to doubt that the London Bureau has enough strength, under present conditions, to call even its members alone to a "peace congress" in November. In any case, we haven't the least interest in promising our participation and in providing a certain authority to this congress of nobodies which may never see the light of day. We must turn our faces towards the great masses, make inroads into the mass organizations *at any price, by any means, without allowing ourselves to be influenced or paralyzed by a conservative intransigence.* But before these masses we must preserve our independence, avoid any compromise with vainglorious centrists, any erasing of borders between them and us — in a word, any criminal reconciliation.

With best of greetings,
Leon Trotsky

55

THE REACTIONARY COWARDICE OF THE POPULAR FRONT

July 30, 1936

Let's go on now to the question of Nin. Some people (for example, Rosmer) consider my sharp critique of his policies to be sectarian. If it is sectarianism, then all of Marxism is only sectarianism, since it is the doctrine of the class struggle and not of class collaboration. The present events in Spain in particular show how criminal was Nin's rapprochement with Azaña: the Spanish workers will now pay with thousands of lives for the reactionary cowardice of the Popular Front, which has continued to support with the people's money an army commanded by the executioners of the proletariat. Here it is a question, my dear Victor Serge, not of splitting hairs, but of the very essence of revolutionary socialism. If Nin today were to pull himself together and realize how discredited he is in the eyes of the workers, if he should draw all the necessary conclusions, then we would help him as a comrade; but we cannot permit the spirit of chumminess in politics.

From your amendments to the theses on the revolutionary upsurge, I got the idea that some important groups will be breaking away on the left of the Socialist and Communist parties (I have already alluded to that without developing the idea); on the other hand, I unfortunately cannot accept your other amendments, for I consider them fundamentally wrong. A marvelous historian of the Russian Revolution, you refuse, I do not know why, to apply its most important lessons to other countries. Everything you say about the Popular Front applies to the bloc of Mensheviks and Social Revolutionaries with the Cadets (the Russian "Radicals"), and yet, we led a merciless struggle against that Popular Front, which alone made it possible for us to win.

Your practical propositions concerning Spain are excellent and correspond completely to *our* line. But try to find a dozen people capable of accepting your propositions, not in words but in deeds, outside of our "sectarian" organization! The fact

Excerpt from a letter to Victor Serge. From *Le Mouvement communiste en France,* 1919-1939. Translated for this volume from the French by Naomi Allen.

that you put forward such magnificent *practical* propositions bears witness in my opinion to the fact that for all practical purposes we have our feet on common ground, and I am patiently awaiting your verification of your a priori conceptions in the living political experience, and your drawing the necessary conclusions from them. I do not doubt for a single instant that your conclusions will correspond with ours, conclusions that we have formulated *collectively,* in *different* countries, basing ourselves on the experience of *great* events. Despite our so-called sectarianism, we are steadily growing and expanding, while our critics have been able to build nothing.

That's enough for today. I have answered your frankness completely frankly. I think that we will follow that path in the future, to our mutual advantage. I clasp your hand warmly.

Leon Trotsky

56   *THE LESSON OF SPAIN*

July 30, 1936

Europe has become a harsh and terrible school for the proletariat. In one country after another events have unfolded that have exacted great and bloody sacrifices from the workers but have so far ended in victory for the enemies of the proletariat (Italy, Germany, Austria). The policy of the old labor parties clearly shows how *impossible* it is for them to lead the proletariat, how *incapable* they are of preparing for victory.

At the present time, while this is being written, the civil war in Spain has not yet terminated. The workers of the entire world feverishly await news of the victory of the Spanish proletariat. If this victory is won, as we firmly hope, it will be necessary to say: the workers have triumphed this time in spite of the fact that their leadership did everything to bring about

From the September 1936 *Socialist Appeal*, then the magazine of a left wing in the Socialist Party, which the Trotskyists had joined earlier that year.

their defeat. All the greater honor and glory to the Spanish working class!

In Spain, the Socialists and communists belong to the Popular Front, which already betrayed the revolution once, but which, thanks to the workers and peasants, once again attained victory, and in February created a "republican" government. Six months afterwards, the "republican" army took the field against the people. Thus it became clear that the Popular Front government had maintained the military caste with the people's money, furnished them with authority, power, and arms, and given them command over young workers and peasants, thereby facilitating the preparations for a crushing attack on the workers and peasants.

More than that, even now, in the midst of civil war, the Popular Front government does everything in its power to make victory doubly difficult. A civil war is waged, as everybody knows, not only with military but also with political weapons. From a purely military point of view, the Spanish revolution is much weaker than its enemy. Its strength lies in its ability to rouse the great masses to action. It can even take the army away from its reactionary officers. To accomplish this, it is only necessary to seriously and courageously advance the program of the socialist revolution.

It is necessary to proclaim that, from now on, the land, factories, and shops will pass from the hands of the capitalists into the hands of the people. It is necessary to move at once toward the realization of this program in those provinces where the workers are in power. The fascist army could not resist the influence of such a program for twenty-four hours; the soldiers would tie their officers hand and foot and turn them over to the nearest headquarters of the workers' militia. But the bourgeois ministers cannot accept such a program. Curbing the social revolution, they compel the workers and peasants to spill ten times as much of their own blood in the civil war. And to crown everything, these gentlemen expect to disarm the workers again after the victory and to force them to respect the sacred laws of private property. Such is the true essence of the policy of the Popular Front. Everything else is pure humbug, phrases, and lies!

Many supporters of the Popular Front now shake their heads reproachfully at the rulers of Madrid! Why didn't they foresee all this? Why didn't they purge the army in time? Why didn't they take the necessary measures? More than anywhere else, these criticisms are being voiced in France, where, however, the policy of the leaders of the Popular Front can in no way be distinguished from the policy of their Spanish colleagues. In spite of the harsh lesson of Spain, one can say in advance that the Léon Blum government will accomplish no serious purge of the army. Why? Because the workers' organizations remain in a coalition with the Radicals and consequently are the prisoners of the bourgeoisie.

It is naive to complain that the Spanish republicans or the Socialists or the communists foresaw nothing, let something slip. It is not at all a question of the perspicacity of this or that minister or leader, but of the general direction of the policy. The workers' party that enters into a political alliance with the radical bourgeoisie by that fact alone renounces the struggle against capitalist militarism. Bourgeois domination, that is to say, the maintenance of private property in the means of production, is inconceivable without the support of the armed forces for the exploiters. The officers' corps represents the guard of capital. Without this guard, the bourgeoisie could not maintain itself for a single day. The selection of the individuals, their education and training, make the officers as a distinctive group uncompromising enemies of socialism. Isolated exceptions change nothing. That is how things stand in all bourgeois countries. The danger lies not in the military braggarts and demagogues who openly appear as fascists; incomparably more menacing is the fact that at the approach of the proletarian revolution the officers' corps becomes the executioner of the proletariat. To eliminate four or five hundred reactionary agitators from the army means to leave everything basically as it was before. The officers' corps, in which is concentrated the centuries-old tradition of enslaving the people, must be dissolved, broken, crushed in its entirety, root and branch. The troops in the barracks commanded by the officers' caste must be replaced by the *people's militia,* that is, the democratic organization of the armed workers and peasants. There is no other solution. But such an army is incompatible with the domination of exploiters big and small. Can the republicans agree to such a measure? Not at all. The Popular Front government, that is to say, the government of the coalition of the workers with the bourgeoisie, is in its very essence a

government of capitulation to the bureaucracy and the officers. Such is the great lesson of the events in Spain, now
being paid for with thousands of human lives.

The political alliance of the working class leaders with the
bourgeoisie is disguised as the defense of the "republic." The
experience of Spain shows what this defense is in actuality.
The word "republican," like the word "democrat," is a deliberate charlatanism that serves to cover up class contradictions. The bourgeois is a republican so long as the republic
protects private property. And the workers utilize the republic to overthrow private property. The republic, in other words,
loses all its value to the bourgeois the moment it assumes
value for the workers. The Radical cannot enter into a bloc
with workers' parties without the assurance of support in the
officers' corps. It is no accident that Daladier is at the head
of the Ministry of War in France. The French bourgeoisie
has entrusted this post to him more than once and he has
never betrayed them. Only people like Maurice Paz or Marceau
Pivert[4] can believe that Daladier is capable of purging the
army of reactionaries and fascists, in other words, of dissolving the officers' corps. But no one takes such people seriously.

But here we are interrupted by the exclamation, "How can
one dissolve the officers' corps? Doesn't this mean destroying
the army and leaving the country disarmed in the face of
fascism? Hitler and Mussolini are only waiting for that!" All
these arguments are old and familiar. That's how the Cadets,
the Social Revolutionaries, and the Russian Mensheviks reasoned in 1917, and that's how the leaders of the Spanish Popular Front reasoned. The Spanish workers half-believed these
ratiocinations until they were convinced by experience that the
nearest fascist enemy was to be found in the Spanish fascist
army. Not for nothing did our old friend Karl Liebknecht teach:
"The main enemy is in our own country!"

L'Humanité tearfully begs that the army be purged of fascists. But what is this plea worth? When you vote credits to
maintain the officers' corps, when you enter into an alliance
with Daladier and through him with finance capital, confide
the army to Daladier, and at the same time demand that this
entirely capitalist army serve the "people" and not capital, then
you have either become a complete idiot or else you are consciously deceiving the working masses.

"But we've got to have an army," repeat the Socialist and

communist leaders, "because we must defend our democracy and with it the Soviet Union against Hitler!" After the lesson of Spain, it is not difficult to foresee the consequences of this policy for democracy as well as for the Soviet Union. Once they have found a favorable moment, the officers' corps, hand in hand with the dissolved fascist leagues, will assume the offensive against the working masses, and if victorious, will crush the miserable remnants of bourgeois democracy and extend their hands to Hitler for a common struggle against the USSR.

The articles appearing in *Le Populaire* and *L'Humanité* on the events in Spain fill one with rage and disgust. These people learn nothing. They do not want to learn. They consciously shut their eyes to the facts. The principal lesson for them is that it is necessary at all costs to maintain the "unity" of the Popular Front, that is to say, unity with the bourgeoisie and friendship with Daladier.

Unquestionably Daladier is a great "democrat." But can one doubt for a moment that side by side with the official work in Blum's ministry, he is working unofficially in the general staff of the officers' corps? There one finds serious people who look facts in the face, who do not get drunk on hollow rhetoric the way Blum does. These people are prepared for every eventuality. No doubt Daladier and the military leaders are coming to an understanding with respect to the necessary measures to take in case the workers take the road toward revolution. To be sure, the generals are of their own accord far ahead of Daladier. And among themselves the generals say: "Let's support Daladier until we are through with the workers, and then we will put a stronger man in his place." At the same time the Socialist and communist leaders repeat from day to day: "Our friend Daladier." The worker ought to reply to them: "Tell me who your friends are and I will tell you who you are." People who entrust the army to that old agent of capital, Daladier, are unworthy of the workers' confidence.

Certainly, the Spanish proletariat, like the French proletariat, does not want to remain disarmed before Mussolini and Hitler. But to defend themselves against these enemies, it is first necessary to crush the enemy in one's own country. It is impossible to overthrow the bourgeoisie without crushing the officers' corps. It is impossible to crush the officers' corps without overthrowing the bourgeoisie. In every victorious counterrevolution, the officers have played the decisive role. Every victorious revolution that had a profound social character destroyed the old officers' corps. This was the case in the Great French Revolution at the end of the eighteenth century, and this was the case in the October Revolution in 1917.

To decide on such a measure one must stop crawling on one's knees before the Radical bourgeoisie. A genuine alliance of workers and peasants must be created against the bourgeoisie, including the Radicals. One must have confidence in the strength, initiative, and courage of the proletariat, and the proletariat will know how to bring the soldier over to its side. This will be a genuine and not a fake alliance of workers, peasants, and soldiers. This very alliance is being created and tempered right now in the fire of civil war in Spain. The victory of the people means the end of the Popular Front and the beginning of Soviet Spain. The victorious social revolution in Spain will inevitably spread out over the rest of Europe. For the fascist hangmen of Italy and Germany, it will be incomparably more terrible than all the diplomatic pacts and all the military alliances.

57   *LETTER TO JEAN ROUS*

August 16, 1936
Dear Comrade:

I got your unexpected telegram. Unfortunately, it could be interpreted here as evidence of direct interference by me in Spanish affairs at this time when the question is pending —

From the December 5, 1970, issue of *Le Monde*, a Paris daily. Translation from the original French appears in the January 18, 1971, *Intercontinental Press*. Jean Rous (1908-   ) was the representative of the Trotskyist movement in Barcelona in 1936. This letter is Trotsky's response to a telegram from Rous transmitting a proposal from the POUM leaders to intervene on Trotsky's behalf to get him a visa to Spain, and inviting him to contribute regular articles to *La Batalla*. The letter never reached its destination because it was intercepted by Mussolini's agents in Barcelona. It was discovered in 1970 in the archives of the Italian police by the Italian historian Paolo Spriano.

so far as I know — of my being able to get a visa to return to Barcelona. Needless to say, I would be very happy to do so. Is this possible?

You are aware of the situation I have been subjected to here — the fascist attack on the one hand and the infamous TASS statement on the other.[5] I do not know what position the government will take. It doesn't have the slightest notion of the criminal infamy of the Stalin-Yagoda clique.[6]

Natalia and I would be completely ready to go at once to Barcelona. The matter — to succeed — must be approached with the greatest possible discretion.

You well understand that I cannot give you any advice from here. Direct armed struggle is now under way and the situation shifts from day to day. The level of information reaching me stands at zero. People are talking about the disappearance of Maurín. What does it mean? I hope he hasn't been killed. As for Nin, Andrade, and the others, it would be criminal to let ourselves be guided now in this great struggle by memories of the preceding period. Even after the experiences we have had, if there are differences in program and method, these divergences must in no way impede a sincere and lasting rapprochement. Further experience would do the rest. As for me personally, I would be entirely ready to aid in the battle, if only as a mere observer from afar.

The question most on my mind concerns relations between the POUM and the syndicalists. It seems to me it would be extremely dangerous to let oneself be guided *exclusively* or even *primarily* by doctrinal considerations. At all costs, it is necessary to improve relations with the syndicalists, despite all their prejudices. The common enemy must be defeated. The confidence of the best syndicalists must be won in the course of the struggle. These considerations may certainly seem commonplace to you and I apologize in advance. I am not sufficiently familiar with the situation to offer any concrete advice. I would only like to note that before October we made every effort to work together even with the purest Anarchists.

The Kerensky government often tried to use the Bolsheviks against the Anarchists. Lenin resolutely opposed this. In that situation, he said, one Anarchist militant was worth more than a hundred hesitating Mensheviks. During the civil war forced on you by the fascists, the greatest danger is lack of decisiveness, a spirit of equivocation, in a word — Menshevism.

Again all this is too vague. I am willing to do everything to make my suggestions as precise as possible. But in order to do that, the distance separating us must be overcome. . . . For my part, I can pledge the sincerest desire to reach a mutual understanding with the comrades in struggle, in spite of all possible differences. It would be shameful pettiness to turn toward the past if the present and the future open the way for common struggle.

With the help of a dictionary, I will try to follow the course of battle at close range. But I will not be back home for four or five days.

My warmest greetings to all our friends and also and especially for those who feel they have reason to be dissatisfied with me.

[The following note was attached to the letter.]

My dear Rous:

You can show the attached letter — if you consider it useful — to Nin and the others. What I say in the letter is not at all a diplomatic maneuver. Once again flexibility must be combined with firmness. I feel bound hand and foot. Best wishes from Natalia and me.

Sincerely,
L. T.

58   *FOR COLLABORATION IN CATALONIA*

August 18, 1936
Dear Victor Lvovich:

. . . What you write me about the Spanish Anarchists, or more exactly the Catalan Anarchists, is completely correct, and I am delighted to the extent that this expresses our unity of opinions on that *essential* question at this time. Unfortunately, you and I are only spectators. . . .

Excerpt from a letter to Victor Serge. French translation provided by Pierre Broué, with the authorization of Colette Chambelland and Jean Maitron. Translated for this volume from the French by Naomi Allen.

242 *The Spanish Revolution (1931-39)*

At this time, the most important thing would be to find organic forms of collaboration between the POUM and the trade unions in Catalonia (juntas, councils, soviets, action committees?), even at the price of large organizational concessions. But one can only solve those problems on the spot. . . .

I shake your hand warmly.

Yours,

L. Trotsky

59 INTERVIEW WITH HAVAS

February 19, 1937

Have I or have I not given "instructions" to aid the republican front with volunteers? I have given "instructions" to no one. In general, I do not give "instructions." I express my *opinion* in articles. *Only cowards, traitors, or agents of fascism can renounce aid to the Spanish republican armies.* The elementary duty of every revolutionist is to struggle against the bands of Franco, Mussolini, and Hitler.

On the left wing of the Spanish governmental coalition, and partly in the opposition, is the POUM. This party is no "Trotskyite." I have criticized its policies on many occasions despite my warm sympathy for the heroism with which the members of this party, above all the youth, struggle at the front. The POUM has committed the error of participating in the electoral combination of the "Popular" Front; under the cover of this combination, General Franco during the course of several months boldly prepared the insurrection which is now ravaging Spain. A revolutionary party did not have the right to take upon itself, either directly or indirectly, any responsibility for a policy of blindness and criminal tolerance

---

From the April 17, 1937, issue of *Labor Action*, a revolutionary socialist paper edited by J. P. Cannon, and published under the auspices of the Socialist Party in California. Havas was the French newspaper agency. The interview is reprinted in *The Case of Leon Trotsky*, Merit Publishers, New York, the book containing the proceedings of the Dewey Commission of Inquiry into the Charges Made Against Leon Trotsky in the Moscow Trials. The hearings were held in Mexico, April 10-17, 1937.

It was obliged to call the masses to vigilance. The leadership of the POUM committed the second error of entering the Catalan coalition government; in order to fight hand in hand with the other parties at the front, there is no need to take upon oneself any responsibility for the false governmental policies of these parties. Without weakening the military front for a moment, it is necessary to know how to rally the masses politically under the revolutionary banner.

In civil war, incomparably more than in ordinary war, *politics dominates strategy.* Robert Lee, as an army chieftain, was surely more talented than Grant, but the program of the liquidation of slavery assured victory to Grant. In our three years of civil war the superiority of military art and military technique was often enough on the side of the enemy, but at the very end it was the Bolshevik program that conquered. The worker knew very well what he was fighting for. The peasant hesitated for a long time, but comparing the two regimes by experience, he finally supported the Bolshevik side.

In Spain the Stalinists, who lead the chorus from on high, have advanced the formula to which Caballero, president of the cabinet, also adheres: *First* military victory, and *then* social reform. I consider this formula fatal for the Spanish revolution. Not seeing the radical differences between the two programs in reality, the toiling masses, above all the peasants, fall into indifference. In these conditions, fascism will inevitably win, because the purely military advantage is on its side. *Audacious social reforms represent the strongest weapon in the civil war and the fundamental condition for the victory over fascism.*

The policies of Stalin, who has always revealed himself as an opportunist in revolutionary situations, are dictated by a fear of frightening the French bourgeoisie, above all the "200 families" against whom the French Popular Front long ago declared war — on paper. Stalin's policies in Spain repeat not so much Kerensky's policies in 1917 as they do the policies of Ebert-Scheidemann in the German revolution of 1918. Hitler's victory was the punishment for the policies of Ebert-Scheidemann. In Germany the punishment was delayed for fifteen years. *In Spain it can come in less than fifteen months.*

However, would not the social and political victory of the Spanish workers and peasants mean European war? Such prophecies, dictated by reactionary cowardice, are radically false. If fascism wins in Spain, France will find itself caught in a vise from which it will not be able to withdraw. *Franco's dictatorship would mean the unavoidable acceleration of European war,* in the most difficult conditions for France. It is useless to add that a new European war would *bleed the French people* to the last drop and lead it into its decline, and by the same token would deal a terrible blow to all humanity.

On the other hand, the victory of the Spanish workers and peasants would undoubtedly shake the regimes of Mussolini and Hitler. Thanks to their hermetic, totalitarian character, the fascist regimes produce an impression of unshakable firmness. Actually, *at the first serious test they will be the victims of internal explosions. The victorious Russian revolution sapped the strength of the Hohenzollern regime. The victorious Spanish revolution will undermine the regimes of Hitler and Mussolini. For that reason alone the victory of the Spanish workers and peasants will reveal itself at once as a powerful force for peace.*

The task of the true Spanish revolutionists consists in strengthening and reinforcing the military front, in demolishing the political tutelage of the Soviet bureaucracy, in giving a bold social program to the masses, in assuring thereby the victory of the revolution and, precisely in that way, upholding the cause of peace. Therein alone lies the salvation of Europe!

60   *A STRATEGY FOR VICTORY*

February 25, 1937

Some comrades, affected by the terrible struggle under way in Spain, and especially by the extremely difficult situation of the POUM, tend to adapt themselves passively to the political line of the POUM leadership. They approve it with a number of secondary reticences.

This attitude seems to me to be false and even harmful. One does not demonstrate one's friendship for a revolutionary

---

An excerpt from a letter from Trotsky to Harold Isaacs. From the personal archives of George Novack.

organization in a difficult situation by closing one's eyes to its mistakes and the dangers arising from them. The situation in Spain can be saved only by an energetic, radical, and heroic comeback of the left wing of the proletariat; thus an immediate regroupment is necessary. It is necessary to open up an implacable campaign against the bloc with the bourgeoisie, and for a socialist program. It is necessary to denounce the Stalinist, Socialist, and Anarchist leaders precisely because of their bloc with the bourgeoisie. It is not a question of articles more or less confined to the columns of *La Batalla*. No. It is a question of marshaling the masses against their leaders, who are leading the revolution to complete destruction.

The policy of the POUM leadership is a policy of adaptation, expectation, hesitation, that is to say, the most dangerous of all policies during civil war, which is uncompromising. Better to have in the POUM 10,000 comrades ready to mobilize the masses against treason than 40,000 who suffer the policies of others instead of carrying out their own. The 40,000 members of the POUM (if the figure is accurate) cannot by themselves assure the victory of the proletariat if their policy remains hesitant. But 20,000, or even 10,000, with a clear, decisive, aggressive policy, can win the masses in a short time, just as the Bolsheviks won the masses in eight months.

The present policy of the POUM leadership is that of Martov, not of Lenin.[7] And for victory, the policy of Lenin is needed.

61 *THE PROPOSED BARCELONA CONFERENCE*

March 20, 1937

I'm not sure that the Barcelona conference, which the papers set for May 1, will really take place, given the events in Spain and elsewhere. It is very difficult for me to formulate an opinion on this projected conference because my information is

From *Information Bulletin*, International Bureau for the Fourth International, July 1937. Signed "Lund." The conference was called at the Brussels conference of the London Bureau in 1936, but was never held.

not only incomplete but almost nil. I can only express some general considerations.

The course of events puts all the groups, tendencies, and factions to terrible tests. We have seen ultraleftism of pure culture (Bordigists) explode under the shock that came from Spain. We have seen in our own ranks how formal intransigence is transformed in a few weeks into miserable desertion (the opponents of entry, Schmidt, Stein de Zeeuw, Muste).8 We have also seen other intransigent non-entrists, who yesterday made an alliance against us with Schmidt, Stein de Zeeuw, and Muste, look anew for political support against us from the opportunistic leadership of the POUM (Sneevliet and Vereecken). These lessons are decisive. But there are others.

The ILP and SAP become Stalinist at the very moment when Stalinism is revealed as the veritable syphilis of the workers' movement. The London Bureau, with which not only Schmidt but Sneevliet and Vereecken were flirting, expires or is ready to fold up. The different intermediate groups, terrified by their own inconsistency, seek support at the last minute from the Spanish revolution. All the leaders of the ILP and SAP, in supporting Nin against us, have done everything they could do to hamper victory in Spain. They think now they can hide their definitive bankruptcy in the shadow of the heroic Spanish and Catalan proletariat. In vain. Victory is possible only by the road that we have indicated time and again. Either Nin, Andrade, Gorkin must change their policy radically, that is to say, change from the path of Martov to that of Lenin, or they will lead the POUM to a split and perhaps even to a terrible defeat. Revolutionary words (editorials, solemn discourses, etc.) do not advance the revolution a step. The struggle of the POUMist workers is magnificent, but without resolute leadership it cannot bring victory. It is a question of rousing the masses with supreme courage against the traitorous leaders. There is the beginning of wisdom.

Break with the phantom bourgeoisie who stay in the Popular Front only to prevent the masses from making their own revolution. That is the first order of the day. Rouse the Anarchists, Stalinists, and Socialists against their leaders, who do not want to break with their bourgeois ministers, those scarecrows protecting private property. That is the second step. Without that, everything else is verbiage, prattle, and lies. They have wasted five years for Leninist policy. I am

ot sure that they still have five months or five weeks in which
 to try to correct the errors committed.

If Sneevliet, after flirting with London, tries now to create
 new international with Nin, so much the worse for him.
He will come out of the endeavor only the more compromised.
 You are going to participate in the Barcelona conference
 it is really held. That decision seems correct to me. It would
 e absurd to imitate the "non-entrists" at any cost. We will
 ater or we will not, according to circumstances. That is not
 he decisive thing. You must know what you are going to do
 t the conference. To take part in the style of Vereecken and
 neevliet would be fatal. It is necessary to participate with
 ll independence, without the least concession on questions
 f principle and without sparing in the least the faults and
 rimes of the other participants. Naturally, the form of our
 xposures and our criticisms must be adapted to the Spanish
 ituation and the mentality of the workers who are not yet
 ith us. It seems to me the Moscow trials [9] are the touch-
 tone for each group that lays claim to revolutionary prin-
 iples. Average workers may not have an opinion on these
 ials; we shall patiently explain the truth to them. But the
 eaders" who presume to create a new international cannot be
 vasive and solidarize themselves in secret with the GPU, as
 o the Brandler and Walcher scum.[10] The least that you can
 sk at the conference is complete support for an international
 ommission of investigation. If the majority refuses, it will
 e necessary to quit the conference demonstratively. If the
 najority supports the proposition, you must pitilessly stigma-
 ze the minority that opposes it in a statement in which all
 ne agents of the GPU should be enumerated and character-
 ed. Do not let the charlatans come to tell us that in view
 f the interests of the Spanish revolution we must not open
 ebates on the Russian question, or as that miserable lackey
 Malraux[11] says, on "personal questions." It is precisely in
 iew of the interests of the Spanish revolution and in the face
 f the approaching war that it is necessary to distinguish clear-
 y where the revolutionists are, and even the honest semirevo-
 ntionists-semicentrists, and where the falsifiers, those agents
 f the Bonapartist caste who have demonstrated by the Moscow
 ials that they are capable and ready at any moment to be-
 ray the supreme interests of the proletariat in order to safe-
 uard their privileges.

The discussion on programmatic and political questions, while we preserve all our intransigence, may at the same time be very calm and even amicable toward the elements who have the minimum courage necessary to oppose the Bonapartists of Moscow. As for the others, we must on every occasion deal with them whip in hand.

I am speaking only of tactical questions because our comrades are sufficiently armed on theoretical and political points. They have nothing to change, nothing to revise. It is a question only of adapting what we have acquired by experience to the present situation. These are the few remarks that I can make from here on the Barcelona conference.

62

TO THE EDITORIAL BOARD OF "LA LUTTE OUVRIERE"

March 23, 1937
Dear Comrades:

I find in number 9 of your paper, dated Saturday, February 27, 1937, an article taken from *Spanish Revolution*, the organ of the POUM, with a eulogistic introduction by yourselves. I can't conceal from you that your solidarity not with the struggle of the workers of the POUM but with the policy of its leadership seems to me not merely an error but a crime against which I shall publicly protest with all my strength.

The article that you reprint is false from beginning to end, and the manner in which it is false is extremely revealing of the equivocation and ambiguity of the policy of Nin and his associates. They carry on a polemic against "bourgeois antifascism" and the program of a "bourgeois neo-republic." But how and why did Nin come to be minister of that "bourgeois neo-republic"? Did he openly recognize his error, which to tell the truth was a betrayal? How can one combat the bourgeois republic while being in its government? How can one

From *Information Bulletin*, International Bureau for the Fourth International, July 1937. Signed "Lund."

mobilize the workers to overthrow the bourgeois state while at the same time representing oneself as a minister of bourgeois "justice"? Is one taking things seriously or making fun of the program and ideas of the proletariat?

The article is false from beginning to end. It speaks of the "leaders of the petty bourgeoisie" who "have risen through the disappearance of monopoly capitalism." The characterization of the function of Azaña, Companys, et al. is wholly false. [12] These gentlemen are not the petty bourgeoisie. The real petty bourgeoisie, ruined, declassed, are the peasants, artisans, and employees (clerks). Azaña and his sort are the political exploiters of the little bourgeoisie in the interests of the big bourgeoisie. They remain in the camp of the popular masses like scarecrows — and the crows are the leaders of the Socialists, reformists, and also, alas, the POUMists. They (Azaña, Companys, et al.) dare not touch private property, and they stoop even to the role of defender of "justice" based on private property. That is the truth, and all the rest is only a lie. "Monopoly capitalism" is pretending to be dead only until the victory of Franco. Azaña and Companys carry on its business in the meantime, and *La Batalla* says that they can't carry on its business "without the POUM or against the POUM."

Everything is false in the article, retrospect as well as perspective. "Cohabitation" (i.e., collaboration of the classes, if you please) has been possible only "thanks to the war against freedom." But this "cohabitation" (that is to say, this collaboration of the POUM with the leaders of the bourgeois neo-republic) has terribly paralyzed the upsurge of the workers and peasants and piled up defeat on defeat. They say nothing of that, but they smuggle in: "But today, even the conduct of the war makes necessary a decision [by whom?] as to the road to be taken." Why "today"? Because the policy of yesterday led to the brink of the abyss? And even at the edge of the abyss, the POUM continues to preach sermons to the traitorous leaders instead of rousing the armed masses against them.

This is where Bolshevism begins. Instead of playing the vaudeville role of minister of the bourgeois neo-republic, it was necessary to mobilize the workers courageously, openly, for the purpose of driving out the bourgeois ministers and making it possible to replace the Socialist and Stalinist ministers. Instead of this unrelenting work in and through the

masses, they write ambiguous articles on the necessity of taking
a position for the workers' state.

"To carry on the war is to assure collectivization and so-
cialization. . . ." An utterly abstract syllogism to cover up
an utter lack of revolutionary courage. To pursue the war
without collectivization means defeat. To assure victory, the
bourgeoisie must be chased out and the treacherous leaders
driven into a corner by the direct pressure of the armed masses. The abstract syllogism is not enough. Action is necessary.
But it is precisely here that Nin, the Spanish Martov, capit-
ulates.

"The proletariat of Catalonia have in their hands a strong
war industry that puts the central government of the republic
in a state of vassalage [!] in respect to war needs." The state
of vassalage is . . . that of the leaders of the POUM in respect to the government of the bourgeois neo-republic. That
is the truth. If this policy continues, the Catalan proletariat
will be the victim of a terrible catastrophe comparable to that
of the Paris Commune of 1871.

For six years, Nin has made nothing but mistakes. He has
flirted with ideas and eluded difficulties. Instead of battle, he
has substituted petty combinations. He has impeded the creation of a revolutionary party in Spain. All the leaders who
have followed him share in the same responsibility. For six
years they have done everything possible to subject this energetic and heroic proletariat of Spain to the most terrible
defeats, and in spite of everything the ambiguity continues.
They do not break the vicious circle. They do not rouse the
masses against the bourgeois republic. They accommodate
themselves to it and then, to make up for it, they write articles from time to time — on the proletarian revolution. Such
wretchedness! And you reproduce that with your approba-
tion instead of flaying the Menshevik traitors who cover themselves with quasi-Bolshevik formulas.

Do not tell me that the workers of the POUM fight heroically, etc. I know it as well as others do. But it is precisely
their battle and their sacrifice that forces us to tell the truth
and nothing but the truth. Down with diplomacy, flirtation,
and equivocation. One must know how to tell the bitterest
truth when the fate of a war and of a revolution depend on
it. We have nothing in common with the policy of Nin, nor
with any who protect, camouflage, or defend it.

63

REVOLUTIONARY STRATEGY IN
THE CIVIL WAR

April 14, 1937

Beals: I would like to ask one question along these lines, since we are talking about it. I would like to ask one question since we are talking about the world war: the most imminent danger of war in Spain. Are you responsible for the Trotskyites in Spain?

Trotsky: What is "Trotskyites in Spain"?

Beals: Are you responsible for the various factions in Spain who use the name of "Trotskyites"?

Trotsky: There are no Trotskyites. The situation is such that everybody who opposes the politics of the Comintern is named by the Comintern "Trotskyite." Because Trotskyite means fascism in the Comintern propaganda. It is a simple argument. The Trotskyites in Spain are not numerous — the genuine Trotskyites. I regret it, but I must confess, they are not numerous. There is a powerful party, the POUM, the Workers Party of Marxist Unification. That party alone recognizes that I am not a fascist. The youth of that party has sympathy with our ideas. But the policy of that party is very opportunistic, and I openly criticize it.

Beals: Who is the head of it?

Trotsky: Nin. He is my friend. I know him very well. But I criticize him very sharply.

Beals: One reason I bring this out is that the charge has been made that the faction of Trotskyites sabotage the loyalist movement in Spain.

Trotsky: That we allegedly sabotage the loyalist movement. I believe that I have expressed it in many interviews and articles: The only way possible to assure victory in Spain is to say to the peasants: "The Spanish soil is your soil." To say to the workers: "The Spanish factories are your factories." That is the only possibility to assure victory. Stalin, in order not to

An excerpt from *The Case of Leon Trotsky.* Carleton Beals, a leading authority on Latin America, and Benjamin Stolberg, an American journalist, were members of the full Commission of Inquiry into the Charges Made Against Leon Trotsky in the Moscow Trials. John Finerty, a defense lawyer famous for his work in the Sacco-Vanzetti trial, was the Commission's legal counsel. Albert Goldman was Trotsky's attorney.

frighten the French bourgeoisie, has become the guard of private property in Spain. The Spanish peasant is not very interested in fine definitions. He says: "With Franco and with Caballero, it is the same thing," because the peasant is very realistic. During our civil war — I do not believe that we were victorious principally because of our military science. It is false. We were victorious because of our revolutionary program. We said to the peasant: "It is your soil." And the peasant, who at one time went away and then went to the Whites, compared the Bolsheviks with the White Guards and said, "The Bolsheviks are better." Then when the peasantry, the hundreds and millions of Russian peasantry, were of the conviction that the Bolsheviks were better, we were victorious.

Beals: Would you expand a little further the statement that Stalin is guarding private property in Spain?

Trotsky: He says, and the Comintern declared with regard to Spain, that the social reforms will come after the victory. "Now, it is war. Our job now is war. Social reforms will come after the victory." The peasant becomes indifferent. "It is not my war; I am not interested in the victory of the generals. The generals are fighting one another." That is his opinion. You know, in his primitive way, he is right. I am with this primitive Spanish peasant against the fine diplomats.

Beals: Then you don't think it is of great importance which side wins the war in Spain? It does not make a great deal of difference which side wins the war?

Trotsky: No, the workers must win the war. It is necessary that the workers win. But I assure you that by the policy of the Comintern and Stalin you have the surest way of losing the revolution. They lost the revolution in China, they lost the revolution in Germany, and now they are preparing the defeat in France and in Spain. We had only one victory of the proletarian revolution. That was the October Revolution, and it was made directly in opposition to the method of Stalin.

Beals: Now, what steps would you take in the case of Spain today, if you were in Stalin's place?

Trotsky: I could not be in his place.

Beals: Say, if you were in Stalin's place — if you had the destiny of the Soviet Union in your hands, what would be your action in Spain?

Trotsky: It is not a question of the Soviet Union. It is a question of the revolutionary parties of the Comintern, it is a question of the parties. Naturally, I would remain in opposition to all the bourgeois parties.

Stolberg: Mr. Trotsky, may I ask a question which relates to Carleton Beals's question? If you had been in power from 1923 on, in that case, from your point of view, the Chinese revolution would have been either saved or would have gained additionally. There would have been no German fascism. I mean, if your position had been victorious back in 1923. There would have been the situation in Spain, but it could not have occurred exactly that way. But you lost. The Comintern politics in China and Germany brought about a defeat. Now we have the Spanish situation. I am merely presenting what I think is your position. Then I will ask the question. We have the Spanish situation on top of the mistakes made in the last fourteen years. We have a civil war in Spain. Surely a purely orthodox or puristic position does not answer the problem. With whom would you side at the present time in Spain?

Trotsky: I gave the answer in many interviews and articles. Every Trotskyite in Spain must be a good soldier, on the side of the left. Naturally, it is so elementary a question — you know it is not worth discussing. A leader or any other member in the government of Caballero is a traitor. A leader of the working class cannot enter the bourgeois government. We did not enter the government of Kerensky in Russia. While we defended Kerensky against Kornilov, we did not enter his government. As I declared that I am ready to enter into an alliance with Stalin against the fascists, or an alliance with Jouhaux[13] against the French fascists. It is an elementary question.

Finerty: Mr. Trotsky, if you were in power in Russia today and your help was asked by the loyalists in Spain, you would condition your help on the basis that the land was given to the peasants and the factories to the workers?

Trotsky: Not on the condition — not this question. The first question would be the attitude of the Spanish revolutionary party. I would say, "No political alliance with the bourgeoisie," as the first condition. The second, "You must be the best soldiers against the fascists." Third, "You must say to the soldiers, to the other soldiers and the peasants: 'We must transform our country into a people's country. Then, when we win the masses, we will throw the bourgeoisie out of office, and then we will be in power and we will make the social revolution.'"

Finerty: Then, to make effective any help, you will have to have an alliance with the Marxist party in Spain?

Trotsky: Naturally, I would help Caballero with all the material means against fascism, but at the same time I would give the advice to the Communist Party not to enter into the government, but to remain in a critical position against Caballero and to prepare the second chapter of the workers' revolution.

Beals: Isn't that one of the reasons that the Azaña government, when first in office, brought in the reaction, precisely because of that policy?

Trotsky: Because of a conservative bourgeois policy: because he tried to make half a revolution, a third of a revolution. My opinion is that the revolution must be — better not begin that way. If you begin the revolution, do it to the end. To the end signifies the social revolution.

Beals: This would mean, by the policy you follow, the probable victory of Franco, would it not?

Trotsky: The victory of Franco is assured by the present policy of the Comintern. The Spanish revolution, the Spanish proletariat and peasantry, by their efforts and energy and devotion during the past six years, could have assured five victories or six victories — every year a victory. But the ruling stratum of the working class did everything to hinder, sabotage, and betray the revolutionary power of the masses. The revolution is based upon the elementary forces of the proletariat, and on the political direction of its leaders. It is a very important problem, and the leadership in Spain was miserable all the time. The Spanish proletariat shows that it is of the best material, the best revolutionary force we have seen for the last decade. In spite of that, it is not victorious. I accuse the Communist International and the Second International of hindering the victory by their perfidious policy, which is based on cowardice before the bourgeoisie, the bourgeoisie and Franco. They remain in a government with the bourgeoisie, which is the symbol of private property. And Caballero himself bows before the symbol of private property. The masses, however, do not see the difference between the two regimes.

Goldman: Do you exclude the possibility of a victory, of a military victory of Caballero over Franco?

Trotsky: It is very difficult to say — a military victory. It is possible that even by a military victory, the victorious regime can in a very short time be transformed into a fascist regime, if the masses remain dissatisfied and indifferent and the new military organization created by the victory is not a socialist organization.

Goldman: But the masses in Spain might be under the illusion that they are actually in the struggle against Franco and the fascists — they are actually struggling for their own proletarian interests.

Trotsky: Unfortunately, the majority of the masses have lost all their illusions. And this explains the dragging character of the civil war, because the Popular Front government prepared an army for Franco. The new government issued from the Popular Front, from the victory, and protected the army and Franco, so that under the government of the Popular Front the army was prepared for the insurrection. Then began the civil war, and the bourgeoisie said to the people: "You must await victory. Then we will be very generous, but after the victory."

Goldman: Now, you didn't answer the question asked a half hour ago.

Beals: I didn't quite finish. I don't yet see, Mr. Trotsky, how you or Mr. Stalin is going to save the situation in Spain. It seems to me that both of the policies you have indicated will have the most immediate results of winning the war for Franco. I can't see, personally, anything in favor of Franco at all. I don't quite clearly get your point. It seems to me that in the meantime Mr. Franco will have won the war.

Trotsky: I can only repeat that I gave the key, a little key to my friends and everybody who is of the same conviction, and my first advice is to be the best soldiers now in the camp of Caballero. That is the first thing. You know there is a group of the Fourth International, a company of our comrades in the trenches. It is so elementary that I will not dwell on it. It is necessary to fight. But, you know, it is not sufficient to fight with a gun. It is necessary to have ideas and give these same ideas to others, to prepare for the future. I can fight with the simple peasant, but he understands very little in the situation. I must give him an explanation. I must say: "You are right in fighting Franco. We must exterminate the fascists, but not in order to have the same Spain as before the civil war, because Franco issued from this Spain. We must exterminate the foundation of Franco, the social foundation of Franco, which is the social system of capitalism. Are you satisfied with my ideas?" you ask the peasant. He will say: "Yes, I believe so." Then explain the same thing to the workers.

Beals: Why would you send the soldier to fight Franco and yet refuse to enter the government of Caballero to assist in the same purpose?

Trotsky: I explained it. We refused categorically to enter the Kerensky government, but the Bolsheviks were the best fighters against Kornilov. Not only that, the best soldiers and sailors were Bolsheviks. During the insurrection of Kornilov, Kerensky must go to the sailors of the Baltic fleet and demand of them to defend them in the Winter Palace. I was at that time in prison. They took him to the guard, and sent a delegation to me to ask me what must be done: to arrest Kerensky or defend him? That is a historical fact. I said: "Yes, you must guard him very well now; tomorrow we will arrest him." [Laughter]

Goldman: Are you through?

Beals: Yes.

64   *IS VICTORY POSSIBLE IN SPAIN?*

April 23, 1937

Let us once more review the basic facts. Franco's army was built under the direct protection of Azaña, that is, of the Popular Front, including the Socialist and Stalinist, and later even the Anarchist, leaders.

The prolonged character of the war is the direct result of the conservative bourgeois program of the Popular Front, i. e., of the Stalinist bureaucracy.

The longer the politics of the Popular Front keep their hold over the country and the revolution, the greater the danger of the exhaustion and disillusionment of the masses and of the military victory of fascism.

The responsibility for this situation rests entirely upon the

From the Russian *Bulletin of the Opposition*, no. 56-57, July-August 1937. Signed "Crux." Translated for this volume from the Russian by George Saunders.

Stalinists, Social Democrats, and Anarchists, more precisely, on their leaders, who, on the model of Kerensky, Tseretelli, Ebert, Scheidemann, Otto Bauer, and the like, subordinated the revolution of the people to the interests of the bourgeoisie.

Does this mean that, with the continuation of the present policies, the *military* victory of Largo Caballero over Franco is inconceivable? To calculate beforehand the material and moral resources of the two opposing camps is not possible. Only the course of the struggle itself can test out the actual relation of forces. But we are not interested in *military* victory in and of itself, but in the victory of the *revolution*, that is, the victory of one class over another. It is necessary to aid the republican troops with all one's strength; but the victory of Largo Caballero's army over Franco's would still not mean, by far, the victory of the revolution.

"What kind of revolution do you have in mind," the philistines of the Popular Front demand of us, "democratic or socialist? The victory of Largo Caballero's army over Franco's would mean the victory of democracy over fascism, that is, the victory of progress over reaction."

One cannot listen to these arguments without a bitter smile. Before 1934 we explained to the Stalinists tirelessly that even in the imperialist epoch democracy continued to be preferable to fascism; that is, in all cases where hostile clashes take place between them, the revolutionary proletariat is obliged to support democracy against fascism.

However, we always added: We can and must defend bourgeois democracy not by bourgeois democratic means but by the methods of class struggle, which in turn pave the way for the replacement of bourgeois democracy by the dictatorship of the proletariat. This means in particular that in the process of defending bourgeois democracy, even with arms in hand, the party of the proletariat takes no responsibility for bourgeois democracy, does not enter its government, but maintains full freedom of criticism and of action in relation to all parties of the Popular Front, thus preparing the overthrow of bourgeois democracy at the next stage.

Any other policy is a criminal and hopeless attempt to use the blood of the workers as cement to hold together a bourgeois democracy that is *inevitably doomed to collapse regardless of the immediate outcome of the civil war.*

"But you ignore the peasantry!" cries some muddlehead who

has read his fill of the miserable Comintern compilations of 1923-29 vintage.14   The readiest of all to cry out about "ignoring" the peasantry are those gentlemen who are betraying the *revolutionary interests* of the peasantry in the name of a united front with the landed property owners. The Spanish peasantry has shown well enough its eager desire to stand shoulder to shoulder with the proletariat. All that is necessary is for the proletariat to actually enter the road of expropriation of the landed exploiters and usurers. But it is precisely the Stalinists and their new pupils, the "Socialists" and "Anarchists" (?!), who have prevented the proletariat from putting forward a revolutionary agrarian program.

The government of Stalin-Caballero tries with all its might to imbue its army with the character of a "democratic" guard for the defense of private property. That is the essence of the Popular Front. All the rest is phrasemongering. Precisely for that reason, the Popular Front is preparing the triumph of fascism. Whoever has not understood this is deaf and blind.

Is a *military* victory of the democratic guardian of capital possible over its fascist guard? It is possible. But since in the present epoch the fascist guard corresponds much more to the requirements of capital, the military victory of Stalin-Caballero could not be firm or lasting. *Without the proletarian revolution the victory of "democracy" would only mean a roundabout path to the very same fascism.*

Andrés Nin admits that as a result of the heroic struggle of the Spanish proletariat the revolution has been "thrown back." Nin forgets to add: with the direct collaboration of the leadership of the POUM, which "critically" adapted to the Socialists and Stalinists, that is, to the bourgeoisie, instead of counterposing its party at every step to all the other parties and thereby preparing the victory of the proletariat. The consequences of this fatal policy of vacillation and adaptation we predicted to Nin six years ago, at the very start of the Spanish revolution. We advise every thinking worker to reread our polemic with Nin, in hundreds of letters and articles. Nin's present vacillations flow completely from his vacillations of yesterday.

Nin says: "From the time that we were expelled from the Catalan government, reaction has intensified." In fact it would have been appropriate to say: "Our participation in the Catalan government more readily provided the bourgeoisie with the chance to strengthen itself, drive us out, and openly enter the road of reaction." The POUM as a matter of fact even now partly remains in the Popular Front. The leaders of the POUM plaintively try to *persuade* the government to take the road of socialist revolution. The POUM leaders respectfully try to make the CNT leaders understand at last the Marxist teaching about the state. The POUM leaders view themselves as "revolutionary" advisors to the leaders of the Popular Front. This position is lifeless and unworthy of revolutionaries.

It is necessary to openly and boldly mobilize the masses against the Popular Front government. It is necessary to expose, for the syndicalist and Anarchist workers to see, the betrayals of those gentlemen who call themselves Anarchists but in fact have turned out to be simple liberals. It is necessary to hammer away mercilessly at Stalinism as the worst agency of the bourgeoisie. It is necessary to feel yourselves leaders of the revolutionary masses, not advisors to the bourgeois government.

A purely military victory of the democratic army of the bourgeois Stalin-Caballero regime is, of course, possible. But what would be its immediate results?

The present acts of violence against the workers' organizations, especially the left wing, in the name of "discipline" and "unity of the army" represent nothing less than a school of Bonapartism. What is involved is not the internal discipline of the proletarian army but the military subordination of the proletariat to the bourgeoisie. A military victory would raise the self-consciousness of the commanding circle of the "republican" army to an extraordinary degree and would saturate it through and through with Bonapartist tendencies. On the other hand, a military victory paid for with the blood of the workers would raise the self-consciousness and determination of the proletarian vanguard. In other words, *the victory of the republican army of capital over the fascist army would inevitably mean the outbreak of civil war in the republican camp.*

In this new civil war, the proletariat could conquer only if it has at its head a revolutionary party that knows how to win the confidence of the majority of the workers and the semi-proletarian peasants. If such a party is not present at the critical moment, the civil war within the republican camp threatens to lead to a victory of Bonapartism that would differ very little in character from the dictatorship of General Franco. That is why the politics of the Popular Front are a round-about path to the very same fascism.

As Azaña prepared and armed Franco's army, so Caballero, that Azaña Number 2 with the mask of a Socialist, prepares the army of Franco Number 2, a kind of Spanish Cavaignac or Galliffet,15 behind the mask of a "republican" general. Who-ever cannot see this deserves only scorn!

In *La Batalla* of April 4, we find the "thirteen points for victory." All the points have the character of *advice* that the Central Committee of the POUM is offering to the authorities. The POUM demands the "calling of a delegated congress of workers' and peasants' syndicates and of soldiers." In form, what seems to be involved is a congress of workers', peasants', and soldiers' deputies. But the trouble is that the POUM re-spectfully proposes that the bourgeois-reformist government itself call such a congress, which then ought to "peacefully" substitute itself for the bourgeois government. A revolutionary slogan is turned into empty phrases!

The fourth point proclaims: "For the creation of an army controlled by the working class." The bourgeoisie in alliance with the reformists should create an army that Nin will control. On the most crucial question, the army, the lifelessness of the positions of the POUM leaders appears in the most deadly form. The army is a weapon of the ruling class and cannot be anything else. The army is controlled by whoever com-mands it, that is, by whoever holds state power. The prole-tariat cannot "control" an army created by the bourgeoisie and its reformist lackeys. The revolutionary party can and must build its cells in such an army, preparing the advanced sections of the army to pass over to the side of the workers. This basic revolutionary task is glossed over by the Central Committee of the POUM with sugary utopias about workers' "control" over the army of the bourgeoisie. The POUM's of-ficial position is shot through with ambivalence. It cannot be otherwise: ambivalence is the heart of centrism.

"The revolution has fallen back," profoundly declaims Nin, getting ready in fact for . . . his own backsliding. Or perhaps Nin is getting ready to stop the downward-falling revolution at the *democratic stage*? How? Obviously, with the help of hot-air brakes. If Nin were able to think his own words through, he would understand that *so long as these gentlemen leaders keep the revolution from rising to the dictatorship of the proletariat, it will inevitably fall to fascism.* So it was in Germany, so it was in Austria, so it will be in Spain — only in a much shorter time. It is necessary to think one's position through to the end.

When Nin says that the Spanish workers can still seize power by peaceful means today, he is stating an outright falsehood. Even now power is in the hands of the military leaders and the bureaucracy in alliance with the Stalinists and anarcho-reformists. In their struggle against the workers all these gentlemen rely on the foreign bourgeoisie and the Soviet bureaucracy. To speak of peacefully gaining power under these conditions is to deceive oneself and the working class.

In the same speech (at the end of March) Nin said that they want to take the guns away from the workers and recommended that the workers not surrender their arms. This advice, of course, is correct. But when one class wants to disarm another, and the other class, namely the proletariat, refuses to surrender its arms, that means imminent civil war. The false and sugary perspective of gaining power peacefully upsets all of Nin's radical argumentation about the dictatorship of the proletariat. Moreover, the essence of Nin's politics is precisely the sugary perspective. It permits him to avoid drawing practical conclusions from his radical arguments and to continue the policy of centrist vacillation. Nin's reactionary persecution of "Trotskyists," i. e., of true revolutionaries who interfere with Nin's pretense of being a Bolshevik, is a direct result of his need for a rosy perspective.

It is extremely typical that Nin will not say clearly and precisely *exactly who* wants to take the arms from the workers, though it is the direct duty of a revolutionary to name the authors of counterrevolutionary plans, to brand them and their parties, and to render them hateful in the eyes of the masses of people.

It is not enough to tell the workers: "Don't give up your arms." It is necessary to teach the workers to disarm those who would take the arms from the workers.

The politics of the POUM both in content and in tone fail completely to correspond to the urgency of the situation. The

POUM leadership consoles itself by thinking that it is "more advanced" than the other parties. But that is not enough. The comparison should be not with the other parties but with events, with the course of the class struggle. The outcome of the revolution will be decided in the last analysis not by these pompous ministers nor by party committees, with their intrigues and combinations, but by the millions of workers and peasants, on the one hand, and the Spanish and world bourgeoisie, on the other.

Nin's international policies are just as wrong as his domestic policy. "We are not for the Fourth International; we are not Trotskyists," the POUM leaders swear and apologize at every step. At the same time, they declare that they base themselves on the ideas of Marx and Lenin. Untrue! Outside the line of the Fourth International there is only the line of Stalin-Caballero. The POUM leadership describes helpless zigzags between these two lines. The art of Nin, Andrade, Gorkin — in contradictions to the teachings of Marx and Lenin — lies in avoiding the clear formulation of problems, precise analysis, and honest reply to criticism. For that very reason every new stage of the revolution catches them unaware. And the worst experiences still lie ahead!

Tell me your friends and I'll tell you who you are! The POUM leadership is connected with the pitiful opportunist clique of the German SAP, which plays the lackey to the Stalinists; with the leaders of the British Independent Labour Party, which has lost all right to existence; and with other half-opportunist, half-adventurist groupings, without any program, without revolutionary training, and without a future. Tell me your friends and I'll tell you who you are. The international policy of the POUM leaders only supplements their centrist vacillations on the domestic level.

It is necessary to break — sharply, decisively, boldly — the umbilical cord of bourgeois public opinion. It is necessary to break from the petty-bourgeois parties including the syndicalist leaders. It is necessary to think the situation through to the end. It is necessary to descend to the masses, to the lowest and most oppressed layers. It is necessary to stop lulling them with illusions of a future victory that will come by itself. It is necessary to tell them the truth, however bitter it may be. It is necessary to teach them to distrust the petty-bourgeois agencies of capital. It is necessary to teach them to trust in themselves. It is necessary to tie your fate to theirs inseparably. It is necessary to teach them to build their own combat organizations — soviets — in opposition to the bourgeois state.

Can one hope that the present leadership of the POUM will carry out this turn? Alas, the experience of six years of revolution leaves no room for such hopes. The revolutionists inside the POUM, as well as outside, would be bankrupt if they limited their role to "persuading," "winning over" Nin, Andrade, Gorkin, the way the latter try to win over Largo Caballero, Companys, et al. The revolutionists must turn to the workers, to the depths, against the vacillations and waverings of Nin. Unity of the proletarian front does not mean capitulation to the centrists. The interests of the revolution are higher than the formal unity of the party.

How many members does the POUM now have? Some say 25,000; others, 40,000. This question, however, does not have a decisive significance. Neither 25,000 nor 40,000 in and of themselves can guarantee victory. The question is decided by the relations between the party and the working class, on the one hand, and between the working class and the oppressed masses of the village, on the other. Forty thousand members with a wavering and vacillating leadership are able only to disperse the proletariat and thereby to pave the way for catastrophe. Ten thousand, with a firm and perceptive leadership, can find the road to the masses, break them away from the influence of the Stalinists and Social Democrats, the charlatans and loudmouths, and assure them not just the episodic and uncertain victory of the republican troops over the fascist troops, but *a total victory of the toilers over the exploiters.* The Spanish proletariat has shown three times that it is able to carry out such a victory. The whole question is in the leadership!

65 THE INSURRECTION IN BARCELONA
(Some Preliminary Remarks)

May 12, 1937

The news we have here of the most recent events is not only incomplete but also deliberately distorted. Under these conditions, the conclusions we formulate can have only a hypothetical and provisional character.

It seems that the insurrection was "spontaneous" in character, that is, it broke out unexpectedly for the leaders, including those of the POUM. This fact alone shows what an abyss had been dug between the Anarchist and POUM leaders, on the one side, and the working masses, on the other. The conception propagated by Nin that "the proletariat can take power through peaceful means" has been proven absolutely false. We know nothing, or almost nothing, of the real position of the POUM at the time of the insurrection. But we do not believe in miracles. The position of the leaders of the POUM at the decisive moment must have been a simple continuation of their position during all the preceding period. More exactly, it is precisely in a decisive moment that the inconsistency of left centrism must be revealed in the most striking and tragic fashion. Such was, for example, the fate of Martov in the events of 1905 and 1917.

Even in our own ranks, the false idea of Martov as a representative of left centrism is often expressed. In his criticism of the Kerensky-Tseretelli-Dan regime, Martov came close to the Bolsheviks. In the radicalism of his criticism and the largeness of his perspectives, Martov greatly surpassed the editors of *La Batalla*. But in the depths of his consciousness he al-

From *Information Bulletin*, International Bureau for the Fourth International, July 1937. Signed "Lund." In the beginning of May 1937, the Communist Party, through its control of the Barcelona police, ordered the seizure of the telephone exchange, which had been operated by the Anarchist union since they had captured it from the fascists in July 1936. This provocation triggered a new upsurge in Barcelona, with the workers fighting for control of the city against the police and government forces. However, the POUM and Anarchist leaders settled for a truce, and central government forces occupied the city. Shortly thereafter began the final crackdown against the POUM and the CNT.

ways hoped to convince his adversaries and not to oppose
the proletariat to the class enemy. That is why, at the moment when the workers passed over to action, Martov, frightened
by the harshness of the struggle, jumped aside to play the
role not of a *leader* of revolutionary action but of an *attorney*
for the defeated masses. Fortunately, on Martov's left was a
revolutionary party that knew what it wanted.

The situation in Spain is very different. The leadership of
the POUM appeared to the masses up to yesterday to be the
expression of the most resolute tendency. The working class
vanguard, at least in Catalonia, took the POUM literature
very seriously. But just at the moment when the masses prepared to realize this criticism by action, they found themselves
practically decapitated. Was it otherwise at the time of the
last insurrection? I fear not.

Or was the miracle perhaps produced in spite of everything,
and did the pressure of the masses impose on Nin a Bolshevik
position? That would indeed be magnificent, and we would
rejoice here at the possibility of common work with Nin on the
basis of new historic experiences. But until new word comes,
we have not the least reason to change our estimate of the
official policies of the POUM.

What is the meaning of the armistice in Barcelona that the
dispatches mention: the defeat of the insurgents determined
primarily by the inconsistency of the leadership, or the direct
capitulation of the leaders, frightened by the pressure of the
masses? We do not yet know. For the moment the struggle
seems to be continuing outside Barcelona. Is a resumption of
the offensive in Barcelona possible? Will not the repression
on the part of the Stalinist-reformist scum give a new impulse
to the action of the masses? We refrain from predicting here for
lack of accurate information. Criticism of the leadership in any
case retains its decisive importance, whatever the immediate
course of events may be. In spite of the mistakes and weak-
nesses of the insurrection, we remain before the outside world
indissolubly bound to the defeated workers. But this does not
mean sparing the leadership, hiding its inconsistency, and keeping silent about its mistakes under the pretext of a purely sentimental solidarity.

It seems very probable that this impressive experience will
provoke a split in the POUM. The elements that excluded the

Trotskyists and fraternized with the Brandlerist and SAP leaders — the cast-off rubbish of Stalinism — will definitely betray the revolution by seeking the mercy and then the favor of the Moscow bureaucracy. On the other hand, the revolutionary elements must understand that there is no intermediary between the Fourth International and betrayal. To facilitate and accelerate this political differentiation, our criticism should be frank, open, and even adamant. In the first place, all our comrades must understand the inconsistency of the policy of passive indulgence sanctioned by our friends Victor Serge, Sneevliet, Vereecken, and others. We must know how to draw from great events all the conclusions necessary to prepare the future.

The analogy with the events of July 1917 is too evident for us to dwell on it. What must be emphasized above all are the differences. The POUM still remains a Catalan organization. Its leaders prevented its timely entry into the Socialist Party, covering their fundamental opportunism with a sterile intransigence. It is to be hoped, however, that the events in Catalonia will produce fissures and splits in the ranks of the Socialist Party and the UGT. In this case, it would be fatal to be confined within the cadres of the POUM, which moreover will be much reduced in the weeks to come. It is necessary to turn towards the Anarchist masses in Catalonia, towards the Socialist and communist masses elsewhere. It is not a question of preserving the old external forms, but of creating new points of support for the future.

Even if the defeat is severe (and we cannot measure its severity from here), it is far from being definitive. New elements in Spain itself or in France can determine a new revolutionary upswing.

It is certainly very difficult to predict, expecially from afar, when and how the Spanish October will come. Nobody can, in any case, affirm in advance that the revolutionary force of the admirable Iberian proletariat is exhausted. But to prepare for October, the revolutionary vanguard must be forewarned against everything that is ambiguous, confused, and equivocal in the upper layer of the proletariat, nationally and internationally. Whoever does not have the courage to counterpose the Fourth International to the Second and Third will never have the courage to lead the workers in the decisive combats. Whoever remains connected with the Brandlers, the SAP people, the Maxtons, the Fenner Brockways, can only betray the proletariat on the very eve of combat or during combat. The Iberian workers should be made to understand now that the Fourth International means the scientific program of social revolution, confidence in the masses, mistrust of the centrists of every stamp, and the will to lead the struggle to the very end.

66 THE MURDER OF ANDRES NIN BY AGENTS OF THE GPU

August 8, 1937

When Andrés Nin, the leader of the POUM, was arrested in Barcelona, there could not be the slightest doubt that the agents of the GPU would not let him out alive. The intentions of Stalin were revealed with exceptional clarity when the GPU, which holds the Spanish police in its clutches, published an announcement accusing Nin and the whole leadership of the POUM of being "agents" of Franco.

The absurdity of this accusation is clear to anyone who is acquainted with even the simplest facts about the Spanish revolution. The members of the POUM fought heroically against the fascists on all fronts in Spain. Nin is an old and incorruptible revolutionary. He defended the interests of the Spanish and Catalan peoples against the agents of the Soviet bureaucracy. That was why the GPU got rid of him by means of a

From the Russian *Bulletin of the Opposition*, no. 58-59, September-October 1937. Signed "L. T." Translated for this volume from the Russian by Iain Fraser.

The November-December 1971 issue of *La Batalla*, which is published by the POUM in exile in France, reprinted Trotsky's letter with a note on the factual errors it contained. It was not known until long after the civil war was over that Nin had not been executed in the jail in Barcelona. The GPU took him immediately from Barcelona; his torture and assassination took place in Alcalá de Henares, on a date that is still not precisely known.

well-prepared "raid" on the Barcelona jail. What role in this matter was played by the official Spanish authorities remains a matter for speculation.

The newspaper dispatch inspired by the GPU calls Nin a "Trotskyist." The dead revolutionary often protested against this appellation, and with complete justification. Both under the leadership of Maurín and under that of Nin, the POUM remained hostile to the Fourth International. It is true that during the years 1931-1933, Nin, who was not then a member of the POUM, kept up a friendly correspondence with me. But as early as the beginning of 1933, differences of opinion on questions of principle led to a complete break between us. In the course of the last four years, we have exchanged only polemical articles. The POUM excluded Trotskyists from its ranks. The GPU calls everyone who is in opposition to the Soviet bureaucracy a Trotskyist. This makes their bloody vengeance easy.

Quite apart from the differences of opinion that separate me from the POUM, I must acknowledge that in the struggle that Nin led against the Soviet bureaucracy, it was Nin who was right. He tried to defend the independence of the Spanish proletariat from the diplomatic machinations and intrigues of the clique that holds power in Moscow. He did not want the POUM to become a tool in the hands of Stalin. He refused to cooperate with the GPU against the interests of the Spanish people. This was his only crime. And for this crime he paid with his life.

67   THE CIVIL WAR IN SPAIN

August 16, 1937

A civil war can be won only by advancing a bold program that satisfies the aspirations of the people. Franco's military

---

From the January 1938 *Quatrième Internationale*, the magazine of the Parti Ouvrier Internationaliste, under the title "Answers to Questions of *México al Día*." Translated from the French for this volume by A. L. Preston.

successes are the result of the policy Stalin imposes on the Negrín government16 — a policy of preserving the social system, which is directed against the masses of workers and peasants.

After a series of defeats, Stalin is trying to shift the responsibility onto the left wing, calling its leaders agents of Franco — hence the shameful assassination of Nin and other leaders of the POUM by the GPU. If this policy continues for another month or two, the defeat of the revolution will become a fait accompli.

The Spanish people must be freed from the domination of the Moscow bureaucracy. They must be given a revolutionary program and a revolutionary government. This will assure the total victory of the revolution.

68   *A TEST OF IDEAS AND INDIVIDUALS THROUGH THE SPANISH EXPERIENCE*

August 24, 1937
To all organizations adhering to the Fourth International:

The Spanish revolution has enormous significance in the eyes of advanced workers, not only as a historical event of primary importance, but also as a school of revolutionary strategy. Ideas and individuals are being submitted to an exceptionally important, one may say an infallible test. It is an obligation for every serious Marxist to study not only the events of the revolution but also the political positions that are taken in our own ranks by various groups and isolated militants with regard to the Spanish events.

Comrade Vereecken and Comrade Sneevliet

In this letter I would like to dwell on a particular case, but one that is instructive in the highest degree: to examine the position of Comrade Vereecken, one of the leading members of our Belgian section. Vereecken gave the report on the Span-

From the *Internal Bulletin*, Organizing Committee for the Socialist Party Convention, no. 1, October 1937. Signed "Crux."

ish question at the meeting of the Central Committee of the Revolutionary Socialist Party held at the end of June this year. The report on his speech, published in the internal bulletin of the Belgian section for June-July, is extremely short, perhaps twenty-five lines at most, but it nevertheless gives a clear enough picture of Comrade Vereecken's mistakes, mistakes that are as dangerous for our Belgian section as for the whole International.

Comrade Sneevliet, head of the Dutch RSAP, has been in complete solidarity, as is known, with the policy of the POUM, and has thus shown clearly to what extent he has become divorced from revolutionary Marxism. Comrade Vereecken's case is somewhat different. Vereecken is more cautious. His arguments, in the past as well as now, are mingled with reservations: "on the one hand," "on the other hand." With regard to the POUM he has a "critical" position, borrowing numerous arguments from our common arsenal. But fundamentally his centrist position is much more likely to bring confusion into our ranks than the position of Comrade Sneevliet. For this reason it is necessary to submit the conception of Vereecken to careful criticism.

Optimistic fatalism, a feature of centrism

Vereecken gave his report before the crushing of the POUM and before the vile assassination of its head by the agents of Stalin in Spain (Antonov-Ovsëenko and others).17 We will unshakably defend the memory of Nin and his companions against the slanders of the scoundrels in Moscow and elsewhere. But the tragic fate of Nin cannot change our political estimates, dictated by the historical interests of the proletariat and not by sentimental considerations.

For a long time, Comrade Vereecken has been completely mistaken in his evaluation of the POUM, thinking that under the pressure of events this party would, so to speak, evolve "automatically" toward the left and that our policy in Spain would be limited to a "critical" support of the POUM. Events have absolutely disproved this fatalistic and optimistic prognosis, extremely characteristic of centrist, but by no means of Marxist thinking. It is enough to recall here that this same fatalistic optimism imbued the whole policy of the POUM, whose leadership had adapted itself to the Anarchist leaders, in the hope that they would enter automatically the path of the proletarian revolution, just as Vereecken had adapted himself to the leaders of the POUM. All these expectations were completely destroyed: events hurled the Anarchist leaders, as well as the leaders of the POUM, not to the left but to the right. Instead of openly recognizing the falseness of his policy, Vereecken tries to pass over surreptitiously to a new position, distinguished from that of the day before only by an even greater confusion.

Characterization of the POUM

"In distinction to the CNT and the FAI, which have existed for dozens of years"—so Vereecken begins his report—"the POUM is recent, heterogeneous, its left wing is weak." This description represents a radical condemnation not only of Sneevliet's position but also of Vereecken's own previous position. For where is the promised evolution toward the left? At the same time, this characterization of the POUM is purposely vague. The "left wing is weak." The word "left" means nothing in this context. Is he referring to the Marxist faction in the POUM or to the left centrist faction? Vereecken intentionally refrains from answering this question. We will answer for him: no Marxist faction of any consequence, since the exclusion of the "Trotskyites," has existed in the POUM. But even the left faction of the centrists is weak. On this point Vereecken is right. But this means only that after six years of experience in the revolution, the policy of the POUM is determined by the right centrists. Such is the unvarnished truth.

Comrade Vereecken "criticizes" the POUM

Now let us hear how Vereecken criticizes the POUM: "Mistakes of the POUM: rallying to the Popular Front at the time of the elections. They repaired this error on the nineteenth of July by armed struggle. Another mistake: participation in the government and the dissolution of the committees. But after they came out of the government a clarification took place in the POUM."

All this reminds one, at first glance, of Marxist criticism. Actually, Vereecken uses sterilized fragments of Marxist criticism not to unveil but on the contrary to mask the opportunist tactics of the POUM—and his own. Above all one is struck by the fact that for our critic it is a question of isolated "mistakes" on the part of the POUM and not of a Marxist appraisal of their whole policy. There can be "mistakes" in any organization. Marx made mistakes, Lenin made mistakes, also the Bolshevik Party as a whole. But these mistakes were corrected in time, thanks to the accuracy of the fundamental line. For the POUM, it is a question not of isolated "mistakes" but of a fundamental line that is nonrevolutionary, centrist, that is to say, essentially opportunist. In other words, for a revolutionary party "mistakes" are the exception; for the POUM, the exception is a few isolated correct steps.

The nineteenth of July, 1936

Vereecken reminds us that on the nineteenth of July, 1936, the POUM participated in the armed struggle. Of course! Only a *counterrevolutionary* organization would not have been able to participate in this struggle, which comprised the whole proletariat: none of us, obviously, have so characterized the POUM. But how could participation in the struggle of the masses, who in those days imposed *their* policy on both the Anarchists and the Socialists as well as the POUMists, "repair the error" of participation in the Popular Front? Perhaps the POUM changed the fundamental direction of its policy? Not at all! The struggle of the nineteenth of July, in spite of the real victory of the workers, ended in the ambiguity of dual power only because no organization had the necessary clear-headedness and courage to carry the struggle through to the end. The participation of the POUM in the Popular Front was not a fortuitous "mistake" but the infallible sign of its opportunist character. In the July days only the external situation had changed, but not the centrist character of the party. The POUM adapted itself to the electoral mechanism of the Popular Front. The zigzag of centrism to the left complemented its zigzag to the right, but in no way repaired it. And during the zigzag to the left, the POUM held its hybrid position wholly intact and precisely in doing this prepared the catastrophe of the future.

Participation in the government

"The other mistake," says Vereecken, "was the participation in the government and the dissolution of the committees." Where could this "other mistake" have come from, if participation in the July insurrection had "repaired" the previous false policy?

Actually, participation in the government was a new zigzag that originated in the centrist nature of the party. Comrade Sneevliet has written that he "understands" this participation. Alas, this ambiguous formula shows only that Sneevliet *does not* understand the laws of the class struggle in the epoch of the revolution.

The July days of 1936, when the Catalan proletariat with correct leadership could, without additional efforts or sacrifices, have seized power and opened the era of the dictatorship of the proletariat throughout Spain, ended, largely through the fault of the POUM, in a regime between the proletariat (committees) and the bourgeoisie, represented by its lackeys (Stalinist, Anarchist, and Socialist leaders). The interest of the workers was to do away with the equivocal and dangerous situation as rapidly as possible, by handing over all power to the committees, that is, to the Spanish soviets. The task of the bourgeoisie, on the other hand, was to do away with the committees in the name of "unity of power." The participation of Nin in the government was a corporate part of the plan of the bourgeoisie, directed against the proletariat. If Sneevliet "understands" such a thing, so much the worse for him. Vereecken is more cautious: he speaks of the participation in the government as the "other mistake." Not bad, this "mistake" that consisted in directly supporting the government of the bourgeoisie against the workers' committees!

"But," Vereecken hastens to break the point of his criticism, "after they had come out of the government a clarification took place in the POUM." This is an obvious untruth that Vereecken himself has refuted in his characterization of the POUM, already quoted, as a *heterogeneous* party in which the left is weak. In what then does this "clarification" consist, after which even the left centrists constitute a feeble minority in the party? Or perhaps by "clarification" we should understand . . . the exclusion of the Bolshevik-Leninists?

Criticism of the International Secretariat

Vereecken goes even farther in defending the case of centrism. After enumerating the "mistakes" of the POUM, he immediately goes on to enumerate, in the interest of symmetry, the "mistakes" of the International Secretariat. Let us look again at his actual words.

"Mistakes of the International Secretariat: ten days after the

nineteenth of July, they had no position in Paris. They did
not understand the importance of the events. They did not at-
tend the Brussels conference; *they applied too literally the Paris
resolution.* They should have profited by this occasion to push
the POUM toward a revolutionary policy. They cut themselves
off from Nin by the publication of Trotsky's letter."

One cannot believe one's own eyes in reading this accu-
mulation of "accusations"! Naturally, the International Secretariat [IS] may have been guilty of certain practical negli-
gences and even of certain political mistakes. But to place these
on the same level as the opportunistic policy of the POUM is
to assume the inappropriate role of arbiter between a party
which is hostile to us and our own international organization. Comrade Vereecken reveals here, not for the first time,
a dispiriting lack of a sense of proportion. However, let us
examine his accusations more closely.

"Ten days" after the nineteenth of July, the IS had no position! Admitting that this is correct, what was the reason for
it? Lack of information? Excessive caution? Vereecken does
not explain. Of course, it is better to have a "position" immediately. But on one condition: that it should be correct. The
IS is the supreme administrative institution. It had to be very
cautious in taking a political position, the more so as it was
not immediately directing and could not direct the struggle
in Spain. But if "ten days after" the IS had no position, one
year after the nineteenth of July, Comrade Vereecken occupies
a wholly false position. This is incomparably worse.

The Brussels conference[18]

It was necessary, you see, to take part once again in the
pitiful and paltry conference of centrists in Brussels, in order
"to push the POUM toward a revolutionary policy." The POUM
should have been influenced, it appears, not in Barcelona
but in Brussels, not in front of the revolutionary masses but
in the closed chambers of a conference. As if it were the first
time that we had encountered the leaders of the POUM! As if
for six years we had not attempted to "push" them onto the
road of revolutionary policy! We used every method and every
path: abundant correspondence, sending of delegates, organizational connections, numerous articles and entire pamphlets,

finally, public criticism. Nevertheless, instead of adopting a Marxist policy, the leaders of the POUM, frightened by the inexorable requirements of the revolution, definitely adopted the line of centrism. For Vereecken, all this is evidently a slip of no importance. What would have had enormous importance, it seems, is . . . the centrist conference in Brussels, where Vereecken, before one or two POUM leaders, would have given a speech that *at best* would have repeated what had been said and written hundreds of times before the conference. This time again Comrade Vereecken rounds out the centrist with the sectarian.

For the sectarian the supreme moment of existence is that in which he exhibits himself at the thousand and first conference!

Trotsky's letter

Finally, the last accusation: the publication of Trotsky's letter. The letter, as far as I know, was not designed for publication. But one must really have lost the last shreds of political insight to see in the publication of this letter an important determining factor in our relations with the POUM. The letter described the participation in the bloc with the bourgeoisie as a *betrayal* of the proletariat. Is this right or wrong?

We have never suspected the purity of Nin's intentions. But the political evaluation of his participation in the Popular Front as an act of betrayal was absolutely correct. How, therefore, could the publication of this letter "cut us off" from Nin? Even before the publication of the letter, we were sufficiently cut off from him, and not by accident: his whole policy went in the opposite direction from ours. It was not for some whim that Nin broke with us three years before the publication of Trotsky's letter. Or does Vereecken mean perhaps that after the elections Nin was evolving toward us, and that the publication of the letter stopped this evolution?

Vereecken's words can have no other meaning, admitting that they have even a shadow of meaning. Actually, as we know, Nin and his friends continued to think that their participation in the Popular Front and afterwards in the government was correct, and they demanded even the renewal of this participation. There too it was a question not of a "mistake" but of an entire political line.

Finally, if one admits even that the POUM understood the "mistake" of having participated in the Popular Front, how could the publication of the letter, containing a sharp analysis of this mistake, prevent the evolution of the POUM? Is Vereecken trying to say (if he is trying to say anything!) that Nin was so offended by the letter that he decided to return to his previous incorrect position? But such an opinion is too insulting to Nin, who was guided by political ideas and not by considerations of petty personal self-conceit.

Such are the "mistakes" of the IS which Vereecken puts on the same level as the centrist policies of the POUM. In this he shows only that he himself occupies an intermediary position between Marxism and centrism.

The preparation for the May days (1937)

Vereecken then proceeds to the events of May of this year.

"It can be maintained," he says, "that the POUM was expecting them and was arming. The scope of the events took the party unawares. But any party would have been taken unawares."

Every sentence is a mistake; moreover not an accidental mistake, but the product of a false political line. The events of May could be "foreseen" and prepared for in only one way: by declaring an uncompromising struggle against the governments of Catalonia and Spain; by refusing all political collaboration with them; by opposing their own party to all other parties, that is, to their directing centers, particularly and above all to the leadership of the CNT; by not allowing the masses for one instant to confuse the revolutionary leaders with the lackeys of the bourgeoisie! An uncompromising policy of this kind, with, of course, active participation in the military struggle and in the revolutionary actions of the masses, would have assured the POUM of an unshakable authority among all the workers, above all among the Anarchists who constitute the great majority of the Catalan proletariat. Instead of that, the POUM demanded the reentrance of its leaders into the counterrevolutionary government and at the same time asserted in every issue of *La Batalla* that the workers could take power without a fight. It was even with this goal that the POUM launched the infantile project of a special congress to be convoked by the bourgeois government in order to . . .

hand over the power to the workers and peasants. This is precisely why the POUM was taken unawares and why the events of May were for it only another stage on the road to catastrophe.

"But," cried Vereecken, "any party would have been taken unawares." This unbelievable sentence shows once again that Vereecken does not know the difference between a centrist and a Marxist party. One can, of course, recognize that a real mass insurrection goes beyond, *to a greater or lesser degree,* any revolutionary party. But the difference lies precisely in the *degree:* here too quantity turns into quality. A centrist party is carried away by events and is drowned in them, whereas a revolutionary party in the final showdown dominates them and assures victory.

"Defensive and not offensive"

"On the fourth and fifth of May," Vereecken continues, "its policy (the POUM's) was correct: defensive and not offensive. To march on to the taking of power would have been adventurism in the contingencies of the moment. The great mistake of the POUM was that it threw out illusions during the retreat and passed off the defeat as a victory."

You see with what apothecary's precision Vereecken weighs and balances the "correct" actions and the "mistakes" of the POUM. However, his whole argument is nothing but error. Who said — and where — that to go on in May to taking power was adventurism? This was not, above all, the opinion of the POUM itself. The day before it was still assuring the workers that if they wanted to, they would take power without a fight. The workers "wanted to." Wherein is the adventurism? The element of vile provocation on the part of the Stalinists, from the point of view that interests us here, is of secondary importance. All the reports after the events show that with a leadership with any seriousness and confidence in itself the victory of the May insurrection would have been assured. In this sense the POUM was right when it said that the workers could take power if they "wanted to." It forgot only to add: unfortunately you have no revolutionary leadership. The POUM could not lead the Catalan proletariat to the revolutionary offensive because — and only because — all its previous policy had rendered it incapable of such initiative.

"The July days" of 1917 and "the May days" of 1937

At this point, Comrade Vereecken can, however, retort: "But even the Bolsheviks in July 1917 did not decide to seize power and limited themselves to the defensive, leading the masses out of the line of fire with as few victims as possible. Why then was this policy not suitable for the POUM?"

Let us examine this argument. Comrades Sneevliet and Vereecken are very fond of reminding us that Spain "is not Russia," that it is impossible to apply "Russian" methods there, etc. Abstract homilies of this kind make no serious impression. Whether well or poorly done, we have endeavored during the past six years to analyze the concrete conditions of the Spanish revolution. Even at the beginning, we warned that one must not expect a rapid rhythm in the development of events, in the manner of Russia in 1917. On the contrary, we used the analogy of the Great French Revolution, which began in 1789 and passed through a series of stages before attaining its culmination in 1793. But it is precisely because we are not at all inclined to schematize historic events that we do not consider it possible to transport the tactics of the Bolsheviks in July 1917 in Petersburg to the events of May 1937 in Catalonia. "Spain is not Russia." The differentiating features are too obvious.

The armed demonstration of the Petersburg proletariat broke out four months after the beginning of the revolution, three months after the Bolshevik Party had launched a truly Bolshevik program (Lenin's April theses). The overwhelming mass of the population of the gigantic country was only just beginning to emerge from the illusions of February. At the front was an army of twelve million men who were only then being touched by the first rumors about the Bolsheviks. Under these conditions, the isolated insurrection of the Petersburg proletariat would have led inevitably to their being crushed. It was necessary to gain time. These were the circumstances that determined the tactic of the Bolsheviks.

In Spain the May events took place not after four months but after six years of revolution. The masses of the whole country have had a gigantic experience. A long time ago, they lost the illusions of 1931, as well as the warmed-over illusions of the Popular Front. Again and again they have shown to every part of the country that they were ready to go through to the end. If the Catalan proletariat had seized power in May 1937 — as it had really seized it in July 1936 — they would have found support throughout all of Spain. The bourgeois-Stalinist reaction would not even have found two regiments with which to crush the Catalan workers. In the territory occupied by Franco not only the workers but also the peasants would have turned toward the Catalan proletariat, would have isolated the fascist army and brought about its irresistible disintegration. It is doubtful whether under these conditions any foreign government would have risked throwing its regiments onto the burning soil of Spain. Intervention would have become materially impossible, or at least extremely dangerous.

Naturally, in every insurrection, there is an element of uncertainty and risk. But the subsequent course of events has proven that even in the case of defeat the situation of the Spanish proletariat would have been incomparably more favorable than now, to say nothing of the fact that the revolutionary party would have assured its future.

But on what does Vereecken base his categorical statement that taking power in Catalonia would have been, in the contingencies of the moment, "adventurism"? On absolutely nothing, unless . . . on the desire to justify the impotence of centrism and at the same time his own policy, which was and remains only the left shadow of centrism.

Vereecken defends the exclusion of the Bolshevik-Leninists

The concluding lines of the record are on the level of the whole report: "they say that there is no democracy in the POUM; but if the Bordigists wanted to enter our party, we would undoubtedly accept, though without the rights of a faction." Who says this? A lawyer for centrism or a revolutionary who numbers himself among the Bolshevik-Leninists? It is hard to tell. Vereecken is fully satisfied with the democracy of the POUM. The opportunists exclude the revolutionaries from their party. Vereecken says: the opportunists are right because the naughty revolutionaries build factions.

Let us recall once more what Vereecken said of the POUM at the beginning: it is "recent, heterogeneous, its left wing is weak." From this heterogeneous party, in its essence composed entirely of factions and sub-factions, the POUM excludes not

the avowed reformist, nor the petty-bourgeois Catalan nationalist, nor, of course, the centrist, but *only* the Bolshevik-
Leninist. This should be clear. Nevertheless, the "Bolshevik-
Leninist" Vereecken approves of the repressions of the centrists.
He is preoccupied, you see, by the juridical question of the
rights of factions, and not by the political question of their
program and tactics.

In the eyes of a Marxist, the revolutionary faction inside
a centrist party is a positive fact; the sectarian or opportunist
faction in the revolutionary party is a negative fact. That
Vereecken should reduce the question to the simple right of
factions to exist shows only that he has completely wiped out
the line of demarcation between centrism and Marxism. Here is
what a true Marxist would say: "They say there is no democracy in the POUM. This is not true. Democracy does exist
there—for the right-wingers, for the centrists, for the confusionists, but not for the Bolshevik-Leninists." In other words, the
extent of democracy in the POUM is determined by the real
content of its centrist policy, radically hostile to revolutionary
Marxism.

Unpardonable sally

But Vereecken does not stop even there. In the interest of
defending the POUM, he resorts to a direct calumny (there is
no other word for it!) against our comrades in Catalonia. "The
Bolshevik-Leninist section of Barcelona," he says, "was made
up of careerists and adventurers." One cannot believe one's
own eyes! Who is saying this? A Social Democrat? A Stalinist?
A bourgeois enemy? No, it is said by a responsible member
of our Belgian section. This is what it means to cling to
mistakes uncovered by the whole march of events! Tomorrow
the agents of the GPU in Barcelona, if the Belgian bulletin
falls into their hands, will say: "By Vereecken's own confession,
the Bolshevik-Leninists are careerists and adventurers. They
must be done away with accordingly!"

I think that it is the duty of all our sections to declare that
we reject with indignation this inadmissible sally of Comrade
Vereecken and that with all our international authority we
support our young Barcelona organization. I will add here:
as is shown by their programmatic call of the nineteenth of
July of this year, our comrades in Barcelona understand the

tasks of the revolution with incomparably greater depth and seriousness than Vereecken. The real "mistake" of the International Secretariat consists rather in that up to the present time, it has not condemned Vereecken's statement and has not insisted on its condemnation by our Belgian section.

Once more we must help Comrade Vereecken to return to the correct line

We have not the slightest intention of aggravating disagreements. We have encountered Comrade Vereecken in various conditions and at different stages of the development of the Belgian section and of the international organization. All of us have learned to appreciate the devotion of Comrade Vereecken to the cause of the working class, his energy, his eagerness to give all his strength disinterestedly to this cause. Young workers should learn this from Comrade Vereecken. But as for his political position, unfortunately, it is most often several yards to the right or to the left of the Marxist line, which, however, does not incline Comrade Vereecken to indulgence for those who remain on this line. In the past we have had to struggle above all against the *sectarian* tendencies of Comrade Vereecken, which have caused no little harm to the Belgian section. But even then it was no secret for us that sectarianism is only a bud from which can always bloom the full flower of opportunism. We now have before us an exceptionally striking confirmation of this law of political botany. Comrade Vereecken has given proof of sectarianism in questions of secondary importance or in formal questions of organization, only to arrive at opportunism in a political question of gigantic historical importance.

The internal life of the Fourth International is founded on the principles of democracy. Comrade Vereecken makes very wide, at times even anarchist, use of this democracy. Nevertheless, the advantage of the democratic regime consists in that the overwhelming majority, relying on experience and on comradely discussion, can formulate freely its authoritative opinion and can at the right moment call back to order a minority that has become engaged in a dangerous path. This is the best service that one can render at the present moment to our Belgian and at the same time to our Dutch sections.

69
ANSWER TO QUESTIONS
ON THE SPANISH SITUATION
(A Concise Summary)

September 14, 1937

1. The difference between Negrín and Franco is the difference between decaying bourgeois democracy and fascism.

2. Everywhere and always, wherever and whenever revolutionary workers are not powerful enough immediately to overthrow the bourgeois regime, they defend even rotten bourgeois democracy from fascism, and they especially defend their own position inside bourgeois democracy.

3. The workers defend bourgeois democracy, however, not by the methods of bourgeois democracy (Popular Fronts, electoral blocs, government coalitions, etc.) but by their own methods, that is, by the methods of revolutionary class struggle. Thus, by participating in the military struggle against fascism they continue at the same time to defend their own organizations, their rights, and their interests from the bourgeois-democratic government.

4. Bourgeois democracy decomposes together with capitalism, which engendered it. The very possibility of fascist insurrection against bourgeois democracy is a sign that its days are numbered. Thus the "regeneration" of bourgeois democracy cannot be a *program* of the proletariat. The defense of bourgeois democracy against fascism is only a *tactical* episode submitted to our line: to overthrow bourgeois democracy and establish the dictatorship of the proletariat.

5. A coalition with the bourgeoisie under the name of Popular Front; participation in the government of the Popular Front; political support of such a government; the renunciation of independent agitation and organization for the revolutionary overthrow of the bourgeois government can, in the best case, only prolong the death agony of bourgeois democracy and more easily prepare the triumph of fascism. The policies not only of the Stalinists and the Socialists, the direct lackeys of the counterrevolution, but also of the leaders of the CNT, and the POUM as well, were and remain pernicious from the point of view of proletarian interests.

From the *Internal Bulletin,* Organizing Committee for the Socialist Party Convention, no. 1, October 1937. Signed "Crux."

6. But if it is true — and it is true — that the government of Stalin-Negrín and the government of Franco are both watchdogs of capitalism; if it is true that the politics of Stalin-Negrín must inevitably lead to the triumph of fascism; it is nevertheless absolutely false to conclude that in the struggle between the armies of Stalin-Negrín and of Franco, the proletariat should take a *neutral* position. The Spanish as well as the world proletariat are interested: (a) in militarily crushing Franco; (b) in a policy during the civil war that is capable of preparing for the earliest overthrow of the government of Stalin-Negrín.

7. One can object to this: during a war between two bourgeois *states,* the revolutionary proletariat, independent of the political regime in its country, must take the position that "the defeat of our own government is the lesser evil." Is this rule not applicable also to the civil war in which two bourgeois governments are fighting against one another?

It is not applicable. In a war between two bourgeois states, the purpose is one of imperialist conquest, and not a struggle between democracy and fascism. In the Spanish civil war, the question is: democracy or fascism.

For the capitalist class, the difference between democracy and fascism is not decisive. It uses democracy or fascism for its own purpose, depending upon circumstances. But for the petty-bourgeois agents of capitalism — the leaders of the Social Democracy, the Stalinists, and the Anarchists — democracy signifies the source of their existence and influence; fascism signifies for them debacle and extermination. The revolutionary proletariat should not put both fighting camps in the same bag; it must use their fight for its own interests. The revolutionaries can be successful not by the politics of neutrality but by dealing military blows to the number one foe: fascism.

8. Franco is an obvious, immediate, and deadly foe, hated by the majority of the workers and peasants. Negrín, Stalin, Caballero, and the others are less obvious, more camouflaged foes who still lead millions of workers and peasants. With Franco the only possible fight is a *physical* one; with Negrín a physical fight at present is impossible because the revolutionary elements are in a minority, and the physical fight, which is inevitable, should be prepared for *politically.* The most important means for this political preparation is to denounce and expose the bad conduct of the war by the govern-

ment and to explain to the masses that the reason for this bad conduct is the servility of the government to the interests of capital.

9. It can be objected that the two imperialist camps (Italy and Germany on one side, and England, France, and the USSR on the other) conduct their struggle on the Iberian Peninsula and that the war in Spain is only an "episode" of this struggle.

In the sense of a historical possibility, it is true. But it is impermissible to identify a historical possibility with the actual, concrete course of the civil war today. The intervention of the imperialist countries has indisputably great influence upon the development of the events in Spain. But until today it has not changed the fundamental character of these events as a struggle between the camp of the Spanish bourgeois democracy and the camp of Spanish fascism.

10. If the war continues on the same basis, the political difference between the two camps can be reduced to zero. But that is only a possibility. As of today it is not a fact. It is necessary therefore to use the situation as it is. The situation can change also in another direction: under the influence of the military blows from Franco, the Negrín government can be forced to make more concessions to the workers, as Kerensky did in August 1917 under the blow from Kornilov. We will use these concessions also for better preparation of the overthrow of Negrín.

11. If Caballero, for example, had been capable of initiating a struggle against Negrín, as was hoped by many, we would have taken the most active part in this struggle without accepting any political responsibility for Caballero. On the contrary, we would have accused him of a lack of revolutionary program and the necessary resoluteness in the fight. But Caballero cowardly fled from his own army, the UGT, from the Anarchist workers, the CNT, who had pushed him on the road of struggle. The flight of this vaudeville hero dispels many illusions, creates more elbowroom for the genuine revolutionists and gives the possibility during the *military* struggle against Franco to mobilize the masses *politically* against Negrín.

12. Let's take an example: two ships with armaments and munitions start from France or from the United States — one for Franco and the other for Negrín. What should be the attitude

of the workers? To sabotage both ships? Or only the one for Franco?

We are not neutral. We will let the ship with the munitions for the Negrín government pass. We have no illusions: from these bullets, only nine of every ten would go against the fascists, at least one against our comrades. But out of those marked for Franco, ten out of every ten would go to our comrades. We are not neutral. We do not let the ship with the munitions for Franco pass. Of course, if an armed insurrection began in Spain, we would try to direct the ships with munitions into the hands of the rebellious workers. But when we are not that strong, we choose the lesser evil.

13. Will we, as a revolutionary party, mobilize new volunteers for Negrín? That would be to send them into the hands of the GPU. Collect money for the Negrín government? Absurd! We will collect money for our own comrades in Spain. If we send comrades across the border, it will be conspiratorially, for our own movement.

14. Our attitude toward such committees as the North American Committee for Spanish Democracy, towards meetings, trade union actions, etc?

We will defend the idea that the trade unions should collect money not for the government but for the Spanish trade unions, for the workers' organizations. If anyone objects that the Spanish trade union leaders are connected with the government and that it is thus impermissible to send them money, we will answer by pointing to a single example: during the miners' strike in Great Britain in 1926, we sent money to the miners' trade union, the leaders of which were closely connected with the British government. Strike committees can be reformists; they can betray; they have connections with the bosses. But we can't avoid them as long as the workers are not capable of changing them. And thus we send them the money with the risk that they will betray the workers. We warn the workers of this, and when it occurs, we say, "You see, your leaders have betrayed you."

15. The Salemme resolution[19] says: "The Cannon-Shachtman-Goldman line of 'preferring a loyalist victory' is identical with the approach of the Stalinists. This open degeneration into the swamp of 'lesser evil' Popular Front politics explodes the pretense that material aid does not involve political support. . . . Workers who refuse to surrender their arms, that is, refuse

to give the government military or material aid, are shot by the government's Stalinist Cheka."[20]

Yes, we know that our comrades are shot by the government's Cheka, but what conclusion does the Salemme group draw? Do they propose desertion from the loyalist army, or a military insurrection? If desertion, where to? Surely not into the camp of Franco. If the government mobilized the workers and peasants, what does refusal to give it military aid signify? It can only signify desertion or insurrection. Or do they mean a general strike? A general strike, especially during a war, can only be with the aim of overthrowing the government, can only be an introduction to an insurrection. I agree fully that if we can call the people to insurrection, we must do so. But can we do it? I would like to know how numerous are the Salemme regiments in Spain, if its resolution was written for Spain and not for the political satisfaction of the author. If we ask the soldier not to fight, then we must ask the worker (who by working in the munitions factory gives "material aid" to the loyalist government) not to work. But if, as is the case, we are not strong enough now to seize power, we must *militarily* fight against Franco under the material conditions determined by the relationship of forces, while at the same time we *politically* prepare for the insurrection against Negrín.

16. Their resolution further states: "Revolutionary workers must not become defenders of a bourgeois government; they can defend only a workers' government. On the other hand, they must become revolutionary defeatists only in an imperialist clash. The class interests of the proletariat in the Spanish civil war demand that revolutionists not only avoid but also struggle against all programs calling for revolutionary defeatism or defensism."

But the war against fascism is more than a defense of the Negrín government. We have our workers' organizations. In Spain, especially in Catalonia, there is socialist property, collectivized farms. The Negrín government is against that, but so far it must tolerate it. We must defend those conquests against Franco.

17. The Salemme resolution says: "In no case must revolutionists raise slogans calling for the sabotage of the military struggle against Franco, [since] to do this would be to slip into the position of revolutionary defeatism."

This announcement speaks for itself. These "revolutionists"

are so revolutionary that they feel condemned by their own position and proclaim that they will not call for "sabotage of the military struggle against Franco." Is this assurance not a bit . . . humiliating for these "revolutionists"? Not less interesting is the fact that the authors speak only against "sabotage" of the republican army. Do they stand for the sabotage of the Franco army? Are the authors for sabotage in the fascist army? Why do they keep silent? This "omission" is very characteristic for the whole position of the group; under the cover of vehement expressions and terribly radical formulas, they try to conceal their lack of confidence in themselves. That is not surprising. The school of purely formal intransigence is condemned at every step to close its eyes to reality, and when a pupil of such a school accidentally opens his eyes, he becomes an opportunist. We now have such a striking example in Belgium with Comrade Vereecken.

18. The Salemme resolution further states: "The Social Democrats who criminally preferred the victory of Hindenburg to that of Hitler, and got both, or the Stalinists who preferred Roosevelt to Landon, are no more politically degenerate than the Cannons and Shachtmans who prefer the victory of the Negríns over the Francos and will get either a Negrín military dictatorship or a Negrín-Franco truce."

The civil war between Negrín and Franco does not signify the same thing as the electoral competition of Hindenburg and Hitler. If Hindenburg had entered into an open *military* fight against Hitler, then Hindenburg would have been a "lesser evil." We do not choose the "greater evil," we choose the "lesser evil." But Hindenburg was not the "lesser evil"—he did not go into open warfare against Hitler; the Social Democrats hoped for that—that was stupid—but that was not the case. But here we do have a war of the Social Democrats against fascism. To support Hindenburg against Hitler meant to give up political independence. Here too we do not support Negrín politically. If we were to have a member in the Cortes, he would vote against the military budget of Negrín.* We charge Negrín

---

* To vote for the military budget of the Negrín government signifies to vote him *political* confidence. We cannot do it. To do it would be a crime. How can we explain our vote to the Anarchist workers? Very simply: We have not the slightest confidence in the capacity of this government to conduct the war and assure victory. We accuse this government of protecting the rich and starving the poor. This gov-

with the political responsibility for the conduct of the war. But at the same time, we must repulse the fascist hordes until the moment when we ourselves can take into our hands the conduct of the war.

To affirm that to fight together with the Negrín forces against Franco is the same as to vote for Hindenburg against Hitler is an expression, I am sorry to say, of what is known as parliamentary cretinism. The war against fascism cannot be resolved by parliamentary means because fascism is an army of reaction that can be crushed only by force. That's why we were against the policy of the Social Democrats in Germany — the pure parliamentary combination with Hindenburg against Hitler. We called for the creation of workers' militias, etc. But here we do have a fight against fascism. It is true that the general staff of the "democratic" army is capable of tomorrow making a truce with Franco, but it is not a fact today. And we can't overlook the real events. Tactically we must use the war of the republicans against the fascists for the purpose of a strategical aim: the overthrow of the capitalist regime.

19. The Salemme resolution states: "Cannon and Shachtman say in the plenum report, July 30: 'Whoever would, for example, refuse to support the government in the war against the fascists by such material aid as fighting in the Loyalist army, *would be criminally remiss in his elementary proletarian duty*' (Our emphasis). We ask Cannon-Shachtman: Were the revolutionary workers of Catalonia who fought against the encroachments of bourgeois military discipline — were they remiss in their elementary proletarian duty? Were they remiss when they refused to give arms, that is, material aid, to the bourgeois Loyalist army? . . . Were they acting then as agents of the Fifth Column, as Burnham[21] accused us of acting when we refused to give military aid to the Popular Front?"

Everything here is put in the same bag. The Catalan workers fought against the government on May 3-7. Not conscious-

ernment must be smashed. So long as we are not strong enough to replace it, we are fighting under its command. But on every occasion we express openly our nonconfidence in it; it is the only possible way to mobilize the masses *politically* against this government and to prepare its overthrow. Any other politics would be a betrayal of the revolution. — Crux [L. T.]

ly but instinctively they fought for power, which could give them the opportunity to better continue the war against Franco. But they tried this without the necessary revolutionary leadership and they were defeated. Now they are ten times weaker than before the May events. The workers now ask: What should we do now, not in the Bronx or Manhattan, but in Spain? Try to overthrow Negrín by insurrection? But we are too weak, we are now disarmed. The Salemme group will answer us with our own words: you must prepare the masses *politically* for the future overthrow of the Negrín government. Good. But this requires time. And meanwhile Franco is approaching. Should we not try to crush him?

The slogan "Neither victory nor defeat" or "We are neither defensists nor defeatists" is false from a principled point of view and politically pernicious. It is devoid of every agitational value. Imagine a revolutionist standing between two camps of civil war with a banner: Neither victory nor defeat. This is a slogan for a club of Pontius Pilates, not for a revolutionary party. We are for the defense of the workers' organizations and the victory of the revolution over Franco. We are "defensists." The "defeatists" are Negrín and Stalin and their ilk. We participate in the struggle against Franco as the best soldiers, and at the same time, in the interests of the victory over fascism, we agitate for the social revolution and we prepare for the overthrow of the defeatist government of Negrín. Only such an attitude can give us an approach to the masses.

70   *LETTER TO JAMES P. CANNON*

September 21, 1937
Dear Comrade Cannon:

I am a bit disquieted by the letter of Comrade Shachtman that I received yesterday. The last thesis on Spain accepted by the National Committee seemed to me not satisfactory.

From the personal archives of J. P. Cannon, who was soon to be elected national secretary of the Socialist Workers Party. A copy to Shachtman was indicated.

I discussed the matter with Comrade Weber when he was here.[22] The question of the so-called material aid to the Negrín government was too generally formulated and could thus give a certain basis for the "left" opposition — Salemme and others. I was and still remain sure that it is not a question of fundamental disagreement but only of an unsatisfactory formulation. I gave my answers to the questions of Comrade Dick Lorre of Los Angeles in written form in order to make more precise the thesis of the National Committee and to counterpose more concretely the Marxist position to that of the Oehlerites, etc.[23] But the letter of Comrade Shachtman aroused some doubts in my mind. I hope that the doubts are not justified.

A vote in parliament for the financial budget is not a "material" aid, but an act of political solidarity. If we can vote for Negrín's budget, why can't we delegate our representative to his government? It can also be interpreted as a "material aid."

The French Stalinists give their full confidence to the Popular Front government but officially they don't participate in it. We call this kind of nonparticipation the worst, most pernicious kind of participation. To give Blum and Chautemps[24] all the means they need for their actions signifies political participation in the government coalition.

The question of Comrade Shachtman: "How can we refuse to devote a million pesetas to the purchase of rifles for the front?" was a hundred and a thousand times put to the revolutionary Marxists by the reformists: "How can you vote against the millions and millions necessary for schools, for roads, not to speak of national defense?" We recognize the necessity of schools and roads no less than the necessity of the fight against Franco. We use the "capitalist" railroads; our children go to the "capitalist" schools; but we refuse to vote for the budget of the capitalist government.

During our fight against Kornilov, we never voted in the soviet in a way that could have been interpreted as political solidarity with Kerensky.

From the point of view of agitation, we would not now have in Spain the slightest difficulty explaining our negative vote: "We asked for two million for rifles and they gave only one million. We asked for distribution of the rifles under workers' control; they refused. We asked that the police be disarmed and their rifles given to the front; they refused. How can we *voluntarily* give our money and our confidence to this government?" Every worker would understand and approve of our action.

All the Negrín government does is done under the sign of war necessities. If we accept political responsibility for *their* management of the war necessities, we would politically vote for every serious governmental proposition. In the same way, we would praise them in our press, at our meetings. Thus we would become a governmental party a la POUM. How can we, under such conditions, prepare for the overthrow of the Negrín government? The whole sense of my answers is: we fight against Franco militarily in spite of the existence of the Negrín government, and simultaneously we prepare polit- ically for the overthrow of the Negrín government. If we agree on this fundamental principle, we can't disagree on the practical consequences.

Did you receive my polemical letter against Comrade Vereecken on the Spanish question? Will you publish it also in your bulletin? It seems to me doubly necessary now: (1) to expose the absolutely opportunist position of Vereecken; (2) to show how easily the people who are ultraleft on minor questions become opportunists in the face of great events.

In the last two weeks I read all our international bulletins from the International Secretariat, from our Barcelona organi- zation, from the French and German sections, and I was greatly impressed by the high level of analysis, especially concerning the Spanish events. I don't know if all this precious material is being read and studied by the leading comrades in the United States. The best articles should be translated into English, some for the internal bulletins and others for the *New International.* [25]

With best greetings,
Trotsky

[From a postscript to a letter to Shachtman and Cannon on other subjects]

September 25, 1937

P. S. In the *Socialist Appeal* of November 1, 1936, I find on the first page, in the editorial, the following sentence: "Revo- lutionary workers must continue their agitation for arms for the Spanish workers and peasants, not for the Spanish bour- geois-democratic government."

It was written at the time of Largo Caballero, before the

bloody repressions against the revolutionary workers. How then could we vote for the military budget for the Negrín government?

L. T.

71

ULTRALEFTS IN GENERAL AND INCURABLE ULTRALEFTS IN PARTICULAR
(A Few Theoretical Considerations)

September 28, 1937

Marxist thought is concrete, that is, it looks upon all the decisive or important factors in any given question, not only from the point of view of their reciprocal relations, but also from that of their development. It never dissolves the momentary situation within the general perspective, but by means of the general perspective makes possible an analysis of the momentary situation in all its peculiarities. Politics has its point of departure in precisely this sort of concrete analysis. Opportunist thought and sectarian thought have this feature in common: they extract from the complexity of circumstances and forces one or two factors that appear to them to be the most important (and sometimes are, to be sure), isolate them from the complex reality, and attribute to them unlimited and unrestricted powers.

In that way, for the long epoch preceding the world war, reformism made use of the very important but temporary factors of that time, such as the powerful development of capitalism, the rise in the standard of living of the proletariat, and the stability of democracy. Today sectarianism makes use of these most important factors and tendencies: the decline of capitalism, the falling standard of living of the masses, the decomposition of democracy, etc. But like reformism in the preceding epoch, sectarianism transforms historic tendencies into omnipotent and absolute factors. The "ultralefts" conclude their analysis just where it should really begin. They counter-

From the *Internal Bulletin,* Organizing Committee for the Socialist Party Convention, no. 1, October 1937.

pose a ready-made schema to reality. But since the masses live in the sphere of reality, the sectarian schema does not make the slightest impression on the mentality of the workers. By its very essence, sectarianism is doomed to sterility.

Imperialist capitalism is no longer capable of developing the productive forces of humanity. For this reason it can grant the workers neither material concessions nor effective social reforms. All this is correct. But it is only correct on the scale of an entire epoch. There are branches of industry that have developed since the war with prodigious force (automotives, aviation, electricity, radio) despite the fact that the general level of production has not risen, or has risen very little, above the prewar and wartime levels. Moreover, this decrepit economy has its ebbs and flows. The workers are almost continually passing from one struggle to another, and sometimes they are victorious. Of course, capitalism takes from the workers with its right hand what it has given them with its left. That is how the rise in prices is wiping out the great gains of the Léon Blum era. But this result, determined by the intervention of various factors, in its turn impels the workers upon the road of struggle. It is precisely this potent dialectic of our epoch that opens up a revolutionary perspective.

A trade union leader who would let himself be guided by the general tendency of rotting capitalism in order to abandon all economic and partial struggle would be, in actuality, in spite of his "revolutionary" concepts, an agent of reaction. A Marxist trade union leader must not only grasp the general tendencies of capitalism, but also analyze the specific features of the situation, the conjuncture, the local conditions — the psychological element included — in order to propose a position of struggle, of watchful waiting, or of retreat. It is only on the basis of this practical activity, intimately linked with the experience of the great mass, that the trade union leader is able to lay bare the general tendencies of decomposing capitalism and to educate the workers for the revolution.

It is a truism that our epoch is characterized politically by a relentless struggle between socialism (communism) and fascism. But unfortunately this does not mean that the proletariat is already and everywhere conscious of this alternative, nor that in any given country, at any given moment, it may ignore the partial struggle to safeguard its democratic liberties. The fundamental alternative, communism or fascism, established by Lenin, has become for many a hollow formula, which the left centrists use only too often to cover up their capitulations, or the sectarians to justify their inaction.

Upon entering the government of the Catalan Generalitat, [26] the unfortunate Andrés Nin began his broadcast declarations with the following thesis: "The struggle that is beginning is not the struggle between bourgeois democracy and fascism, as some think, but between fascism and socialism." This formula, moreover, was in current usage by the POUM. All the articles of *La Batalla* were only interpretations and variations of it. We saw some sectarians, in Belgium, for example, seize upon this formula in order to find in it the complete or partial justification of the policy of the POUM. However, in practice, Nin transformed the Leninist formula into its opposite: he entered a bourgeois government whose objective was the spoliation and the stifling of all the gains, all the props of the incipient socialist revolution. The substance of his thoughts was the following: since this revolution is a socialist revolution "in essence," our entry into the government can only aid it. And the pseudo-revolutionary sectarian exclaimed: "Nin's participation in the government is perhaps a mistake, but it would be a crime to exaggerate its importance. Hasn't Nin recognized that the revolution is socialist 'in essence'?" Yes, he proclaimed it, but only in order to justify the policy that sapped the foundations of the revolution.

The socialist character of the revolution, determined by the fundamental social factors of our epoch, is not, however, given ready-made and completely guaranteed right from the beginning of revolutionary development. No, from April 1931 onward, the great Spanish drama has taken on the character of a "republican" and "democratic" revolution. During the years that followed, the bourgeoisie was able to impose its stamp upon events, even though the Leninist alternative, communism or fascism, retained — in the last analysis — all its value. The more the left centrists and the sectarians transform this alternative into a suprahistorical law, the less they are capable of tearing the masses away from the grip of the bourgeoisie. Still worse, they only strengthened this grip. The POUM paid dearly for this experience — moreover, unfortunately, without drawing the necessary lessons.

If the left centrists hide behind Lenin in order to imprison the revolution within its original framework, that is, the framework of bourgeois democracy, the ultralefts draw from the same Leninist alternative the right to ignore and to "boycott" the real development of the revolution.

"The difference between the Negrín government and that of Franco," I said in reply to an American comrade, "is the difference between decaying bourgeois democracy and fascism." It is with this elementary consideration that our political orientation begins. What! exclaim the ultralefts, you want to restrict us to a choice between bourgeois democracy and fascism? But that's pure opportunism! The Spanish revolution is fundamentally a struggle between socialism and fascism. Bourgeois democracy does not offer the slightest solution. . . . And so on.

The alternative, *socialism or fascism,* merely signifies, and that is enough, that the Spanish revolution can be victorious only through the dictatorship of the proletariat. But that does not at all mean that its victory is assured in advance. The problem still remains, and therein lies the whole political task, *to transform this hybrid, confused, half-blind and half-deaf revolution into a socialist revolution.* It is necessary not only to say what is but also to know how to use "what is" as one's point of departure. The leading parties, even those who speak about socialism, including the POUM, are doing everything they can to prevent the transformation of this despoiled and disfigured halfway revolution into a conscious and completed revolution. At the moment of revolutionary upsurge, the working class, impelled by its instinct, succeeded in establishing important landmarks on the road to socialism. But these are landmarks that have been swept away by the leading parties. It is not at all difficult to skip over this contradictory reality by contenting oneself with a few sociological generalizations. But that does not advance developments by a hairsbreadth. It is necessary to overcome material difficulties in action, that is, by means of a tactic suited to reality.

The military struggle in Spain is at the present time being conducted by Franco on one side, and by Stalin-Negrín on the other. While Franco represents fascism, Stalin-Negrín do not at all represent socialism. On the contrary, they represent a "democratic" brake that obstructs the movement toward socialism. The *historic* alternative, communism or fascism, has not yet achieved its *political* expression. Far from it. Since

July 1936, the Spanish revolution has even been thrown far behind the objective that Nin formulated without understanding it. But the civil war in Spain remains, in spite of everything, a fact of capital importance. It is necessary to understand this fact for what it is, that is, an armed struggle between two armed camps, subordinated on the one hand to bourgeois democracy and on the other to avowed fascism. It is necessary to find a correct attitude toward this hybrid struggle in order to transform it from within into a struggle for the proletarian dictatorship.

The Stalin-Negrín government is a quasi-democratic obstacle on the road to socialism; but it is also an obstacle, not a very reliable or durable one, but an obstacle nonetheless, on the road to fascism. Tomorrow or the day after tomorrow, the Spanish proletariat may perhaps be able to break through this obstacle and seize power. But if it aided, even passively, in tearing it down today, it would only serve fascism. The task consists not merely of theoretically evaluating the two camps at their true worth, but moreover of utilizing their struggle in practice in order to make a leap forward.

The left centrists as well as the incurable ultralefts often cite the example of Bolshevik policy in the Kerensky-Kornilov conflict, without understanding anything about it. The POUM says: "But the Bolsheviks fought alongside Kerensky." The ultralefts reply: "But the Bolsheviks refused to give Kerensky their confidence even under the threat of Kornilov." Both are right . . . halfway; that is, both are completely wrong.

The Bolsheviks did not remain neutral between the camp of Kerensky and that of Kornilov. They fought in the first camp against the second. They accepted the official command as long as they were not sufficiently strong to overthrow it. It was precisely in the month of August, with the Kornilov uprising, that a prodigious upswing of the Bolsheviks began. This upswing was made possible only thanks to the double-edged Bolshevik policy. While participating in the front lines of the struggle against Kornilov, the Bolsheviks did not take the slightest responsibility for the policy of Kerensky. On the contrary, they denounced him as responsible for the reactionary attack and as incapable of overcoming it. In this way they prepared the political premises of the October Revolution, in which the alternative Bolshevism or counterrevolution (communism or fascism) evolved from a historic tendency into a living and immediate reality.

We must teach this lesson to the youth. We must inculcate the Marxist method into them. But as to the people who are a few decades past school age and who persist in counterposing to us at all times — to us as well as to reality — the same formulas (which they have, by the way, taken from us), it is necessary to recognize them publicly as incurables who must be kept a few feet away from the general staffs who are elaborating revolutionary policy.

September 29, 1937

It appears that while we were writing these lines, a new "purge" was being carried on in Spain on a grand scale. Insofar as it is possible to understand the reports, which are deliberately confused, the blows are directed this time against the anarchosyndicalists especially. It is possible that this is a preparation for a conciliation between Stalin-Negrín and Franco. But it is not excluded that the Moscow bureaucracy, which thinks that everything can be solved by means of the GPU, is in this way preparing a "victory" of the sort that is continually escaping it. In reality, it can prepare only the triumph of Franco or the military dictatorship of some "republican" Miaja,27 which will resemble that of Franco as one drop of water resembles another.

Only complete imbeciles can have any illusions on the objectives or methods of the Stalinist clique or of Negrínist democracy. The struggle between the two camps can very well cease in an instant. The new situation thus created would dictate a new tactic, in line with the same strategic goal. But for the present, the military struggle between Negrín and Franco still continues, and the tactic for today must be dictated by the situation as it is today.

72   *THE POUM AND THE CALL FOR SOVIETS*

October 1, 1937

I had a very interesting correspondence with Andrés Nin — I
will publish it. On every question the POUM utilized the conceptions of the Bolshevik-Leninists for opportunist purposes.
This is the first time I have heard that they claim that it did
no good calling for soviets as the workers didn't build them.
As to the question of soviets — here is its history:

In 1931, at the beginning of the revolution, I wrote that
I believed that it would not be advisable to begin with the
slogan for soviets. During massive strikes, as in Russia in
1905, strike committees were built, but the workers didn't understand at that time that this was the beginning of soviets. At
present the word "soviet" signifies the Soviet government. The
worker who is involved in a strike cannot understand what
connection that has with a soviet. The Socialists and Anarchists
would oppose it as the dictatorship of the proletariat. My opinion, therefore, was that it was necessary to create mass
organizations but not to give them the name of "soviets," rather
to name them "juntas," a traditional Spanish name, and not
so concrete as "soviet." But instead an artificial organization
was created, not representative of the wide masses, with delegates
from the old organizations: Anarchists, three members; Socialists, three; and delegates from the CP and the POUM. And
they imposed the same relationship in every town.

Revolution is a very dynamic process, with the political
sense of the masses developing to the left while the bourgeois
classes swing to the right. During one month, the situation
changes rapidly. The revolution in its development sweeps
away the old organizations, the old conservative parties, and
the trade unions. The new leadership in every plant, in every
factory, is younger, more active, more courageous. The old
organization becomes the greatest brake upon the revolution.
It was absolutely necessary to build juntas — or we can call
them soviets; we know what we mean — that's the only way
to give the revolution a unified expression.

As to the necessity of unification, our fight with the POUM

An excerpt from "Answers to Questions," in the *Internal Bulletin*, SWP,
no. 3, August 1938. Signed "Crux." Full text is in *Writings of Leon
Trotsky* (1937-38)

was not over unification — but over the question, will the policy unify the bourgeoisie or the new creative elements from the proletariat? It is not a question of a mathematical unification — it is a class question, not an administrative one. How can they say that the workers didn't build soviets? They built committees everywhere and these committees took over industry. It was only a question of unifying these committees, of developing them, and that would have been the Soviet of Barcelona.

73   *FOR AID TO THE SPANISH VICTIMS OF STALIN-NEGRIN*

October 6, 1937

Esteemed Comrade Tresca:

With warm sympathy I respond to your call for action to help the Spanish revolutionary victims of Stalin-Negrín. The militants of the CNT incontestably occupy first place among these victims.

As a Marxist, I am an adversary of anarchism. Even more irreconcilably am I an adversary of the present opportunism of the leaders of the CNT. But this cannot hinder me from seeing and recognizing that in the ranks of this organization are concentrated the elite of the Spanish proletariat. Profound revolutionary solidarity binds me to the Anarchist workers, whereas in the pseudo-Marxist cliques of Stalin-Negrín I see only masked class foes.

I totally share your indignation at the attitude of the *Nation* and the *New Republic*.[28] The executioner is hideous, but more hideous is the priest in the service of the executioner. As the agent of imperialism, Stalin's GPU invokes hatred, but completely nauseating are the long-haired democratic preachers who pander to the Stalinist executioners.

The struggle for the liberation of humanity is impossible

A letter to Carlo Tresca, from *Socialist Appeal,* October 23, 1937. Carlo Tresca was a well-known Italian-American Anarchist and editor of *Il Martello.*

without the simultaneous mobilization of contempt for such courtesans, sycophants, lackeys, bigots as the *Nation* and the *New Republic*.

I wish you the best success in your campaign and I shake your hand with revolutionary greetings.

Leon Trotsky

74 ON THE REVOLUTIONARY CALENDAR

October 22, 1937
Dear Friend:

In your letter of May 5, you draw my attention to a supposed contradiction in the appreciation of the May days in Barcelona between the letter of Lund ("The Insurrection in Catalonia — A Few *Preliminary* Remarks") dated May 12, 1937, and my article ("A Test of Ideas and Individuals Through the Experience of the Spanish Revolution") dated August 24, 1937.

This supposed contradiction concerns the analogy with the July days at Petrograd. You predict as well that the pro-POUM-ists are going to be served by this "contradiction." I do not think so, because this would be truly too imprudent. I have reread the text of the two articles, and I do not find the least con'radiction. On the contrary, they complement one another.

The historical analogy

Each concrete event of history is determined by a multitude of fundamental and secondary factors. The dialectic imparts a decisive importance to factors of the second, the third, and the tenth order in a given event. Thus, one can say with assurance that the defeat of the German working class was determined not by the very low level of productive forces, not by the insufficient development of class antagonisms, but directly and even exclusively by the bankruptcy of the working class party. Thus we know that the party occupies the decisive place in the hierarchy of historic factors.

A letter to Jean Rous. From the *Internal Bulletin*, SWP, no. 5, August 1938. Signed "Crux." The date of Rous's letter obviously could not have been May 5.

If one analyzes the July days in Russia thoroughly, one finds from top to bottom all the factors that determined the preceding history of the country: the level of production, the specific weight of the working class, the role of the peasants, the place of Petrograd in the national life, the role of the different parties — without speaking of the influence of the war and the enormous weight of the army. It is then absolutely evident that the July days could never be repeated anywhere. Of what use, then, is the analogy? Solely to clarify a new event from a point of view that we are the most interested in *practically* for the present. In this way I have often invoked the July days as an example of a grave defeat, which was, however, not decisive and which may also be considered as an inevitable stage on the road to victory. It must be added, however, that this victory was by no means "assured" by the defeat, but that it was solely possible under certain supplementary conditions, including a correct revolutionary policy.

"What must be emphasized"

Lund's article, written May 12, 1937, on the basis of telegraphic dispatches "not only incomplete but also deliberately distorted," says: "The analogy with the events of July 1917 is too evident for us to dwell on it. What must be emphasized above all are the differences." The author is then far from content with the analogy. On the contrary, he warns the reader of its insufficiency for analysis and prognosis. *"What must be emphasized above all,"* he says, *"are the differences."* The analogy with the July days was made under conditions that, above all, are for the purposes of immediate *propaganda.* The uppermost purpose was to encourage the vanquished. "The Russians also suffered their defeat in July, and yet they were able to seize power." That is what the analogy is reduced to in this case.

That is why Lund, who did not directly address the masses but rather the leaders, said essentially in his letters: "You naturally use the example of the Russian July to encourage the workers. This is so natural that it is not necessary to insist upon it. But don't forget that independent from this very general analogy, which has its importance for immediate propaganda, the situations are absolutely different, and that our analysis and our prognosis must be based not so much on the common traits as upon the differences." Lund characterizes the movement of May as "'spontaneous' in character, that is, it broke out unexpectedly for the leaders, including those of the POUM." (Again a certain analogy with the July days in Russia.) But in the same letter Lund calls the movement of May by its right name: an *insurrection.* He is far from regarding this insurrection as "premature." He is disquieted by the news of an "armistice" in Barcelona, whereas in Petrograd in July 1917, the Bolsheviks themselves sought the armistice.

Here is what Lund says on this question: "What does the armistice in Barcelona, of which the dispatches speak, signify: the defeat of the insurgents determined primarily by the inconsistency of the leadership or the direct capitulation of the leaders frightened by the pressure of the masses? We do not know yet. For the moment the struggle seems to be continuing outside Barcelona. Is a resumption of the offensive in Barcelona possible?" In sum, the question for Lund is that of an insurrectional movement that whatever its point of departure is directed by the entire objective situation, by the entire preceding history of the revolution towards the conquest of power. The sole question in this situation was that of the attitude of the organizations of the left, the POUM and the Anarchists. Such was the "preliminary" appreciation of Lund, given at the same time as the events.

My article of August 24 was directed primarily against Comrade Vereecken. What constitutes his fault, or rather one of his faults, which are very numerous? He has based his appreciation of the May days upon the purely formal analogy with the July days. In place of studying the situation, such as it was presented in the month of May 1937, after more than six years of revolutionary development, Vereecken finds in the schematic calendar a master key for opening all the enigmas of history and of politics. In other words, Vereecken commits precisely the fault against which Lund has attempted to put us on guard when he wrote: "What must be emphasized above all are the differences."

The capture of power was possible in May

At a distance of some thousands of miles, without having the information that one could find solely at the place of action, one was still able to ask in the month of May whether the conquest of power was not materially possible. But since then documents, reports, innumerable articles have appeared in the press of all the tendencies. All the facts, all the data, all the testimony lead to the same conclusion: the conquest of power was possible, was assured, as much as the issue of the struggle can be assured in general in advance. The most important evidence comes from the Anarchists. Since the May insurrection, *Solidaridad obrera*[29] has not ceased to repeat the same plaintive melody: "We are accused of having been the instigator of the May rebellion. But we were completely opposed to it. The proof? Our adversaries know it as well as we: *if we had wished to take power, we could have accomplished it in May with certainty*. But we are against dictatorship, etc., etc."

The misfortune is precisely that the CNT did not want power. The misfortune is that the leadership of the POUM was passively adapting itself to the leadership of the CNT. The misfortune (of a most modest size) is that Vereecken, Sneevliet, and Victor Serge are passively adapting themselves to the attitude of the POUM. Worse yet, at the decisive moment when we attempted to shake the fatal self-sufficiency of the POUM ("their own" building, "their own" radio station, "their own" printing press, "their own" militia), when we attempted to make comprehensible to the leaders of the POUM that the revolution has its pitiless logic, which does not tolerate half measures (that is, moreover, precisely why the Stalinists have superseded the Socialists and the Anarchists), it is at this critical moment that the Vereeckens, the Sneevliets, the Victor Serges have placed their cudgels between the spokes.

They have found it advantageous to support the leadership of the POUM against us, that is, to support their hesitations, their inconsistencies, their opportunism. The latest events have brought their pitiless verification. Since the so-called July days, the POUM, far from being strengthened, has been virtually crushed. The CNT, of which the POUM was a shadow, is now losing its positions one after the other. We do not know if the Spanish revolution can yet be saved by a new eruption from below. But the CNT and the POUM have done just about everything to assure the victory of the Stalinists, that is, of the counterrevolution. And Vereecken, Sneevliet, and Victor Serge have done everything to support the POUM on that road to ruin.

The decisive question

All our sections have followed with the greatest attention the development of the situation in Spain. If one goes over our international press now, and all the internal bulletins, one can state with satisfaction that the great majority of the organization has known how to apply the Leninist method to Spanish events. We have had correspondence of indisputable Marxist value from Clart, from Moulin, from Braun.[30] Our organization has in this way passed its theoretical test in a question of historic proportions. And at each stage Comrades Sneevliet and Vereecken, with the aid of Victor Serge, have counterposed to our position — and to the position of the crushing majority of the Fourth International — a centrist attitude that was as sharply against the International Secretariat as it was unclear in its perspectives and slogans.

When Comrade Sneevliet broke off every normal relation with our international organization, when he collaborated with our implacable adversaries against us, he constantly used as a pretext the "bad regime," "the incompetence" of the International Secretariat, etc. Comrade Vereecken did the same thing with a few individual variations that are characteristic of him. On the question of the "regime," we shall also have several words to say to our comrade Sneevliet in order to demonstrate that the bureaucratism that stifled the life of the party, and the goodwill of the leader who liked neither program, nor theses, nor discussion, cannot be the norm in the world party of the social revolution. But today it is not a question of the "regime." The question is one of attitude toward the Spanish revolution. The fundamental divergences are revealed. The policy of the POUM was and remains (as much as it remains at all) the policy of Mensheviks. The Fourth International continues and develops the Bolshevik tradition.

Our methods

The Fourth International is only at its beginning. It has a stupendous task of education to accomplish. It is necessary to be patient. If one casts a glance back on our history during the last ten years, one cannot reproach us for lacking patience and endurance. Expulsions have been extremely rare; they can be counted on one's fingers. Our organization has always employed the methods of discussion, of persuasion, leaving to time and to events the verification of the conflicting points of view. The splits and resignations were the product of elements and groups that despite our best will and pedagogical patience have themselves acknowledged the incompatibility of their "tendency" with the Bolshevik organization. Those who have separated themselves from us, alleging the "bad regime" of the Fourth International, have fallen one after the other into nothingness. Every one of these, Landau, Witte, R. Molinier, Oehler, Weisbord, Field, and others, have had to verify by their own lamentable experience that it is not so easy to improvise a tendency outside of the line historically determined by developments during a dozen years, a great historic tradition, and the uninterrupted collective work of Marxist thought. [31]

Comrade Sneevliet thought long ago of severing his party from the international organization. Oh, certainly he has always employed the figure "four" to designate his position. But outside of the fundamental principles, that is, the Bolshevik-Leninist program, outside of our collective work on that basis, the formula of the Fourth International becomes a hollow phrase, good for nothing. This situation, more and more equivocal, has already lasted for almost three years, that is, a little too long for a "revolutionary calendar." Needless to say, we do not want the separation of our Dutch section, rather to the contrary. What we do want is that it effectively enter into our international framework, that it really participate in our collective life. No international organization can tolerate one of its sections remaining separated by a watertight partition, nor can it tolerate hearing "accusations" of greater and greater sharpness, of greater and greater unjustifiableness from Comrade Sneevliet against our "regime," against our "manners," for the sake of hiding in this way his fundamental differences with the Bolshevik-Leninists. And naturally Vereecken never misses an occasion to support a twisted policy; whether it is to the right or to the left is a trifling matter to him.

We must have a thorough discussion with our sister party in Holland. This is the only possibility of preventing a split in the dark, bureaucratically prepared and bureaucratically realized. Our Belgian section will naturally participate in this discussion, which should be the preparation for the next international conference. We shall know how to avoid the split. We shall, at the same time, know how to stop those who are preparing the split. We shall come out of the discussion more matured and more united. Great events are approaching. We haven't the right to repeat the same mistakes two or three times. The Spanish revolution, whatever its importance, is nothing more than a "rehearsal" for events many times greater. It is necessary to draw all the lessons from this experience lived by the new generation. This cannot be done through casuistic interpretations of such and such a question with which somebody will be able to divert us from our road. Events have spoken. The international conference will know how to interpret their voice.

75

THE LESSONS OF SPAIN: THE LAST WARNING

December 17, 1937

Menshevism and Bolshevism in Spain
All general staffs are studying closely the military operations in Ethiopia, in Spain, in the Far East, in preparation for the great future war. The battles of the Spanish proletariat, heat lightning flashes of the coming world revolution, should be no less attentively studied by the revolutionary staffs. Under this condition and this condition alone will the coming events not take us unawares.

Three ideologies fought — with unequal forces — in the so-called republican camp, namely, Menshevism, Bolshevism, and anarchism. As regards the bourgeois republican parties, they were without either independent ideas or independent political significance and were able to maintain themselves only by climbing on the backs of the reformists and Anarchists. Moreover, it is no exaggeration to say that the leaders of Spanish anarcho-syndicalism did everything to repudiate their doctrine

From *Socialist Appeal,* January 8 and 15, 1938, in a translation from the Russian by John G. Wright.

and virtually reduce its significance to zero. Actually two doctrines in the so-called republican camp fought — Menshevism and Bolshevism.

According to the Socialists and Stalinists, i.e., the Mensheviks of the first and second instances, the Spanish revolution was called upon to solve only its "democratic" tasks, for which a united front with the "democratic" bourgeoisie was indispensable. From this point of view, any and all attempts of the proletariat to go beyond the limits of bourgeois democracy are not only premature but also fatal. Furthermore, on the agenda stands not the revolution but the struggle against the insurgent Franco.

Fascism, however, is not feudal but bourgeois reaction. A successful fight against bourgeois reaction can be waged only with the forces and methods of the proletarian revolution. Menshevism, itself a branch of bourgeois thought, does not have and cannot have any inkling of these facts.

The Bolshevik point of view, clearly expressed only by the young section of the Fourth International, takes the theory of permanent revolution as its starting point, namely, that even purely democratic problems, like the liquidation of semi-feudal land ownership, cannot be solved without the conquest of power by the proletariat; but this in turn places the socialist revolution on the agenda. Moreover, during the very first stages of the revolution, the Spanish workers themselves posed in practice not merely democratic problems but also purely socialist ones. The demand not to transgress the bounds of bourgeois democracy signifies in practice not a defense of the democratic revolution but a repudiation of it. Only through an overturn in agrarian relations could the peasantry, the great mass of the population, have been transformed into a powerful bulwark against fascism. But the landowners are intimately bound up with the commercial, industrial, and banking bourgeoisie, and the bourgeois intelligentsia that depends on them. The party of the proletariat was thus faced with a choice between going with the peasant masses or with the liberal bourgeoisie. There could only be one reason to include the peasantry and the liberal bourgeoisie in the same coalition at the same time: to help the bourgeoisie deceive the peasantry and thus isolate the workers. The agrarian revolution could have been accomplished only *against* the bourgeoisie, and therefore only through measures of the dictatorship of the proletariat. There is no third, intermediate regime.

From the standpoint of theory, the most astonishing thing about Stalin's Spanish policy is the utter disregard for the ABC of Leninism. After a delay of several decades — and what decades! — the Comintern has fully rehabilitated the doctrine of Menshevism. More than that, the Comintern has contrived to render this doctrine more "consistent" and by that token more absurd. In czarist Russia, on the threshold of 1905, the formula of "purely democratic revolution" had behind it, in any case, immeasurably more arguments than in 1937 in Spain. It is hardly astonishing that in modern Spain "the liberal labor policy" of Menshevism has been converted into the reactionary anti-labor policy of Stalinism. At the same time the doctrine of the Mensheviks, this caricature of Marxism, has been converted into a caricature of itself.

"Theory" of the Popular Front

It would be naive, however, to think that the politics of the Comintern in Spain stem from a theoretical "mistake." Stalinism is not guided by Marxist theory, or for that matter by any theory at all, but by the empirical interests of the Soviet bureaucracy. In their intimate circles, the Soviet cynics mock Dimitrov's "philosophy" of the Popular Front.[32] But they have at their disposal for deceiving the masses large cadres of propagators of this holy formula, sincere ones and cheats, simpletons and charlatans. Louis Fischer, with his ignorance and smugness, with his provincial rationalism and congenital deafness to revolution, is the most repulsive representative of this unattractive brotherhood.[33] "The union of progressive forces!" "The triumph of the idea of the Popular Front!" "The assault of the Trotskyists on the unity of the antifascist ranks!" . . . Who will believe that the *Communist Manifesto* was written ninety years ago?

The theoreticians of the Popular Front do not essentially go beyond the first rule of arithmetic, that is, addition: "Communists" plus Socialists plus Anarchists plus liberals add up to a total which is greater than their respective isolated numbers. Such is all their wisdom. However, arithmetic alone does not suffice here. One needs as well at least mechanics. The law of the parallelogram of forces applies to politics as well.

In such a parallelogram, we know that the resultant is shorter, the more the component forces diverge from each other. When political allies tend to pull in opposite directions, the resultant may prove equal to zero.

A bloc of divergent political groups of the working class is sometimes completely indispensable for the solution of common practical problems. In certain historical circumstances, such a bloc is capable of attracting the oppressed petty-bourgeois masses whose interests are close to the interests of the proletariat. The joint force of such a bloc can prove far stronger than the sum of the forces of each of its component parts. On the contrary, the political alliance between the proletariat and the bourgeoisie, whose interests on basic questions in the present epoch diverge at an angle of 180 degrees, as a general rule is capable only of paralyzing the revolutionary force of the proletariat.

Civil war, in which the force of naked coercion is hardly effective, demands of its participants the spirit of supreme self-abnegation. The workers and peasants can assure victory only if they wage a struggle for their own emancipation. Under these conditions, to subordinate the proletariat to the leadership of the bourgeoisie means beforehand to assure defeat in the civil war.

These simple truths are least of all the products of pure theoretical analysis. On the contrary, they represent the unassailable deduction from the entire experience of history, beginning at least with 1848. The modern history of bourgeois society is filled with all sorts of Popular Fronts, i. e., the most diverse political combinations for the deception of the toilers. The Spanish experience is only a new and tragic link in this chain of crimes and betrayals.

Alliance with the bourgeoisie's shadow

Politically most striking is the fact that the Spanish Popular Front lacked in reality even a parallelogram of forces. The bourgeoisie's place was occupied by its shadow. Through the medium of the Stalinists, Socialists, and Anarchists, the Spanish bourgeoisie subordinated the proletariat to itself without even bothering to participate in the Popular Front. The overwhelming majority of the exploiters of all political shades openly went over to the camp of Franco. Without any theory of "permanent revolution," the Spanish bourgeoisie understood from the outset that the revolutionary mass movement, no matter how it starts, is directed against private ownership of land and the means of production, and that it is utterly impossible to cope with this movement by democratic measures.

That is why only insignificant debris from the possessing classes remained in the republican camp: Messrs. Azaña, Companys, and the like — political attorneys of the bourgeoisie but not the bourgeoisie itself. Having staked everything on a military dictatorship, the possessing classes were able, at the same time, to make use of their political representatives of *yesterday* in order to paralyze, disorganize, and afterward strangle the socialist movement of the masses in "republican" territory.

Without in the slightest degree representing the Spanish bourgeoisie, the left republicans still less represented the workers and peasants. They represented no one but themselves. Thanks, however, to their allies — the Socialists, Stalinists, and Anarchists — these political phantoms played the decisive role in the revolution. How? Very simply. By incarnating the principles of the "democratic revolution," that is, the inviolability of private property.

The Stalinists in the Popular Front

The reasons for the rise of the Spanish Popular Front and its inner mechanics are perfectly clear. The task of the retired leaders of the left bourgeoisie consisted in checking the revolution of the masses and thus in regaining for themselves the lost confidence of the exploiters: "Why do you need Franco if we, the republicans, can do the same thing?" The interests of Azaña and Companys fully coincided at this central point with the interests of Stalin, who needed to gain the confidence of the French and British bourgeoisie by proving to them in action his ability to preserve "order" against "anarchy." Stalin needed Azaña and Companys as a cover before the workers: Stalin himself, of course, is for socialism, but one must take care not to repel the republican bourgeoisie! Azaña and Companys needed Stalin as an experienced executioner, with the authority of a revolutionist. Without him, so insignificant a crew never could nor would have dared to attack the workers.

The classic reformists of the Second International, long ago derailed by the course of the class struggle, began to feel a new tide of confidence, thanks to the support of Moscow. This support, incidentally, was not given to all reformists but only to those most reactionary. Caballero represented that face of the Socialist Party that was turned toward the workers' aristocracy. Negrín and Prieto always looked towards the bourgeoisie. Negrín won over Caballero with the help of Moscow. The left Socialists and Anarchists, the captives of the Popular Front, tried, it is true, to save whatever could be saved of democracy. But inasmuch as they did not dare to mobilize the masses against the gendarmes of the Popular Front, their efforts at the end were reduced to plaints and wails. The Stalinists were thus in alliance with the extreme right, avowedly bourgeois wing of the Socialist Party. They directed their repressions against the left — the POUM, the Anarchists, the "left" Socialists — in other words, against the centrist groupings who reflected, even in a most remote degree, the pressure of the revolutionary masses.

This political fact, very significant in itself, provides at the same time a measure of the degeneration of the Comintern in the last few years. I once defined Stalinism as *bureaucratic centrism,* and events brought a series of corroborations of the correctness of this definition. But it is obviously obsolete today. The interests of the Bonapartist bureaucracy can no longer be reconciled with centrist hesitation and vacillation. In search of reconciliation with the bourgeoisie, the Stalinist clique is capable of entering into alliance only with the most conservative groupings among the international labor aristocracy. This has acted to fix definitively the counterrevolutionary character of Stalinism on the international arena.

Counterrevolutionary superiorities of Stalinism

This brings us right up to the solution of the enigma of how and why the Communist Party of Spain, so insignificant numerically and with a leadership so poor in caliber, proved capable of gathering into its hands all reins of power, in the face of the incomparably more powerful organizations of the Socialists and Anarchists. The usual explanation that the Stalinists simply bartered Soviet weapons for power is far too superficial. In return for munitions, Moscow received Spanish gold.

According to the laws of the capitalist market, this covers everything. How then did Stalin contrive to get power in the bargain?

The customary answer is that the Soviet government, having raised its authority in the eyes of the masses by furnishing military supplies, demanded as a condition of its "collaboration" drastic measures against revolutionists and thus removed dangerous opponents from its path. All this is quite indisputable but it is only one aspect of the matter, and the least important at that.

Despite the "authority" created by Soviet shipments, the Spanish Communist Party remained a small minority and met with ever-growing hatred on the part of the workers. On the other hand, it was not enough for Moscow to set conditions; Valencia had to accede to them. This is the heart of the matter. Not only Zamora, Companys, and Negrín, but also Caballero, during his incumbency as premier, were all more or less ready to accede to the demands of Moscow. Why? Because these gentlemen themselves wished to keep the revolution within bourgeois limits. Neither the Socialists nor the Anarchists seriously opposed the Stalinist program. They feared a break with the bourgeoisie. They were deathly afraid of every revolutionary onslaught of the workers.

Stalin with his munitions and with his counterrevolutionary ultimatum was a savior for all these groups. He guaranteed them, so they hoped, military victory over Franco, and at the same time, he freed them from all responsibility for the course of the revolution. They hastened to put their Socialist and Anarchist masks into the closet in the hope of making use of them again after Moscow reestablished bourgeois democracy for them. As the finishing touch to their comfort, these gentlemen could henceforth justify their betrayal to the workers by the necessity of a military agreement with Stalin. Stalin on his part justified his counterrevolutionary politics by the necessity of maintaining an alliance with the republican bourgeoisie.

Only from this broader point of view can we get a clear picture of the angelic toleration which such champions of justice and freedom as Azaña, Negrín, Companys, Caballero, García Oliver, and others showed towards the crimes of the GPU.[34] If they had no other choice, as they affirm, it was not at all because they had no means of paying for airplanes and tanks other than with the heads of the revolutionists and the rights of the workers, but because their own "purely democratic," that is, antisocialist, program could be realized by no other measures save terror. When the workers and peasants enter on the path of *their* revolution — when they seize factories and estates, drive out the old owners, conquer power in the provinces — then the bourgeois counterrevolution — democratic, Stalinist, or fascist alike — has no other means of checking this movement except through bloody coercion, supplemented by lies and deceit. The superiority of the Stalinist clique on this road consisted in its ability to apply instantly measures that were beyond the capacity of Azaña, Companys, Negrín, and their left allies.

Stalin confirms in his own way the correctness of the theory of permanent revolution

Two irreconcilable programs thus confronted each other on the territory of republican Spain. On the one hand, the program of saving *at any cost* private property from the proletariat, and saving *as far as possible* democracy from Franco; on the other hand, the program of abolishing private property through the conquest of power by the proletariat. The first program expressed the interests of capitalism through the medium of the labor aristocracy, the top petty-bourgeois circles, and especially the Soviet bureaucracy. The second program translated into the language of Marxism the tendencies of the revolutionary mass movement, not fully conscious but powerful. Unfortunately for the revolution, between the handful of Bolsheviks and the revolutionary proletariat stood the counterrevolutionary wall of the Popular Front.

The policy of the Popular Front was, in its turn, not at all determined by the blackmail of Stalin as a supplier of arms. There was, of course, no lack of blackmail. But the reason for the success of this blackmail was inherent in the inner conditions of the revolution itself. For six years, its social setting was the growing onslaught of the masses against the regime of semifeudal and bourgeois property. The need of defending this property by the most extreme measures threw the bourgeoisie into Franco's arms. The republican government had promised the bourgeoisie to defend property by "democratic" measures, but revealed, especially in July 1936, its complete bankruptcy. When the situation on the property front became even more threatening than on the military front, the democrats of all colors, including the Anarchists, bowed before Stalin; and he found no other methods in his own arsenal than the methods of Franco.

The hounding of "Trotskyists," POUMists, revolutionary Anarchists and left Socialists; the filthy slander; the false documents; the tortures in Stalinist prisons; the murders from ambush — without all this the bourgeois regime under the republican flag could not have lasted even two months. The GPU proved to be the master of the situation only because it defended the interests of the bourgeoisie against the proletariat more consistently than the others, i. e., with the greatest baseness and bloodthirstiness.

In the struggle against the socialist revolution, the "democrat" Kerensky at first sought support in the military dictatorship of Kornilov and later tried to enter Petrograd in the baggage train of the monarchist general Krasnov. On the other hand, the Bolsheviks were compelled, in order to carry the democratic revolution through to the end, to overthrow the government of "democratic" charlatans and babblers. In the process they put an end thereby to every kind of attempt at military (or "fascist") dictatorship.

The Spanish revolution once again demonstrates that it is impossible to defend democracy against the revolutionary masses otherwise than through the methods of fascist reaction. And conversely, it is impossible to conduct a genuine struggle against fascism otherwise than through the methods of the proletarian revolution. Stalin waged war against "Trotskyism" (proletarian revolution), destroying democracy by the Bonapartist measures of the GPU. This refutes once again and once and for all the old Menshevik theory, adopted by the Comintern, in accordance with which the democratic and socialist revolutions are transformed into two independent historic chapters, separated from each other in point of time. The work of the Moscow executioners confirms in its own way the correctness of the theory of permanent revolution.

Role of the Anarchists

The Anarchists had no independent position of any kind in the Spanish revolution. All they did was waver between Bolshevism and Menshevism. More precisely, the Anarchist workers instinctively yearned to enter the Bolshevik road (July

19, 1936, and May days of 1937) while their leaders, on the contrary, with all their might drove the masses into the camp of the Popular Front, i.e., of the bourgeois regime.

The Anarchists revealed a fatal lack of understanding of the laws of the revolution and its tasks by seeking to limit themselves to their own trade unions, that is, to organizations permeated with the routine of peaceful times, and by ignoring what went on outside the framework of the trade unions, among the masses, among the political parties, and in the government apparatus. Had the Anarchists been revolutionists, they would first of all have called for the creation of soviets, which unite the representatives of all the toilers of city and country, including the most oppressed strata, who never joined the trade unions. The revolutionary workers would have naturally occupied the dominant position in these soviets. The Stalinists would have remained an insignificant minority. The proletariat would have convinced itself of its own invincible strength. The apparatus of the bourgeois state would have hung suspended in the air. One strong blow would have sufficed to pulverize this apparatus. The socialist revolution would have received a powerful impetus. The French proletariat would not for long have permitted Léon Blum to blockade the proletarian revolution beyond the Pyrenees. Neither could the Moscow bureaucracy have permitted itself such a luxury. The most difficult questions would have been solved as they arose.

Instead of this, the anarcho-syndicalists, seeking to hide from "politics" in the trade unions, turned out to be, to the great surprise of the whole world and themselves, a fifth wheel in the cart of bourgeois democracy. But not for long; a fifth wheel is superfluous. After García Oliver and his cohorts helped Stalin and his henchmen to take power away from the workers, the Anarchists themselves were driven out of the government of the Popular Front. Even then they found nothing better to do than jump on the victor's bandwagon and assure him of their devotion. The fear of the petty bourgeois before the big bourgeois, of the petty bureaucrat before the big bureaucrat, they covered up with lachrymose speeches about the sanctity of the united front (between a victim and the executioners) and about the inadmissibility of every kind of dictatorship, including their own. "After all, we could have taken power in July 1936. . . ." "After all, we could have taken power in May 1937. . . ." The Anarchists begged Stalin-Negrín to recognize and reward their treachery to the revolution. A revolting picture!

In and of itself, this self-justification that "we did not seize power not because we were unable but because we did not wish to, because we were against every kind of dictatorship," and the like, contains an irrevocable condemnation of anarchism as an utterly antirevolutionary doctrine. To renounce the conquest of power is voluntarily to leave the power with those who wield it, the exploiters. The essence of every revolution consisted and consists–in putting a new class in power, thus enabling it to realize its own program in life. It is impossible to wage war and to reject victory. It is impossible to lead the masses towards insurrection without preparing for the conquest of power.

No one could have prevented the Anarchists after the conquest of power from establishing the sort of regime they deem necessary, assuming, of course, that their program is realizable. But the Anarchist leaders themselves lost faith in it. They hid from power not because they are against "every kind of dictatorship"—in actuality, grumbling and whining, they supported and still support the dictatorship of Stalin-Negrín—but because they completely lost their principles and courage, if they ever had any. They were afraid of everything: "isolation," "involvement," "fascism." They were afraid of Stalin. They were afraid of Negrín. They were afraid of France and England. More than anything these phrasemongers feared the revolutionary masses.

The renunciation of conquest of power inevitably throws every workers' organization into the swamp of reformism and turns it into a toy of the bourgeoisie; it cannot be otherwise in view of the class structure of society. In opposing the *goal*, the conquest of power, the Anarchists could not in the end fail to oppose the *means*, the revolution. The leaders of the CNT and FAI not only helped the bourgeoisie hold on to the shadow of power in July 1936; they also helped it to reestablish bit by bit what it had lost at one stroke. In May 1937, they sabotaged the uprising of the workers and thereby saved the dictatorship of the bourgeoisie. Thus anarchism, which wished merely to be antipolitical, proved in reality to be antirevolutionary, and in the more critical moments — counterrevolutionary.

The Anarchist theoreticians, who after the great test of 1931-37 continue to repeat the old reactionary nonsense about Kronstadt,[35] and who affirm that "Stalinism is the inevitable result of Marxism and Bolshevism," simply demonstrate by this they are forever dead for the revolution.

You say that Marxism is in itself depraved and Stalinism is its legitimate progeny? But why are we revolutionary Marxists engaged in mortal combat with Stalinism throughout the world? Why does the Stalinist gang see in Trotskyism its chief enemy? Why does every approach to our views or our methods of action (Durruti, Andrés Nin, Landau, and others)[36] compel the Stalinist gangsters to resort to bloody reprisals? Why, on the other hand, did the leaders of Spanish anarchism serve, during the time of the Moscow and Madrid crimes of the GPU, as ministers under Caballero-Negrín, that is, as servants of the bourgeoisie and Stalin? Why even now, under the pretext of fighting fascism, do the Anarchists remain voluntary captives of Stalin-Negrín, the executioners of the revolution, who have demonstrated their incapacity to fight fascism?

By hiding behind Kronstadt and Makhno, the attorneys of anarchism will deceive nobody.[37] In the Kronstadt episode and in the struggle with Makhno, we defended the proletarian revolution from the peasant counterrevolution. The Spanish Anarchists defended and continue to defend bourgeois counter-revolution from the proletarian revolution. No sophistry will delete from the annals of history the fact that anarchism and Stalinism in the Spanish revolution were on one side of the barricades while the working masses with the revolutionary Marxists were on the other. Such is the truth which will forever remain in the consciousness of the proletariat!

Role of the POUM

The record of the POUM is not much better. In point of theory, it tried, to be sure, to base itself on the formula of the permanent revolution (that is why the Stalinists called the POUMists Trotskyists). But the revolution is not satisfied with theoretical avowals. Instead of mobilizing the masses against the reformist leaders, including the Anarchists, the POUM tried to convince these gentlemen of the superiorities of socialism over capitalism. This tuning fork gave the pitch to all the articles and speeches of the POUM leaders. In order not to quarrel with the Anarchist leaders, they did not form their own nuclei inside the CNT, and in general did not conduct any kind of work there. To avoid sharp conflicts, they did not carry on revolutionary work in the republican army. They built instead "their own" trade unions and "their own" militia, which guarded "their own" institutions or occupied "their own" section of the front.

By isolating the revolutionary vanguard from the class, the POUM rendered the vanguard impotent and left the class without leadership. Politically the POUM remained throughout far closer to the Popular Front, for whose left wing it provided the cover, than to Bolshevism. That the POUM nevertheless fell victim to bloody and base repressions was due to the failure of the Popular Front to fulfill its mission, namely to stifle the socialist revolution — except by cutting off, piece by piece, its own left flank.

Contrary to its own intentions, the POUM proved to be, in the final analysis, the chief obstacle on the road to the creation of a revolutionary party. The platonic or diplomatic partisans of the Fourth International like Sneevliet, the leader of the Dutch Revolutionary Socialist Workers Party, who demonstratively supported the POUM in its halfway measures, its indecisiveness and evasiveness, in short, in its centrism, took upon themselves the greatest responsibility. Revolution abhors centrism. Revolution exposes and annihilates centrism. In passing, the revolution discredits the friends and attorneys of centrism. That is one of the most important lessons of the Spanish revolution.

The problem of arming

The Socialists and Anarchists who seek to justify their capitulation to Stalin by the necessity of paying for Moscow's weapons with principles and conscience simply lie and lie unskillfully. Of course, many of them would have preferred to disentangle themselves without murders and frame-ups. But every goal demands corresponding means. Beginning with April 1931, that is, long before the military intervention of Moscow, the Socialists and Anarchists did everything in their power to check the proletarian revolution. Stalin taught them how to carry this work to its conclusion. They became Stalin's criminal accomplices only because they were his political co-thinkers.

Had the Anarchist leaders in the least resembled revolutionists, they would have answered the first piece of blackmail from Moscow not only by continuing the socialist offensive but also by exposing Stalin's counterrevolutionary conditions before the world working class. They would have thus forced the Moscow bureaucracy to choose openly between the socialist revolution and the Franco dictatorship. The Thermidorean bureaucracy fears and hates revolution. But it also fears being strangled in a fascist ring. Besides, it depends on the workers. All indications are that Moscow would have been forced to supply arms, and possibly at more reasonable prices.

But the world does not revolve around Stalinist Moscow. During a year and a half of civil war, the Spanish war industry could and should have been strengthened and developed by converting a number of civilian plants to war production. This work was not carried out only because Stalin and his Spanish allies equally feared the initiative of the workers' organizations. A strong war industry would have become a powerful instrument in the hands of the workers. The leaders of the Popular Front preferred to depend on Moscow.

It is precisely on this question that the perfidious role of the Popular Front was very strikingly revealed. It thrust upon the workers' organizations the responsibility for the treacherous deals of the bourgeoisie with Stalin. Insofar as the Anarchists remained in the minority, they could not, of course, immediately hinder the ruling bloc from assuming whatever obligations they pleased toward Moscow and the masters of Moscow: London and Paris. But without ceasing to be the best fighters on the front, they could and should have openly dissociated themselves from the betrayals and betrayers; they could and should have explained the real situation to the masses, mobilized them against the bourgeois government, and augmented their own forces from day to day in order in the end to conquer power and with it the Moscow arms.

And what if Moscow, in the absence of a Popular Front, should have refused to give arms altogether? And what, we answer to this, if the Soviet Union did not exist altogether? Revolutions have been victorious up to this time not at all thanks to high and mighty foreign patrons who supplied them with arms. As a rule, counterrevolution enjoyed foreign patronage. Must we recall the experience of the intervention of French, English, American, Japanese, and other armies against the Soviets? The proletariat of Russia conquered domestic reaction and foreign interventionists without military support from the outside. Revolutions succeed, in the first place, with the help of a bold social program, which gives the masses the possibility of seizing weapons that are on their territory and disorganizing the army of the enemy. The Red Army seized French, English, and American military supplies and drove the foreign expeditionary corps into the sea. Has this really been already forgotten?

If at the head of the armed workers and peasants, that is, at the head of so-called republican Spain, were revolutionists and not cowardly agents of the bourgeoisie, the problem of arming would never have been paramount. The army of Franco, including the colonial Riffians and the soldiers of Mussolini, was not at all immune to revolutionary contagion. [38] Surrounded by the conflagration of the socialist uprising, the soldiers of fascism would have proved to be an insignificant quantity. Arms and military "geniuses" were not lacking in Madrid and Barcelona; what was lacking was a revolutionary party!

Conditions for victory

The conditions for victory of the masses in a civil war against the army of exploiters are very simple in their essence.

1. The fighters of a revolutionary army must be clearly aware of the fact that they are fighting for their full social liberation and not for the reestablishment of the old ("democratic") forms of exploitation.

2. The workers and peasants in the rear of the revolutionary army as well as in the rear of the enemy must know and understand the same thing.

3. The propaganda on their own front as well as on the enemy front and in both rears must be completely permeated with the spirit of social revolution. The slogan "First victory, then reforms," is the slogan of all oppressors and exploiters from the Biblical kings down to Stalin.

4. Politics are determined by those classes and strata that participate in the struggle. The revolutionary masses must have a state apparatus that directly and immediately expresses their will. Only the soviets of workers', soldiers', and peasants' deputies can act as such an apparatus.

5. The revolutionary army must not only proclaim but also immediately realize in life the more pressing measures of social

revolution in the provinces won by them: the expropriation of provisions, manufactured articles, and other stores on hand and the transfer of these to the needy; the redivision of shelter and housing in the interests of the toilers and especially of the families of the fighters; the expropriation of the land and agricultural inventory in the interests of the peasants; the establishment of workers' control and soviet power in place of the former bureaucracy.

6. Enemies of the socialist revolution, that is, exploiting elements and their agents, even if masquerading as "democrats," "republicans," "Socialists," and "Anarchists," must be mercilessly driven out of the army.

7. At the head of each military unit must be placed commissars possessing irreproachable authority as revolutionists and soldiers.

8. In every military unit there must be a firmly welded nucleus of the most self-sacrificing fighters, recommended by the workers' organizations. The members of this nucleus have but one privilege: to be the first under fire.

9. The commanding corps necessarily includes at first many alien and unreliable elements among the personnel. Their testing, retesting, and sifting must be carried through on the basis of combat experience, recommendations of commissars, and testimonials of rank-and-file fighters. Coincident with this must proceed an intense training of commanders drawn from the ranks of revolutionary workers.

10. The strategy of civil war must combine the rules of military art with the tasks of the social revolution. Not only in propaganda but also in military operations it is necessary to take into account the social composition of the various military units of the enemy (bourgeois volunteers, mobilized peasants, or as in Franco's case, colonial slaves); and in choosing lines of operation, it is necessary to rigorously take into consideration the social structure of the corresponding territories (industrial regions, peasant regions, revolutionary or reactionary, regions of oppressed nationalities, etc.). In brief, revolutionary policy dominates strategy.

11. Both the revolutionary government and the executive committee of the workers and peasants must know how to win the complete confidence of the army and of the toiling population.

12. Foreign policy must have as its main objective the awak-

ening of the revolutionary consciousness of the workers, the exploited peasants, and oppressed nationalities of the whole world.

Stalin guaranteed the conditions of defeat

The conditions for victory, as we see, are perfectly plain. In their aggregate they bear the name of the socialist revolution. Not a single one of these conditions existed in Spain. The basic reason is — the absence of a revolutionary party. Stalin tried, it is true, to transfer to the soil of Spain, the outward practices of Bolshevism: the Politburo, commissars, cells, the GPU, etc. But he emptied these forms of their social content. He renounced the Bolshevik program and with it the soviets as the necessary form for the revolutionary initiative of the masses. He placed the technique of Bolshevism at the service of bourgeois property. In his bureaucratic narrow-mindedness, he imagined that "commissars" by themselves could guarantee victory. But the commissars of private property proved capable only of guaranteeing defeat.

The Spanish proletariat displayed first-rate military qualities. In its specific gravity in the country's economic life, in its political and cultural level, the Spanish proletariat stood on the first day of the revolution not below but above the Russian proletariat at the beginning of 1917. On the road to its victory, its own organizations stood as the chief obstacles. The commanding clique of Stalinists, in accordance with their counter-revolutionary function, consisted of hirelings, careerists, declassed elements, and in general, all types of social refuse. The representatives of other labor organizations — incurable reformists, Anarchist phrasemongers, helpless centrists of the POUM — grumbled, groaned, wavered, maneuvered, but in the end adapted themselves to the Stalinists. As a result of their joint activity, the camp of social revolution — workers and peasants — proved to be subordinated to the bourgeoisie, or more correctly, to its shadow. It was bled white and its character was destroyed.

There was no lack of heroism on the part of the masses or courage on the part of individual revolutionists. But the masses were left to their own resources while the revolutionists remained disunited, without a program, without a plan of action. The "republican" military commanders were more concerned with crushing the social revolution than with scoring military victories. The soldiers lost confidence in their commanders, the masses in the government; the peasants stepped aside; the workers became exhausted; defeat followed defeat; demoralization grew apace. All this was not difficult to foresee from the beginning of the civil war. By setting itself the task of rescuing the capitalist regime, the Popular Front doomed itself to military defeat. By turning Bolshevism on its head, Stalin succeeded completely in fulfilling the role of gravedigger of the revolution.

It ought to be added that the Spanish experience once again demonstrates that Stalin failed completely to understand either the October Revolution or the Russian civil war. His slow-moving provincial mind lagged hopelessly behind the tempestuous march of events in 1917-21. In those of his speeches and articles in 1917 where he expressed his own ideas, his later Thermidorean "doctrine" is fully implanted. In this sense, Stalin in Spain in 1937 is the continuator of Stalin of the March 1917 conference of the Bolsheviks. But in 1917 he merely feared the revolutionary workers; in 1937 he strangled them. The opportunist had become the executioner.

"Civil war in the rear"

But, after all, victory over the governments of Caballero and Negrín would have necessitated a civil war in the rear of the republican army! — the democratic philistine exclaims with horror. As if apart from this, in republican Spain no civil war has ever existed, and at that the basest and most perfidious one — the war of the proprietors and exploiters against the workers and peasants. This uninterrupted war finds expression in the arrests and murders of revolutionists, the crushing of the mass movement, the disarming of the workers, the arming of bourgeois police, the abandoning of workers' detachments without arms and without help on the front, and finally, the artificial restriction of the development of war industry.

Each of these acts is a cruel blow to the front, direct military treason, dictated by the class interests of the bourgeoisie. But "democratic" philistines — including Stalinists, Socialists, and Anarchists — regard the civil war of the bourgeoisie against the proletariat, even in areas most closely adjoining the front, as a natural and inescapable war, having as its task the safeguarding of the "unity of the Popular Front." On the other hand, the civil war of the proletariat against the "republican" counterrevolution is, in the eyes of the same philistines, a criminal, "fascist," Trotskyist war, disrupting . . . "the unity of the antifascist forces." Scores of Norman Thomases, Major Attlees, Otto Bauers, Zyromskys, Malrauxes, and such petty peddlers of lies as Duranty and Louis Fischer spread this slavish wisdom throughout our planet. [39] Meanwhile the government of the Popular Front moves from Madrid to Valencia, from Valencia to Barcelona.

If, as facts attest, only the socialist revolution is capable of crushing fascism, then on the other hand a successful uprising of the proletariat is conceivable only when the ruling classes are caught in the vise of the greatest difficulties. However, the democratic philistines invoke precisely these difficulties as proof of the impermissibility of the proletarian uprising. Were the proletariat to wait for the democratic philistines to tell them the hour of their liberation, they would remain slaves forever. To teach the workers to recognize reactionary philistines under all their masks and to despise them regardless of the mask is the first and paramount duty of a revolutionist!

The outcome

The dictatorship of the Stalinists over the republican camp is not long-lived in its essence. Should the defeats stemming from the politics of the₁ Popular Front once more impel the Spanish proletariat to a revolutionary assault, this time successfully, the Stalinist clique will be swept away with an iron broom. But should Stalin — as is unfortunately the likelihood — succeed in bringing the work of gravedigger of the revolution to its conclusion, he will not even in this case earn thanks. The Spanish bourgeoisie needed him as executioner, but it has no need for him at all as patron or tutor. London and Paris on the one hand, and Berlin and Rome on the other, are in its eyes considerably more solvent firms than Moscow. It is possible that Stalin himself wants to cover his traces in Spain before the final catastrophe; he thus hopes to unload the responsibility for the defeat on his closest allies. After this Litvinov will solicit Franco for the reestablishment of diplomatic relations. [40] All this we have seen more than once.

Even a complete military victory of the so-called republican army over General Franco, however, would not signify the triumph of "democracy." The workers and peasants have twice placed bourgeois republicans and their left agents in power: in April 1931 and in February 1936. Both times the heroes of the Popular Front surrendered the victory of the people to the most reactionary and the most serious representatives of the bourgeoisie. A third victory, gained by the generals of the Popular Front, would signify their inevitable agreement with the fascist bourgeoisie on the backs of the workers and peasants. Such a regime will be nothing but a different form of military dictatorship, perhaps without a monarchy and without the open domination of the Catholic church.

Finally, it is possible that the partial victories of the republicans will be utilized by the "disinterested" Anglo-French intermediaries in order to reconcile the fighting camps. It is not difficult to understand that in the event of such a variant the final remnants of the "democracy" will be stifled in the fraternal embrace of the generals Miaja (communist!) and Franco (fascist!). Let me repeat once again: victory will go either to the socialist revolution or to fascism.

It is not excluded, by the way, that tragedy might at the last moment make way for farce. When the heroes of the Popular Front have to flee their last capital, they might, before embarking on steamers and airplanes, perhaps proclaim a series of "socialist" reforms in order to leave a "good memory" with the people. But nothing will avail. The workers of the world will remember with hatred and contempt the parties that ruined the heroic revolution.

The tragic experience of Spain is a terrible — perhaps final — warning before still greater events, a warning addressed to all the advanced workers of the world. "Revolutions," Marx said, "are the locomotives of history." They move faster than the thought of semirevolutionary or quarter-revolutionary parties. Whoever lags behind falls under the wheels of the locomotive, and consequently — and this is the chief danger — the locomotive itself is also not infrequently wrecked.

It is necessary to think out the problem of the revolution to the end, to its ultimate concrete conclusions. It is necessary to adjust policy to the basic laws of the revolution, i.e., to the movement of the embattled classes and not the prejudices or fears of the superficial petty-bourgeois groups who call themselves "Popular" Fronts and every other kind of front. During revolution the line of least resistance is the line of greatest disaster. To fear "isolation" from the bourgeoisie is to incur isolation from the masses. Adaptation to the conservative prejudices of the labor aristocracy is betrayal of the workers and the revolution. An excess of "caution" is the most baneful lack of caution. This is the chief lesson of the destruction of the most honest political organization in Spain, namely, the centrist POUM. The parties and groups of the London Bureau obviously either do not wish to draw the necessary conclusions from the last warning of history or are unable to do so. By this token they doom themselves.

By way of compensation, a new generation of revolutionists is now being educated by the lessons of the defeats. This generation has verified in action the ignominious reputation of the Second International. It has plumbed the depths of the Third International's downfall. It has learned how to judge the Anarchists not by their words but by their deeds. It is a great inestimable school, paid for with the blood of countless fighters! The revolutionary cadres are now gathering only under the banner of the Fourth International. Born amid the roar of defeats, the Fourth International will lead the toilers to victory.

76   THE FIFTH WHEEL

January 27, 1938

The so-called International Workers' Association (AIT), representing the anarcho-syndicalist groupings in various countries, convened in Paris December 8-17. As is well known, the only large section of this international is the Spanish CNT. All the other organizations (Swedish, Portuguese, French, Latin American) are completely insignificant in size.

Of course, even a small organization can be quite significant if it has an independent revolutionary position that anticipates the future development of the class struggle. But, as can be seen from the brief account printed in the *Information Bulletin of the AIT* (number 67 of the German edition of the *Boletín de información*), the special congress in Paris ended with

From the February 12, 1938, *Socialist Appeal,* which was by then the official paper of the Socialist Workers Party.

the full victory of the politics of García Oliver, that is, the politics of capitulation to the bourgeoisie.

During the past year, a few Anarchist publications, especially the French, have mildly criticized the Spanish CNT's methods of action. There are quite enough bases for this criticism: instead of building stateless communism, the leaders of the CNT became ministers in a bourgeois state! This circumstance did not, however, hinder the Paris congress of the AIT from "approving the line of the CNT." In turn the leaders of Spanish anarcho-syndicalism explained to the congress that if they had betrayed the socialist revolution in the interests of saving the bourgeoisie, that was merely due to the "insufficient solidarity of the international proletariat."

The congress invented nothing new. All reformist betrayers have always laid the blame for their betrayal upon the proletariat. If social patriots support their "national" militarism, it is, of course, not because they are lackeys of capital but because the masses are not "matured yet for real internationalism." If the leaders of the trade unions appear as strikebreakers, it is because the masses "have not matured" for the struggle.

The account does not say a word about revolutionary criticism at the Paris congress. In this respect, as in many others, the gentlemen Anarchists fully imitate the bourgeois liberals. Why let the rabble hear of differences among the higher circles? This can only shake the authority of the anarcho-bourgeois ministers. It is very likely that in answer to the "left" criticism from the French Anarchists, the latter were reminded of their own conduct during the last imperialist war.

We have already heard from some Anarchist theoreticians that at the time of such "exceptional" circumstances as war and revolution, it is necessary to renounce the principles of one's own program. Such revolutionists bear a close resemblance to raincoats that leak only when it rains, i. e., in "exceptional" circumstances, but during dry weather they remain waterproof with complete success.

The decisions of the Paris congress are entirely on the same level as the politics of García Oliver and his kind. The leaders of the AIT have resolved to appeal to the Second, Third, and Amsterdam Internationals[41] with a proposal to create a "united international antifascist front." Not one word about the struggle against capitalism! The methods of battle are announced: "boycott of fascist goods" and . . . "pressure upon democratic governments"—the most reliable methods with which to liberate the proletariat.

Evidently with the aim of exerting "pressure," the leader of the Second International, Blum, became premier in "democratic" France and did everything to crush the revolutionary movement of the French proletariat. Together with Stalin, and with the cooperation of García Oliver, Blum helped Negrín and Prieto stifle the socialist revolution of the Spanish proletariat. In all these acts, Jouhaux took a most prominent part.

With such actions, the united front of the three internationals for the struggle against the revolutionary proletariat has already been conducted for a long time. In this front, the leaders of the CNT have occupied not a conspicuous place but a sufficiently shameful one!

The Paris congress signifies the imposition of the betrayal of the Spanish Anarchists upon anarchism throughout the world. This finds its expression particularly in the fact that from now on the general secretary of the AIT will be appointed by the Spanish CNT. In other words, the general secretary will from now on be an official of the Spanish bourgeois government.

Gentlemen Anarchist and semi-Anarchist theoreticians and semitheoreticians, what do you have to say about all this? Following the example of the Spanish anarcho-syndicalists, do you agree to play the role of fifth wheel on the cart of bourgeois democracy?

Many Anarchists do not, of course, feel completely at ease. But to overcome this uneasiness they change the subject of conversation. Why, indeed, occupy oneself with Spain or the Paris congress of the AIT . . . when one can talk about . . . Kronstadt or Makhno? . . the most burning issues.

In its decomposition and decay, the Anarchist International evidently does not wish to lag behind the Second and Third Internationals. All the sooner will the honest Anarchist workers find the Fourth International.

77 *TRAITORS IN THE ROLE OF ACCUSERS*

October 22, 1938

The newspaper dispatches inform us that *Solidaridad obrera* blames the world proletariat for not having rendered sufficient support to the Spanish revolution. What hypocrisy! The charge comes from those very gentlemen who not only refused to support the proletarian revolution but also indirectly participated in its suppression. It may be stated as a law: every revolution develops the power of international attraction in proportion to the social program realized by the insurgent masses. The entire world proletariat followed the course of the Spanish revolution with bated breath as long as it was a genuine movement of the masses toward socialism. The sympathy of the workers turned to amazement, indignation, and worse still, indifference, when Stalin, Negrín, and their associates began to stifle the Spanish revolution with the support of Anarchists from *Solidaridad obrera.*

The hypocrisy of the charges directed against the world proletariat becomes especially clear in the light of the Barcelona trial of the POUMists.42 We shall not dwell on the accusations that the leaders of the POUM had relations with the fascists. No thinking person in the whole world believes this filthy fabrication! The only *serious* charge in the prosecutor's mouth is that the POUM, by its "extremist" revolutionary conduct, *compromised the Spanish revolution in the eyes of democracy abroad,* that is, England and France. That is what the indictment literally says. This means that the Barcelona government wanted to carry out a revolution . . . with the permission of the English and French imperialists. The task of the GPU was to prevent the masses from going beyond the limits of what was acceptable to King George, Chamberlain, President Lebrun, etc. This great goal could not be reached except by suppressing the workers' and peasants' movement, destroying the revolutionary party, and organizing kangaroo courts. The world proletariat can give the accusers from *Solidaridad* (!) *obrera* this reply: "Shut your mouths, traitors!"

From the Russian *Bulletin of the Opposition,* no. 72, December 1938. Unsigned. Translated for this volume from the Russian by Iain Fraser.

78   THE TRAGEDY OF SPAIN

February 1939

One of the most tragic chapters of modern history is now
drawing to its conclusion in Spain. On Franco's side there is
neither a staunch army nor popular support. There is only
the greed of proprietors ready to drown in blood three-fourths
of the population if only to maintain their rule over the remaining one-fourth. However, this cannibalistic ferocity is not
enough to win a victory over the heroic Spanish proletariat.
Franco needed help from the opposite side of the battlefront.
And he obtained this aid. His chief assistant was and still is
Stalin, the gravedigger of the Bolshevik Party and the proletarian revolution. The fall of the great proletarian capital,
Barcelona, comes as direct retribution for the massacre of the
uprising of the Barcelona proletariat in May 1937.

Insignificant as Franco himself is, however miserable his
clique of adventurists, without honor, without conscience, and
without military talents, Franco's great superiority lies in this,
that he has a clear and definite program: to safeguard and
stabilize capitalist property, the rule of the exploiters, and
the domination of the church; and to restore the monarchy.

The possessing classes of all capitalist countries — whether
fascist or democratic — proved, in the nature of things, to be
on Franco's side. The Spanish bourgeoisie has gone completely
over to Franco's camp. At the head of the republican camp,
there remained the cast-off "democratic" armor-bearers of the
bourgeoisie. These gentlemen could not desert to the side of
fascism, for the very sources of their influence and income
spring from the institutions of bourgeois democracy, which
require (or used to require!) for their normal functioning law-
yers, deputies, journalists, in short, the democratic champions
of capitalism. The program of Azaña and his associates is
nostalgia for a day that has passed. This is altogether
inadequate.

The Popular Front resorted to demagogy and illusions in
order to swing the masses behind itself. For a certain period,
this proved successful. The masses who had assured all the

From *Socialist Appeal,* February 10, 1939.

previous successes of the revolution still continued to believe that the revolution would reach its logical conclusion, that is, achieve an overturn in property relations, give land to the peasants, and transfer the factories into the hands of the workers. The dynamic force of the revolution was lodged precisely in this hope of the masses for a better future. But the honorable republicans did everything in their power to trample, to besmirch, or simply to drown in blood the cherished hopes of the oppressed masses.

As a result, we have witnessed during the last two years the growing distrust and hatred of the republican cliques on the part of the peasants and workers. Despair or dull indifference gradually replaced revolutionary enthusiasm and the spirit of self-sacrifice. The masses turned their backs on those who had deceived and trampled upon them. That is the primary reason for the defeat of the republican troops. The inspirer of deceit and of the massacre of the revolutionary workers of Spain was Stalin. The defeat of the Spanish revolution falls as a new indelible blot upon the already bespattered Kremlin gang.

The crushing of Barcelona deals a terrible blow to the world proletariat, but it also teaches a great lesson. The mechanics of the Spanish Popular Front as an organized system of deceit and treachery of the exploited masses have been completely exposed. The slogan of "defense of democracy" has once again revealed its reactionary essence, and at the same time, its hollowness. The bourgeoisie wants to perpetuate its rule of exploitation; the workers want to free themselves from exploitation. These are the real tasks of the *fundamental* classes in modern society.

Miserable cliques of petty-bourgeois middlemen, having lost the confidence and the subsidies of the bourgeoisie, sought to salvage the past without giving any concessions to the future. Under the label of the Popular Front, they set up a joint stock company. Under the leadership of Stalin, they have assured the most terrible defeat when all the conditions for victory were at hand.

The Spanish proletariat gave proof of extraordinary capacity for initiative and revolutionary heroism. The revolution was brought to ruin by petty, despicable, and utterly corrupted "leaders." The downfall of Barcelona signifies above all the downfall of the Second and Third Internationals, as well as of anarchism, rotten to its core.

Forward to a new road, workers! Forward to the road of the international socialist revolution!

79   SPAIN, STALIN, AND YEZHOV

March 4, 1939

Yezhov, the former head of the GPU, fell into disgrace for a number of reasons. But undoubtedly connected with his fall are the Spanish events. The rout of the armies of the republican government, which was brought about with the direct and most active participation of the GPU, represents a very great danger for both the GPU and its masters in the Kremlin.

Innumerable crimes committed on the Iberian Peninsula by the international scoundrels in Stalin's employ must now inevitably come out into the open. Scores, hundreds, and thousands of witnesses, victims, and participants are now departing and fleeing from Spain to all parts of the world. They will carry with them everywhere their testimony concerning the crimes of the GPU in Spain. Truth will become accessible to broad circles of the population in all countries.

If the republicans had been victorious, many would have been inclined to condone Stalin's crimes: "Conquerors are not brought to judgment." But it has now become perfectly clear that the infamous murders of revolutionists only served to facilitate Franco's victory. The blinders will fall from the eyes of many a blinded man.

In pursuance of his traditional method, Stalin has tried by a timely removal of Yezhov to say: "Yezhov is guilty of all this — not I." But after all this, who will believe this cowardly cunning which begins to look more and more like stupidity? For the crimes in Spain, Stalin himself is personally answerable to the world working class — both for the perfidious policy of

From *Socialist Appeal*, April 21, 1939. Unsigned. Nicholas Yezhov, the successor to Yagoda as head of the GPU, disappeared after the third Moscow trial.

the Comintern and for the murderous policy of the GPU.

Almost in every country in the world there are people who have passed in one way or another through the hands of the GPU. After the massacre of Spain, the number of such individuals has enormously increased. When forced to free their victims from the clutching claws, the agents of the GPU usually say: "Remember we have far-reaching hands." The fear of this threat seals many a lip.

We must now do all in our power to make the terrified ones speak up. Our comrades in all countries must explain to all former victims and semi-victims of the GPU that it is their direct duty to tell everything they know. Their relatives in the USSR will not suffer if the revelations assume a mass character. The organizations of the Fourth International can and must give these revelations a mass character. At present, this is an extremely urgent task in the struggle against the international Stalinist Mafia.

80   *MYSTERIES OF IMPERIALISM*

March 4, 1939

The Socialist Léon Blum and the Conservative Chamberlain, in equal measure friends of "peace," were for nonintervention in the Spanish affair. Hand in hand with them went Stalin, the ex-Bolshevik, through his ambassador Maisky, the ex-Menshevik. Nuances of programs did not hinder them from friendly collaboration in the name of one and the same high aim.

Now, however, Chamberlain declares that if, after recognition of Franco, Italy and Germany do not withdraw the so-called volunteers from Spain, England is prepared to take the most serious measures, not short of war. The Radical Socialist Daladier, another well-known supporter of the policy of "nonintervention," completely supports Chamberlain in this question. From love of peace, these gentlemen refused to defend

From the Russian *Bulletin of the Opposition*, no. 75-76, March-April 1939. Unsigned. Translated for this volume from the Russian by Iain Fraser.

democracy with arms. But there is a limit to everything, even
to the love of peace of these experienced friends of humanity.
Chamberlain openly says: the arrival of Italian and German
soldiers on the Iberian Peninsula would break the "balance"
in the Mediterranean. This cannot be endured! England and
France were not at all inclined to support Spanish democracy;
but now, when they have helped Franco to stifle it, they are
fully prepared to support with arms the "balance" in the Mediterranean, which mysterious technical term is to be understood as meaning the defense by the enslavers of their colonial
possessions and the seaways leading to them.

We humbly ask the gentlemen of the Second and Third Internationals exactly what historical, political, and other conditions are required to establish the promised grand alliance
in defense of democracy in the whole world? The government
of France relied on the Popular Front. The struggle of the
Popular Front in Spain was waged in the name of democracy.
What other example can be invented in which the duty to defend democracy would appear in a more imperative form?
If a "Socialist" government supported by a "National Front"
refused to defend a democracy also headed by "Socialists,"
then the question arises just where and when will what kind
of government occupy itself with the task of defending democracy? Perhaps the augurs of Social Democracy and the Comintern can, nevertheless, manage to explain that?

In fact, the two imperialist democracies, in the person of
their ruling classes, were from the very beginning completely
on the side of Franco; they merely did not at first believe
in the possibility of his victory, and were afraid of compromising themselves by premature disclosure of their sympathies.
As Franco's chances improved, however, the real faces of the
possessing classes of the "great democracies" were revealed ever
more clearly, ever more openly, ever more shamelessly. Both
Great Britain and France know perfectly well that it is considerably easier to control colonies, semicolonies, and simply
weak nations through a military dictatorship than through a
democratic or even semidemocratic regime.

Alliance with the Conservative [Chamberlain] government
is just as immutable a commandment for the "Socialist" petty
bourgeois Blum as for the most extreme reactionaries of the
French Chamber of Deputies. This commandment emanates

from the French stock exchange. England's plan in relation to Spain was fixed from the very start: let them fight; whoever wins will need money to revive the economy of the country. Neither Germany nor Italy will be able to give this money; consequently, the victor will have to turn to London, and partly to Paris. Thus it will be possible to dictate terms.

Blum was initiated into the English plan perfectly well from the beginning. He could have no plan of his own because his semisocialist government was completely dependent on the French bourgeoisie, and the French bourgeoisie on Great Britain. Blum shouted about the preservation of peace as an even more sacred task than the salvation of democracy. But in fact he was concealing the plan of British capital. After he had carried out this piece of dirty work, he was thrown into the opposition camp by the French bourgeoisie, and again obtained the possibility of shouting about the sacred duty of helping the Spanish republicans. Without a cheap left phrase, he would not have preserved the possibilities of again rendering other just as treacherous services to the French bourgeoisie at a critical moment.

The Moscow diplomats also, of course, speak somewhat through gritted teeth in favor of Spanish democracy, the very thing they have destroyed by their policy. But in Moscow they now express themselves very carefully, because they are groping for a way to Berlin. The Moscow Bonapartists are ready to betray all the democracies in the world, not to speak of the international proletariat, just to prolong their rule for an additional week. It is possible that both Stalin and Hitler have started with bluff; each wants to frighten Chamberlain, Daladier, and even Roosevelt. But if the "democratic" imperialists are not frightened, the bluff may go considerably further than was at first supposed in Moscow and Berlin. To cover up their maneuvers, the Kremlin clique needs the assistance of the leaders of the Second and Third Internationals, the more so as that does not cost too much.

Crudely speaking, the social-patriotic gentlemen can be divided into conscious rogues and semi-sincere fools. However, there are a considerable number of intermediary and combined types. In their time, these gentlemen have endured the nasty comedy of "nonintervention," helping Stalin to slaughter proletarian Spain. When it turned out that republican Spain had been slaughtered along with it, they began to wave their hands in protest, without, however, rejecting in the slightest either the Popular Front or the "alliance of the democracies." In the rituals of imperialism, these people invariably fill the most humiliating and shameful roles.

In the veins of the Spanish people, there still remains unshed blood. Who will dispose of it, Hitler and Mussolini or Chamberlain with his French accomplices, is a question that will be decided by the relations of the imperialist forces in the near future. The struggle for peace, for democracy, for race, for authority, for order, for balance, and for dozens of other high and imponderable things means the struggle for a new division of the world. The Spanish tragedy will go down in history as an episode on the path of preparation of a new world war. The ruling classes of all shades are afraid of it and at the same time are preparing for it with all their might. The charlatanism of Popular Fronts serves one part of the imperialists to conceal their plans from the popular masses, as the other gang uses phrases about blood, honor, and race for the same purpose. The petty-bourgeois windbags and phrasemongers only make it easier for the imperialists to prepare war, by preventing the workers from seeing the naked truth.

Thus, from various ends and by various methods, a new carnage of the people is being prepared. Humanity can be saved from ruin and destruction only by tearing the vanguard of the proletariat away from imperialism and its lackeys; by complete independence of proletarian policy; by complete mistrust of the rituals of imperialism, fascist and democratic; by merciless struggle against the Second and Third Internationals; by stubborn, systematic, untiring preparation for the international proletarian revolution!

81

ONCE AGAIN ON THE CAUSES OF THE DEFEAT IN SPAIN

March 4, 1939

The inventors of the umbrella

An old French humorist once wrote an account of how a petty bourgeois came to invent the umbrella. Walking the street in the rain, he began pondering how fine it would be if the streets were covered with roofs. . . . But that would interfere with the free circulation of air. . . . It would have to be moved by the pedestrian, holding some sort of lever in his hands, etc., etc. Finally, our inventor exclaimed, "Bah! Why, that's an umbrella!" Inventors of the umbrella can nowadays be encountered at every step among the "leftists"!

In its time, Bolshevism discredited reformist politics for a number of years. But with the coming of reaction, the Stalinists together with all their underlings have begun inventing anew the umbrella of reformism: "the Popular Front," (coalition with the bourgeoisie); the duty of the proletariat to defend the democratic fatherland (social patriotism); and so on. And they do it with all the vigor of ignorance!

Another newly invented umbrella

In the Mexican newspaper *El Popular,* which has achieved almost international fame for the profundity of its erudition, its honesty of thought, and the revolutionary character of its politics, Guillermo Vegas León, who is not altogether unknown to our readers, comes to the defense of the policies of the Spanish Popular Front with the aid of a newly invented umbrella. The war in Spain, you see, is not a war for socialism but rather a war against fascism. In the war against fascism, it is impermissible to engage in such adventures as the seizure of factories and land. Only the friends of fascism are capable of proposing such plans. And so forth and so on. Historical events obviously exercise no sway over people who live in the kingdom of cheap newspaper copy.

Mr. León is unaware that the same umbrella was used in

From *Socialist Appeal,* March 21, 1939. Unsigned.

their operations by the Russian Mensheviks and Social Revolutionaries (the party of Kerensky). They never tired of repeating that the Russian Revolution was "democratic" and not socialist; that in a war with Germany, which was menacing the young democratic republic, any attempt to engage in such adventures as the expropriation of the means of production was to give aid to Hohenzollern. And inasmuch as there were not a few scoundrels among them, they also asserted that the Bolsheviks did all this for some secret reason. . . .

The class character of the revolution

Whether a revolution is "antifascist" or proletarian, bourgeois or socialist, is determined not by political labels but by the class structure of a given nation. For León, the development of society from approximately the middle of the nineteenth century has passed unnoticed. Yet this development in capitalist countries has washed away the petty and the middle bourgeoisie, pushing them into the background, degrading and lowering them. The principal classes in modern society — including Spain — are the bourgeoisie and the proletariat. The petty bourgeoisie cannot — at all events, for any lengthy period — wield power; that must be either in the hands of the bourgeoisie or in the hands of the proletariat. In Spain, the bourgeoisie, driven by fear for its property, went completely over into the camp of fascism. The only class capable of waging a serious struggle against fascism is the proletariat. It alone could have rallied the oppressed masses, above all, the Spanish peasantry. But workers' power could only be socialist power.

The example of China and Russia

But, objects Mr. León, the immediate goal is the struggle against fascism. All our forces must be centered on this immediate goal, etc., etc. Of course, of course! But tell us, pray, why during a struggle against fascism must the land belong to the landlords and the factories and mills to the capitalists, all of whom are in Franco's camp? Is it perhaps because the peasants and workers "have not matured" for the seizure of land and factories? But they proved their maturity by seizing on their own initiative the lands and factories. Reactionaries, who call themselves republicans, under the leadership of the Stalinists, were able to smash this powerful movement allegedly in the name of "antifascism," but in reality in the interest of bourgeois proprietors.

Let us take another example. At present China is engaged in a war against Japan, a just, defensive war against plunderers and oppressors. With this war as a pretext, the government of Chiang Kai-shek, aided by Stalin's government, has crushed all revolutionary struggle and above all the struggle of the peasants for the land. The exploiters and the Stalinists say: "Now is not the time to solve the agrarian question. Now it is a question of a common struggle against the Mikado." Yet it is self-evident that were the Chinese peasants precisely at the present time in possession of the land, they would defend it tooth and nail against the Japanese imperialists. We must recall once again that if the October Revolution was able to triumph in a war of three years duration over countless enemies, including the expeditionary forces of the mightiest imperialist powers, it was only because this victory was assured above all by the fact that *during the war* the peasants had gained possession of the land while the workers held the mills and factories. Only the fusion of the socialist overturn with the civil war made the Russian Revolution unconquerable.

Gentlemen like Mr. León determine the character of a revolution by the name given it by bourgeois liberals and not by the manner in which it is expressed in the actual class struggle, nor by how it is sensed — even if not always clearly understood — by the revolutionary masses. But we look upon the Spanish revolution not through the eyes of the liberal philistine Azaña but through the eyes of the workers of Barcelona and Asturias, and the peasants of Seville who were fighting for the mills and factories, for the land, for a better future, and not at all for the old parliamentary umbrella of the Popular Front.

The empty abstraction of "antifascism"

The very concepts of "antifascism" and "antifascist" are fictions and lies. Marxism approaches all phenomena from a class standpoint. Azaña is "antifascist" only to the extent that fascism hinders bourgeois intellectuals from carving out parliamentary or other careers. Confronted with the necessity of choosing between fascism and the proletarian revolution, Azaña will always prove to be on the side of the fascists. His entire policy during the seven years of revolution proves this.

On the other hand, the slogan "Against fascism, for democracy!" cannot attract millions and tens of millions of the populace if only because during wartime there was not and is not any democracy in the camp of the republicans. Both with Franco and with Azaña there have been military dictatorship, censorship, forced mobilization, hunger, blood, and death. The abstract slogan "For democracy!" suffices for liberal journalists but not for the oppressed workers and peasants. They have nothing to defend except slavery and poverty. They will direct all their forces to smashing fascism only if, at the same time, they are able to realize new and better conditions of existence. In consequence, the struggle of the proletariat and the poorest peasants against fascism cannot in the social sense be defensive but only offensive. That is why León goes wide of the mark when, following the more "authoritative" philistines, he lectures us that Marxism rejects utopias, and the idea of a socialist revolution during a struggle against fascism is utopian. In point of fact, *the worst and most reactionary form of utopianism is the idea that it is possible to struggle against fascism without overthrowing the capitalist economy.*

Victory was possible

Truly astonishing is the total ignorance of these people. They have no inkling of the existence, beginning with Marx and Engels, of a world literature in which the very concept of the democratic revolution and its inner class mechanism have been subjected to analysis. It is obvious that they never read the basic documents of the first four congresses of the Communist International nor the theoretical research of the Fourth International, which prove and explain and enable even an infant to digest the fact that the struggle against fascism is unthinkable in modern conditions other than by the methods of the proletarian class struggle for power.

These gentlemen picture history as painstakingly preparing the conditions for the socialist revolution, apportioning roles, inscribing in large letters on a triumphal arch: ENTRANCE TO THE SOCIALIST REVOLUTION, guaranteeing victory and then politely inviting the honorable leaders to assume the prominent posts of ministers, ambassadors, etc. No. The question stands somewhat differently; it is far more complex, difficult, and dangerous. Opportunists, reactionary blockheads, and petty-bourgeois cowards never have recognized and never will recognize the situation that places the socialist overturn on the agenda. To do so one must be a revolutionary Marxist, a Bolshevik; to do so one must be able to despise the public opinion of the "educated" petty bourgeoisie, which reflects only the egotistic class fears of capitalism.

The proletariat was strong enough

The leaders of the CNT and FAI themselves declared after the uprising of May 1937: "Had we wished, we could have seized power at any time, because all the forces were on our side, but we did not want any dictatorship," etc., etc. What the Anarchist servitors of the bourgeoisie did or did not want is in the long run a secondary issue. They did, however, admit that the insurrectionary proletariat was strong enough to have conquered power. Had it possessed a revolutionary and not a treacherous leadership, it would have purged the state apparatus of all the Azañas, instituted the power of the soviets, given the land to the peasants, the mills and factories to the workers — and the Spanish revolution would have become socialist and unconquerable.

But because there was no revolutionary party in Spain, and because there was instead a multitude of reactionaries imagining themselves as Socialists and Anarchists, they succeeded under the label of the Popular Front in strangling the socialist revolution and assuring Franco's victory.

It is simply ridiculous to justify the defeat by references to the military intervention of Italian fascists and German Nazis, and to the perfidious conduct of the French and British "democracies." Enemies will always remain enemies. Reaction will always intervene whenever it can. Imperialist "democracy" will always betray. This means that the victory of the proletariat is impossible in general! But what about the victory of fascism in Italy and Germany itself? No intervention there. Instead we had there a powerful proletariat and a very large Socialist Party and, in the case of Germany, a large Communist Party as well. Why then was there no victory gained over fascism? Precisely because the leading parties tried to reduce the question in both these countries to a struggle "against fascism" when only a socialist revolution can defeat fascism.

The Spanish revolution was the supreme school. It is impermissible to allow the slightest frivolity toward its dearly bought lessons. Down with charlatanism, phrasemongering, smug ignorance, and intellectual parasitism! We must study seriously and honestly and prepare for the future.

82   *THE CULPABILITY OF LEFT CENTRISM*

March 10, 1939
Dear Comrade Guérin:
. . . In my letter to Pivert I expressed my surprise at seeing that your party was still able, after the experience of the last years, to find itself in political alliance with the Independent Labour Party (ILP) of England, with the POUM and other similar organizations — against us. . . .

The POUM
What is the situation with the POUM? According to the words of Pivert, your whole party is "unanimously" ready to defend the POUM against our criticism. I leave aside the question of the "unanimity": I am not sure that the members of your organization know in detail the history of the Spanish revolution, the history of the struggle of the various tendencies in its midst,

---

An excerpt from a letter to Daniel Guérin, published in *The New International,* May 1939, under the title "Centrism and the Fourth International." Signed "L. T." *The New International* was the predecessor of *Fourth International.* The full text is in *Leon Trotsky on France* (1934-39).

Daniel Guérin was expelled from the SFIO (the French Socialist Party) in 1938, and was a co-founder with Marceau Pivert of the PSOP (Workers and Peasants Socialist Party). He wrote a number of books on revolutionary history, the workers' movement, and sociological topics, among them *Fascism and Big Business* and *Negroes on the March.*

in particular the critical work which the representatives of the Fourth International contributed in the questions of the Spanish revolution. But it is clear in any case that the *leadership* of your party has absolutely not understood the fatal mistakes of the POUM, which flow from its *centrist, nonrevolutionary, non-Marxist* character.

Since the beginning of the Spanish revolution, I found myself in very close contact with a certain number of militants, in particular with Andrés Nin. We exchanged hundreds of letters. It is only after the experience of quite a number of months that I came to the conclusion that Nin, honest and devoted to the cause, was not a Marxist but a centrist, in the best case a Spanish Martov, that is to say, a Menshevik of the left. Pivert does not distinguish between the policy of Menshevism and the policy of Bolshevism in the revolution.

The leaders of the POUM did not pretend for a single day to play an independent role; they did everything to remain in the role of good "left" friends and counsellors of the leaders of the mass organizations.* This policy, which flowed from the lack of confidence in itself and in its ideas, doomed the POUM to duplicity, to a false tone, to continual vacillations that found themselves in sharp contradiction with the amplitude of the class struggle. The mobilization of the vanguard against the reaction and its abject lackeys, including the anarcho-bureaucrats, the leaders of the POUM replaced by quasi-revolutionary homilies addressed to the treacherous leaders, declaring in self-justification that the "masses" would not understand another, more resolute policy.

Left centrism, especially under revolutionary conditions, is always ready to adopt in words the program of the socialist revolution and is not niggardly with sonorous phrases. But the fatal malady of centrism is not being capable of drawing courageous tactical and organizational conclusions from its general conceptions. They always seem to it to be "premature"; "the opinion of the masses must be prepared" (by means of

---

*Just as for a long time, too long a time, Marceau Pivert did everything to remain the left-wing friend and the counsellor of Blum and his associates, I greatly fear that even today Marceau Pivert and his closest ideological companions have not understood that Blum does not represent an ideological adversary but an avowed, and moreover dishonest, class enemy. — L. T.

equivocation, of duplicity, of diplomacy, etc.); in addition, it fears to break its habitual amicable relations with the friends on the right; it "respects" personal opinions; that is why it delivers all its blows . . . *against the left*, thus endeavoring to raise its prestige in the eyes of serious public opinion.

Such is also the political psychology of Marceau Pivert. He absolutely does not understand that a pitiless manner of posing the fundamental questions and a fierce polemic against vacillations are only the necessary ideological and pedagogical reflection of the implacable and cruel character of the class struggle of our time. To him it seems that this is "sectarianism," lack of respect for the personality of others, etc., that is, he remains entirely on the level of petty-bourgeois moralizing. Are these "serious differences"? Yes, I cannot imagine more serious differences inside the labor movement. With Blum and his associates we do not have "differences": we simply find ourselves on different sides of the barricades.

The cause of the defeat in Spain

Following all the opportunists and centrists, Marceau Pivert explains the defeat of the Spanish proletariat by the bad behavior of French and British imperialism and the Bonapartist clique of the Kremlin. This is quite simply to say that a victorious revolution is always and everywhere impossible. One can neither expect nor ask for a movement of greater scope, greater endurance, greater heroism on the part of the workers than we were able to observe in Spain. The imperialist "democrats" and the mercenary rabble of the Second and the Third Internationals will always behave as they did towards the Spanish revolution. What then can be hoped for? Whoever invokes the ignominy of the bourgeoisie and its lackeys, instead of analyzing the bankrupt policy of the revolutionary or quasi-revolutionary organizations, is a criminal. It is precisely against them that a correct policy is needed!

An enormous responsibility for the Spanish tragedy falls upon the POUM. I have all the greater right to say so because in my letters to Andrés Nin, since 1931, I predicted the inevitable consequences of the disastrous policy of centrism. By their general "left" formulas the leaders of the POUM created the illusion that a revolutionary party existed in Spain and prevented the appearance of the truly proletarian, intransigent tendencies. At the same time, by their policy of adaptation to all the forms of reformism, they were the best auxiliaries of the Anarchist, Socialist, and Communist traitors. The personal honesty and heroism of numerous workers of the POUM naturally provoke our sympathy; against the reaction and the rabble of Stalinism we are ready to defend them to the utmost. But that revolutionist is worth precious little who, under the influence of sentimental considerations, is incapable of considering objectively the real essence of a given party.

The POUM always sought the line of least resistance, it temporized, ducked, played hide-and-seek with the revolution. It began by trying to retrench itself in Catalonia, closing its eyes to the relationship of forces in Spain. In Catalonia, the leading positions in the working class were occupied by the Anarchists; the POUM began by ignoring the Stalinist danger (in spite of all the warnings!) and attuning itself to the Anarchist bureaucracy. So as not to create any "superfluous" difficulties for themselves, the POUM leaders closed their eyes to the fact that the anarcho-bureaucrats were not worth one whit more than all the other reformists, that they only covered themselves with a different phraseology.

The POUM refrained from penetrating into the midst of the CNT in order not to disturb relations with the summits of this organization and in order to retain the possibility of remaining in the role of counsellor to them. That is the position of Martov. But Martov, be it said in his honor, knew how to avoid mistakes as crude and shameful as participation in the Catalan government! To pass over openly and solemnly from the camp of the proletariat to the camp of the bourgeoisie! Marceau Pivert closes his eyes to such "details."

For the workers who, during the revolution, direct all the force of their class hatred against the bourgeoisie, the participation of a "revolutionary" leader in a bourgeois government is a fact of enormous importance: it disorients and demoralizes them. And this fact did not fall from the sky. It was a necessary link in the policy of the POUM. The leaders of the POUM spoke with great eloquence of the advantages of the socialist revolution over the bourgeois revolution; but they did nothing serious to prepare this socialist revolution because the preparation could only consist of a pitiless, audacious, implacable mobilization of the Anarchist, Socialist, and Communist workers against their treacherous leaders. It was necessary not to fear separation from these leaders, to change into a "sect" during the early days, even if it were persecuted by everybody; it was necessary to put forth exact and clear slogans, foretell the morrow, and basing oneself on the events, discredit the official leaders and drive them from their positions.

In the course of eight months, the Bolsheviks, from the small group that they were, became a decisive force. The energy and the heroism of the Spanish proletariat gave the POUM several years in which to prepare. The POUM had the time on two or three occasions to emerge from its swaddling clothes and to become an adult. If it did not, it is in no way the fault of the "democratic" imperialists and the Moscow bureaucrats, but the result of an internal cause: its own leadership did not know where to go or what paths to take.

An enormous historical responsibility falls upon the POUM. If the POUM had not marched at the heels of the Anarchists and had not fraternized with the "Popular Front," if it had conducted an intransigent revolutionary policy, then, at the moment of the May 1937 insurrection and most likely much sooner, it would naturally have found itself at the head of the masses and would have assured the victory. The POUM was not a revolutionary party but a centrist party raised by the wave of the revolution. That is not at all the same thing. Marceau Pivert does not understand this even today, for he is himself a centrist to the marrow of his bones.

83   *INTERVIEW WITH SYBIL VINCENT*

March 18, 1939

If the Spanish revolution had been victorious, it would have given a powerful impulse to the revolutionary movement in France and in other countries of Europe. In this case it would have been possible to hope confidently that the victorious socialist movement would forestall the imperialist war, making

From *Socialist Appeal*, April 4, 1939. Full text is in *Writings of Leon Trotsky* (1938-39). Sybil Vincent was from the London *Daily Herald*.

it useless and impossible. But the socialist proletariat of Spain was strangled by the coalition of Stalin-Azaña-Caballero-Negrín-García Oliver, even before it was definitively crushed by Franco's bands. The defeat of the Spanish revolution postponed a revolutionary perspective for the imperialist war. Only the blind cannot see that! . . .

My opinion about the civil war in Spain? I have expressed myself on this subject in the press many times.

The Spanish revolution was socialist in its essence: the workers attempted several times to overthrow the bourgeoisie, to seize the factories; the peasants wanted to take the land. The Popular Front led by the Stalinists strangled the socialist revolution in the name of an outlived bourgeois democracy. Hence the disappointment, the hopelessness, the discouragement of the masses of workers and peasants, the demoralization of the republican army, and as a result, the military collapse.

To invoke the treacherous policy of England and France explains nothing. Of course the "democratic" imperialists were with the Spanish reaction with all their hearts and helped Franco as much as possible. It was so and will always be so. The British were naturally on the side of the Spanish bourgeoisie, which passed entirely to the side of Franco. However, in the beginning Chamberlain did not believe in the victory of Franco, and feared to compromise himself by a premature revelation of his sympathies. France, as ever, executed the will of the French bourgeoisie. The Soviet government played the role of hangman toward the revolutionary Spanish workers, in order to demonstrate its trustworthiness and loyalty to London and Paris. The fundamental cause of the defeat of a powerful and heroic revolution is the treacherous anti-socialist policy of the so-called Popular Front. If the peasants had seized the land and the workers the factories, Franco would never have been able to wrest this victory from their hands!

Can the regime of Franco maintain itself? Not, of course, for a thousand years, as the boasting National Socialism of Germany promises. But Franco will maintain himself for a certain time, thanks to the same conditions as Hitler. After great efforts and sacrifices, after terrible defeats, in spite of these sacrifices, the Spanish working class must be disappointed to the bottom of their hearts in the old parties: Socialists, Anarchists, Communists, who by their common forces, under the banner of the Popular Front, strangled the socialist revolution. The Spanish workers will now pass inevitably through a period of discouragement before they begin slowly and stubbornly to look for a new road. The period during which the masses lie prostrate will coincide precisely with the time of Franco's domination.

84   *THEIR FRIEND MIAJA*

March 24, 1939

As I see from the last issue of the *Socialist Appeal* received here, the Stalinists are trying to link us with Miaja and his staff. The *Socialist Appeal* has already given a clear answer to this frame-up. In this connection, permit me to quote from my article "The Lessons of Spain — The Last Warning," written in December 1937. Analyzing the possibility, under certain circumstances, of a rapprochement between the leaders of the fighting camps, I wrote: "It is not difficult to understand that in the event of such a variant the final remnants of the 'democracy' will be stifled in the fraternal embrace of the generals Miaja (communist!) and Franco (fascist!)."

Marxist theory makes it possible to foresee some things even on a personal plane. Stalinist practice (here there is no theory at all) consists of combinations of betrayals and frame-ups.

A letter to *Socialist Appeal,* printed March 31, 1939. On March 4, 1939, General Miaja had joined General Casado in broadcasting a manifesto repudiating the Negrín government and calling for surrender to the fascists.

85   *FIGHTING AGAINST THE STREAM*

April 1939

In Spain the same reasons played the same role (as in France: the strength of the Popular Front current) with the supplementary factor of the deplorable conduct of the Nin group. He was in Spain as [a] representative of the Russian Left Opposition, and during the first year we did not try to mobilize, to organize our independent elements. We hoped that we would win Nin to the correct conception, and so on. Publicly the Left Opposition gave him its support. In private correspondence we tried to win him and push him forward, but without success. We lost time. Was it correct? It is difficult to say.

If in Spain we had had an experienced comrade, our situation would be incomparably more favorable, but we did not have one. We put all our hopes on Nin, and his policy consisted of personal maneuvers in order to avoid responsibility. He played with the revolution. He was sincere, but his whole mentality was that of a Menshevik. It was a tremendous handicap, and to fight against this handicap only with correct formulas falsified by our own representatives in the first period, the Nins, made it very difficult.

An excerpt from the discussions in "The Fourth International in Europe," printed in *Internal Bulletin,* SWP, December 20, 1939. In this initial form, Trotsky was identified as Crux. C. L. R. James, who participated in the discussions under the name of Johnson, is the West Indian author of *The Black Jacobins* and *World Revolution.* He later left the Fourth Internationalist movement. The full text is in *Writings of Leon Trotsky* (1938-39).

86

THE COUNTERREVOLUTIONARY ROLE OF THE KREMLIN

July 1, 1939

It is difficult to conceive of a sillier invention than the references of Hitler and Mussolini to the Spanish events as proof of the revolutionary intervention of the Soviet Union. The Spanish revolution, which exploded without Moscow and unexpected by it, soon revealed a tendency to take a socialist character. Moscow feared above all that the disturbance of private property in the Iberian Peninsula would bring London and Paris nearer to Berlin against the USSR. After some hesitations, the Kremlin intervened in the events in order to restrict the revolution within the limits of the bourgeois regime.

All the actions of the Moscow agents in Spain were directed toward paralyzing any independent movement of the workers and peasants and reconciling the bourgeoisie with a moderate republic. The Spanish Communist Party stood in the right wing of the Popular Front. On December 21, 1936, Stalin, Molotov, and Voroshilov,[43] in a confidential letter to Largo Caballero, insistently recommended to the Spanish premier at that time that there be no infringement of private property, that guarantees be given to foreign capital against violation of freedom of commerce and for maintaining the parliamentary system without tolerating the development of soviets. This letter, recently communicated by Largo Caballero to the press through the former Spanish ambassador in Paris, L. Araquistain (*New York Times*, June 4, 1939),[44] summed up in the best manner the Soviet government's conservative position in the face of the socialist revolution.

We must, moreover, do justice to the Kremlin—the policy did not stay in the domain of words. The GPU in Spain carried out ruthless repression against the revolutionary wing ("Trotskyists," POUMists, left Socialists, left Anarchists). Now, after the defeat, the cruelties and frame-ups of the GPU in Spain are voluntarily revealed by the moderate politicians, who largely utilized the Moscow police apparatus in order to crush their revolutionary opponents.

An excerpt from "The Kremlin in World Politics," in *The New International*, October 1942. Full text is in *Writings of Leon Trotsky* (1938-39).

87 *NO GREATER CRIME*

July 15, 1939

Pivert strives to defend the personal memory of Andrés Nin against base calumnies and this is of course excellent. But when he depicts Nin's politics as a revolutionary model then it is impermissible to call this anything but a crime against the proletariat. In the heat of revolutionary war between the classes Nin entered a *bourgeois* government whose goal it was to destroy the workers' committees, the foundation of *proletarian* government. When this goal was reached, Nin was driven out of the bourgeois government. Instead of recognizing after this the colossal error committed, Nin's party demanded the re-establishment of the coalition with the bourgeoisie. Does Pivert dare deny this? It is not words that decide but facts. The politics of the POUM were determined by capitulation before the bourgeoisie at all critical times, and not by this or that quotation from a speech or article by Nin. *There can be no greater crime than coalition with the bourgeoisie in a period of socialist revolution.*

Instead of mercilessly exposing this fatal policy Pivert reprints in its justification all the old articles of Kurt Landau. Like Nin, Landau fell victim to the GPU. But the most ardent sympathy for the victims of Stalin's executioners does not free one from the obligation of telling the workers the truth. Landau, like Nin, represented one of the varieties of left Menshevism, was a disciple of Martov and not of Lenin. By supporting Nin's mistakes, and not our criticism of these mistakes, Landau, like Victor Serge, like Sneevliet, like Pivert himself, played a regrettable role in the Spanish revolution. Within the POUM a left opposition is now beginning to raise its head (José Rebull and his friends). The duty of Marxists is to help them draw the final conclusions from their criticisms. Yet Pivert supports the worst conservatives of the Gorkin type in the POUM. No, Pivert has not drawn the conclusions of his break with Blum!

An excerpt from "'Trotskyism' and the PSOP" in the October 1939 *New International.* The full text of this article is in *Leon Trotsky on France* (1934-39).

88

NO CONFIDENCE
IN THE NEGRIN GOVERNMENT

January 24, 1940

Shachtman, as we have already seen, persistently demands the citation of precedents: when and where in the past have the leaders of the opposition manifested petty-bourgeois opportunism? The reply that I have already given him on this score must be supplemented here with two letters that we sent each other on the question of defensism and methods of defensism in connection with the events of the Spanish revolution. On September 18, 1937, Shachtman wrote me:

> . . . You say, "If we would have a member in the Cortes he would vote *against* the military budget of Negrín." Unless this is a typographical error, it seems to us to be a *non sequitur*. If, as we all contend, *the element of an imperialist war* is not dominant at the present time in the Spanish struggle, and if instead the decisive element is still the struggle between decaying bourgeois democracy, with all that it involves, on the one side, and fascism, on the other, and further if we are obliged to give military assistance to the struggle against fascism, we don't see how it would be possible to vote in the Cortes against the military budget. . . . If a Bolshevik-Leninist on the Huesca front were asked by a Socialist comrade why his representative in the Cortes voted against the proposal by Negrín to devote a million pesetas to the purchase of rifles for the front, what would this Bolshevik-Leninist reply? It doesn't seem to us that he would have an effective answer. . . . [My emphasis — LT]

This letter astounded me. Shachtman was willing to express confidence in the perfidious Negrín government on the purely negative basis that the "element of an imperialist war" was not dominant in Spain.

On September 20, 1937, I replied to Shachtman:

> To vote for the military budget of the Negrín government signifies to vote him *political* confidence. . . . To do

---

An excerpt from *In Defense of Marxism.* The full text is available in book form from Pathfinder Press, New York.

it would be a crime. How [can] we explain our vote to the Anarchist workers? Very simply: We have not the slightest confidence in the capacity of this government to conduct the war and assure victory. We accuse this government of protecting the rich and starving the poor. This government must be smashed. So long as we are not strong enough to replace it, we are fighting under its command. But on every occasion we express openly our nonconfidence in it; it is the only one possibility to mobilize the masses *politically* against this government and to prepare its overthrow. Any other politics would be a betrayal of the revolution.

The tone of my reply only feebly reflects the . . . amazement that Shachtman's opportunist position produced in me. Isolated mistakes are of course unavoidable, but today, two and a half years later, this correspondence is illuminated with new light. Since we defend bourgeois democracy against fascism, Shachtman reasons, we therefore cannot refuse confidence to the bourgeois government. In applying this very theorem to the USSR, it is transformed into its converse — since we place no confidence in the Kremlin government, we cannot, therefore, defend the workers' state. Pseudoradicalism in this instance, too, is only the obverse side of opportunism.

89 THE CLASS, THE PARTY, AND THE LEADERSHIP
Why Was the Spanish Proletariat Defeated?
(Questions of Marxist Theory)

(Unfinished, August 20, 1940)

The extent to which the working class movement has been thrown backward may be gauged by the condition not only of the mass organizations, but also of the ideological groupings and those theoretical inquiries in which so many groups are engaged. In Paris there is published a periodical *Que faire*

The rough drafts and fragmentary notes for this article were found among Trotsky's papers shortly after his death. The article was published in *Fourth International,* December 1940.

(What To Do), which for some reason considers itself Marxist but in reality remains completely within the framework of the empiricism of the left bourgeois intellectuals and those isolated workers who have assimilated all the vices of the intellectuals.

Like all groups lacking a scientific foundation, without a program and without any tradition, this little periodical tried to hang on to the coattails of the POUM—which seemed to open the shortest avenue to the masses and to victory. But the result of these ties with the Spanish revolution seems at first entirely unexpected; the periodical did not advance but on the contrary retrogressed. As a matter of fact, this is wholly in the nature of things. The contradictions between petty-bourgeois conservatism and the needs of the proletarian revolution have developed in the extreme. It is only natural that the defenders and interpreters of the policies of the POUM found themselves thrown far back both in political and theoretical fields.

The periodical *Que faire* is in and of itself of no importance whatever. But it is of symptomatic interest. That is why we think it profitable to dwell upon this periodical's appraisal of the causes for the collapse of the Spanish revolution, inasmuch as this appraisal discloses very graphically the fundamental features now prevailing in the left flank of pseudo-Marxism.

"Que faire" explains

We begin with a verbatim quotation from a review [in *Que faire*] of the pamphlet *Spain Betrayed* by Comrade Casanova:[45]

> Why was the revolution crushed? 'Because,' replies the author [Casanova], 'the Communist Party conducted a false policy which was unfortunately followed by the revolutionary masses.' But why, in the devil's name, did the revolutionary masses who left their former leaders rally to the banner of the Communist Party? 'Because there was no genuinely revolutionary party.' We are presented with a pure tautology. A false policy of the masses; an immature party either manifests a certain condition of social forces (immaturity of the working class, lack of independence of the peasantry) which must be explained by proceeding from facts, presented among others by Casanova himself; or it is the product of the actions of certain

malicious individuals or groups of individuals, actions
which do not correspond to the efforts of 'sincere individuals'
alone capable of saving the revolution. After groping for
the first and Marxist road, Casanova takes the second.
We are ushered into the domain of pure demonology; the
criminal responsible for the defeat is the chief Devil, Stalin,
abetted by the anarchists and all the other little devils;
the God of revolutionists unfortunately did not send a
Lenin or a Trotsky to Spain as He did in Russia in 1917.

The conclusion then follows: "This is what comes of seeking
at any cost to force the ossified orthodoxy of a chapel upon
facts." This theoretical haughtiness is made all the more magnificent by the fact that it is hard to imagine how so great
a number of banalities, vulgarisms, and mistakes quite spe-
cifically of conservative philistine type could be compressed
into so few lines.

The author of the above quotation avoids giving any explanation for the defeat of the Spanish revolution; he only
indicates that profound explanations, like the "condition of
social forces," are necessary. The evasion of any explanation
is not accidental. These critics of Bolshevism are all theoretical
cowards, for the simple reason that they have nothing solid
under their feet. In order not to reveal their own bankruptcy,
they juggle facts and prowl around the opinions of others.
They confine themselves to hints and half-thoughts as if they
just haven't the time to delineate their full wisdom. As a matter of fact they possess no wisdom at all. Their haughtiness is
lined with intellectual charlatanism.

Let us analyze step by step the hints and half-thoughts of
our author. According to him, a false policy of the masses
can be explained only as it "manifests a certain condition of
social forces," namely, the immaturity of the working class
and the lack of independence of the peasantry. Anyone search-
ing for tautologies couldn't find in general a flatter one. A
"false policy of the masses" is explained by the "immaturity"
of the masses. But what is "immaturity" of the masses? Obviously, their predisposition to false policies. Just what the false
policy consisted of, and who were its initiators, the masses
or the leaders — that is passed over in silence by our author.
By means of a tautology, he unloads the responsibility on

the masses. This classical trick of all traitors, deserters, and their attorneys is especially revolting in connection with the Spanish proletariat.

Sophistry of the betrayers

In July 1936 — not to refer to an earlier period — the Spanish workers repelled the assault of the officers who had prepared their conspiracy under the protection of the Popular Front. The masses improvised militias and created workers' committees, the strongholds of their future dictatorship. The leading organizations of the proletariat, on the other hand, helped the bourgeoisie to destroy these committees, to liquidate the assaults of the workers on private property, and to subordinate the workers' militias to the command of the bourgeoisie, with the POUM moreover participating in the government and assuming direct responsibility for this work of the counterrevolution.

What does "immaturity" of the proletariat signify in this case? Self-evidently only this, that despite the correct political line chosen by the masses, they were unable to smash the coalition of Socialists, Stalinists, Anarchists, and the POUMists with the bourgeoisie. This piece of sophistry takes as its starting point a concept of some absolute maturity, i. e., a perfect condition of the masses in which they do not require a correct leadership, and more than that, are capable of conquering against their own leadership. There is not and there cannot be such maturity.

But why should workers who show such correct revolutionary instinct and such superior fighting qualities submit to treacherous leadership?, object our sages. Our answer is: there wasn't even a hint of mere submission. The workers' line of march at all times cut a certain angle to the line of the leadership. And at the most critical moments this angle became 180 degrees. The leadership then helped directly or indirectly to subdue the workers by armed force.

In May 1937 the workers of Catalonia rose not only without their own leadership but also against it. The Anarchist leaders — pathetic and contemptible bourgeoisie masquerading cheaply as revolutionists — have repeated hundreds of times in their press that had the CNT wanted to take power and set up their dictatorship in May, they could have done so without any difficulty. This time the Anarchist leaders speak the unadulterated truth. The POUM leadership actually dragged at the tail of the CNT, only they covered up their policy with a different phraseology. It was thanks to this and this alone that the bourgeoisie succeeded in crushing the May uprising of the "immature" proletariat.

One must understand exactly nothing in the sphere of the interrelationships between the class and the party, between the masses and the leaders, in order to repeat the hollow statement that the Spanish masses merely followed their leaders. The only thing that can be said is that the masses who sought at all times to blast their way to the correct road found it beyond their strength to produce in the very fire of battle a new leadership corresponding to the demands of the revolution. Before us is a profoundly dynamic process, with the various stages of the revolution shifting rapidly, with the leadership or various sections of the leadership quickly deserting to the side of the class enemy, and our sages engage in a purely static discussion: Why did the working class as a whole follow a bad leadership?

The dialectical approach

There is an ancient epigram from the evolutionist and liberal conception of history: Every people gets the government it deserves. History, however, shows that one and the same people may in the course of a comparatively brief epoch get very different governments (Russia, Italy, Germany, Spain, etc.), and furthermore that the order of these governments doesn't at all proceed in one and the same direction: from despotism to freedom as was imagined by the liberal evolutionists. The secret is that a people is comprised of hostile classes, and the classes themselves are comprised of different and in part antagonistic layers that fall under different leadership; furthermore every people falls under the influence of other peoples who are likewise comprised of classes. Governments do not express the systematically growing "maturity" of a "people" but are the product of the struggle between different classes and the different layers within one and the same class, and finally, the action of external forces — alliances, conflicts, wars, and so on. To this should be added that a government, once it has established itself, may endure much longer than the relationship of forces that produced it. It is precisely out of this historical contradiction that revolutions, coups d'etat, counterrevolutions, etc., arise.

The very same dialectical approach is necessary in dealing with the question of the leadership of a class. Imitating the liberals, our sages tacitly accept the axiom that every class gets the leadership it deserves. In reality leadership is not at all a mere "reflection" of a class or the product of its own free creativeness. A leadership is shaped in the process of clashes between the different classes or the friction between the different layers within a given class. Having once arisen, the leadership invariably rises above its class and thereby becomes predisposed to the pressure and influence of other classes. The proletariat may "tolerate" for a long time a leadership that has already suffered a complete inner degeneration but has not as yet had the opportunity to express this degeneration amid great events.

A great historic shock is necessary to reveal sharply the contradiction between the leadership and the class. The mightiest historical shocks are wars and revolutions. Precisely for this reason the working class is often caught unawares by war and revolution. But even in cases where the old leadership has revealed its internal corruption, the class cannot immediately improvise a new leadership, especially if it has not inherited from the previous period strong revolutionary cadres capable of utilizing the collapse of the old leading party. The Marxist interpretation, that is, the dialectical and not the scholastic interpretation of the interrelationship between a class and its leadership, does not leave a single stone unturned of our author's legalistic sophistry.

How the Russian workers matured

He conceives of the proletariat's maturity as something purely static. Yet during a revolution the consciousness of a class is the most dynamic process directly determining the course of the revolution. Was it possible in January 1917 or even in March, after the overthrow of czarism, to give an answer to the question whether the Russian proletariat had sufficiently "matured" for the conquest of power in eight to nine months?

The working class was at that time extremely heterogeneous

socially and politically. During the years of the war it had been renewed by 30-40 percent from the ranks of the petty bourgeoisie, often reactionary, from backward peasants, from women, and from youth. The Bolshevik Party in March 1917 was followed by an insignificant minority of the working class, and furthermore there was discord within the party itself. The overwhelming majority of the workers supported the Mensheviks and the "Social Revolutionaries," that is, conservative social patriots. The situation was even less favorable with regard to the army and the peasantry. We must add to this: the general low level of culture in the country, the lack of political experience among the broadest layers of the proletariat, especially in the provinces, let alone the peasants and soldiers.

What were the advantages of Bolshevism? A clear and thoroughly thought-out revolutionary conception at the beginning of the revolution was held only by Lenin. The Russian cadres of the party were scattered and to a considerable degree bewildered. But the party had authority among the advanced workers. Lenin had great authority with the party cadres. Lenin's political conception corresponded to the actual development of the revolution and was reinforced by each new event. These advantages worked wonders in a revolutionary situation, that is, in conditions of bitter class struggle. The party quickly aligned its policy to correspond with Lenin's conception; to correspond, that is, with the actual course of the revolution. Thanks to this, it met with firm support among tens of thousands of advanced workers. Within a few months, by basing itself upon the development of the revolution, the party was able to convince the majority of the workers of the correctness of its slogans. This majority, organized into soviets, was able in its turn to attract the soldiers and peasants.

How can this dynamic, dialectical process be exhausted by a formula of the maturity or immaturity of the proletariat? A colossal factor in the maturity of the Russian proletariat in February or March 1917 was Lenin. He did not fall from the skies. He personified the revolutionary tradition of the working class. For Lenin's slogans to find their way to the masses, cadres had to exist, even though numerically small at the beginning; the cadres had to have confidence in the leadership, a confidence based on the entire experience of the past. To cancel these elements from one's calculations is simply to ignore the living revolution, to substitute for it an abstraction, the "relationship of forces"; because the development of the revolution precisely consists of the incessant and rapid change in the relationship of forces under the impact of the changes in the consciousness of the proletariat, the attraction of the backward layers to the advanced, the growing assurance of the class in its own strength. The vital mainspring in this process is the party, just as the vital mainspring in the mechanism of the party is its leadership. The role and the responsibility of the leadership in a revolutionary epoch is colossal.

Relativity of "maturity"

The October victory is a serious testimonial to the "maturity" of the proletariat. But this maturity is relative. A few years later the very same proletariat permitted the revolution to be strangled by a bureaucracy that rose from its ranks. Victory is not at all the ripe fruit of the proletariat's "maturity." Victory is a strategical task. It is necessary to utilize the favorable conditions of a revolutionary crisis in order to mobilize the masses; taking as a starting point the given level of their "maturity," it is necessary to propel them forward, to teach them to understand that the enemy is by no means omnipotent, that it is torn asunder with contradictions, that behind the imposing facade panic prevails. Had the Bolshevik Party failed to carry out this work, there couldn't even be talk of the victory of the proletarian revolution. The Soviets would have been crushed by the counterrevolution and the little sages of all countries would have written articles and books on the keynote that only uprooted visionaries could dream in Russia of the dictatorship of the proletariat, so small numerically and so immature.

Auxiliary role of peasants

Equally abstract, pedantic, and false is the reference to the "lack of independence" of the peasantry. When and where did our sage ever observe in capitalist society a peasantry with an independent revolutionary program or a capacity for independent revolutionary initiative? The peasantry can play a very great role in the revolution, but only an auxiliary role.

In many instances, the Spanish peasants acted boldly and fought courageously. But to rouse the entire mass of the peasantry, the proletariat had to set an example of a decisive uprising against the bourgeoisie and inspire the peasants with faith in the possibility of victory. In the meantime, the revolutionary initiative of the proletariat itself was paralyzed at every step by its own organizations.

The "immaturity" of the proletariat, the "lack of independence" of the peasantry are neither final nor basic factors in historical events. Underlying the consciousness of the classes are the classes themselves, their numerical strength, their role in economic life. Underlying the classes is a specific system of production which is determined in its turn by the level of the development of productive forces. Why not then say that the defeat of the Spanish proletariat was determined by the low level of technology?

The role of personality

Our author substitutes mechanistic determinism for the dialectical conditioning of the historical process. Hence the cheap jibes about the role of individuals, good and bad. History is a process of the class struggle. But classes do not bring their full weight to bear automatically and simultaneously. In the process of struggle the classes create various organs, which play an important and independent role and are subject to deformations. This also provides the basis for the role of personalities in history. There are naturally great objective causes which created the autocratic rule of Hitler but only dull-witted pedants of "determinism" could deny today the enormous historic role of Hitler. The arrival of Lenin in Petrograd on April 3, 1917, turned the Bolshevik Party in time and enabled the party to lead the revolution to victory.

Our sages might say that had Lenin died abroad at the beginning of 1917, the October Revolution would have taken place "just the same." But that is not so. Lenin represented one of the living elements of the historical process. He personified the experience and the perspicacity of the most active section of the proletariat. His timely appearance on the arena of the revolution was necessary in order to mobilize the vanguard and provide it with an opportunity to rally the working class and the peasant masses. Political leadership in the crucial moments of historical turns can become just as decisive a factor as is the role of the chief command during the critical moments of war. History is not an automatic process. Otherwise, why leaders? why parties? why programs? why theoretical struggles?

Stalinism in Spain

"But why, in the devil's name," asks the author as we have already heard, "did the revolutionary masses who left their former leaders rally to the banner of the Communist Party?" The question is falsely posed. It is not true that the revolutionary masses left all of their former leaders. The workers who were previously connected with specific organizations continued to cling to them, while they observed and checked. Workers in general do not easily break with the party that awakens them to conscious life. Moreover the existence of mutual protection within the Popular Front lulled them: since everybody agreed, everything must be all right. The new and fresh masses naturally turned to the Comintern as the party which had accomplished the only victorious proletarian revolution and which, it was hoped, was capable of assuring arms to Spain.

Furthermore the Comintern was the most zealous champion of the idea of the Popular Front; this inspired confidence among the inexperienced layers of workers. Within the Popular Front, the Comintern was the most zealous champion of the bourgeois character of the revolution; this inspired the confidence of the petty and in part the middle bourgeoisie. That is why the masses "rallied to the banner of the Communist Party."

Our author depicts the matter as if the proletariat were in a well-stocked shoe store, selecting a new pair of boots. Even this simple operation, as is well known, does not always prove successful. As regards new leadership, the choice is very limited. Only gradually, only on the basis of their own experience through several stages, can the broad layers of the masses become convinced that a new leadership is firmer, more reliable, more loyal than the old. To be sure, during a revolution, i.e., when events move swiftly, a weak party can quickly grow into a mighty one provided it lucidly understands the course of the revolution and possesses staunch cadres that do not become intoxicated with phrases and are not terrorized by persecution. But such a party must be available prior to the revolution inasmuch as the process of educating the cadres requires a considerable period of time and the revolution does not afford this time.

Treachery of the POUM

To the left of all the other parties in Spain stood the POUM, which undoubtedly embraced revolutionary proletarian elements not previously firmly tied to anarchism. But it was precisely this party that played a fatal role in the development of the Spanish revolution. It could not become a mass party because in order to do so it was first necessary to overthrow the old parties and it was possible to overthrow them only by an irreconcilable struggle, by a merciless exposure of their bourgeois character.

Yet the POUM, while criticizing the old parties, subordinated itself to them on all fundamental questions. It participated in the "Popular" election bloc; entered the government that liquidated workers' committees; engaged in a struggle to reconstitute this governmental coalition; capitulated time and again to the Anarchist leadership; conducted, in connection with this, a false trade union policy; and took a vacillating and nonrevolutionary attitude toward the May 1937 uprising.

From the standpoint of determinism in general, it is possible, of course, to recognize that the policy of the POUM was not accidental. Everything in this world has its cause. However, the series of causes engendering the centrism of the POUM is by no means a mere reflection of the condition of the Spanish or Catalan proletariat. Two causalities moved toward each other at an angle, and at a certain moment they came into hostile conflict.

It is possible by taking into account previous international experience, Moscow's influence, the influence of a number of defeats, etc., to explain politically and psychologically why the POUM unfolded as a centrist party. But this does not alter its centrist character, nor does it alter the fact that a centrist party invariably acts as a brake upon the revolution, must each time smash its own head, and may bring about the collapse of the revolution. It does not alter the fact that the Catalan masses were far more revolutionary than the POUM, which in turn was more revolutionary than its leadership.

In these conditions to unload the responsibility for false policies on the "immaturity" of the masses is to engage in sheer
charlatanism frequently resorted to by political bankrupts.

Responsibility of leadership

The historical falsification consists in this, that the responsibility for the defeat of the Spanish masses is unloaded on
the working masses and not those parties that paralyzed or
simply crushed the revolutionary movement of the masses.
The attorneys of the POUM simply deny the responsibility
of the leaders, in order thus to escape shouldering their own
responsibility. This impotent philosophy, which seeks to reconcile defeats as a necessary link in the chain of cosmic developments, is completely incapable of posing and refuses to
pose the question of such concrete factors as programs, parties, and personalities that were the organizers of defeat. This
philosophy of fatalism and prostration is diametrically opposed to Marxism as the theory of revolutionary action.

Civil war is a process wherein political tasks are solved
by military means. Were the outcome of this war determined
by the "condition of class forces," the war itself would not be
necessary. War has its own organization, its own policies,
its own methods, its own leadership by which its fate is directly determined. Naturally, the "condition of class forces"
supplies the foundation for all other political factors; but just
as the foundation of a building does not reduce the importance of walls, windows, doors, roofs, so the "condition of
classes" does not invalidate the importance of parties, their
strategy, their leadership. By dissolving the concrete in the
abstract, our sages really halted midway. The most "profound"
solution of the problem would have been to declare the defeat of the Spanish proletariat as due to the inadequate development of productive forces. Such a key is accessible to
any fool.

By reducing to zero the significance of the party and of
the leadership, these sages deny in general the possibility of
revolutionary victory, because there are not the least grounds
for expecting conditions more favorable. Capitalism has ceased
to advance, the proletariat does not grow numerically; on
the contrary, it is the army of unemployed that grows, which
does not increase but reduces the fighting force of the proletariat and has a negative effect also upon its consciousness.

There are similarly no grounds for believing that under the regime of capitalism the peasantry is capable of attaining a higher revolutionary consciousness. The conclusion from the analysis of our author is thus complete pessimism, a sliding away from revolutionary perspectives. It must be said — to do them justice — that they do not themselves understand what they say.

As a matter of fact, the demands they make upon the consciousness of the masses are utterly fantastic. The Spanish workers, as well as the Spanish peasants, gave the maximum of what these classes are able to give in a revolutionary situation. We have in mind precisely the class of millions and tens of millions.

Que faire represents merely one of these little schools, or churches or chapels that, frightened by the course of the class struggle and the onset of reaction, publish their little journals and their theoretical etudes in a corner, on the sidelines, away from the actual developments of revolutionary thought, let alone the movement of the masses.

Repression of Spanish revolution

The Spanish proletariat fell victim to a coalition composed of imperialists, Spanish republicans, Socialists, Anarchists, Stalinists, and on the left flank, the POUM. They all paralyzed the socialist revolution, which the Spanish proletariat had actually begun to realize. It is not easy to dispose of the socialist revolution. No one has yet devised other methods than ruthless repression, massacre of the vanguard, execution of the leaders, etc. The POUM, of course, did not want this. It wanted, on the one hand, to participate in the republican government and to enter as a loyal peace-loving opposition into the general bloc of ruling parties; and on the other hand, to achieve peaceful comradely relations at a time when it was a question of implacable civil war. For this very reason the POUM fell victim to the contradictions of its own policy.

The most consistent policy in the ruling bloc was pursued by the Stalinists. They were the fighting vanguard of the bourgeois-republican counterrevolution. They wanted to eliminate the need for fascism by proving to the Spanish and world bourgeoisie that they were themselves capable of strangling the proletarian revolution under the banner of "democracy." This was the gist of their policies. The bankrupts of the Spanish

Popular Front are today trying to unload the blame on the GPU. I trust that we cannot be suspected of leniency toward the crimes of the GPU. But we see clearly and we tell the workers that the GPU acted in this instance only as the most resolute detachment in the service of the Popular Front. Therein was the strength of the GPU; therein was the historic role of Stalin. Only ignorant philistines can wave this aside with stupid little jokes about the Chief Devil.

These gentlemen do not even bother with the question of the social character of the revolution. Moscow's lackeys, for the benefit of England and France, proclaimed the Spanish revolution as bourgeois. Upon this fraud were erected the perfidious policies of the Popular Front, policies that would have been completely false even if the Spanish revolution had really been bourgeois. But from the very beginning, the revolution expressed much more graphically the proletarian character than did the revolution of 1917 in Russia. In the leadership of the POUM, gentlemen sit today who consider that the policy of Andrés Nin was too "leftist," that the really correct thing was to have remained the left flank of the Popular Front. The real misfortune was that Nin, covering himself with the authority of Lenin and the October Revolution, could not make up his mind to break with the Popular Front.

Victor Serge, who is in a hurry to compromise himself by a frivolous attitude toward serious questions, writes that Nin did not wish to submit to commands from Oslo or Coyoacán. Can a serious man really be capable of reducing to petty gossip the problem of the class content of a revolution? The sages of *Que faire* have no answer whatever to this question. They do not understand the question itself. Of what significance indeed is the fact that the "immature" proletariat founded its owۡ organs of power, seized enterprises, sought to regulate production while the POUM tried with all its might to keep from breaking with bourgeois Anarchists who, in an alliance with the bourgeois republicans and the no less bourgeois Socialists and Stalinists, assaulted and strangled the proletarian revolution! Such "trifles" are obviously of interest only to representatives of "ossified orthodoxy." The sages of *Que faire* possess instead a special apparatus that measures the maturity of the proletariat and the relationship of forces independently of all questions of revolutionary class strategy. . . .

Appendix

THE TROTSKY-NIN CORRESPONDENCE

By Way of Preface

February 21, 1933

Comrade Nin, who is in practically permanent conflict with the leadership of the International Opposition and with the leaders of all the other sections, at the same time denies the existence of theoretical or political differences. He often refers in this sense to his correspondence with me, without, however, giving details.

But in reality my correspondence with Comrade Nin, which has lasted two and a half years, was nothing else than a constant polemic, in spite of its most friendly form. This polemic covered almost all the questions that deal with the life and the activity of the International Opposition. It is true that Comrade Nin formally accepted the fundamental premises, but when the situation called for it, he always refused to draw from them the necessary conclusions. He held back for a long time the formation of the Spanish Opposition. He did everything to isolate it and oppose it to the International Opposition.

I am sorry that I cannot reproduce the whole correspondence; it would make a large volume. Two comrades who help me in my work have undertaken to select the most characteristic excerpts. It is regrettable to have to lose time on such work, unless the Spanish comrades attentively take note of those excerpts in order better to understand the history of the differences and to help the International Opposition to lead its Spanish section onto the right road.

L. D. Trotsky

From the *International Bulletin* of the Communist Left Opposition, no. 2/3, March 1933. Released by Trotsky's secretaries in French and English editions for internal circulation.

Letters from Nin to Trotsky

October 23, 1930

In France I saw very few people. Thanks to you I informed myself as to the internal situation of the Opposition. For their part, they had spoken to me about it only very vaguely, presenting the existing disharmony as having a purely personal character. As for the rest, they are satisfied with the work.

Now we have: (1) the official party, which has no effective force and no authority among the masses; (2) the Communist Federations of Catalonia and Valencia, which have been excluded from the party, and which in reality, together with the most influential groups of Asturia and a few other places, constitute in fact an independent party; (3) the Catalan Communist Party, which has a good elite leadership, counts on a certain influence among the dock workers of Barcelona and dominates the workers' movement in Lerida; and (4) the Left Opposition. The latter has no force in Catalonia.

November 12, 1930

The situation in France disturbs me very much. A split in our ranks would have catastrophic results. Let us hope that an agreement which you have recently reached will not prove transitory and that work in common will be possible. Personally I am very little in touch with the existing differences. Your letters have contributed a little to my orientation. I am expecting letters that the French comrades have told me about in order to form a more complete idea of the situation.

Official Communist Party: It has some branches in Biscay, Asturia, and Andalusia. Its authority is nil. . . .

Catalan-Balearic Communist Federation: Until very recently it belonged to the official party. Its most prominent leader is Maurín. On his arrival in Spain, the Central Committee, which has never regarded this comrade favorably (for, in spite of his hesitations, he is very intelligent, and above all a very honest comrade), asked him to make a declaration against "Trotskyism" and to renounce his "former errors." He refused to give this declaration and then was expelled. The Catalan Federation, having declared its solidarity with him, was expelled in a bloc. . . .

The Federation has an organ, a weekly, *La Batalla*, with a

circulation of 8,000. The paper is highly confusionist. . . .
For this reason no great importance should be given to the
publication in its pages of the unfortunate report of Stalin.
They published this as they might have published anything
else. Perhaps it was put in for lack of copy. This same paper,
for instance, on the anniversary of October published the pic-
tures of the leaders of the revolution, and among them
yours. . . .

The difficulty of our task results from the fact that we still
don't have a party. . . . With people whom we have to teach
the first notions of communism, we cannot begin by making
Opposition propaganda. . . . In Spain, I repeat, there is no
party. . . . In the unified party or in the existing groups, we
will demand our right to defend our position. A few words on
Maurín. I don't know whether you know that I am bound
to him by a very old friendship. Maurín is very close to us
and I am sure that he will end up in a short time by declaring
himself for the Opposition. That would be an acquisition of
great value, for as I have told you, he is very well thought
of and honest. We could spoil everything if we were to attack
him in a manner that was too unjustified.

December 3, 1930
I am convinced that in Spain the proletariat will organize its
party outside of the official party (which does not exist in
fact), and in spite of it. . . .

I would like to say a few words to you on the French matters but this letter is already too long and I reserve the subject
for a future letter.

January 17, 1931
And we reach an essential question. Here the party will be
formed outside of the official party. . . .

I should add that the Catalan Federation counts on the sympathy of the best elements in the rest of Spain and that a joint
action is quite possible.

My own conduct seems quite clear to me (and I say *to me*
because I am officially the only member of the Left Opposition
here): I ought to enter the Federation. Andrade and Lacroix,
the best elements that we have in Spain, share my opinion.
I have already carried on negotiations and I shall surely be

admitted, naturally without giving up my position in any way. . . . We must act with a certain tact. Most of the militants (except Maurín, who is the most intelligent and is really with us) say they are not with the Opposition; but (an astonishing thing!) they are ours without suspecting it; when I don't speak to them about the Opposition but explain to them our point of view on the essential questions of strategy, tactics, and organization, they show they are in agreement with us. . . . Here is a striking example. Next month the unification congress is to take place. Maurín is charged with the task of drawing up the theses on the political question and the tasks of the party. Well, taking advantage of the fact that we are "neighbors" (he lives next door to me), we are drawing up the theses together. . . . It would be stupid to give up a joint action when it is possible on a political platform that is completely acceptable. . . .

Now a few words on the French crisis. I subscribe completely to your theses. But I must confess to you that I still orient myself a little poorly on the real causes of the crisis. Rosmer wrote me a long letter several weeks ago to prove to me that he had no divergences in principle and that everything was confined to the incompatibility between them and Molinier, whom he represents as a "shifty" fellow, very much discredited in the French labor movement. It must be said that other comrades, who do not belong to the Opposition, have expressed the same opinion to me. What have you to say about that? That naturally does not reach the bottom of the question, but it also has its importance. Moreover, I am at pains to assert that I share your opinion on Naville. He suffers a little from the malady of many French militants, which is the result of their lack of direct contact with the working masses.

January 26, 1931

I speak of a *fundamental* agreement because I do not entirely share your viewpoint in detail. . . . Let us begin with the question of the Cortes. . . . Should we boycott it? Among the republicans there is opinion very favorable to abstention. . . . If the majority of the opposition parties boycott the parliament, I think that the communists will have to do the same. . . .

You speak of my candidacy. The Catalan Communist Federation (this is the section that has broken with the Comintern and whose *leader* is Maurín) should be unified without much trouble at a congress and should fix upon a line for the elections. The Barcelona section and the provisory executive committee have accepted the theses presented by Maurín and me (I edited them almost in their entirety), and have decided to present candidates in several places in cases where the opposition parties do not decide upon a boycott. One of the resolutions adopted is to present my candidacy in the Vendrell district. . . .

An indispensable condition for success is merciless struggle against the republican parties. Since my arrival, we have advanced a good deal in this direction. When I arrived, not only the anarcho-syndicalists but also a good section of the communists were following at the tail of the "left" bourgeoisie and petty bourgeoisie. That has come to an end.

February 5, 1931

We are entirely in agreement on the general line and I am greatly overjoyed at this. The political theses of the Catalan Federation, I think I told you, which were edited by Maurín and me, are inspired in exactly the same sense. I add yet more: the Federation has entrusted me with editing the official reply in the pages of *La Batalla* to the "Political Declaration" of the party. Is that not interesting?

March 7, 1931

I should have struggled energetically against the idea of creating a "Workers and Peasants Party." This idea has now been rejected. However, I could not prevent the adoption of a project for the creation of a "Workers and Peasants Bloc." But I have succeeded in obtaining the necessary guarantees. The Bloc will be *provisional*; its program will be that of the party. . . .

The Catalan Federation considers that my direct adherence in it may aggravate its relations with the Comintern. This is correct. But we have found a formula: I shall adhere to the Bloc, and as a member of it I shall participate in all the *meetings*. On the other hand, I will write every week in *La Batalla* under a pseudonym. If the rupture with the Comintern becomes definite (and it is inevitable), I would immediately be admitted into the Federation.

I am completely ignorant of divergences existing among us (the members of the Spanish Opposition). Nobody has ever said anything to me about them. It is certainly extraordinary! At least if there were some differences, that would indicate the Opposition is alive.

March 15, 1931
In April we shall have (or ought to have) municipal elections. . . . Here we shall have a communist candidacy presented under the banner of the Workers and Peasants Bloc (a "communist" candidate would not be authorized, for the party is illegal). . . . Despite this formality, the Bloc will be presented under an openly communist platform. . . . After all probabilities are weighed, I should be a candidate. . . . The candidacy is composed of members of the Catalan-Balearic Federation, and of the "Catalan party" group which has not fused with the latter, and myself. Therefore this is the first attempt at a communist united front. I also proposed to invite the official party. My proposal was met with a good deal of resistance, but it is not impossible that it may ultimately be accepted. . . .

Recently I received your letter on the German crisis, [1] * which has interested me tremendously. I must admit to you that I understand this crisis more clearly than that of the French Opposition.

April 4, 1931
Open propaganda for the principles of the Opposition has provoked my rupture with the Catalan Federation, or to put it better, with its leaders. The workers hold a very different attitude and demonstrate obvious sympathy with me.

[Letter to the International Secretariat]

April 5, 1931
The crisis of the Left Opposition in Germany may have disastrous consequences for the entire future of our movement, if we do not adopt energetic and speedy measures. We can strike at the roots of the crisis by the effective means that the methods

---

*Notes for the Appendix begin on p. 426.

of democratic centralism offer us. In this sense the proposals formulated by Comrade Trotsky in his letter of February 17 appear entirely correct and I hereby unreservedly associate myself with them.*

April 10, 1931
Let us pass on to the "well known" differences with the Madrid comrades. . . . As it appears, it is on the question of my so-called unconditional entrance into the Catalan Federation that the most serious difference existed. Seeing that the Madrid comrades have never said anything on this subject, I cannot clarify wherein these differences lie.

April 12, 1931
In my opinion if we should begin by suddenly attacking the Federation with violence, the results would be utterly regrettable. . . . We must enter the Federation, carry on systematic work in it, and create our faction in it. That is quite possible. I am certain that, if my entrance is not possible today, it soon will be, perhaps before a month.

April 15, 1931
The Catalan Federation has come to ask my aid. I could not refuse it, so here I am working in an immediate manner (actually in a large measure leading) in the Central Committee of the organization. . . . We publish a daily sheet of which I am editor.

May 25, 1931
Your fears are exaggerated so far as concerns the possibility of premature action in Catalonia. . . . The entire tactic of the anarcho-syndicalists, who exercise hegemony over the movement, consists in checking the actions of the proletariat. As for the communists, the Catalan Federation (the only one here that can be reckoned as a communist force) has a quite correct conception of the movement (exactly like ours) and is decidedly antagonistic to all adventurist or putschist policies.

* This proposal (Trotsky-Nin) was accepted. After that, Nin accused the International Opposition of having a false policy toward Landau. — L. T.

June 25, 1931
The Catalan Federation, whose policies I do not defend and
have never defended, did not adopt a policy of conciliation
toward the anarcho-syndicalists.

June 29, 1931
[The Catalan Federation's] orientation is, as always, variable,
indefinite. My relations with its leaders have evolved through
various stages: collaboration, rupture, new collaboration, new
rupture. Right now we stand in the latter situation . . . up to
the unification congress [the ellipsis is Nin's].

July 7, 1931
Until now we haven't materialized any consistent and organized work. . . . We couldn't do it any other way. A cell of
the Opposition has recently begun operating without having
been created or existing formally.

July 9, 1931
In a few days the supplementary elections will take place at
Barcelona. . . . There have been official understandings between the Esquerra (of Macía) and Maurín.[2] The former will
officially support the latter, and by means of this it is almost
certain that he will be elected. . . . The Esquerra officially made
some gestures to me to present my candidacy. I replied that
I shall accept only in the event that I should be presented by
the Catalan Federation and on condition that the Esquerra
would make no gesture in favor of my candidacy. The Federation naturally presented Maurín. There still remained the
province of Barcelona where three deputies are to be elected.
The Federation is presenting no candidates. Friends in the
province proposed to me that I should be presented as an
"independent communist," but I flatly refused.

July 13, 1931
For the third number of the review [*Comunismo*], I wrote
an article against the mistakes of Maurín. We cannot maintain
silence on them without the greatest danger for the movement.
The electoral campaign that the Bloc has carried on these
last few days has had little of a communist nature.

July 15, 1931
We are still a very small nucleus in Spain. . . . We work in perfect agreement and with the greatest enthusiasm. . . . Of the IS comrades I know only Mill. He made a good impression on me. I have heard the most contradictory opinions on Molinier and Frank and I ought to declare to you that I incline more to the side of the less favorable reports. But, I repeat, all this is merely suppositions, *presentiments*. And J still do not judge myself informed enough to express a definite opinion, as I did for example on Germany, because I knew the persons and saw the conflict clearly.

A few words on one of the points that wrongly suggest disturbances to you, where you see in my attitude some "elements" of "diplomacy." I want to speak of Rosmer's visit. I must tell you above all that I am convinced of having spoken to you about it. But, in actuality, there was no important matter to speak of. He was sober enough in his judgment and did not express himself as far as the Spanish affairs are concerned in the sense that you indicate. On the French questions, he related some things to me that I know well enough. I must *see* Molinier and Frank personally and talk with them.

July 20, 1931
If we could only have a weekly in Barcelona! It would rapidly become an organizing center. If I had a thousand pesetas, I would spend it immediately.

August 25, 1931
I have the opportunity to establish communist organizations here in several cities. To what organization should they adhere? To the Bloc or to the official party? I have a good deal of hesitation on this point. To make them adhere to the official party is quite difficult, for there is practically no organization in Catalonia. On the other hand, the political position of the Bloc is at present so false that it is no less difficult to advise their adherence to this organization. Still I am inclined in favor of this second solution. . . .

For us the most important task is now the publication of the weekly. Molinier passed by here and will pass by again in two or three days. We shall meet, all three together, with Lacroix at Barcelona, in order definitely to settle the plan of work. He has already supplied a little money. . . .

A few words on the French situation. Either I expressed myself poorly (which is quite possible, for due to lack of time, I write with great haste) or else you did not understand me well. I certainly do not subordinate (which would be absurd) the political questions to personal questions; I merely believe (and you do too, in my opinion) that persons play a big role. I have not had the time to make a thorough study of the documents concerning the French question. I am in the act of doing that right now and it is surely due to this circumstance that I do not see clearly enough. Your manner of viewing the trade union problem seems absolutely correct to me, generally speaking. But I still have been unable to estimate to what extent the errors that you indicate *actually* exist. And it is here that the personal problems may play a role. Sometimes we attribute to people concepts that they have never held. This is not an accusation that I make against you (that is the furthest thing from my intentions); but this hypothesis is not excluded *on the French side*. I repeat it, these are only conjectures. A profound study of the documents will undoubtedly help me to arrive at precise conclusions. On the other hand, I have met Molinier (a circumstance that has its importance) and I must tell you that the impression he produced on me was excellent. I shall not fail to acquaint you with my definite opinion. As far as Rosmer is concerned, I completely share your viewpoints.

September 6, 1931
I insist upon thinking that our most urgent task is the founding of a weekly organ of struggle at Barcelona. . . .

P. S. — All the letters in the list you sent me have arrived.

September 18, 1931
During these last two weeks I have thoroughly studied all the documents concerning the French question. I have spoken at great length on this question with Molinier, who as you know, is among us. And truly all my doubts have been dispelled. I am now convinced that Rosmer and Naville are not right. (I did not see Rosmer this time.) Moreover, I was very

glad to become acquainted with Molinier, whose devotion I appreciate, and whom I regard as a genuine revolutionary. . . . I must confess to you that what Rosmer said about Molinier produced a certain impression on me. But, I repeat, I no longer have any doubts on the matter. Molinier's position seems to me absolutely correct and I estimate the acquisition of militants like him as a great benefit to the Opposition. . . .

We have considered at length with some comrades from Barcelona as well as with Molinier and Lacroix the problem of the eventual adherence of the organizations to the Bloc or the party. Naturally, from a principled point of view, you are right; we must make them adhere to the party. But the complexity of our situation demands a combined solution. In Barcelona, we shall make everyone adhere to the party. In the Catalan provinces we shall make them adhere to the Bloc. Here, for the time being, is the only possible solution. In the first place, it would be difficult to make the organizations adhere to the party (they would not want to go into it); in the second place because — do not forget this — in Catalonia the party actually does not exist. In all these groups the best elements are with us, and under our leadership they will be able to contribute actively to the decomposition of the Bloc.

We considered it absolutely inadmissible and impossible to make these groups adhere to the Opposition and to demand of them that they adhere to the party. In the first place, it is not a question of groups composed of Oppositionists but of *recent* communists among whom there are some Oppositionists. Even in cases where we should be able to make them adhere integrally to the Opposition (should that be desirable), we ought not to be inclined to that solution: they would not be admitted into the official party and in fact we would be laying the basis for a new party. Inside the Bloc these groups will be a very fruitful basis of work for us; they will be the *pioneers* for unity and the most implacable adversaries of the policy of the leadership. It is true that for the tactic you recommend you consider an Opposition center in Catalonia necessary. And you add textually: "If you remember, I have insisted upon this from the first day of your arrival in Barcelona, but alas, without success." Now we have that center. That it was necessary I have never doubted. But to achieve it we required almost a year.

October 7, 1931
Some other day I will write to you at length on the question
of a "narrow" or "broad" faction. I have translated your letter
and we are going to discuss it in our organizations. I prefer
to transmit my personal opinion to you along with that of all
the comrades. Nevertheless, I am taking pains to inform you
that I do not share your viewpoint which seems to me to be
dictated by insufficient information on the situation.

[Letter to the IS]

November 7, 1931
The governor's persecution of *El Soviet* allowed us to suspend
publication in an "honorable" manner. . . .

Indeed, we foresaw all the difficulties to which we were exposing ourselves. In accordance with this, and because of it,
we did not push the weekly publication sooner. But Comrade
Molinier made us solemn promises in the name of the IS. . . .

But these promises remained thin air, and our economic situation became grave. The one directly culpable for all this is
Comrade Molinier who acted with unjustifiable irresponsi-
bility. . . .

Truly, a conscious saboteur of the Opposition could not
have done better than Molinier.

November 24, 1931
Undoubtedly the IS has sent you a copy of the letter I mailed
it on this subject (the suspension of *El Soviet*). . . . It is my
purpose solely to add that the Spanish Opposition is unanimous
in asserting the ruinous role that Molinier is playing in the
French League and in the International Opposition. All the
information I possess (in addition to your own experiences)
confirms me in this opinion. . . .

Our work is proceeding very well, and there is not the least
difference among us (in the Spanish section).

There are no differences on the question of "broad" factions.
It was a misunderstanding among us and nothing more.

December 7, 1931
You say that the present regime in Spain can be compared
to "Kerenskyism." . . . I do not think so. "Kerenskyism" was

the bourgeoisie's last card. It was the announcement for October. Azaña announces Lerroux, that is, Miliukov, the big bourgeoisie.

February 7, 1932
I have nothing further to add to what I have written you in my previous letters on the question that causes our differences. What makes the situation especially serious is not its political aspect, but its personal aspect. In the case of France, that has decisive importance.

June 7, 1932
Your letter of May 29 surprised me excessively through its tone and content. I had made a sincere effort to resume a correspondence whose usefulness to our movement (each day more important) is incontestable. I did not find the same goodwill on your part. . . . Your direct collaboration is precious to us; but even without it (since you refuse it), we are consecrating all our energies up to the present to the task of creating a strong Left Communist force in Spain. . . .

I am still trying to emphasize that there is no political difference between us, and that it is very unfortunate that the fact that we do not share your opinion on a French militant (a militant?) . . . has determined an actual break, the responsibility for which rests entirely on you.

November 25, 1932
Neither the Spanish Opposition as such nor I personally have ever said that the Spanish revolution was finished. This is an incredible monstrosity. We consider the publication of a resolution from the Central Committee on this matter entirely superfluous, for no one here has accused us of having supported a viewpoint that is in fundamental opposition to our political position.

Letters from Trotsky to Nin

September 13, 1930

I have no doubt that in Paris you will be put in touch with the internal struggle of the League. That is why I find it necessary to expound for you my viewpoint on this question. . . .

If you enter into all these internal matters in Paris (I think you should do so), it is necessary that you hear both sides. I would be pleased if you would write me the detailed impressions you bring away from it.*

November 21, 1930

Insofar as the Western European Opposition generally has not lived a permanent ideological and political life, has not reacted to the important questions, has not mingled in the party's internal life, its casual followers (Urbahns, Overstraeten, Souvarine, Paz)[3] were able to appear to themselves and others as our partisans. But at bottom they contributed the greatest damage by blocking the road to the ideas of the Left Opposition in the party, which they all declared liquidated and dead, conceding that this is much simpler and offers the opportunity of living peaceably in a corner, to devote one hour a week to Oppositionist conversations. . . .

In your letter occurs the sentence: "A split in our ranks [in France] would have catastrophic results." Obviously every split has an abnormal character. Obviously the withdrawal of Comrade Rosmer would deal a blow to *La Vérité,* and personally, for my part, I am ready to do everything to avoid that. It is in this sense that I wrote to the French comrades and to Rosmer himself. But I must say that such a split cannot be catastrophic for us. . . .

In order that the small national groups, without adequate theoretical basis, without tradition, without experience, may not lose themselves on the road in the process of patient clarification, there must be a firm link between them; there must be continuous reciprocal verification; there must be organized

---

* Nin did not do this, confining himself to a conversation with the Rosmer group. — L. T.

ideological control; there must be double and triple ideological implacability. . . .

You write that Landau announced your correspondence without your authorization. But, in that case, where did he obtain your correspondence?

November 29, 1930
You speak of the backwardness of the Spanish workers and of the necessity for making them acquainted with the fundamental ideas of communism before posing the questions of the Left Opposition. . . .

For myself, I assert that I do not consider myself able to give a lecture on communism to the most backward workers without at the same time posing the questions of the Left Opposition. . . . If I were to hold a conference on communism with the most backward groups of workers, Spanish or otherwise, I would mark out the road from the very beginning by the following declaration: "There are several currents in communism. I belong to such and such a current and I shall expound to you how this current conceives the tasks of the working class."

In conclusion I should summon the workers to join the organization that defended the viewpoints I had just expounded. Without that propaganda and agitation we acquire an academic character, are deprived of an organizational axis, and ultimately aid our adversaries, i. e., the centrists and right wingers.

December 12, 1930
I think that even though the Left Opposition may be weak, if it takes the initiative of posing the political (agrarian) and organizational problems of the revolution, it can in a very short space of time occupy the leading position in the movement.

I tell you frankly, I am very much afraid that the historians of the future may have to accuse the Spanish revolutionists of not having known how to take advantage of an exceptional revolutionary situation.

January 12, 1931
According to the press, the bourgeois opposition parties are

preparing to boycott the elections to the Cortes. All the more then should the workers have recourse to the tactic of the boycott.

In the immediate situation, it certainly appears that we could invalidate Berenguer's elections by an energetically applied boycott tactic; in 1905 that was how we invalidated the election of a legislative Duma that was merely consultative. What is the policy of the communists on this point? Do they distribute leaflets, appeals, proclamations on this subject?

January 31, 1931

From a revolutionary viewpoint, the question is resolved in this manner: does the Catalan party aspire to political and organizational independence? Or has it really considered itself from the beginning as a regional organization of the Spanish party? We can allow federalism in the state but under no circumstances in the party. . . .

Although the official party as it is today may be feeble and insignificant, nevertheless it possesses all the external historic possibilities in it, in the USSR, and everything that is linked up with the USSR. That is why to guide yourself empirically solely on the immediate relation of forces seems dangerous to me. . . .

The entrance of the Left Communists into larger and broader organizations is justified in Spain more than anywhere else by the condition of the communist ranks on the one hand, by the revolutionary situation on the other. But this tactic creates the immediate danger of the dissolution of the Left Oppositionists into other currents and factions. That is why the creation of a center of the Left Opposition seems to me the necessary and urgent condition for the entrance of the lefts into other organizations. A paper of the Left Opposition and an internal bulletin, these are necessary.

February 5, 1931

As for the boycott, I do not regard myself convinced. . . . The communists obviously committed an error by failing to take the initiative in the boycott. They alone, at the head of the revolutionary workers, could have given the boycott campaign a bold and militant character. The sentiment for boycott, nevertheless, is evidently very widespread in the opposition parties and is a reflection and symptom of the profound restlessness among the popular masses. The latest dispatches seem to confirm the news that the republicans and Socialists have come out in favor of the boycott. If the communists had vigorously confronted them at the proper time, the republicans and Socialists would have infinitely more difficulty in renouncing this plan for a boycott.

February 13, 1931
The fact that the Catalan Federation entrusts you with the editing of its principal documents, including therein the reply to the party's political declaration, is a very valuable conquest that holds much promise. . . .

But nevertheless I am renewing my proposal for publishing in Madrid (or in another city) a bulletin of the Spanish Left Opposition as a politically and theoretically solid monthly organ. . . . Without that, the new stage of the revolution can catch the Left Opposition off its guard, and with the weakness of the party and the confusion of the Catalan Federation, that could bring about the most terrific irreparable disasters.

February 15, 1931
. . . Unfortunately the communists were not the stars in the boycotters' performance. That is why they did not achieve any important victories in the campaign of the last two or three months. In periods of stormy revolutionary flux, the authority of the party grows rapidly, feverishly — if, in decisive turns, at new stages, the party immediately advances the necessary slogan, whose correctness is soon confirmed by the events. . . . In the course of the last weeks and months, opportunities have been allowed to escape. But it does no good to look back now. We must look ahead. The revolution is only beginning. We can win back a hundredfold what we have allowed ourselves to lose. . . .

It is necessary to create immediately a well-organized faction of the Left Opposition, no matter how small it may be to begin with, which will publish its own bulletin and its own theoretical organ. Of course, this does not exclude the participation of the Left Communists in broader organizations; on the contrary, it assumes it, but at the same time, organizing the Left Opposition is the indispensable condition for this participation.

March 4, 1931

The political experience of the Berenguer period demonstrates that the proletarian party must firmly adopt a position of boycott of the admiral's Cortes. The Socialists, the republicans can abandon the positions of boycott assumed by them if they are not continually driven to the left. At the present stage of the revolution, the communist organization can play the role of the small but strong flywheel that compels all the toothed gear wheels of the Socialists, republicans, and even the partisans of the constituent Cortes to revolve — in order that the flywheel may not break the teeth of the Socialist and constitutional wheels.

We must put forward the slogan of an active boycott; that means not simply abstaining from participation in the elections, but also developing an energetic offensive to smash the falsely constituted Cortes (by public meetings, proclamations, demonstrations, denouncing the names of the official candidates as enemies of the people, public boycott of those participating in the election, etc.). I think the tactic of an active boycott would allow the creation of workers' boycott committees which, at the opportune moment, could be transformed into workers' juntas. . . .

In my preceding letters, I wrote in detail on the cohesion of the Left Opposition and on its attitude toward the official party. I do not know whether you have received my letters and I am waiting impatiently for you to inform me of your viewpoints on these questions and the practical measures taken by you and your comrades. Questions of revolutionary strategy and tactics have a meaning only on condition that there exists "the subjective factor" of this strategy, namely, a revolutionary organization, even if very small in numbers at the start.

March 15, 1931

How will your participation in the Bloc be defined and politically explained, as that of a representative of a communist faction or as that of a revolutionist known to be isolated? It is possible that some elements of the Federation, in case of need to reach an agreement with the bureaucracy of the Comintern, will later declare that they formed a bloc with the peasantry and the revolutionary petty bourgeoisie in the person of Nin. To exist without a political passport, especially during the revolution, is very dangerous.

March 29, 1931
I receive from Paris letters showing more and more uneasiness on the subject of the situation in Spain. I must tell you that I share this uneasiness. In Spain the situation is revolutionary; in Spain we have entirely qualified representation of the Left Opposition. By correspondence, articles, etc., we have elaborated something like a draft program of the Left Opposition. All eyes are turned toward Spain. And yet the Left Opposition as an official and active organization does not exist in Spain. And every day lost will have heavy repercussions in the decisive moments. Nobody outside of the Left Opposition is capable of giving a correct orientation nor of laying down a proper policy in the revolutionary conditions in Spain. And yet the Left Opposition does not exist; that provokes uneasiness among many of the comrades, and I share that uneasiness. . . .

Where is the way out? The Madrid comrades believe that with the assistance of the Asturian comrades it is possible to publish a monthly theoretical paper. They are also ready to publish a bulletin of the left faction. It seems to me that we must support them with all our forces. By preserving a permanent liaison between you and Madrid, on the one hand, and between Spain, Paris, and Constantinople, on the other, we can achieve the necessary political, theoretical, and organizational harmony. I await your reply on this question with a good deal of impatience, all the more so because my previous letters have remained unanswered on this point. . . .

The presentation of your candidacy in the municipal elections is obviously a very important point. But you will manifestly agree with me that in politics, above all during the revolution, only those conquests are important which are translated into the growth of the party or, in the immediate case, of the faction. Without that, the tempest of the revolution will completely sweep away the individual initiative, in the event of victory for the revolution as well as in the event of defeat.

April 1, 1931
I am extremely pleased at your conference and your successes.

Your intention of occupying yourself during your trip with the organization of a Left Opposition faction gives me even more hope. It is important to have a crystal prepared; the development of the revolution will create a saturated solution.

April 12, 1931

I have just received your letter in which you inform me for the first time of your break with the Catalan Federation and the appearance in a short while of an organ of the Left Opposition, *Comunismo.* The latter news fills me with so much joy that I refuse to regret the several months lost in the matter of forming a Left Opposition. I do not doubt that you will win back a hundred times the period of time lost.

April 20, 1931

In your second letter you show the necessity of influencing the Catalan Federation in a friendly manner and tactfully. I am in full agreement with you. . . .

But I cannot fail to emphasize from here, from far off, the second side of the matter. Two or three months ago you estimated that the organization would be won over by you with no difficulties; together with Maurín you elaborated the theses, etc. A little while later it was asserted that the Federation, because of its equivocal relations with the Comintern, finds your direct entrance into its ranks inopportune. This record is, in my eyes, an argument against the attempts to influence the Federation only personally, individually, pedagogically — with the lack of an organized left faction acting everywhere with its own banner displayed. Work inside the Federation? Yes, certainly. Work patiently, in a friendly manner, without fear of being checked? Yes, yes, yes. But work openly, as an accredited Left Oppositionist, as a Bolshevik-Leninist belonging to a faction, and as one who demands for it the freedom of criticism and of expounding his opinions.

April 22, 1931

The most important information in your letter is the fact of your entrance into the Central Committee of the Catalan Federation and your editing of the daily publication of the Federation. I cannot state what tremendous significance this fact has. However, the political premises are unfortunately not clear to me. Several weeks ago, you wrote that you were obliged to

break with the Federation because its leaders considered your
adherence to the Left Opposition incompatible with adherence
to the Federation. In other words, the leaders showed themselves extremely hostile to us and employed the methods and
phraseology of the Stalinist bureaucracy.

After that, your entrance at the end of several weeks into
the leading positions of the Federation, I assure you, disorients
me to a large extent. What has happened to the Federation?
Has the composition of the leadership changed? Has their
state of mind radically altered under the influence of the republican overthrow and the general softening of manners?
Have they lost hope of being reconciled with the bureaucracy
of the Comintern? On what condition did you enter the Federation? On all these questions I shall await your reply with
great impatience. . . .

You wrote that you are disposed to utilize your journey
for the organization of the left faction. Unfortunately there
is no mention of this in your letter.

Now as to the general political angle of these facts. The
Catalan Federation, according to what I understand, has not
sought and does not seek a general Spanish organization.
If this is so, then it is leading itself and the Catalan labor
movement into defeat. . . . The strength of the Left Opposition
in Barcelona as well as in Madrid can and should lie in raising all these questions to a historical level, not permitting
isolated groups and sects to destroy the revolution by pro-
vincialism, by passive or active nationalism, by bureaucratic
myopia, etc. We have lost much time on this field, and time
is a very precious factor in the revolution. A new loss of time
will be a crime. On the Spanish communists and on you personally, dear friend, rests a tremendous historical responsibility. The Catalan Federation is only an arena for influence,
but not a sure lever. Without a serious principled basis, without a clear strategic line, the Catalan Federation, encrusted
with numerous prejudices, would not itself stand up under
the tests of the revolution and would be defeated at the next
sharp turn. A small but firm Marxist nucleus, understanding
precisely what it wants, can save not only the Catalan Federation but also the Spanish revolution; but only on one condition: the small nucleus must march under its own clear
program and under its own banner.

I beg you to reply to me as quickly as you possibly can,

precisly on these questions, conceding that in my eyes they
have decisive importance. *

May 26, 1931
I am forced to observe that in your letters you prefer to inform
me about facts with which I am generally familiar from the
newspapers, and at the same time you consistently avoid questions that appear to be of crucial importance. Undoubtedly
I have no right demanding current news from you or even
brief replies (yes and no) to the questions I ask you. But
you should understand that diplomatic correspondence cannot
satisfy me.

As a result of numerous and increasing attempts at achieving
minimum clarity through our correspondence I have gotten
the impression that you do not seek this same clarity. Why?
Evidently this is because you have taken a contradictory position, you are letting things ride while waiting for them to
work out by themselves. Experience and theory have shown
that such politics have fatal consequences.

May 30, 1931
You see that at the end of my new work on the Spanish revolution ["The Spanish Revolution in Danger"], I attach a considerable number of my letters addressed to you, at the same
time eliminating everything that had a personal or "polemical"
character, no matter how friendly; I left only the principled
and political considerations. **

May 31, 1931
Unfortunately I cannot assimilate the reassuring observations
you make concerning the situation in Spain and especially
in Catalonia. You find that there is no reason to fear premature events in Catalonia, even granting that the anarcho-
syndicalists who have hegemony in the labor movement hold
on to the workers with all their power. According to you,
the Catalan Federation is acting in the same direction. I see
in this information, which is in agreement with the informa-

* Nin has never replied to these questions and has never explained
on what basis he entered the Central Committee of the Federation.
— L. T.

** Nin expunged all these letters from the Spanish edition. — L. T.

tion of the bourgeois press on the anarcho-syndicalists, a source not of mitigation, but on the contrary, of disquiet.

As far as I can judge, the anarcho-syndicalists are follow- ing a policy of conciliation toward the despicable regime of Colonel Macía, the Barcelonese agent of the Madrid impe- rialists. The anarcho-syndicalist leaders have probably become the sub-lieutenants, and in fact the agents, of national civil peace in Catalonia.

As far as I can tell from your letter, the Catalan Federa- tion has adopted a conciliatory position toward the anarcho- syndicalists; that is to say, it has replaced the revolutionary policy of the united front with the opportunist policy of de- fending and flattering the Macía regime. It is precisely in this that I see one of the sources of explosion that can be so dan- gerous at a certain stage. It is not the task of the trade unions to hold back the workers, but on the contrary, to mobilize and organize them for the offensive. . . .

So that the restraining of actions that are premature and unreasonable cannot be transformed into a Menshevik suf- focation of the revolution, we must have a clear strategic line, and the advanced workers must understand it well so that they can tirelessly explain it to the broad masses. The Catalan Federation obviously has no strategic line. Its leaders are afraid to ponder on the fundamental problems of the rev- olution; otherwise they would not have that infantile and stu- pid fear of "Trotskyism," which expresses the entire extent of their political thought. Solidarity with such leaders instead of opposition to them with a serious and tenacious policy, even in the friendliest tone, means rushing headlong with open arms toward tragic errors. But on that I have often written and I shall not return to it.

June 29, 1931
To win over the proletarian nucleus of the Catalan Federa- tion, it is necessary to create a firm nucleus of the Left Op- position in Catalonia and corresponding publications — at the very least, a bulletin in the Catalan language. We must sub- mit Maurín to pitiless and incessant criticism; events will com- pletely confirm our criticism. . . .

The fact that the Stalinists in Barcelona have drawn to their side several dozen unemployed — as you write — is, in my opinion, an important symptom that speaks against the Catalan Federation. How can the leading revolutionary organization fail to influence the unemployed, who represent the left flank of the movement? I think that the reason for this is the opportunism of the Federation, the absence of activity and vigor on its part, its premature "wisdom," that is, opportunism. During the revolution, the workers pass quickly from one organization to another.

July 2, 1931

My criticism was not that you write little or seldom, but that in your correspondence you obstinately avoid certain questions. . . .

There was still one moment that disquieted me. You cannot be ignorant of Rosmer's political position. On this question, I have been awaiting more frankness on your part. If you consider that I have committed such and such an error towards Rosmer, I am ready to hear any criticism whatsoever, even the harshest, and I am ready to do anything to mend the situation, which has been intensified entirely and exclusively because of Rosmer. But I insist that the fact that you keep me uninformed regarding Rosmer's visit, not informing me of what he wants, proposes, and of what, in your opinion and estimation, I should do on this question, disturbs me a good deal. In my opinion, this is what contains an element òf "diplomacy."

July 27, 1931

I admit that the part of your letter devoted to Rosmer has produced a bizarre impression on me. You write that we cannot separate political significance from personal significance. That is correct: I insist upon that all the time. Now it seems to me that not only do you separate political from personal significance, but you also are inclined to subordinate political to personal significance.

We have undergone a series of separations on an international scale. We have freed ourselves from Overstraeten, who represented a Belgian edition of Maurín, and whom Rosmer half-supported (he does everything by halves); with enormous efforts, we have separated ourselves from the Monattists and semi-Monattists whom Rosmer has obstinately supported; we have carried on a struggle against the syndicalist backsliders (Gourget) who approached us only through Rosmer's fault;[4] for a year Rosmer openly and clearly prevented a polemic with the Bordigists; finally, he supported the Landau clique on the methods and viewpoints about which I have written in a sufficiently detailed manner in the circular letter. It seems that all those questions are superpolitical, very often even programmatic. . . . But you write that you want to see Molinier and Frank to decide on which side you stand. I can in no way comprehend that. . . .

How, as an international organization, could we act in case of new principled divergences in the different sections? Are we going to transport the representatives of the two groups to every capital in the world? Is there some misunderstanding — which is still not clear to me — of a profoundly principled or episodic character?

Perhaps, being too occupied with Spanish matters, you do not read foreign publications of the Opposition, among others, *La Vérité,* the Russian *Bulletin,* and above all, the *International Bulletin*?[5] Otherwise, I should have to understand it thus: all the ideological work of the last two years is nonexistent for you; in its place should be substituted personal impressions. But that would be impressionism and not Marxism. It is obvious that this cannot be your policy. . . .

August 26, 1931
You complain of not receiving a letter from me. However, I have written to you no less often than you have to me. In particular, I sent you a long letter concerning Rosmer. Up to the present, I do not know if you have received it. On the other hand, the Berlin comrades complain that you do not reply to anyone's letters. . . .

I see myself obliged to declare, in an absolutely formal manner, the following: Long before the conflict, we knew about all those personal "accusations" that Rosmer projects against Molinier, and together with Rosmer, we considered these accusations to be slanders and took measures to force the slanderers to accept responsibility. Rosmer has stooped to bringing forth these accusations again only after a political conflict had arisen between him and Molinier.

September 1, 1931
I have received your letter of August 25. You ask yourself

the question: shall we summon the workers to join the party or the Federation? . . .

If we consider the present results of our collaboration with the Federation, we find that it is bringing us more harm than benefit. The entire press of the Comintern, and *Pravda* in particular, has held us responsible for Maurín's opportunist confusionism. Comrade Mill's articles in *La Vérité* also contributed greatly to this. Despite this collaboration, we have been forced to break with the Federation and we have left almost empty-handed. In other words, the experience of collaboration with the Federation has weakened us in Spain as a whole, as well as internationally, without helping us any in Catalonia.

It is time to strike a balance. In my opinion, we ought to execute an abrupt political turn to avoid being confused with Maurín any longer — a confusion that has been to his advantage and our own disadvantage.

The most correct procedure would be to call upon the workers to join the Left Communist faction, to build it, and to demand admission into the party. But such a policy requires an official center, no matter how small, of the Left Opposition in Catalonia. If you remember, I have insisted on this from the first day of your arrival in Barcelona, but alas, without success. Even now I see no other road. . . .

Without a doubt, it seems to Rosmer that his opponents are inventing differences. That is explained because Rosmer stops precisely where the question only begins. This man has tremendous personal qualities and a very estimable past. But he has three faults: (1) he is not a Marxist; (2) he is not a revolutionary; (3) he is not a politician. . . .

My differences with Rosmer began almost on the first day of his return from Prinkipo to Paris. Put back into his own environment, he almost automatically resumed his old relations and habits of thought. *La Vérité,* at one fell swoop, obviously adopted a syndicalist deviation. On the subject of MacDonald and his party, Rosmer wrote not otherwise than in this spirit: that they "do not understand" how necessary it is to defend the interests of the working class. If Cuvier distinguishes between animals by the dissecting knife,[6] by these words "do not understand" Rosmer's manner of thinking is distinguished. He considered that the party is one thing and

La Vérité is another. He feels no need for the international organization. He had the relations with it that one has with a heavy burden. He protected Overstraeten, the Bordigists, and everything that is confused and undetermined, thereby seeking a point of support for his own lack of determination. If it were a question of a young comrade, we could doubtless say to ourselves: "He will learn." But unfortunately, everybody was waiting for Rosmer to teach others, and very speedily everyone was disillusioned. From this arose the conflict of the live and revolutionary elements with the Rosmer group. Persuading and criticizing Rosmer in personal letters, I have, at the same time, done everything I could do to safeguard not only the unity of the organization, but also Rosmer's responsible position within it. However, he arrived at no compromise. He wanted to crush those young comrades who, basically, were correct against him.

September 27, 1931

First of all, I should like to clear up for myself the disputed question in the Left Opposition: a narrow or broad faction? . . .

Yesterday, with regard to Catalonia, as I can see from your letter, the question was posed in the following manner: should we call upon the workers to enter the official Communist Party or the Catalan Federation? . . . But is it still possible to speak seriously of the Left Opposition calling on the workers to enter the Catalan Federation? I cannot understand it! . . . It would be the most monstrous mistake and would not only weaken but even disgrace the Left Opposition. . . .

Formally, the question of the official party is posed differently. . . . It has always appeared to me that many comrades have underestimated the possibilities for the development of the official Communist Party in Spain. I have written to you about this more than once. To ignore the official party as a fictitious quantity, to turn our back on it, seems to me to be a great mistake. On the contrary, with regard to the official party, we must stick to the path of uniting the ranks. Nevertheless this task is not so simple. As long as we remain a weak faction, this task is in general unachievable. We can only produce a tendency toward unity inside the official party when we become a serious force.

The opponents of the "broad faction" reply to this: But if we group about us a broad section of workers, we automatically transform ourselves into a second party. I must admit that this argument astonishes me. If we are to reason in such a formal manner, then in order to avoid the danger of a second party, the Bolshevik-Leninists must altogether disappear from the face of the earth. That is just what the Stalinists want. Political Malthusianism is the most unnatural of all the varieties of Malthusianism. Any political tendency that has confidence in its forces cannot help looking forward to uniting the largest possible masses around it. . . .

The Left Opposition would become a sect if it were to come to the conclusion that its task is only *criticism* of the actions of the official party and of the mass organizations of the proletariat. The Spanish revolution is a fact. There has already been a tremendous amount of time lost without all this, including time lost by the Spanish Left Opposition. Next year we will not be able, merely by snapping our fingers, to reproduce the revolutionary situation that we are passing up today. It is precisely in Spain that the Opposition can grow within a brief time into a large force. But the first condition for that is not to be afraid of becoming a force but to strive toward that. . . .

November 19, 1931

You write about the "honorable" suspension of *El Soviet* for refusing to submit to the formal censorship of the governor. I find this manner of posing the question incorrect in principle. A revolutionary organization cannot suspend publication as a simple political demonstration. This act is worthy of a democrat but not of a Marxist. A Marxist should make use of the legal possibilities to the very end, complementing them with illegal actions. There is nothing "shameful" in submitting to censorship, if you do not have the force to do away with it; it is a question of the relationship of forces, not of abstract morality. To cease publishing a paper without replacing it with an illegal publication simply signifies desertion. In that I see nothing "honorable."

Then what could we have done? Explained openly and clearly to the workers the existing conditions: the internal support on the part of the workers is insufficient; the support promised by friends does not come; we are obliged temporarily to cease publishing *El Soviet* as a weekly; but we are stepping back only the better to leap forward. Workers, help us! That is how,

in my opinion, you should have motivated the temporary suspension of the weekly. . . .

November 28, 1931
On the grossest errors in Spanish politics, we confined ourselves
in correspondence to mutual persuasion, and we did not un-
necessarily transport the discussions onto the international
arena, even in the most friendly form. But Mill's entirely false
and opportunistic letters from Spain remained without any
open reply (this I consider a mistake). However, the misunderstanding arising on the basis of the budget has become the
object of an international intrigue. I shall not conceal from you
that this incident creates an extremely unfavorable impression
upon me. I think you should be required to explain your first
letter, to take back your accusations, which are absolutely
impermissible in form just as much as in basis, and to state
whether you intended your letter for international circulation.
In this way, we could consider the incident liquidated and the
necessity for an international polemic would disappear.

December 16, 1931
As it appears (incidentally you write the same thing) you have
not read the thesis on the world situation with sufficient care;
otherwise your objection is incomprehensible. Everything
depends on the manner in which "Kerenskyism" is seen: as the
last bourgeois government after which the bourgeoisie must
perish, or as the last left government, the furthest left which
the bourgeoisie can advance in the struggle for its regime,
and which must enable the bourgeoisie to save itself (and
hardly perish) or yield its place to a fascist government. Everything depends upon the relationship of forces and above all
upon the existence of a solid revolutionary party, which there
is not in Spain.

In Spain there is a liberal-Socialist coalition government.
Those about me assert that it is the "last" or the "next to the
last" left government, that is, that there is still open the possibility of a government further to the left, a "socialist" government, which by no means can infallibly mark the end of the
bourgeoisie. Let us recall that in Germany the Social Democratic
"soviet" government (that is, the furthest left there could possibly
have been) saved the bourgeoisie. The same thought is further
developed in my opinion in relation to the situation in England.

. . . The International Opposition gave exceptional attention to the Spanish Opposition, if we take into consideration the weakness of our forces. The world crisis struck with indirect but very real forces at all the comrades who have the opportunity to give financial support. Unemployment grew unbearably severe everywhere in alarming proportions. Among the German Oppositionist comrades, many are completely deprived of means. The entire German Opposition did not receive half so much attention as the Spanish Opposition received, although *right now* in Germany the situation is incomparably more acute than in Spain. Under these conditions, to rake up an international scandal because two or three comrades did not give regularly enough due to financial difficulties, when they were thoroughly relied upon to contribute support to the Spanish publication — no, that is impermissible. In this we have a certain spirit that is foreign to us, which is neither revolutionary, nor proletarian, nor communist.

The Spanish comrades made a great number of mistakes; they lost time; they lost months and months. A number of comrades saw these mistakes, observed them with uneasiness, kept accusing me of excessive indulgence. . . . But to the very end, we manifested with regard to the Spanish comrades much more extreme patience in questions of tremendous political significance. Confronted with the first financial difficulty, the Spanish comrades stirred up an international scandal.

The only explanation I can find is this: the Spanish comrades looked for occasions to support Rosmer directly. Having no principled basis for this, that is, without risking open defense of a scandalous political position, the Spanish comrades — unfortunately, you are one of these — profited from the first advantageous or disadvantageous opportunity to lend indirect support to Rosmer. That is the sole psychological explanation for the Spanish comrades' manner of acting.

January 17, 1932

My impression of the role the Spanish Opposition is playing in international affairs remains exceedingly unfavorable. . . . During the three years of my foreign exile a process of selection took place between the truly revolutionary elements in the Opposition and the philistines who are simply deserters. In this task the Spanish comrades took no part. They intervened on international questions only in cases where they considered themselves personally affronted, and in these cases, they intervened in such a manner that they aided the deserters from our ranks. . . .

June 13, 1932

Your letter of June 7 contained a series of strange misunderstandings:

1. If several of your letters containing certain political questions to which I have not replied were lost, it was necessary simply to pose the questions again instead of losing time on general considerations about the value of the correspondence. Now I repeat this proposal: enumerate for me, I beg you, these questions on which you have received no reply from me; I will undertake to reply immediately this time, as I have always done in the past.

2. You write that I refuse aid to the Spanish Opposition. I can only reply to this matter by shrugging my shoulders. I send you all my works, letters, circulars, etc., that is, all the documents that I send to all the national sections. None of these sections accuses me of denying support to it. Perhaps you mean right now I do not concern myself particularly with Spanish problems? That is true, but that is explained by objective political reasons. In the development of the Spanish revolution, I see no new problems of pressing nature. During these last months, there have arisen in the USSR, in Germany, and in the Orient altogether new problems of the greatest importance. In arranging my work schedule, I am guided by political ideas. I have sent you all the manuscripts devoted to German affairs at the same time I've sent them to Germany. I think that the German problems affect the Spanish comrades more closely than do the Spanish problems. I recognize that you regard the question otherwise.

3. Finally, you write that I have ceased "to give aid" after we were no longer of the same opinion about different questions and different comrades. Everything has its limits, Comrade Nin. You think that my appraisal of this or that comrade obliges me to change my political relations with a revolutionary organization; and in spite of that you insist on our correspondence and you declare that it is "very useful." I can't understand this at all.

4. Once again you repeat that we have no political differences with you. I would be very happy if the matter had been really

so! But even before this incident with the French comrades, which so long ago lost its significance, I wrote you that your letters had a purely diplomatic character. You confined yourself to abstractions, to banalities, and you never answered the concrete political questions. If you have a file of my letters to you (and I myself keep the complete file of them), then you would be persuaded without effort that beneath a formal agreement can be uncovered each time an essential disagreement. It is for that reason I think that my aid to the Spanish Opposition would have been greater if, on these contentious questions, we had exchanged our opinions not by private letters remaining without result, as the entire past has convinced me, but by public or semipublic letters, for example in the Spanish bulletin, in order that the Spanish comrades would have been able to take part in the collective elaboration of opinions on all disputed questions. I think that a whole series of disputed questions both Spanish and international can and should be submitted to a serious principled discussion, without hiding behind personal sympathies and antipathies, because I think that such a method is not only incorrect but also impermissible in the revolutionary ranks, above all in the ranks of the Marxists.

September 20, 1932
Several weeks ago I wrote you asking you to say precisely what questions you had raised in your letters to me that I had not received. I have not received a reply to the letter. It was sent registered just as the present letter is sent registered.

November 14, 1932
From different sources, I received the tidings that some Spanish comrades, especially you personally, have evaluated the situation in Spain and concluded that the revolution has ended. It is needless to say how serious this question is in determining political perspectives. It seems to me absolutely necessary to completely clarify this question. It would be preferable that the new Central Committee define its viewpoint on this question in a separate resolution; this would definitely put an end to false interpretations. Perhaps, for that matter, your Central Executive Committee has already taken a position on this question; so much the better.

1. Before the *Chinese Revolution of* 1925-27, and under Stalin's orders, the Chinese communists entered the bourgeois nationalist Kuomintang (People's Party), which was led by Chiang Kai-shek, and rather than pursuing an independent revolutionary policy, hailed Chiang as a great revolutionary. They only changed that policy when Chiang massacred the Shanghai communists and trade unionists.

2. The policy of forming *united fronts* with other working class tendencies was formulated by Lenin and Trotsky and endorsed by the early congresses of the Comintern. Under Stalin, however, the CI blocked the achievement of united fronts with Social Democrats and other organizations that were not Stalinist controlled, while it continued to assert that it was actually in favor of united fronts, provided only that they be "united fronts from below," that is, that they be negotiated with the ranks of the non-Stalinist organizations and not with their leaders.

3. The USPD, or *Independent Socialist Party of Germany*, was composed of Social Democratic centrists who were in a minority in the Socialist Party. They split with it in 1916, but returned in 1922.

4. *The theory of "social fascism,"* a brainchild of Stalin, held that Social Democracy and fascism were not opposites but twins. Since the Social Democrats were only a variety of fascists, and since just about everyone but the Stalinists was some kind of fascist (a liberal-fascist, or a labor-fascist, or a Trotsky-fascist), then it was impermissible for the Stalinists to engage in united fronts with any other tendency against the plain ordinary fascists. No theory was or could have been more helpful to Hitler in the years leading up to his winning power in Germany. The Stalinists finally dropped the theory in 1934, and were soon wooing not only the Social Democrats but also capitalist politicians like Roosevelt, Daladier, and Azaña.

5. *Social Democracy.* The Second International was organized in 1889 as a loose association of national Social Democratic and labor parties, uniting both revolutionary and reformist elements; its strongest and most authoritative section was the German Social Democracy. Its progressive role had ended by 1914, when its major sections violated the most elementary socialist principles and supported their own imperialist governments in World War I. It fell apart during the war, but was revived as a completely reformist organization in 1923.

6. *Karl Liebknecht* (1871-1919) was a left-wing German Social Demo-

crat and antimilitarist. He was the first to vote against war credits in the Reichstag in 1914. Imprisoned for antiwar activity from 1916 to 1918, he was a leader of the Berlin uprising of 1919. He was assassinated by government officers in January 1919.

7. *The Left Social Revolutionaries* were the left wing of the Social Revolutionary Party, which was a petty-bourgeois party in Russia with wide support among the peasantry. Its right wing was led by Kerensky. In October 1917, the party split, with the left wing forming a coalition government with the Bolsheviks. The coalition fell apart when the Left SRs turned against the Soviet government for signing the peace of Brest-Litovsk with Germany.

8. *The Menshevik-Internationalists* were a group of left Mensheviks in Russia led by Martov, who were friendly to the Bolsheviks on many issues. The Mensheviks were a moderate socialist party claiming allegiance to Karl Marx, but believing that the working class must combine with the liberal bourgeoisie to overthrow czarism and establish a democratic republic. They were formed after a split in the Russian Social Democratic Labor Party in 1903, and remained within the Second International, while the Bolsheviks went on to form the Russian Communist Party.

9. *The Anglo-Russian Trade Union Unity Committee* was formed by Soviet and British union representatives in May 1925. The British used it as a cheap device to demonstrate their "progressivism" and to shield themselves against criticism from the left, especially useful at that time, not long before the British general strike of 1926. The Russians continued to support the committee even when the British members betrayed the general strike. The committee collapsed only in 1927, when the British members, no longer needing it, walked out.

10. *The Kuomintang* (People's Party) of China was the bourgeois nationalist party founded by Sun Yat-sen in 1911 and led after 1926 by Chiang Kai-shek, butcher of the Chinese revolution of 1925-27 and ruler of the country until he was overthrown by the 1949 revolution.

11. *The Canton insurrection* took place on December 11, 1927. It was crushed fifty hours later at the cost of 5,700 workers' lives. The uprising was the culminating disaster of the period of adventurism that followed the collapse of the revolutionary movement in August.

12. *March* 1 *elections*. The municipal elections were finally held on April 12.

13. *Spain's African adventures* tied down the Spanish army in wars subduing Morocco until 1927.

14. In 1930, the *peseta* was worth U. S. 11.6¢. In 1972, it was worth U. S. 1.5¢.

15. *Charles V* (1500-1558) was Holy Roman Emperor, 1519-56; as Carlos I, he was also king of Spain, 1516-56.

16. *War with Napoleon.* The Spanish monarchy surrendered to Napoleon in 1808, but the British army under the Duke of Wellington drove out the French in a war of independence, and Ferdinand VII was brought to the throne.

17. *The Jacobins* were the most radical political faction in the French Revolution. They dominated French politics from the overthrow of the Gironde in 1791 until Thermidor in 1794.

18. *The Barcelona uprising of* 1909 resulted in the so-called "Tragic Week," when demonstrations broke out protesting an order sending Catalan reservists to Morocco. During the uprising forty-eight churches were burned. The demonstrations were crushed by the central government.

19. *L. Tarquin* was a pseudonym for Andrés Nin, the leader of the Spanish Left Opposition until it broke with Trotsky in 1935 and merged with Maurin's Workers and Peasants Bloc to form the POUM (Workers Party of Marxist Unification).
    La Lutte de classes was the monthly theoretical review of the French Left Opposition.

20. *Antonio Cánovas del Castillo* was a conservative politician who drew up the constitution under the monarchy that was restored after the first republic.
    Count Alvaro de Figueroa y Torres de Romanones (1863-1950) was a monarchist statesman, a large landowner in Guadalajara, and the most important owner of real estate in Madrid.

21. *The Bulygin Duma* was named after the czar's minister of internal affairs and was a pseudoparliamentary body established in 1905 which possessed little power. Elected by greatly restricted suffrage, it was considered by the czar as a consultative, not a legislative, body. The czar reserved the right to convene or disband it at will.

22. *Mikhail Bakunin* (1814-1887) was a contemporary of Marx in

the First International, and was the founder of anarchism. He put
forth a theory of a stateless federation of autonomous communities.

23. *The Comintern* (Communist or Third International) was organized under Lenin's leadership as the revolutionary successor to the
Second International. Trotsky regarded the theses of the Comintern's
first four congresses as the programmatic cornerstone of the Left Opposition and later of the Fourth International.

   Dimitri Manuilsky (1883-1952), like Trotsky, was a member of
the independent Marxist group that fused with the Bolshevik Party
in 1917. In the 1920s he supported the Stalin faction and served as
secretary of the Comintern from 1931 to 1943. Despite Trotsky's
reference to Manuilsky as "'the leader' of the Latin countries," the
Comintern-appointed head of the "Latin" section of the Comintern
throughout the thirties was Palmiro Togliatti, who had escaped from
Mussolini's Italy in 1924.

24. *The "third period,"* according to the schema proclaimed by the
Stalinists in 1928, was the final period of capitalism, the period of
its immediately pending demise and replacement by soviets. Following
from this, the Comintern's tactics during the next six years were
marked by ultraleftism, adventurism, sectarian "red" unions, and opposition to the united front. In 1934 the theory and practice of the
"third period" were discarded and replaced by those of the Popular
Front, or People's Front (1935-39), but the latter period was not
given a number. The "first period" was 1917-24 (capitalist crisis and
revolutionary upsurge); the "second period" was 1925-28 (capitalist
stabilization).

25. *The events of December* 1930 occurred in the aftermath of the
rebellion of pro-republican generals that month at the Jaca garrison.
The rebellion was quickly crushed, but the public indignation resulting
from the reprisals against the insurgents forced the king to call the
elections that were held in April 1931.

26. *Benito Mussolini* (1883-1945) was the fascist dictator of Italy
from 1922 to 1945.

   Giacomo Matteoti (1885-1924) was a reformist Socialist deputy
who denounced fascist electoral trickery and terrorism in the Italian
parliament, for which Mussolini's henchmen murdered him.

   Ramsay MacDonald (1866-1937) became Prime Minister in the
first British Labour government (1924) and bolted the Labour Party
during his second term (1929-31) to form a "national unity" cabinet
with the Tories (1931-35).

   Chiang Kai-shek (1887-   ) was the military leader of the bourgeois nationalist Kuomintang (People's Party) of China during the revolution of 1925-27. He stood in the right wing of that party, which the Communists had entered on orders from the Comintern. The Stalinists hailed him as a great revolutionary until April 1927, when he conducted a bloody massacre of the Shanghai Communists and trade unionists.

Feodor Dan (1871-1947) was a founder of the Russian Social Democracy and a Menshevik leader on the presidium of the Petrograd Soviet in 1917. He was a pacifist during World War I and an active opponent of the Bolshevik Revolution.

The Abyssinian Negus was the title of Haile Selassie (1891-   ), the emperor of Ethiopia from 1930 to 1936 (and 1941-   ).

27. *Italy after the autumn of* 1920. From the end of World War I the revolutionary movement in Italy grew, and in September 1920 the workers seized the factories and industries. The Social Democrats took fright and jumped back. The proletariat was left leaderless. By November the first major fascist demonstration was held. The Social Democratic leaders hoped to reclaim the confidence of the bourgeoisie against the fascists, and restrained the workers from resisting Mussolini's bands. But the bourgeoisie swung over to the fascists. At the last minute, the Social Democrats called a general strike, but the workers, demoralized and confused, did not respond, and the fascists were able to consolidate their stranglehold. This development is explained fully in the section "Lessons of the Italian Experience," in *The Struggle Against Fascism in Germany*, by Leon Trotsky (Pathfinder Press, New York, 1971).

28. *The first republic* (1873-74) was ended by the enthronement of Alfonso XII.

29. *Epigones* are disciples who corrupt the doctrines of their teachers. Trotsky used the term for the Stalinists, who claim to be followers of Lenin and Marx.

30. *Official centrist faction.* Centrism is the term used by Trotsky for tendencies in the radical movement which stand or vacillate between reformism, the position of the labor bureaucracy and the labor aristocracy, and Marxism, which expresses the historic interests of the working class. Since a centrist tendency has no independent social base, it must be evaluated in terms of its origins, its internal dynamic, and the direction it is taking or being pushed towards by events. Until around 1933, Trotsky saw Stalinism as a special variety of centrism — bureaucratic centrism; thereafter he felt that this term was inadequate to describe what the Soviet bureaucracy was becoming.

Notes for Part II

1. *The left Socialists* were the wing of the Socialist Party led by Francisco Largo Caballero.

2. *The "February regime"* was established in Russia by the February 1917 revolution, which brought Kerensky to power. He held office until the October revolution gave power to the soviets.

3. *The Paris Commune* was the first example of a workers' government. It was in power from March 18 to May 28, 1871, just seventy-two days, before it was overthrown in a bloody series of battles.

4. *The March council and the April conference* were Bolshevik conferences in Petrograd held shortly after the downfall of czarism, when oppositional parties became legal. Lenin returned to Russia just as the March conference was ending, shortly before the April conference, where he took the lead in stemming the conciliationist tendencies among the Old Bolshevik leaders and in beginning the "rearmament" of the party, that is, its reorientation toward fighting for state power. The minutes of the March council are published in Trotsky's *Stalin School of Falsification* (Pathfinder Press, New York).

5. *Andrés Nin* (1892-1937) was a founder of the Spanish Communist Party and secretary of the Red International of Labor Unions (Profintern). He supported the Left Opposition and was expelled from the CP in 1927. He participated in the formation of the International Left Opposition and was the leader of its Spanish section until its break with the ILO in 1935, when it merged with the Workers and Peasants Bloc of Joaquin Maurín to form the POUM (Workers Party of Marxist Unification). For a brief time in 1936 he was the minister of justice in the Catalan government, but he was then arrested by the Stalinists and assassinated.

6. *L'Humanité* is the newspaper of the French Communist Party.

7. *The German revolution of* 1923. The French invasion of the Ruhr in 1923, because Germany had not paid reparations on time, triggered a revolutionary situation that rapidly turned a majority of the German working class toward support of the Communist Party. But the CP leadership vacillated, missed an exceptionally favorable opportunity to conduct a struggle for power, and permitted the German capitalists to recover their balance before the year was ended. The Kremlin's responsibility for this wasted opportunity was one of the factors that led to the formation of the Russian Left Opposition at the end of 1923

8. *Gabriel Péri* (1902-1941) was the foreign editor of *l'Humanité,* the French Communist Party newspaper. He was sent to report the events in Spain, but his correspondence caused considerable resentment among the Spanish readers of the paper because of its falsehoods and misrepresentations. He was shot by the Nazis during World War II.

9. *Niceto Alcalá Zamora* (1877-1949), a large landowner, was the head of the Progressive Party and a liberal Catholic. He was prime minister of the first republican government in April 1931, and president of the republic from June 1931 until May 1936.

10. *The Sixth Congress of the Comintern* was held in 1928, after a lapse of four years since the Fifth Congress. It marked the swing of the Stalinists toward ultraleftism and began the departure from the united front policy that had been developed in earlier congresses.

11. *Alexander Martinov* (1865-1935) was an extreme right-wing Menshevik before 1917 and an opponent of the Bolshevik Revolution. He joined Martov's Menshevik-Internationalists in 1917. He joined the CP only in 1923, and became a vocal opponent of Trotskyism. He was a chief architect of the theory of the "bloc of four classes" in China, which sought to justify the Stalinist tactic of having the Chinese CP join Chiang Kai-shek's bourgeois Kuomintang on the basis that the Kuomintang was a party of the "progressive" bourgeoisie. This was a forerunner of the Popular Front approach.

12. The Marxist theory of *permanent revolution* elaborated by Trotsky states, among other things, that in order to accomplish and consolidate even bourgeois democratic tasks such as land reform in an underdeveloped country, the revolution must go beyond the limits of a democratic revolution into a socialist one, which sets up a workers' and peasants' government. Such a revolution will therefore not take place in "stages" (first a stage of capitalist development to be followed at some time in the future by a socialist revolution), but will be continuous or "permanent," passing immediately to a postcapitalist stage. For a full exposition of the theory, see *The Permanent Revolution and Results and Prospects,* by Leon Trotsky (Pathfinder Press, New York, 1969).

13. *Leon Kamenev* (1883-1936) was an Old Bolshevik. In 1923 he helped Stalin initiate the crusade against Trotskyism, but in 1926 he blocked with the Left Opposition until being expelled from the party in 1927. When Trotsky was exiled, Kamenev capitulated, but was expelled again in 1932. He repented again, but was a victim of the first big Moscow show trial and was executed.

Pavel Miliukov (1859-1943), a leader of the Cadets (Constitutional Democrats), was the minister of foreign affairs in the Russian Provisional Government, March-May 1917, and an outstanding enemy of the Bolshevik Revolution.

Iraklii Tseretelli (1882-1959), a Menshevik leader who supported the war, held ministerial positions March-August 1917; he was an opponent of the Bolsheviks.

Victor Chernov (1876-1952) was a founder and leader of the Russian Social Revolutionaries. He participated in the Zimmerwald conference, served as minister of agriculture in the Kerensky government, and opposed the Bolshevik Revolution.

14. *Wang Ching-wei* (1884-1944) was a government leader in the industrial area of Wuhan in China. Wang was as disappointing as Chiang in the role of revolutionist that the Comintern had assigned to him; his program, like Chiang's, went no further than the preservation of the Chinese bourgeoisie at all costs. Only six weeks after Chiang's coup at Shanghai, Wang attacked the workers in Wuhan. Thus the allies of Stalin drowned the Chinese revolution in blood.

Alejandro Lerroux García (1864-1949) was the leader of the Spanish Radical Party. He was premier from 1933 to 1936.

Ottomar W. Kuusinen (1881-1964) was a Finnish Social Democrat who fled to Moscow after the collapse of the Finnish revolution in April 1918. He became a Stalinist functionary in the Comintern.

15. *The July days* of 1917 in Petrograd broke out without any direction and led to bloody encounters. The Bolsheviks were declared responsible, their leaders arrested, and their papers shut down.

16. *Bonapartism* is a Marxist term describing a dictatorship or a regime with certain features of a dictatorship during a period when class rule is not secure; it is based on the military, police, and state bureaucracy, rather than on the parliamentary parties or a mass movement.

17. *The February revolution of* 1848 in France overthrew Louis Philippe. The liberal bourgeoisie and the workers won the struggle against the monarchy, big financiers, and industrialists, and the second republic was proclaimed.

18. *Colonel Francisco Macía y Llusa* (1859-1933) was the leader of the Catalan Esquerra, the party of the Barcelona lower middle class.

19. *The Madrid autonomous group* was a strong organization in

1931 that had been expelled from the CP for opposition to the bureaucratic methods of the CP's executive committee, and particularly for refusing to follow the directives to split the CNT. While it did not support the platform of the Left Opposition, the Madrid group did permit discussion and participation in its ranks of the local adherents of the Opposition.

20. *Henri Lacroix* was a pseudonym for Francisco Garcia Lavid, one of the first leaders of the Spanish Left Opposition while it was in exile in Belgium. He was arrested in Spain in June 1930 and released after the fall of the monarchy. He became secretary-general of the Spanish Opposition at its second conference in June 1931, and as its chief leader was arrested several times during this period.

After November 1932, he broke with Nin and published a bulletin maintaining that Trotsky had been correct in his criticisms of the Spanish Left Opposition. In 1933 he was expelled from the Spanish section for "misappropriation of funds"; he joined the Socialist Party, later leading a division in the civil war. In January 1939 he was recognized as a former Trotskyist by some officers of the Stalinist "Lister" division, and was arrested and hanged by them only a few dozen yards from the French border.

The editors wish to express their gratitude to Pierre Broué, who provided much of the information in this note and in others in this book.

21. *The Social Revolutionary Party* was founded in Russia in 1900, emerging in 1901-02 as the political expression of all the earlier populist currents; it had the largest share of influence among the peasantry prior to the revolution of 1917. Its right wing was led by Kerensky. The Left SRs were in a coalition government with the Bolsheviks immediately after the October Revolution, but quickly moved into opposition "from the left" thereafter, organizing counterrevolutionary actions.

Alexander F. Kerensky (1882-1970) was an attorney and a member of the Social Revolutionary Party. Elected to the Fourth Duma, he became vice-chairman of the Petrograd Soviet, then bolted from its discipline to assume the ministry of justice in the Provisional Government in March 1917. In May he took the post of minister of war and navy, which he continued to hold when he became premier. After the Kornilov putsch, he appointed himself commander-in-chief as well. Fleeing Petrograd when the Bolsheviks seized power, Kerensky had a long career in exile, where he wrote and rewrote several different versions of what had happened.

Prince George E. Lvov (1861-1925) was a Russian politician and large landowner. After the overthrow of the czar, he became prime minister of the first Provisional Government, March-July 1917.

22. *Kurt Landau,* an Austrian, became a leader of the German Left Opposition. In 1931 he split from the Opposition and formed his own group. He went to Spain and supported the POUM, was kidnapped and killed by Stalin's police.

23. *Joaquín Maurín Julia* (1897-   ) had been a leader of the Spanish Communist Party and had left, forming the Catalan-Balearic Communist Federation, later known as the Workers and Peasants Bloc, of which he was general secretary, and which merged in 1935 with the former Left Oppositionists led by Andrés Nin to create the POUM. He was elected to parliament in February 1936. When the civil war broke out he was arrested by Franco's troops, but escaped execution because the fascists couldn't identify him. Upon his release he went into exile and ceased all political activity.

24. *The "Prometeo" group* was led by Amadeo Bordiga (1889-1970), a founder of the Italian Communist Party who was expelled from the Comintern on charges of "Trotskyism" in 1929. The Left Opposition tried to work with the Bordigists but failed because of the latter's inveterate sectarianism; they opposed the tactic of the united front, for example, "on principle."

25. *Alexander I. Guchkov* (1861-1936) was a member of the First Duma in Russia, a leader of the Octobrists in the Third Duma (1907-12), and was elected its president in 1910. He was minister of war and navy from March to May 1917, when he resigned and left the country.

26. The Spanish *Radical Party* was a bourgeois party that started off left of center and ended up in the camp of the reaction. It held power from September 1933 to January 1936. Its leader was Alejandro Lerroux.

The *Radical Socialists* were also a bourgeois party whose closest sympathies were with Azaña.

27. *General Lavr G. Kornilov* (1870-1918) was a Siberian cossack who became Kerensky's commander-in-chief in July 1917 and led a counterrevolutionary putsch against Kerensky in September 1917. Arrested, he escaped to lead the counterrevolution until April 1918, when he was killed.

28. *Pierre Monatte* (1881-1960) was a French revolutionary syndicalist, and a founder of *Vie ouvrière* in 1909. He was one of the first to oppose World War I. He joined the Communist Party in 1923,

only to leave a year later. In 1926 he founded the Syndicalist League.

29. *Angel Pestaña* was a leader of the Syndicalist Party, the right wing of the CNT.

30. The first *Five-Year Plan* for economic development in the Soviet Union, begun in 1928, projected a modest acceleration of industrial growth and an irresolute policy towards the peasantry. Suddenly the Political Bureau reversed its position and called for fulfilling the Five-Year Plan in four years. The resultant speed-up and forced collectivization of the peasantry led to a period of economic chaos and great hardship for the population.

31. *Indalecio Prieto y Tuero* (1883-1962) was a leader of the right wing of the Socialist Party. He was the minister of navy and air in Largo Caballero's cabinet and remained in Negrin's cabinet until the Stalinists insisted on his expulsion in 1938.

32. *Friedrich Ebert* (1871-1925) was a leader of the right wing of the German Social Democracy. As chancellor, with Scheidemann, he presided over the crushing of the November 1918 revolution, executing Rosa Luxemburg, Karl Liebknecht, and other German revolutionists. He was president of the republic from 1919 to 1925.

33. *La Vérité* was the newspaper of the French Left Oppositionists.*

34. *Vyacheslav Molotov* (1890-   ) was an Old Bolshevik, an editor of *Pravda* prior to the October Revolution. Elected to the Russian party's Central Committee in 1920, he aligned himself with Stalin. He held the post of president of the Council of People's Commissars from 1930 to 1941; in 1939 he became minister of foreign affairs. He was eliminated from the leadership in 1957 when he opposed the Khrushchev "de-Stalinization" program.

35. *The Communist League of France* was formed by supporters of the Left Opposition in April 1930, around the publication of *La Vérité*.

36. *tumultuous strike wave.* Immediately following the June 1931 elections to the Cortes, in which the pro-republican parties won an overwhelming majority, the Anarchist CNT called a series of strikes. The government called out the artillery to crush the strikes, and there were hundreds of casualties on the side of the workers.

37. *M. Mill* was chosen by the Russian Opposition as a member of the Administrative Secretariat of the International Left Opposition,

largely because of his knowledge of Russian; after he was removed from this post in 1932 because of his maneuvers and personal intrigues, he became an agent of Stalinism. Although Isaac Deutscher called him an American (*Prophet Outcast*, p. 59), he was actually a Ukrainian. His real name was Okhun.

38. *"Workers' Control of Production"* was a letter written to a group of German Left Oppositionists. The full text appears in *The Struggle Against Fascism in Germany*.

39. *Francisco Largo Caballero* (1869-1946) was the leader of the left wing of the Spanish Socialist Party. He was premier from September 1936 until May 1937.

40. *Raymond Molinier* (1904-   ) was a cofounder of *La Vérité* and a leader of the French Communist League with whom Trotsky collaborated until 1935.

41. That *Germany was the center of the world revolution* is the thesis of "Germany, the Key to the International Situation," in *The Struggle Against Fascism in Germany*.

42. *Julián Gorkin* had been a figure in the Left Opposition before he joined the Workers and Peasants Bloc under Maurin. He became a top leader of the POUM.

43. The *SAP* (Socialist Workers Party) of Germany was formed in October 1931, after the Social Democrats expelled several left wingers. In the spring of 1932, a split occurred in the German Right Communist Opposition (KPO, the Brandlerites), and a group of about 800, led by Jacob Walcher, entered the SAP and assumed its leadership. In 1933 the SAP signed a declaration proclaiming the need for a new international, but later it became an active opponent of such a formation.

44. *Hugo Urbahns* (1890-1946), a leader of the German Communist Party, was expelled in 1928 and helped found the Leninbund, which was associated with the Left Opposition until 1930.

Otto Bauer (1882-1939), the chief theoretician of Austro-Marxism, was a leader of the Austrian Social Democracy.

Léon Blum (1872-1950) was the head of the French Socialist Party in the thirties and premier of the first Popular Front government in 1936.

45. From the earliest days of the Communist League of France in

1930, Trotsky found himself involved in a number of political, ideological, and organizational disputes with its leaders. Trotsky thought there were important lessons to be learned from these disputes and urged the leaders and members of other sections of the International Left Opposition to follow them attentively and express their opinions.

Alfred Rosmer (1877-1964) was a founding member of the French Communist Party and was on the Executive Committee of the Comintern. He was expelled from the CP in 1924, and was a member of the Trotskyist movement from its beginning until 1930, when he resigned because of political and organizational differences with the majority. He and Trotsky became personally reconciled in 1936.

Pierre Naville (1904-   ) was a founder of the Communist League of France and of *La Vérité.* He opposed the entry of Oppositionists into the French Socialist Party in 1934, although he and his group joined after the majority of the League had done so. He left the Trotskyist movement during World War II.

Francis Gérard was a pseudonym for Gérard Rosenthal, a French Trotskyist and Trotsky's lawyer in France for several years.

Edouard Van Overstraeten was a leader of the Belgian Communist Party who was expelled in 1928 for protesting the suppression of the Russian Left Opposition. A founder of the Belgian Left Opposition, he broke with it after a few years and soon withdrew from politics.

46. *The International Secretariat* (IS) was a committee of the International Communist League, elected by the plenum.

47. *Markin* was a pseudonym for Leon Sedov (1906-1938), Trotsky's son, who was living in Germany in 1932, and who served on occasion as the Russian Opposition's representative to the International Secretariat. After Hitler came to power in 1933, he escaped to Paris, where he lived until his assassination by GPU agents in 1938. "We" refers to the Russian Opposition, "them" to the *Molinier-Frank* group in the French Opposition's leadership with which Trotsky collaborated until 1935.

Pierre Frank (1905-   ) was then a member of the Communist League of France, and later of the International and United Secretariats of the Fourth International. He was Trotsky's secretary from 1932 to 1933. His brief history of the Fourth International, *La Quatrième Internationale* (Maspero, 1969), was serialized in English in *Intercontinental Press,* March 13-June 5, 1972.

48. *defeat of the January general strike.* In January 1932, the FAI had organized an uprising in Catalonia in which the Bolshevik-Leninists took part. It was crushed by the army and its organizers were deported.

49. *General José Sanjurjo Sacanell* (1872-1936), who was known for his repressive role in Morocco in 1927, led an army uprising against the republic in August 1932. An informer warned Azaña, however, and the insurrection was defeated.

50. *The Bulgarian Communist Party* remained neutral in September 1923, when the reactionary Tsankov overthrew the "peasant" government of Stambuliski. Afterwards, having missed the opportunity, the CP organized a fatal putsch against Tsankov and was crushed.

51. *Herbert Hoover* (1874-1964) was the Republican president of the United States from 1929 to 1932.

Franz von Papen (1879-1969) was appointed German chancellor in June 1932 and greased the way for Hitler by dissolving the Social Democratic government of Prussia; he became Hitler's vice-chancellor in January 1933.

Emile Vandervelde (1866-1938) was a Belgian Social Democrat reformist who served as president of the Second International from 1929 to 1936. He was in the war cabinet during World War I, and signed the Versailles Treaty as Belgian's representative.

Mohandas Gandhi (1869-1948) was the leader of the nationalist movement that later became the Congress Party of India. He organized massive opposition to British rule, but insisted on peaceful, nonviolent, passive resistance methods.

Christian Rakovsky (1873-1941) was a leading figure in the Balkan revolutionary movement before the Russian Revolution. In 1918 he became chairman of the Ukrainian Soviet and later served as ambassador to London and Paris. An early leader of the Russian Left Opposition, he was deported to Siberia in 1928; in 1934 he capitulated. In 1938 he was one of the major defendants in the third Moscow show trial, where he was sentenced to twenty years' imprisonment.

52. *The Amsterdam congress* of August 1932 was projected by the Stalinists as a substitute for united front working class activity against war.

General Paul von Schoenaich (1886-1954) was a Junker naval officer turned pacifist who wrote favorable articles about the Soviet Union in the German press.

The French freemasons and the other European masonic societies, with their liberal traditions, had formed a connecting link between the socialist movement and the left wing of the bourgeoisie. They were a mechanism, in Trotsky's view, for corrupting the socialist movement.

Valabhbhai Patel (1877-1950) was a representative of the native Indian bourgeoisie, and a member of the government after the proclamation of India's independence.

53. *Manuel Azaña y Díaz* (1880-1940) was the prime minister of the Spanish republican government in June 1931 and again in 1936. He was president of the republic from May 1936 until his resignation in Paris in 1939.

54. *The Leninbund* was the organization founded by Ruth Fischer, Arkadi Maslow, and Hugo Urbahns after their expulsion from the German Communist Party in 1927. The Leninbund took positions close to the Left Opposition until 1930, when Urbahns took the leadership, expelling those sympathetic to the Opposition.

55. . . . *bitter struggle.* Lacroix had resigned as secretary-general of the Spanish Left Opposition in March 1932, and in November a struggle broke out between him and Nin over issues that were unclear to all observers. Lacroix began publishing a bulletin vindicating Trotsky's criticisms of the leadership of the Spanish section.

In April 1933 the Lacroix group dissolved, and Lacroix was expelled from the Spanish section for "misappropriation of funds."

56. A postconference report by the IS (published in the *Internal Bulletin* of the CLA, no. 11, March 31, 1933) said that the delegate of the Nin group told the conference that he accepted "in principle" the decisions of the conference, "with reservations on those parts which deal with the *application* of these fundamental principles," and with reservations on the ILO's methods, its attitude toward the groups of Rosmer, etc., its views on the Spanish section's change of name, its evaluation of the Spanish section's policies and methods, and the organizational measures it had adopted on the Spanish question.

The IS noted that the preconference had warned that "this method of accepting principles abstractly, with reservations as to their practical application, represents the most dangerous kind of diplomacy in serious political questions," which could lead to the negation of the principles themselves and to a possible split from the ILO.

A "consultative" delegate from the Lacroix tendency told the conference that his group accepted the conference decision without reservation. The preconference took note of this statement but held that its true value could be checked only by extended discussion and activity over a period of time.

57. *The "Declaration to the Antiwar Congress at Amsterdam"* was written July 25, 1932, to be passed out at the congress in August. It was signed by the various sections. Its full text is available in *Writings of Leon Trotsky* (1932), Pathfinder Press, New York.

58. *L. Fersen* was the pseudonym of Enrique Fernández Sendón, who was on the Central Committee of the Spanish Left Opposition.

He supported Nin, and was the delegate of the Nin group at the international preconference held earlier in 1933.

59. *Max Shachtman* (1903-1972) was a leader in the American CP and a founder and leader of the Trotskyist movement. He split from the SWP in 1940 because of differences over defense of the Soviet Union and joined the Socialist Party in 1958.

60. . . . *should have joined the Socialist Party.* After 1933, the radicalization began to take the form of emerging left wings in the old Social Democratic parties. Trotsky proposed the temporary entry of the International Left Opposition into the Socialist parties to link up with the new youthful revolutionaries. This was known as the French turn because it was first applied in France in 1934. The Spanish Left Oppositionists refused to carry out this policy, and as a result the Spanish Socialist Youth merged with the Stalinist Youth in 1935.

61. *Pierre Renaudel* (1871-1935) was a leader of the right wing of the French Socialist Party and of the "Neo" group that was expelled at the end of 1933.

Louis-Oliver Frossard (1889-1946) was a leader of the French Socialist Party who supported its affiliation with the Comintern in 1920, and was then general secretary of the Communist Party. In 1923, he resigned from the CP and rejoined the Socialist Party. He resigned from the SP to become minister of labor, and was a minister in the Popular Front government and then in the first Pétain government.

62. *Philipp Scheidemann* (1865-1939) was a leader of the right wing of the German Social Democracy. He entered the cabinet of Prince Max of Baden in October 1918, and with Ebert presided over the crushing of the German November 1918 revolution. Scheidemann led the Social Democracy in the Reichstag until 1933.

Hermann Müller (1876-1931) was the last Social Democratic chancellor of Germany (1928-1930), and was the functionary who refused Trotsky an entry visa to Germany.

63. *Alexandre Millerand* (1859-1943) in 1899 became the first Socialist to enter a bourgeois cabinet; he was subsequently expelled from the French Socialist Party. He held several ministerial posts and was president of the French Republic from 1920 to 1924.

Aristide Briand (1862-1932) was expelled from the French Socialist Party in 1906 for accepting office in a capitalist cabinet. He was premier several times and representative to the League of Nations.

René Viviani (1863-1925) was a French politician, originally a Socialist. He joined the Clemenceau cabinet in 1906 and was subsequently expelled from the Socialist Party. He entered the Briand cabinet in 1909 and was premier upon the outbreak of war; his cabinet fell in 1915 and he became minister of justice under Clemenceau.

Pierre Laval (1883-1945) was a Socialist in his youth. He was minister of foreign affairs from 1934 to 1935, and negotiated the Franco-Soviet pact. He was premier from 1935 to 1936, and again in 1942, when he pursued a policy of collaboration with Germany. He was executed for treason.

Joseph Paul-Boncour (1873-1972) was a right-wing Socialist until 1931. He was a minister under Sarraut and Blum and was Blum's chief delegate to Geneva. He rejoined the French Socialist Party after World War II.

Adrien Marquet (1884-1955), mayor of Bordeaux, a Neo-Socialist, became minister of labor in the 1934 National Union government. Later he left the Neos and moved further to the right.

64. *La Batalla* was the Spanish-language newspaper of the POUM.

65. *The London Bureau of Revolutionary Socialist Parties,* formerly called the International Labor Community (IAG), was a loose association of centrist parties not affiliated to either the Second or Third International, but opposed to the formation of a Fourth International. Among its members were the SAP of Germany, the Independent Labour Party of Great Britain, the POUM of Spain, and the PSOP (Workers and Peasants Socialist Party) of France.

66. Angel Pestaña's *Syndicalists* were the right wing of the CNT. *Juan Andrade* had been a leader of the Communist Party youth before he was expelled from the CP and joined the Left Opposition. He broke with the Left Opposition at the same time as Nin and became a leader of the POUM.

67. *Fenner Brockway* (1890-   ) was an opponent of the Fourth International and secretary of the London Bureau. He was also a leader of the British *Independent Labour Party* (ILP), which was founded in 1893. The ILP played an influential part in the creation of the British Labour Party, to which it was affiliated and in which it usually occupied a position on the left. Expelled from the Labour Party in 1931, the ILP for some years was attracted by Stalinism; its actual affiliation in the mid-thirties was to the centrist IAG. It later returned to the Labour Party.

68. *James Maxton* (1885-1946) was the principal leader of the Independent Labour Party in the thirties. His pacifism led him to hail Chamberlain's role at Munich in 1938.

69. *The Seventh Congress of the Comintern* was held in August 1935 and called for the Popular Front policy that was already being implemented in France and Spain. Trotsky called the seventh the "liquidation congress" of the Comintern (see *Writings of Leon Trotsky, 1935-36*), and it was in fact the last before Stalin announced its dissolution in 1943 as a gesture to his imperialist allies.

70. The issuance of the *Open Letter for the Fourth International* in the summer of 1935 marked the determination of the Trotskyists around the world to form the Fourth International. It was a statement of principles and purposes of the movement, emphasizing the need for a new international, and was signed by the Workers Party of the United States, the Revolutionary Socialist Workers Party of Holland, the Workers Party of Canada, the French Bolshevik-Leninists, and the International Communist League. The full text is in *Writings of Leon Trotsky* (1935-36).

71. *Léon Lesoil* (d.1942) was one of the founders of the Belgian CP and one of its leaders. He was expelled in 1928 for opposing the repression of the Soviet Opposition. He helped to organize the Belgian section of the Opposition and remained a leader for the rest of his life. Arrested by the Gestapo in June 1941, he died in a concentration camp the following year.

George Vereecken was a representative of a sectarian tendency in the Belgian section of the International Communist League. He opposed the entry of the Belgian section into the Socialist Party.

72. *Jean Longuet* (1876-1938) was a right-wing French Socialist. During World War I, he held a pacifist position but voted for war credits.

Georg Ledebour (1850-1947) was a German Social Democrat who opposed World War I but fought against the German party's joining the Third International in 1920.

Jacob Walcher (1887-   ) left the KPO to join the SAP in 1932, and soon became a dominant figure in that group. He was an active opponent of a new revolutionary international, and after World War II he rejoined the CP.

73. *Henricus Sneevliet* (1883-1942) was a founder of the Communist Party in Holland and in Indonesia. He had been secretary of the Colonial Commission of the Comintern at its Second Congress, and was for a time the Comintern's representative in China. After leaving the CP in 1927, he formed the Revolutionary Socialist Party, which fused with other revolutionary elements and in 1935 formed the Revolutionary Socialist Workers Party, which was allied with the Fourth

Internationalist movement. Because of differences on the POUM and on trade union policy, the RSAP broke with the international Trotskyist movement and did not participate in the founding congress of the Fourth International in 1938. During World War II, Sneevliet was arrested by the Nazis and shot.

74. *The POB* was the Belgian Labor Party, the Belgian section of the Second International.

De Nieuwe Fakkel was the newspaper of the RSAP of Holland.

75. The Russian Constitutional Democrats, called *Cadets,* were the liberal party favoring a constitutional monarchy in Russia or even ultimately a republic; it was a party of progressive landlords, middle bourgeoisie, and bourgeois intelligentsia, headed by Miliukov, a professor of history.

Notes for Part III

1. *Le Populaire* was the daily paper of the French Socialist Party. *Maurice Paz* (1896-   ) was an early leader of the French Left Opposition who broke with Trotsky in 1929, and joined the Socialist Party.

2. *The French Radical Socialist Party* was a liberal bourgeois party with an anti-clerical tradition, and was a stronghold of freemasonry. It was the principal capitalist party of France between the two world wars.

3. *Edouard Daladier* (1884-1970), a Radical Socialist, was premier in 1933 and 1934, when he was ousted during an attempted fascist coup d'etat. He was minister of war under Léon Blum. Later he became premier again, and signed the Munich Pact with Hitler.

4. *Marceau Pivert* (1895-1958) was a member of the Bataille Socialiste group in the French Socialist Party, and an organizer of the Gauche Revolutionnaire group in 1935. He served as an aide of Blum in the 1936 Popular Front government, but when his group was ordered dissolved in 1937 he left the Socialist Party and in 1938 founded the PSOP (Workers and Peasants Socialist Party), which was affiliated with the London Bureau. After World War II he returned to the Socialist Party.

5. *fascist attack . . . and the infamous TASS statement.* During the night of August 4, 1936, Trotsky's home in Norway was raided by members of the fascist formation headed by Major Vidkun Quisling.

The Norwegian Nazis carried off some of Trotsky's papers in an attempt to prove that he was carrying on "Bolshevik agitation" in Norway. On the morning of August 6, 1936, the Norwegian radio broadcast the statement of the prosecution in the Moscow trials accusing Trotsky of directing a "terrorist" campaign against the Soviet Union from Norway.

On August 29, the Soviet ambassador handed an Oslo government official a note threatening that "continued harboring of Trotsky" would lead to a break in diplomatic and trade relations between the USSR and Norway.

In response to this pressure, the Norwegian government placed Trotsky under virtual house arrest for the next three and a half months. For a time it was feared that he would be handed over to Stalin. In December the Cardenas government granted him asylum in Mexico.

6. *Henry Yagoda* was the head of the Soviet secret police in 1934. In 1937, Yagoda, who had supervised the organization of the 1936 Moscow trial, was himself made a defendant and executed.

7. *Julius Martov* (1873-1923) was a founder of the Russian Social Democracy and a close associate of Lenin on the editorial board of *Iskra* until 1903, when he became a Menshevik leader.

8. *Peter J. Schmidt* was the leader of the Independent Socialist Party of Holland, which merged with the Revolutionary Socialist Party in 1935 to become the Revolutionary Socialist Workers Party (RSAP), the Dutch section of the International Communist League.

Stein de Zeeuw was a member of the RSAP.

A. J. Muste (1885-1967), a minister and pacifist, helped to found the Conference for Progressive Labor Action (CPLA), which promoted militancy, union democracy, and industrial unionism in the American Federation of Labor and helped organize the unemployed during the depression. In 1933 the CPLA organized the American Workers Party, which merged with the Communist League of America to form the Workers Party of the United States, of which Muste was secretary. In 1936, when the Workers Party voted to enter the Socialist Party, Muste broke with Marxism and returned to pacifism and the church.

9. From 1936 to 1938, Stalin conducted three big *Moscow confession show trials,* accusing most of the leaders of the Russian Revolution of plotting to restore capitalism. The main defendants in the proceedings were Trotsky, in absentia, and his son, Leon Sedov. Through these trials, Stalin consolidated his personal rule over the Soviet Union.

10. *GPU* was one of the abbreviated names for the Soviet political police; other names were Cheka, NKVD, MVD, KGB, etc., but GPU is often used in their place.

Heinrich Brandler (1881-1967), the leader of the German CP during the early twenties, was made the scapegoat by Moscow for the bungling of the revolutionary situation in 1923, and was expelled in 1929. He and August Thaelheimer founded the Communist Right Opposition (KPO), whose policies paralleled those of the Bukharin-Rykov tendency in the USSR.

11. *André Malraux* (1901-   ), a well-known writer, had expressed sympathy for Trotsky in 1933-34, but became a collaborator of the Stalinists in the Popular Front period, and refused to speak up for Trotsky against the Moscow trial slanders. After World War II he became a Gaullist government official.

12. *Luis Companys y Jover* (1883-1940) became the head of the local government (Generalitat) in Catalonia after Macia's death. His party was the Catalan Esquerra, a bourgeois nationalist party.

13. *Léon Jouhaux* (1870-1954) was the general secretary of the CGT, the chief labor federation in France. He was a reformist, social patriot, and class collaborationist.

14. . . . *peasantry.* One of Stalin's chief charges against Trotsky in the 1920s was that he underestimated the role and ignored the interests of the peasantry.

15. *General Louis Cavaignac* (1802-1857) was the military officer who crushed the Parisian workers in the "June days" of 1848 in some of the bloodiest street fighting ever seen.

Marquis Gaston de Galliffet (1830-1909) was a French general who gained notoriety by his savage suppression of the Paris Commune in 1871.

16. *Juan Negrín López* (1889-1956) displaced Largo Caballero as premier in May 1937 at the insistence of the Stalinists. He was the final premier of the republican government, resigning in exile in France after the civil war was over.

17. *Vladimir A. Antonov-Ovsëenko* (1884-193?) had been a member of the committee that organized the October 1917 insurrection. He arrived in Barcelona as Soviet Consul-General in August 1936, along with an entire coterie of Russian "advisors" including Ernö Gerö, the chief Comintern representative in Catalonia. He was purged following

his return from Spain in the late thirties.

18. Although Trotsky advised against it, both Sneevliet and Vereecken participated in the *Brussels conference* of the London Bureau in 1936. The Brussels conference called for a conference in Barcelona in 1937, but it never took place.

19. *Attilio Salemme* was a member of the Appeal Association, the left wing of the American Socialist Party, which was expelled as Trotskyist in 1937 and became the Socialist Workers Party. Salemme was a leader of the Joerger-Salemme Group inside the Appeal Association, whose position on Spain was "No political or material support to the bourgeois Loyalist government!"

James P. Cannon (1890-   ) was an IWW organizer, a leader of the left wing in the Socialist Party, and a founder of the American CP. Expelled in 1928 for expressing solidarity with Trotsky, he led in the formation of the Left Opposition and later the Socialist Workers Party and the Fourth International.

Albert Goldman was Trotsky's lawyer in the United States and was one of the eighteen defendants convicted in the 1941 Minneapolis Labor Trial, the first use of the Smith Act. He left the SWP in 1946.

20. *Cheka* was the abbreviated name of the first Soviet political police established after the 1917 revolution.

21. *James Burnham* (1905-   ) was then a leader of the left wing in the American SP. He broke with the SWP in 1940 and later became a propagandist for McCarthyism and other ultraright movements, and an editor of the right-wing publication *National Review.*

22. *Jack Weber* was another leader of the Socialist Party left wing. He split away from the Socialist Workers Party near the end of World War II.

23. *The Oehlerites* were a sectarian faction in the Workers Party of the United States in 1935. They opposed on principle the entry of the Workers Party into the SP in order to reach the growing left wing in that party. They were led by Hugo Oehler.

24. *Camille Chautemps* (1885-1963), a French Radical Socialist, was premier in 1930 and in 1933-34, but retired in disgrace because of his involvement in financial scandals. He became premier again in 1937-38.

25. *The New International,* a forerunner of the *International Socialist*

Review, was published in the U. S. by the Communist League of America and later by the Workers Party and the Socialist Workers Party.

26. *The Generalitat* was the local government in Catalonia.

27. *General José Miaja Menant* (1878-1958) was a "republican" career officer who enjoyed special support by the Communist Party and who was left in charge of the defense of Madrid when the government fled to Valencia in November 1936. Toward the end of the war he broadcast a manifesto repudiating the republican government and proposing surrender to the fascists.

28. *The Nation and the New Republic* were liberal magazines published in the United States.

29. *Solidaridad obrera* was the newspaper of the Anarchist FAI.

30. *Clart* was a pseudonym of Jean Rous, who was sent to Spain by the International Secretariat in September 1935 and again in August-September 1936.
   Moulin is a pseudonym for Winter, a German Trotskyist of Czechoslovakian origin. He went to Spain in 1936, and worked closely with the "Friends of Durruti," dissident Anarchists who denounced the capitulation of their leaders. In 1937 he edited *La Voz leninista,* the paper of the Bolshevik-Leninist Section, which was the group that attempted to carry on a revolutionary policy after Nin's followers had merged with Maurin's group to form the POUM; he was also its chief leader. He was arrested by GPU agents in August 1937, and disappeared.
   Nicolle Braun was a pseudonym of Erwin Wolf, a Trotskyist of Czechoslovakian origin, who was Trotsky's secretary while he was in Norway. He was killed by the GPU in Spain in 1937.

31. *Witte,* a representative of the Greek section of the International Communist League, had been a member of the International Secretariat.
   Albert Weisbord had been expelled from the Communist Party in 1929 and formed a small sectarian group, the Communist League of Struggle.
   B.J. Field was a member of the Communist League of America. While leading a New York hotel strike in 1934, he violated party discipline and was expelled. He organized the League for a Revolutionary Workers Party, which soon disappeared.

32. *Georgi Dimitrov* (1882-1949), a Bulgarian communist who had

moved to Germany, attracted world attention in 1933 when the Nazis imprisoned and tried him and others on charges of having set the Reichstag on fire. He defended himself courageously at the trial and was acquitted. He became a Soviet citizen and served as executive secretary of the Comintern from 1934 to 1943. He is credited with being the chief author of the Comintern's Popular Front policy adopted at its Seventh Congress in 1935.

33. *Louis Fischer* (1896-1970) was a European correspondent for the *Nation* whom Trotsky accused of sympathies with Stalinism during the Moscow trials.

34. *José García Oliver* (1901-   ) was a right-wing Spanish Anarchist leader who collaborated with the Stalinists to crush the revolutionary wing of the loyalists. He was minister of justice in the central government from 1936 until the end of the civil war.

35. An uprising of sailors against the Bolshevik regime at the *Kronstadt* naval base near Leningrad in 1921 demanded free elections to the soviets and opposed many of the stern measures the Bolsheviks had taken during the civil war to safeguard the revolution. It was suppressed by the Bolsheviks, but it led to the concessions of the New Economic Policy.

36. *Buenaventura Durruti* (1896-1936) was the leader of the left wing of the FAI and an organizer of the militias; he directed the defense of Madrid, and died in that battle.

37. *Nestor Makhno* (1884 1934) was the leader of small partisan bands of peasants who fought against Ukrainian reactionaries and German occupation forces during the Russian civil war. He refused to integrate his forces into the Red Army and ultimately came into conflict with it. His forces were finally dispersed by the Soviet government.

38. *The Riffians* were Berber tribes in the hilly coastal areas of Morocco.

39. *Norman Thomas* (1884-1968) was the reformist leader of the American Socialist Party and was six times its candidate for president.
    Clement Attlee (1883-1967) was the leader of the British Labour Party after MacDonald and prime minister of Labour governments from 1945 to 1950.
    Jean Zyromsky (1890-) was a left-wing member of the French Socialist Party, a party functionary with pro-Stalinist leanings. An

advocate of "organic unity" in the thirties, he joined the Communist Party after World War II.

Walter Duranty (1884-1957) was a New York Times correspondent in Moscow for many years, and supported the Stalinists against the Oppositionists.

40. *Maxim Litvinov* (1876-1951), an Old Bolshevik, was people's commissar for foreign affairs, 1930-39, ambassador to the United States, 1941-43, and deputy commissar for foreign affairs, 1943-46. Stalin used him to personify "collective security" when he sought alliances with the democratic imperialists and shelved him during the Stalin-Hitler pact and the cold war.

41. *The Amsterdam International* was the popular name of the Social Democratic-dominated International Federation of Trade Unions, revived in July 1919, with headquarters in Amsterdam.

42. *Barcelona trials of the POUMists.* In October 1938, the POUM leaders who had been arrested in mid-1937 were brought to trial. They were acquitted on charges of treason and espionage, but were sentenced to prison for their role in the May 1937 uprising.

43. *Kliment Voroshilov* (1881-1969) was an early supporter of Stalin, a member of the Political Bureau of the Communist Party of the Soviet Union from 1926, president of the revolutionary military council, and people's commissar of defense, 1925-40. He was president of the USSR, 1953-60.

44. *Luis Araquistain Quevedo* (1886-1959) had been editor of the Socialist Party's paper *Claridad* before he was appointed ambassador to France in September 1936, when Largo Caballero became prime minister.

45. *Spain Betrayed* was reprinted in Cahiers de la quatrième Internationale, no. 1, February 1971, ("La Guerre d'Espagne: témoignage d'un combattant trotskyste dans les brigades internationales"), under the title "L'Espagne livrée: comment le Front Populaire a ouvert les portes à Franco." *M. Casanova* was the pseudonym of a Polish Trotskyist.

Notes for Appendix

1. *German crisis.* Trotsky's long letter to all sections of the International Left Opposition, dated February 17, 1931, was entitled "The Crisis of the German Left Opposition," and dealt with ideological and organizational disputes involving a section of the German leadership headed by Kurt Landau, which was soon to split from the Left Opposition. Full text is in *Writings of Leon Trotsky* (1930-31).

2. *The Esquerra* of Macía was the Catalan party of the Barcelona lower middle class. The word "esquerra" is the Catalan word for "left."

3. *Boris Souvarine* (1893-   ) was a founder of the French Communist Party and one of the first serious biographers of Stalin. He was repelled by Stalinism in the 1920s and was the only foreign delegate to the thirteenth congress of the Russian CP to defend Trotsky against the Stalinist slanders. He was expelled from the French party shortly thereafter. In the 1930s he turned against Leninism. For Trotsky he was a prototype of the cynicism and defeatism that characterized the renegades from Bolshevism.

4. *Pierre Gourget* was expelled from the French Communist Party for supporting the Left Opposition. He was a cofounder of *La Vérité* and a leader of the Communist League. He capitulated in 1932 and rejoined the CP.

5. *The Bulletin of the Opposition* was the Russian-language organ of the Left Opposition, published by Trotsky from the beginning of his exile until his death.
   The International Bulletin was the internal discussion bulletin of the International Left Opposition.

6. *Baron Georges Cuvier* (1769-1832) was a French naturalist and an early pioneer in comparative anatomy and paleontology. He originated the natural system of animal classification.

GLOSSARY OF ORGANIZATIONS
AND POLITICAL PARTIES

Catalan Federation: short name of the Catalan-Balearic Communist Federation, the group led by Joaquín Maurín which left the CP in 1930; later known as the Workers and Peasants Bloc.

Communist Party: represented the official centrist faction in the communist movement.

Confederación Nacional del Trabajo (CNT): National Confederation of Labor, was the anarcho-syndicalist trade union federation.

Esquerra: the Catalan party of the Barcelona lower middle class; led by Macía.

Federación Anarquista Ibérica (FAI): Iberian Anarchist Federation, a secret organization under the Primo de Rivera dictatorship, which controlled the much larger CNT; divided into a right wing (led by García Oliver) and a left wing (led by Durruti).

Left Communists: the name adopted by the Spanish Bolshevik-Leninists led by Andrés Nin before they merged with the Catalan Federation to form the POUM.

Left Opposition: the name taken by the followers of Trotsky. It included Nin's group of Spanish Oppositionists until 1935.

Partido Obrero de Unificación Marxista (POUM): Workers Party of Marxist Unification, formed in September 1935 by a fusion of Maurín's Workers and Peasants Bloc with Nin's Left Communists.

Radicals: a bourgeois party led by Alejandro Lerroux that began as a liberal party and moved quickly to the right; held power from September 1933 to January 1936.

Republicans: a general term for those parties and individuals supporting the Popular Front government over the National Front forces of Franco. Several parties had the word "republican" in their names, including Azaña's Republican Left.

Socialist Party: split into a left and right wing, led respectively by Largo Caballero and Indalecio Prieto; held power from 1936 until the end of the civil war.

Syndicalist Party: led by Pestaña, was the right wing of the CNT.

Unión General de Trabajadores (UGT): General Union of Workers, was the second major trade union federation in Spain; led by the Socialist Party.

Workers and Peasants Bloc: the name adopted by the Catalan Federation before it merged with the Left Communists to form the POUM.

GLOSSARY OF PERIODICALS

Adelante: Socialist Party newspaper.

La Batalla: newspaper of the POUM.

Bulletin of the Opposition: publication of the Russian Left Opposition.

Comunismo: magazine of the Spanish Bolshevik-Leninists.

Contra la corriente: first newspaper of the Left Opposition in Spain, published in exile in Belgium under the Primo de Rivera dictatorship.

l'Humanité: organ of the French Communist Party.

La Lutte de classes: monthly theoretical review of the French Left Opposition.

El Mundo obrero: Spanish Communist Party newspaper.

Solidaridad obrera: Spanish Anarchist newspaper.

El Soviet: paper of the Spanish Left Opposition.

La Vérité: organ of the Communist League of France.

386, 387; and International Left
Opposition, 171, 172-73, 174-
79, 188-90, 192, 197-201, 382-
83, 387, 393, 398-99, 409n; and
national question, 155; after for
mation of POUM, 211, 214, 307,
423n; and Socialist Party, 148,
202, 206, 212-13, 216, 266,
416n; and slogan of soviets, 65-
66, 127-28; suppressed, 46, 113,
350; and united front, 61, 92,
195-98; *see also* Nin, Andrés.
Left Opposition (United States),
see Communist League of America; Socialist Workers Party; *and*
Workers Party (United States).
Left Socialists, *see* Socialist Party
(Spain), left wing of.
Left Social Revolutionaries, *see*
Social Revolutionary Party, left
wing of.
Lenin, Vladimir Ilyich, 176, 196,
218, 245, 246, 272, 293, 294,
351, 366, 401n, 404n; on "democratic dictatorship," 122; on
"growing over" of revolution,
119; in Russian Revolution, 130,
143, 145, 152, 240, 278, 359,
361, 406n.
Leninbund (Germany), 192, 412n,
415n.
León, Guillermo Vegas, *see* Vegas
León, Guillermo.
Lerroux, Alejandro, xvi, xvii, 35,
36, 56, 99, 100, 101, 124, 144,
381, 408n, 410n, 427.
Lesoil, Léon, 216, 418n.
"Lesser evils," 185, 285, 287.
Liebknecht, Karl, 62, 237, 401-
02n, 411n.
Litvinov, Maxim, 324, 425n.
Lliga, 101.
London Bureau of Revolutionary
Socialist Parties (IAG), 207, 209-
10, 211, 220, 232, 245n, 246,
247, 326, 417n, 419n; Brussels

conference of, 274-75, 422n.
Longuet, Jean, 217, 418n.
López Sánchez, Juan, 226.
Lorre, Dick, 290.
La Lutte de classes, 76, 135, 138,
403n, 429.
La Lutte ouvrière, 230n, 248.
Luxemburg, Rosa, 411n.
Lvov, Prince George, 136, 143,
409-10n.

MacDonald, Ramsay, 81, 203,
394, 404n.
Macia y Llusa, Francisco, xvi,
126, 134, 135, 136, 152, 376,
391, 408n, 421n, 426n, 427.
Madrid, siege of, xviii, 226, 424n.
Madrid autonomous group, 133,
408-09n.
Maisky, Ivan, 333.
Makhno, Nestor, 317, 328, 424n.
Malraux, André, 247, 324, 421n.
Manuilsky, Dimitri, 81, 82, 112,
113, 404n.
March council (1917, Russia),
108, 323, 406n.
Markin, *see* Sedov, Leon.
Marquet, Adrien, 203, 417n.
Martínez Barrio, Diego de, xvii,
39, 56, 101, 226.
Martinov, Alexander, 120, 124,
407n.
Martov, Julius, 245, 246, 250,
264-65, 343, 345, 351, 402n,
420n.
Marx, Karl, 27, 68, 80, 120, 176,
209, 213n, 262, 272, 325, 340.
Maslow, Arkadi, 415n.
Matteoti, Giacomo, 81, 404n.
Maura y Gamazo, Miguel, xv, 56,
99, 142-44.
Maurín Julia, Joaquín, 140, 146-
47, 152, 153, 154, 161, 162,
173, 210n, 213n, 370, 410n,
427; and Communist Party, 138,
154, 161, 372, 373, 388, 389;

Le Populaire, 230, 238, 419n.

El Popular, 337.

Popular Front, 35, 220-21, 229-30, 282, 308, 336, 337, 407n; 7th Congress of Comintern (1935) calls for, xvii, 29, 210-11, 404n, 418n, 424n.

Popular Front (France), xvii, 33, 41, 208, 210, 230, 237-38, 243, 290, 334, 335, 349, 412n, 416n, 419n.

Popular Front (Spain), comes to power, xvii, 26, 36-37, 101, 102, 208, 214, 225; Anarchists and POUM support, xvii, 28, 36-37, 41, 45, 212, 213, 218-19, 226, 242; colonial policy of, 43-44; Communist Party supports, xvii, xviii, 21, 26, 30, 36-37, 40, 42, 226, 235-39, 307, 309, 310-11, 347; policy of, 231, 233, 237, 255, 256, 258, 260, 308-11, 313, 315, 318, 319, 325, 330-31, 337, 347, 356, 362; Socialist Party supports, 21, 36-37, 40, 208, 226, 235-39; *see also* Socialist Party, bloc with republicans.

Portela Valladares, Manuel, 101.

POUM (Workers Party of Marxist Unification), 30, 39, 40, 43, 49n, 239n, 294; founded, xvii, 34, 206, 403n, 406n, 417n, 427; and anarcho-syndicalists, 240-42, 302, 317-18, 345, 357, 363, 366; and Communist Party, 345; relation to Fourth Internationalist movement, 208, 246-47, 248, 249-50, 262, 268, 275, 318, 342; excludes Trotskyists, 268, 273, 279-80; program of, 208, 209-10, 214, 232, 245, 250, 258-59, 260, 261-62, 263, 264, 265-66, 270-71, 282, 298-99, 304, 317-18, 345-46, 351, 354; joins government, 43, 243, 248-49, 258-59, 271, 272-73, 275, 276, 294, 345, 356, 363, 406n; supports Popular Front, xvii, xviii, 37, 41, 45, 208, 218-19, 232, 242, 248-50, 251, 271-72, 275-76, 295, 346, 356, 363, 365, 366; in May 1937 upsurge, 303, 363, 425n; left opposition within, 351; suppressed, xix, 44, 46-47, 226, 227, 267-68, 269, 270, 303, 314, 329, 350, 425n.

Pravda, 81, 82, 113, 114, 117, 119, 120, 124, 161, 181, 182, 184, 394.

Prieto y Tuero, Indalecio, xviii, 28, 311, 328, 411n, 428; in republic of 1931, 26, 56, 148, 226.

Primo de Rivera, General Miguel, dictatorship of, xv, 25, 55, 56, 57-58, 72, 73, 74, 75, 78, 84, 134, 159; and fascism, 64, 81, 83, 183.

Primo de Rivera, José Antonio, 35, 100.

Progressive Party, 99, 101, 407n.

Proletariat, 159, 169; role of, in 1931 upsurge, 58-59, 73, 75-76; effect of industrialization on, 74-75.

"Prometeo," *see* Bordigists.

PSOP, *see* Workers and Peasants Socialist Party.

Que faire, 353-54, 365, 366.

Quiroga, Casares, xvii, 38-39, 56, 99, 225.

Radical Party (France), *also called* Radical Socialist Party, 229, 230, 231, 236, 237, 239, 422n.

Radical Party (Spain), 56, 99, 100, 101, 144, 229, 230, 232, 408n, 410n, 427.

BOOKS AND PAMPHLETS BY LEON TROTSKY*

The Age of Permanent Revolution

The Basic Writings of Trotsky

The Case of Leon Trotsky

The Chinese Revolution: Problems and Perspectives

The Death Agony of Capitalism and the Tasks of the Fourth International

Europe and America

Fascism: What It Is and How to Fight It

The First Five Years of the Communist International (2 volumes)

The History of the Russian Revolution (3 volumes)

In Defense of Marxism

Lenin: Notes for a Biographer

Leon Trotsky Speaks

Literature and Revolution

Marxism in Our Time

Military Writings

My Life

The New Course

1905

On Black Nationalism and Self-Determination

On Britain

On Engels and Kautsky

On the Jewish Question

On the Labor Party in the U. S.

On Literature and Art

On the Paris Commune

On the Suppressed Testament of Lenin

On the Trade Unions

The Permanent Revolution and Results and Prospects

Problems of the Chinese Revolution

Problems of Civil War

Problems of Everyday Life

The Revolution Betrayed

The Spanish Revolution (1931-39)

Stalin

The Stalin School of Falsification

Stalinism and Bolshevism

The Struggle Against Fascism in Germany

Terrorism and Communism

Their Morals and Ours (with essays by John Dewey and George Novack)

The Third International After Lenin

The Transitional Program for Socialist Revolution

Trotsky's Diary in Exile, 1935

Whither France?

Women and the Family

Writings of Leon Trotsky (1930-31)

Writings of Leon Trotsky (1932)

Writings of Leon Trotsky (1932-33)

Writings of Leon Trotsky (1933-34)

Writings of Leon Trotsky (1934-35)

Writings of Leon Trotsky (1935-36)

Writings of Leon Trotsky (1937-38)

Writings of Leon Trotsky (1938-39)

Writings of Leon Trotsky (1939-40)

The Young Lenin

---

*This list includes all books and pamphlets by Leon Trotsky published in the United States and in print as of 1973.